THE BOOK OF NEGROES

THE BOOK OF NEGROES

African Americans in Exile
After the American Revolution

EDITED BY
GRAHAM RUSSELL GAO HODGES
AND ALAN EDWARD BROWN

Fordham University Press   New York   2021

Original edition published 1996 by Garland Publishing, Inc., as *The Black Loyalist Directory*.

Fordham University Press edition published 2021.

Fordham University Press has no responsibility for the persistence or accuracy of URLs for external or third-party Internet websites referred to in this publication and does not guarantee that any content on such websites is, or will remain, accurate or appropriate.

Fordham University Press also publishes its books in a variety of electronic formats. Some content that appears in print may not be available in electronic books.

Visit us online at www.fordhampress.com.

Library of Congress Control Number: 2021915892

Printed in the United States of America

23 22 21   5 4 3 2 1

Revised and expanded edition

Contents

Acknowledgments   vii

List of Illustrations   ix

Introduction   xi

A Note on the Text   xlviii

Introduction to the 2021 Edition   li

Classroom Use for *The Book of Negroes*   lix

Suggested Readings   lxiii

Black Loyalist Directory   1

    Book One   3

    Book Two   143

    Book Three   193

Appendix 1: Tabular Analysis of the Black Loyalist Directory   215

Appendix 2: The London Black Poor   225

Selected Bibliography   263

Index   271

Illustrations follow page 192

Acknowledgments

My interest in the Black Loyalist Directory began in 1986 during research for a general history of African Americans in New York. I soon recognized the importance of the "Book of Negroe," and put my students to work. Among the Colgate University students who created initial drafts of the transcripts are Paul Townend, Joellen Kelleher, Matt Baldacci, and Charles Grieco. Michael Galligan, formerly of Colgate, and now at Garland, assisted in preparation of the tables in Appendix One. Peter Shaw helped prepare the analysis of family formation in the "Book of the Negroe." In Nova Scotia, Mary Byers and Pearleen Oliver were of great help.

Funding agencies which generously helped me research and prepare this manuscript include the Faculty Research Council of Colgate University, the American Council of Learned Societies and the National Endowment for the Humanities Travel-to-Collections Program. Libraries and archives which aided immensely include the Public Archives of Nova Scotia, National Archives of Canada, New York Public Library, New-York Historical Society, National Archives-Southeast Region, Public Record Office, Kew Gardens, London, the University of Virginia Library, Boston Public Library and the interlibrary loan service at Case Library, Colgate University.

Other individuals gave generously of their time. Ralph Crandall and the members of the New England Historic Genealogical Society underwrote much of the costs of production. Daniel Meaders contributed his valuable research on the Virginia contingent of the Black Loyalists. At Garland Publishing, Inc. Claudia Hirsch has proven a very supportive, enthusiastic and valuable editor and friend. Alan Edward Brown, User Services Technician at Colgate and Master of the Macintosh, formatted several editions of this manuscript with patience and skill. As I worked on the first manuscript, Susan Hawkes Cook, encouraged by Robert Charles Anderson, F.A.S.G., created her own transcript. Mrs. Cook demonstrated true collegiality by preparing several versions of the index and checking the final version of the directory. In addition to Bob Anderson, who read a final draft, Mrs. Cook wishes to thank Gayle Peters, Director of the National Archives-Southeast Region, for making a microfilm version from *Papers of the Continental Congress* available to her. I also acknowledge my indebtedness to my step-daughter, Celeste Creel, my parents, Reverend and Mrs. Graham R. Hodges, and my wife, Margaret Washington for their encouragement. James Creel, my step-son, died just before this book was completed. A traveling spirit, James understood why Black Loyalists searched across the world for freedom and the meaning of life.

This book is dedicated to Clarence L. Cook for his patience, support and encouragement.

Graham Russell Hodges
Hamilton, New York

List of Illustrations

1. A Proclamation by His Excellency the Right Honorable John Earl of Dunmore, his Majesty's Lieutenant and Governor-General of the Colony and Dominion of Virginia . . . . Courtesy of Special Collections, Alderman Library, University of Virginia.

2. Theodor Kaufman, "On to Liberty," 1867. Courtesy of The Metropolitan Museum of Art, Gift of Erving and Joyce Wolf, 1982 (1982.443.3).

3. Pass by Brigadier General Samuel Birch to Cato Ramsay. Courtesy of Public Archives of Nova Scotia.

4–5. Pages 72–73 from "Book of Negroes," British Headquarters Papers, Photostat, Courtesy of New York Public Library. Book photograph by Warren Wheeler.

6. Rose Fortune, Black Loyalist. Courtesy of Public Archives of Nova Scotia.

7. A Black Wood Cutter at Shelburne, Nova Scotia, 1788. Courtesy of National Archives of Canada.

8. "Yankee Doodle or the Negroes Farewell to America." The Words and Music by T.L. Courtesy of Boston Public Library.

9. Plan of Sierra Leone and the Parts Adjacent, 1794. Courtesy of Olin Library, Cornell University.

Introduction

On May 6, 1783, George Washington, Commander-in-Chief of the Continental Army, met with his British counterpart, Sir Guy Carleton, in Orange Town, New York. While discussing implementation of the recently signed peace pact ending the Revolutionary War, Washington asked Carleton about "obtaining the delivery of Negroes and other Property of the Inhabitants' of the United States," as required by article seven of the treaty. Carleton responded that "a number of Negroes" had already embarked with other Loyalists for Nova Scotia. Although rumors about the flight of Black Loyalists had circulated along the Atlantic coast for months, Washington expressed "Surprize" that fugitive slaves were leaving.[1] On May 12, 1783, Carleton wrote Washington confirming that "in the case of the Negroes declared free previous" to his arrival, he "had no right to deprive them of that liberty" given them by proclamations issued by several British generals during the war. Returning the fugitives would be a violation of faith between the English and the Black Loyalists. Infuriated, Washington and other Patriots argued with Carleton, initiating a dispute which lasted for thirty years.[2] Pressured by the Patriot general, Carleton agreed to list each black émigré, providing names, ages, brief descriptions, origins, status, and date of arrival in New York City. Such information, the authorities reasoned, might be useful should the dispute ever entail compensation. The list of 3,000 included 1,336 men, 914 women and 750 children, who left from New York City for Nova Scotia, England, and several German kingdoms during 1783.

This book contributes to previous, excellent works by Ellen Wilson and James W. St. G. Walker on the history of the Black Loyalists by tendering the first printed transcripts of important manuscripts including the "Book of the Negro," as the embarkation list of Black Loyalists of 1783 was known. An appendix includes significant lists of Black Loyalists who turned up in London in the 1780s before departing for Sierra Leone. Both groups of Black

Loyalists are of paramount importance to African American history during the Age of Revolution. They were the first mass group of emancipated African Americans. Along with lesser-known Black Loyalists were seminal black religious, military, and political leaders, whose stories shed light on an emerging black nationalism and republicanism around the Atlantic basin.[3] Within their negotiations with English authorities can be found the earliest moments of the colonization movement which sought to move African Americans back to the land of their ancestors. The Black Loyalists' search for a free land was the first of many calls for reparations to repay for harsh years of servitude. Finally, the war experiences and political and religious beliefs of three thousand African Americans from distant points on the Atlantic Coast helped to forge a black republicanism that set the stage for nineteenth-century black nationalism.

For those unfamiliar with the tale of the Black Loyalists, this introduction provides a brief review of the alliances between African Americans and the British Army during the American Revolution. Second, it delineates the major migrations and struggle of Black Loyalists in Nova Scotia, England, and, later, in Africa. Mirroring the struggles of their black counterparts in the United States, Black Loyalists overcame racism and discrimination to achieve a separate destiny. Although they gained immediate civil freedom, in contrast to the gradual emancipation practiced in the northern United States, the Black Loyalists suffered economic and political deprivation for years, finding full sanctuary primarily in religion and in exile to Africa.[4] Finally, the introduction describes briefly the importance of the Black Loyalists as models for black aspirations in the United States. One inspiration remained clear. Despite the deprivations, the desire for liberty remained paramount among blacks. During the starving years of the 1780s in Nova Scotia, for example, none of the Black Loyalists looked back at slavery with nostalgia. Any of its alleged virtues of food, shelter, or kindly masters "could not satisfy . . . without liberty."[5]

The Black Loyalists' hegira began on November 7, 1775, when, after months of speculation and threats, John Murray, Lord Dunmore, and the last Royal Governor of Virginia, proclaimed freedom to all "indented servants [and] negroes . . . willing to serve His Majesty's forces to end the present rebellion." Hundreds of black fugitives in Virginia, Maryland, and the Carolinas accepted Dunmore's call to join his Æthiopian Regiment. Dunmore's Proclamation probably did more than any other British measure to spur uncommitted white Americans into the camp of rebellion. In the North, angry Long Island farmers burned Dunmore, once governor of New York, in effigy, and worried about slaves "being too fond of British troops." If the proclamation made stronger Patriots of plantation owners and yeoman farmers, it turned many blacks into Tories.[6] After Dunmore's defeat in Norfolk, Virginia, in early 1776, he sailed for New York City, arriving at Staten Island on August 13, 1776. Accompanying him were some one hundred men, the "remains of the Ætheopian Regiment." On Staten Island, these black soldiers joined with other refugee blacks to create a regiment rumored to be over eight hundred strong.[7]

As the conflict unfolded, blacks declared their willingness to fight with either side, but met with sharply different reactions from American Patriots and Tories. American Whigs varied between official rejection of the use of black troops and local needs. Not only did armed slaves pose a danger of black revolt, but slaves were valuable property, made more so by the absence of white laborers in the army. Despite their contributions to the economy, few white Americans regarded blacks as fit recruits.[8] Overcoming official objections, hundreds of blacks served in various capacities for the Americans throughout the war. General George Washington first rejected all black recruits, then changed his mind after Dunmore's Proclamation. Though most Americans spurned Henry Laurens' proposal that the Continental Congress purchase slaves from their masters and then draft them, blacks filtered into the American forces. In smaller states such as Rhode Island and Connecticut, blacks made up significant portions of the regiments.[9]

As Patriots hesitated or refused to include blacks in the battle for freedom, African Americans sided with the British. Americans recognized black preferences for the English. Henry M. Muhlenberg realized early in the war that the Negroes "secretly wished the British army might win, for then all Negro slaves will gain their freedom. It is said that this sentiment is universal amongst all the Negroes in America." In early 1776, patriot Charles Lee sought to impose military order over the black population of Virginia, noting "dominion over the black is based upon opinion, [without] that, authority will fall."[10]

During the Revolution, British army movements attracted tens of thousand of blacks seeking freedom. English policies intended to disrupt the American economy by luring black laborers. Promises of freedom were the best enticements the British could offer, and African Americans of all ages flocked inside the invading army lines. The British organized black regiments as well as free-lance guerrilla units, known as "followers of the flag." They used others as pilots, spies, and waggoneers. In succeeding years, black soldiers, spies and laborers provided important substance to the British military effort around New York City.[11] As British forces marched back and forth through New York, New Jersey, Pennsylvania, Maryland, Virginia, the Carolinas and Georgia, they attracted women as well as men. In the war, black females worked as servants, cooks, and laundresses. Estimates of 25,000 to 55,000 fugitives in the southern states alone added up to the largest black escape in the history of North American slavery. Nothing comparable had ever occurred before or would not again until the Emancipation Proclamation in 1863.[12]

New York City was the securest destination for Loyalists of both races. After the British army and navy occupied the city in 1776, New York remained continually under Crown rule until November, 1783. In 1778 influential Loyalists from several colonies founded the Board of Associated Loyalists to govern their military efforts around the city. New York was the headquarters for the British army; commercial activities were busier than ever during the war. Theaters flourished, newspapers published weekly accounts of social and military activities. The Church of England reestablished services after a brief hiatus. The Black Loyalists population grew steadily. In 1779 a military census counted over twelve hundred blacks living in the city; they were joined in 1782 by over fifteen hundred Black Loyalists evacuated from Savannah and Charleston. Others arrived in the city on privateers.[13]

Black travellers along the road to New York City passed through many dangers. Patriot Americans devised harsh penalties for blacks seeking to join the British. Boston King described one slave arrested for trying to escape from his master. The bondman had been taken prisoner and attempted to escape, but was caught twelve miles off. King sadly wrote: "They tied him to the tail of a horse and in this manner brought him back to Brunswick. When I saw him his feet were fastened in the stocks and at night his hands also."[14]

King related his own flight in dramatic fashion:

> As I was at prayer one evening, I thought the Lord Heard Me, and would mercifully deliver me. Therefore putting my confidence in him, about one o'clock in the morning, I went down to the river side and found the guards were either asleep or in the tavern. I instantly entered the water, but when I was a little distance from the opposite shore, I heard the sentinels disputing among themselves. One said, I am sure I saw a man

cross the river. Another replied, there is no such thing.
When I got a little distance from the shore I got down
on my knees and thanked God for this deliverance. I
travelled until five o'clock in the morning and then
concealed myself until seven o'clock at night, when I
proceeded forward thro' brushes and marshes for fear of
being discovered. When I came to the river, opposite
Staten Island, I found a boat, and altho it was near a
whale-boat, I ventured into it and cutting the rope, I got
safe over. The commanding officer, when informed of
my case, gave me a passport and I proceeded to New
York.[15]

While the British seemed to embrace black hopes for freedom,
their generals were often slippery about promises. Lord Cornwallis
callously abandoned thousands after his surrender at Yorktown.
Dunmore, the erstwhile liberator, deceived others and sold them
into slavery in the Bahamas. This deceit did not immediately sour
black ambitions. The three thousand and more who migrated from
New York City in 1783 to Nova Scotia and London arrived in their
new destinations transformed in profound ways. The war experience
taught them powers of self-reliance, inculcated survival skills, and
imbued them with a deep desire for republican liberty. Their black
republicanism resembled the artisan republicanism motivating the
working classes of American cities in the postwar period. The
ideology of artisan republicanism included deep reverence for the
lessons of the revolution, pride of community and trade, an
inclination towards evangelical religion, and a powerful
egalitarianism. The Black Loyalists held these tenets, adding
modifications based on race and political allegiance. A remarkable
vision recorded on April 16, 1781 demonstrates their fusion of
evangelical religion and military allegiance. About two weeks
earlier, while he was in the barracks of his company on Water
Street in New York City, Murphy Steil of the Black Pioneers heard
a voice "like a Man's (but saw no body)," which told him to inform
British General Sir Henry Clinton that he should send a special
message to General Washington. Stiel heard the voice say several
times that Washington must surrender his troops immediately or the
"wrath of God would fall upon him." God's condemnation, Stiel
understood, meant that He "would raise all of the Blacks in
America to fight against him." Stiel assured Clinton and Lord
Cornwallis not to worry because "the Lord would be on their side."[16]

Other British generals had proven unreliable, but the Black Loyalists found a faithful patron in British Commander-in-Chief Guy Carleton. After consulting his aides in South Carolina, Carleton decided that the Black Loyalists deserved the protection of the King. Lt. General Alexander Leslie told Carleton in June, 1782, that "there are [Blacks] who have been very useful, both at the Siege of Savannah and here, some of them have been guides and from their loyalty have been promised their freedom." There was a drive to give black "followers of the army" brigade status. Some blacks from South Carolina and New York were enlisted in a provincial battalion to build fortifications in Antigua and Jamaica. James Moncrief, before resigning as supervisor of blacks in the engineer's department in South Carolina and New York, recommended to Henry Clinton that black brigade status be "fixed before my departure."[17] Such comments convinced Carleton that blacks deserved protection and transportation to Nova Scotia. His reward was to proclaim the protection of the King and to order that each receive a certificate attesting to their status. Boston King recalled that the proclamation meant "each of us received a certificate from the commanding officer at New-York, which dispelled all our fears and filled us with gratitude."[18]

Now officially part of the British military effort, the Black Loyalists gained compensation. Carleton placed the Black Pioneers on the payroll in New York City from August, 1782 until their departure in the fall of 1783. During this time the Black Loyalists received a £125 payroll for the black noncommissioned officers and private soldiers. Carleton in effect granted the Black Loyalists veterans' status, which the African Americans regarded as a key component of their republicanism. A second aspect of the blacks' ideology was economic independence. This was fostered by Carleton's recommendation that Pioneers each be awarded twenty acres of land in Nova Scotia.[19] The general's determination had immediate practical value. By awarding passports to the Black Loyalists the British superceded the logistical problems of evacuating over thirty thousand Loyalists from America at the close of the war. Transport vessels were extremely scarce. By ruling that only destitute Loyalists would be evacuated on government ships, Carleton insured passage for the Black Loyalists.[20]

These events infuriated white Americans. To the Patriots, the Black Loyalists were runaway slaves. As Americans angrily confronted Carleton and his aides with demands for return of their fugitives, Carleton responded in two ways. First, he ordered protections against former masters seeking return of their escaped chattel. Peace negotiations between the Americans and the British in 1783 encouraged slaveholders to petition Carleton for permission to enter New York City to capture fugitive blacks. Boston King described the terror of seeing old masters from the South, as well as from Philadelphia and New Jersey seizing former slaves off the streets. "The dreadful rumor filled us all with inexpressible anguish and horror." King wrote "for some days we lost our appetite for food and sleep departed from our eyes."[21] Carleton dealt harshly with residents of New York City who aided slave masters intent upon recapturing escaped slaves. Thomas Willis, a police employee, was convicted of forcing Caesar, "a Negro, who came to New York City under a proclamation, onto a vessel which carried him to Elizabeth town in return for a gold coin." Willis tied Caesar's hands behind his back and drove him through the streets by beating him with a stick. After fining Willis fifty guineas, Carleton ordered him transported immediately. In a similar incident the slave of Jacob Duryea of Dutchess County refused to return with his master from New York City after making a delivery. After Duryea tied the slave to his boat, the slave was rescued on the Hudson River by a black guerrilla named Colonel Cuff and helpful Hessian soldiers. The slave was freed and Duryea taken back to New York City and court-martialed.[22]

High-ranking American officials fared little better. General George Washington wrote Commissioner Daniel Parker in New York on April 28, 1783, requesting that he prevent "their carrying off any negroes or other property of the Inhabitants of the United States." Washington also enclosed a "List and description of Negroes which had been sent to me by Governor Harrison of Virginia," in hopes that the fugitives could be captured. Washington noted that "some of my own slaves [and those of Mr. Lund who lives at my home] may probably be in New York, but I am unable to give you their Descriptions, [and] their Names being so easily changed will be fruitless to give you." As these comments suggest, Washington despaired that any slaves would ever be returned to their masters.[23]

To placate angry Americans, Carleton created a Board of Inquiry to handle slave owners' claims. Carleton had already determined that no Black Loyalist would be handed over to the vengeful Americans, but compromised over timing and character of black flight. The board met every Wednesday at noon at Fraunces Tavern. On July 24, 1783, it heard the case of Gerrard Beeckman versus two black children, Peter and Elizabeth, "lately embarked with their Father for Nova Scotia and brought on shore for examination." Beeckman claimed that Pierre Van Cortlandt of Westchester County gave him the two children in 1777, but that Samuel Dobson, the two children's father, rescued them from Van Cortlandt's house and brought them to New York City. Apparently because the two children were too young to have answered any proclamation, the Board awarded them to Beeckman. In another case, the Board ordered Betty from Aquackanonck, New Jersey, though possessing a certificate from Samuel Birch, removed from a ship in the harbor to answer a claim by her former master, Thomas Smith. Smith argued that Betty escaped only last April. Despite her protests that she "came within the British lines under the Sanction and claims the Privilege of the Proclamation," the Board ordered her returned to New Jersey. A third case in which a wife and three children stayed behind while her husband went into the British service meant freedom for the man and continued bondage for his family. In several cases in which blacks clearly demonstrated that they came under British protection, the Board declared themselves unauthorized to determine their fate. American military officials were further hampered by claimants who were unwilling to journey to New York City, a sign that the Board was allowing former slaves' testimony to stand up against agents of their masters.[24]

Loyalists also sought to regain escaped slaves. Judith Jackson fled from her master, John MacLean of Norfolk, Virginia, in 1773. According to an advertisement published by MacLean, Jackson was pregnant and had a one-year-old daughter with her. Shortly after this, MacLean left for Great Britain, leaving his affairs in the hands of Eilbeck, Ross & Company. Jackson remained at large in Norfolk, a sizable shipping town. After Dunmore's Proclamation, she joined his regiment, working as a laundress. Eight years later, she received a certificate from General Birch, entitling her to passage to Nova Scotia. Unexpectedly, Eilbeck, now a Loyalist, arrived to demand possession of Jackson and her children. By her testimony to the board, Jackson revealed that she had joined the troops in Virginia, travelled with them to South Carolina, then voyaged to New York in 1782. Despite Eilbeck's claim as a loyal subject of His Majesty, the board referred Jackson's case to Carleton, who determined that her eight years of service outweighed her old master's property rights.[25]

General Samuel Birch, who issued the coveted passes to Nova Scotia, recognized any claims to freedom older than 1782. Holders of these passports, identified in the lists by GBC and GMC, were guaranteed access to British transport vessels. There were some restrictions. Refugees entitled to passes had to have certificates of good character, which excluded blacks in the guard house imprisoned for crimes ranging from theft and arson to murder. There were 1156 blacks who claimed freedom by the proclamations issued by British generals throughout the war, the very group Carleton most wanted to protect. According to the Book of Negroes, 878 blacks received certificates from General Samuel Birch. After he departed in late 1783, General Thomas Musgrave issued another 278 certificates. Significantly, 485 of this group came from Virginia; nearly all the adults had served the British army for eight years. The second biggest muster in this category came from South Carolina. British Generals Howe and Clinton made two proclamations in New Jersey and New York, which attracted 167 blacks.[26] Many other Black Loyalists could not claim any response to a proclamation. The British gave the benefit of any doubt to 813 blacks who claimed to have abandoned their masters in the heat of the war. Virginia and South Carolina were the homes of over two-thirds of such fugitives. British commanders took black statements about their status at face value, a new acceptance of the validity of black testimony. For this reason, the third largest category, those who claimed to have been born free or who were newly emancipated, indicate assertive statements of African American self-emancipation. New York, despite its highly rigid laws curbing the numbers of free blacks, contributed the largest number with 179 claims. Over half of these free blacks joining the exodus were women and girls.

Other émigrés remained in bondage. British proclamations did not apply to the slaves of Loyalists, and royalist newspapers carried advertisements for fugitive slaves throughout the war.[27] The Loyalist evacuations from Savannah and Charleston carried away hundreds of slaves in preceding years. Among the first blacks to depart in 1783 were the slaves or indentured servants of Loyalists. Not surprisingly, the largest number of these were from New York and New Jersey. Finally, a small number of slaves from New York had been abandoned by their masters.

The 3,000 Black Loyalists departing from New York included 1336 men, 914 women, 339 boys, 335 girls, and 76 children of unidentified gender. Using the methods employed by Ann Patton Malone in her study of Louisiana slaves, I have divided these into solitaires (single people), couples, families with from one to four children, and extended families.[28] I have also counted male and female-headed families. Not surprisingly, given the chaos of war, two thousand or two-thirds of the Black Loyalists were solitaires; totals included 1119 men, 492 women, 215 boys and 174 girls. What is significant about these numbers is the sizable proportion of females. Historically, males accounted for eighty-five to ninety percent of runaway slaves in colonial America.[29] In 1783, the ravages of the war tore American society sufficiently that over forty percent of the departing single Black Loyalists were female. The second surprise is the large number of couples and families. There were eighty-six couples without children and seventy-four families with from one to four children. Finally, there were a number of extended families. For example, one family of freeborn women chose exile; Mary Thomson, 54 years old, her daughter, Margaret, 25, and her three children, Polly 10, Rachell, 3, and Sally, 1, all from Newark, New Jersey, decided to secure their freedom through exile.

The 3,000 Black Loyalists embarking from New York City were the survivors of eight years of war. Scholars have pondered just how much the British appeals to blacks undermined the economies and societies of the American states. Benjamin Quarles estimated the numbers of slaves in flight to the British to be in the tens of thousands. Sylvia Frey has reported that over 6500 departed from East Florida to the Caribbean, and that over ten thousand blacks escaped during the evacuation of Charleston. Frey estimates that between eighty and one hundred thousand Afro Virginians escaped from their masters, many of them contributing to the rapid increase in the black populations of the Bahamas and Jamaica during the war. I have estimated that over five hundred black New Yorkers changed allegiances, while in nearby Bergen County, New Jersey about one hundred or twelve percent of the county's slaves left with the British. Accurate counts are really impossible because of unrecorded casualties, escape to western frontiers, or to ocean vessels.[30]

Numbers alone do not tell the story of human interactions in the heat of war. The lists indicate, for example, how blacks seized the opportunity to reunite families divided by slavery. Cornelius Van Sayl, a thirty year old slave from Monmouth County, New Jersey, fled his master John Lloyd and took with him his wife, Catherine, and daughter, Mary, both of whom formerly belonged to John Van der Meer of Monmouth. In New York, the couple had another child, Peter, and also joined with Cornelius's brother, Peter, who escaped from a master in Tom's River, New Jersey. Even slaves manumitted by masters chose exile from the United States. Isaac Corie, twenty-seven years old, who was manumitted by his former master, William Mott, a Quaker from Great Neck, Long Island, left for Nova Scotia with his wife, Hagar, who was in turn manumitted by her master, Joseph Hewlett, a Quaker of Great Neck. The war also reunited families composed of slaves and free blacks. Prince, a slave from New Jersey, who purchased his freedom from Joseph Stokes of New Jersey, came to New York with his freeborn wife, Margaret, and their son, Mintard. In the city, they connected with their daughter, Elizabeth, her small child, and her husband, Samuel Van Nostrandt, who escaped from his master in Essex County, New Jersey.[31]

There were already small pockets of blacks in Nova Scotia, where slavery had existed since the 1740s. The first known group of free Black Loyalists to arrive in Nova Scotia was the "Company of Negroes" evacuated from Boston with other British forces in 1776. Demonstrating little responsibility towards the company, the British immediately began private negotiations to restore the blacks to their former masters in exchange for reconciliation. Hundreds died of disease in inadequate housing provided for them or starved. Signaling British and Nova Scotian intentions to maintain slavery, the legislature passed a law in 1781 declaring that baptism did not exempt slaves from bondage.[32]

The arrival of 3,000 Black Loyalists, after a ten day voyage from New York to Halifax, immediately enlarged the black communities in the Atlantic provinces. By the close of 1783, 1,485 free blacks lived in Birchtown, while 1,269 servants and free blacks resided in nearby Shelburne, a small port along Nova Scotia's rocky coast.[33] Planning for the creation of Shelburne and Birchtown began in New York City in 1782. Actual work commenced in May, 1783, when the Black Pioneers arrived and surveyed land for settlement. Anglican missionaries left food supplies of barrels of flour and pork "to the pioneers." Under the guidance of surveyor Benjamin Marsden, a Loyalist from Massachusetts, the Black Pioneers and white refugees felled trees and constructed crude huts. Plagued by black flies, and set back by a fire on May 26, their work progressed very slowly. Even with such drawbacks, Afro Nova Scotians labored with an enthusiasm akin to similar work projects conducted by white laborers in the United States.[34]

Social tensions appeared quickly. White and Black Loyalists were inadequately supplied with provisions and housed in tents, or the cramped holds of transport vessels, even during the winter months. More fortunate families had a "single apartment built with sods where men, women, children, pigs, fleas, bugs, mosquitoes and other domestic insects, mingle in society." British officials were not very sympathetic to housing needs, and demanded the removal of "various Negro homes and Hutts" in the spring of 1784. Recognizing that few would have the cash to survive the rugged winter, General Guy Carleton enlisted blacks in Halifax and Port Roseway for one year upon the same terms and pay with the Black Pioneer Company. Promised land distribution became problematic. Most whites received their land within three years, long before the minority of blacks received theirs.[35]

One major difficulty was that Nova Scotia was primarily an agricultural society. A Captain Booth blamed "expectations far too exalted" for the problems of the Black Loyalists. Booth believed they had not "sufficiently examined or reflected whether the land they were seated upon or the water, which partially surrounds them, would be profitable enough to attempt an increase of companies." He regarded the land as a "valley with much stones and a little swampy, but to appearances easily drained and secured." Booth had little confidence in the agricultural abilities of the Black Loyalists, whom he felt had "given no proof of their judgment about farming." Rather, they were "no farmers and very indifferent gardeners . . . . [they need those] able to work the Farmer's Plough and Harrow." Despite Booth's complaints, hundreds of blacks became "sharecroppers," with large and inescapable obligations which reduced them to near-servitude. Others toiled at work related to agriculture. The Pioneers were skilled at land clearance and wood cutting, which "they do for eight dollars, cutting firewood for fires and hunting in the season." Fishing, Booth noted, was the "chief and most profitable employment for their poor . . . though a fisherman requires a little cash to commence his labors."[36]

Many Black Loyalists were trained as artisans. A January 1784 census in Birchtown enumerated over two hundred laborers, forty-six carpenters, thirty-seven sawyers and eleven coopers. Thirty-five black refugees were sailors, ship carpenters, ropemakers, caulkers, and other maritime occupations. Other occupations included blacksmiths, barbers, cooks, bakers, shoemakers, tailors, and chimney-sweeps, reflecting past needs in the American colonies, but with no present advantage in a community with little commerce.[37] A few used entrepreneurial skills to eke out an existence. Boston King built chests which he traded for cornmeal. Later he received £15 and two barrels of fish for working on salmon and herring boats. Rose Fortune from Philadelphia established a baggage handling business in Annapolis in the 1780s. Fortune became an informal port policewoman. Her business survived as the Lewis Transfer Company. Most blacks, too highly skilled for the economy, resembled discontented artisans, anxious about the faltering economy in postwar United States.[38]

Working class white Nova Scotians resented competition from the freed people. Disbanded white soldiers rioted against free blacks in Shelburne in 1784 and "pulled down about 20 of their houses." Employers cheated blacks, sold indentured servants with impunity, or paid only in food and rum. Racial strains materialized as black popular culture appeared in Nova Scotia. On May 12, 1785, authorities distributed handbills forbidding "Negro Dances and Negro Frolicks in the town of Shelburne." A week later several blacks were ordered to the House of Correction for "riotous behavior." A year later frolics remained a problem for Nova Scotia officials, who ordered constables to arrest blacks found dancing and gambling at night. The disorderly house of Hysem Leeds and his wife Sylvia Howell was cited for "giving encouragement to other black people assembling there," and was a noisy disturbance to neighbors. Officials closed a hut occupied by blacks on Charlotte Lane as a "bad house."[39] Authorities punished blacks committing petty crimes with ferocity. Minor thefts earned blacks whippings. David Anderson was confined to the house of correction for thirty days and flogged thirty-nine times for borrowing and selling a watch "to equip him for a negro dance." The new legal statuses of blacks affected African-Americans who arrived as slaves. The Black Loyalists' example of freedom made servitude intolerable and soon the newspapers reported runaways.[40]

The emergence of the first black leader also demonstrated the perils of the new society. Stephen Blucke, leader of the Black Pioneers in New York City, was placed in charge of the development of Birchtown. Captain Booth of the Royal Engineers recalled him as "a man of surprising address, being perfectly polite and, I believe, has had a superior education." Booth noted that Blucke "don't appear to be more than eight and twenty—his wife is a negro woman as is his mother—they are people from Barbados." Within a year Blucke was commissioned Lieutenant-Colonel in command of twenty-one companies of Black Pioneers.[41]

Blucke personified government authority in Birchtown. Late in the summer of 1784, he tried to end wartime privileges. "Cutting and Carrying away, for sale, firewood," had been of great benefit during the hard winters around New York City, but now Blucke complained to the court of "unlicensed persons of Birchtown," taking firewood, "to the great detriment of those inhabitants." The Court agreed with Blucke, ordered such practices ended, and asked Blucke to build a "Gaol of Logs."[42]

Blucke was easily the most prosperous of the early Black Loyalists. He was the first to receive land, owned a rudimentary home, and enjoyed close connections with the Anglican establishment in Nova Scotia. Blucke's reputation grew when he entertained Prince William Henry, later King William IV, at his home in Birchtown. Despite the honor and political recognition this visit entailed, Blucke remained essentially a client of paternalistic whites. In his willingness to exploit poorer comrades, Blucke resembled conservative postwar artisan leaders in the United States. In his assigned role as leader of the Black Loyalists, Blucke was a finely developed product of Anglican missionary efforts. Stephen Skinner, who had been Blucke's patron in revolutionary New Jersey, used the colonel as a conduit for large amounts of money to the black community. Between 1787 and 1791 Skinner loaned Blucke over £200 for his use. Blucke also assisted Skinner when the white Loyalist purchased land from needy blacks at Birchtown. Blucke was perhaps the first African-American to rent a pew at a Church of England, paying twenty shillings for a pew at the Shelburne Anglican Church on January 21, 1790.[43]

The limits of his powers were evident in his negotiations with the English. His first difficulties arose over school financing and land distribution. He became schoolmaster for the black population in Birchtown. With only thirty-eight students, the school was badly under financed. Begging for assistance, Blucke wrote Dr. Bray's Associates in London about "almost naked children at this inclement season," and sought the charity of "clothes, a pair of shoes and a blanket."[44]

Blucke was not alone in his frustrations with Anglican schools. Black enrollment in the Dr. Bray and Society for the Propagation of the Gospel in Foreign Parts (S.P.G.) schools in Nova Scotia expanded upon the charity schools in colonial America. The S.P.G. established three schools for blacks in Nova Scotia under the leadership of Colonel Joseph Barton, a New Jersey Loyalist. Barton hired Joseph Leonard as master of the school in Digby. William Furmage, an assistant to Black Loyalist minister John Marrant, ran the school at Halifax while Blucke was schoolmaster in Birchtown. A few years later Thomas Brownspriggs headed a school at Little Tracadie. By 1791 the combined efforts of the S.P.G. and Dr. Bray's Associates produced five schools enrolling almost three hundred young blacks. All of the teachers were black Anglicans. White inspectors from the two charitable organizations provided books and supplies, but left management to blacks. As James Walker has argued, the schools did not lead to integration, but to the development of a parallel society: black, Christian and educated, separate from white culture, but unquestionably better off than the slave society left behind.[45] The schools' purposes were to produce excellent servants rather than independent citizens. The schools were experiments in industrial training with instruction emphasizing practical tasks such as knitting and sewing.[46]

Land allocation continued to be a logistical nightmare. Blucke was unable to negotiate successfully with Nova Scotian authorities who were overwhelmed by bureaucratic problems and vague about promises. Although Blucke and his men quickly surveyed and cleared land in Shelburne County, British officials and white Loyalists had first preference. Birchtown, destination of the Black Loyalists, was remote and swampy, generally unsuitable for farming. Of 649 black men at Birchtown in 1785, only 184 received any farms at all, averaging about thirty-four acres each. Blucke received two hundred acres but was at least partly responsible for his brethren's late receipt of their shares.[47]

Failing to obtain land or political equality, the Black Loyalists turned to religion. Scholars have established that in the United States, development of independent churches undergirded the creation of a black community and provided blacks with a method of revolutionary expression.[48] Black Loyalists underwent similar trials before sustaining autonomous congregations. At first, attracted to the state church of their British allies, several hundred blacks became Anglican.[49] Unfortunately, Anglicanism in Nova Scotia suffered many of the flaws evident in post revolutionary United States. Though blacks were generally welcome to church services and encouraged to take communion, they had to accept separate pews. On crowded Sundays, blacks were excluded from services. Rector John Breynton of Halifax's St. Paul's Anglican Church, who baptized hundreds of blacks, attempted to solve this problem by commissioning "several capable Negroes who read the Instructions to the Negroes and other pious books to as many of them as assemble for that purpose." Breynton's solution fostered black independence and leadership. Bishop Charles Inglis was later shocked to learn that Joseph Leonard, a black schoolteacher and minister, gave scripture readings and administered communion, baptized, and performed marriage ceremonies for black communicants. Despite Inglis's reproval, Leonard made it plain that he wished to be ordained and "to be entirely independent and separate from the whites, and to have a church."[50]

After an initial rush to membership, blacks grew disaffected from Anglicanism. Leonard's independence stopped short of leaving the Anglican Church. Other blacks were not so hesitant. Off-shoots of Anglicanism such as the Huntingdonians, led by Reverend John Marrant, emphasized "inner light" salvation and supplemented religious worship with daily prayer meetings, revivals and classes for personal instruction. Marrant led a chapel of about forty families in Birchtown while preaching as an itinerant around Nova Scotia to integrated audiences. White evangelists worried about Marrant's separatist tendencies. Freeborn Garretson, visiting from the United States, reported that "a Negro Man named Morant, lately from England, who says he was sent by the Lady Huntingdon, has done much hurt in society among the blacks at Burch town" and has caused "much confusion." Garretson believed that "Satan has sent" Marrant. After his grand tour of the Canadian provinces, Marrant returned to England. Cato Perkins from New York City replaced him as chief pastor in Birchtown.[51]

As their American counterparts did, Black Loyalists found greater freedom along the margins of Methodism. In the 1780s, Methodism was anti-slavery, highly egalitarian regarding the authenticity of religious experience, and open to black membership.[52] Moses Wilkinson, a fiery former slave, was the prime mover of black Methodism in Nova Scotia. He inspired converts Boston and Peggy King to undertake missions in Birchtown where eventually King became pastor of a black congregation. After initial Methodist contact, black ministers and exhorters kept the flames alive, and black congregations developed their own doctrines.[53] Methodists in Nova Scotia used ecstatic "love feasts." William Jessop, a white Methodist minister, reported an evening of preaching at Birchtown. Jessop held a "prayer meeting at night, after we had spent an hour or two in singing and praying most of the people went away, but some were loathe to leave before the power of the Lord came down upon us and a general shout of thanksgiving ascended to the heavens for the space of an hour."[54]

David George, formerly founder in 1773 of the Silver Bluff Baptist Church in South Carolina, the first black congregation in North America, came to Nova Scotia in 1784. George held several camp meetings in Shelburne in late 1784, attracting hundreds of blacks and sympathetic whites. Deeply influenced by Henry Alline and other New Light ministers at work in Nova Scotia in the early 1780s, George quickly became one of the leading black preachers. He used an inspiring and emotional style in mass baptisms of blacks and whites in the river near St. John. George was a charismatic leader who preached simple gospels of faith and total involvement. Angered by his success with whites, soldiers attacked George, entered his chapel during services, beat him, and drove him into the swamp. He fled to Birchtown where he preached from house to house. George was required to take a preaching license which permitted access only to black people.[55]

His highly democratic message, which taught that "a Baptist Church may arise and continue as a self-originating, self-governing body without any consent or approval from without," sparked many congregations. George's problems with whites had two effects. First they foreshadowed the reasons for black emigration in the late 1780s. Secondly, George's strongly democratic methods created a lasting base for black religion in Nova Scotia. By the 1820s, the majority of Nova Scotia blacks were Baptists, with over thirty congregations in a province-wide association. George was, along with Marrant, Leonard, Wilkinson, and others, among the first class of African-American ministers in North America. A few black preachers practicing in the colonial era, except for George, were without churches. Nova Scotia blacks founded their own churches and benevolent organizations in advance of developments in New York and Philadelphia. Marrant, George and the others preceded the activities of Richard Allen, Absalom Jones, George White, and Peter Williams, Jr. working around Philadelphia and New York City in the 1790s.[56]

Despite their religious accomplishments, black Nova Scotians faced dire conditions. Black beggars and paupers became common sights in the streets of Halifax. Charitable groups assisting with bags of seed potatoes enabled David George, for example, to make it through the winter. Throughout the province disastrous conditions increased black dependence on white benevolence. Another sore point was the continued existence of slavery in Nova Scotia. A number of southern Loyalists brought slaves with them. Abuses reappeared in Nova Scotia. Slaves were regularly sold to the West Indies. Courts in Nova Scotia placed the burden of proof on the slave in suits against masters demanding re enslavement. Some blacks took the tragic step of resubmitting to slavery.[57]

Conservative attitudes about slavery held up emancipation in Canada. John Graves Simcoe spearheaded the attack on slavery in Upper Canada (Ontario) and succeeded as governor in 1793 in obtaining limited emancipation. The legislation provided gradual emancipation for all blacks born after 1793 at the age of twenty-five, but discouraged emancipation for those slaves born prior to that date. The bill did, however, make slavery's future doubtful and, although some slave owners sold their chattel to masters in New York State, the law made Canada attractive to fugitive slaves. In

Nova Scotia and New Brunswick, legislators dodged the issue, but slavery became increasingly untenable.[58]

While Nova Scotians struggled, Black Loyalists in England faced similar problems of survival. They arrived filled with republican determination. A song written shortly after the exodus from New York to Nova Scotia and popular among London blacks captures this republican sensibility. Illustration eight portrays the sheet music for "Yankee Doodle; or the Negroes Farewell to America," sung in London in the mid-1780s. The first heady days of freedom soon gave way to deep alienation from English society. Unable to get work or proper housing, buffeted by racism, and allotted a miserable pension of six pence a day,[59] former soldiers, sailors, domestics and runaway slaves, now known as the Black Poor, expressed strong desire to "go to their respective homelands." English liberals, encouraged by the government, devised a "Committee in relief of the Black Poor." The committee and its representatives presented several plans. Black reactions, even in dire poverty, demonstrate their determination to avoid renewed enslavement and clientage. The blacks rejected proposals for emigration to Nova Scotia and the Bahamas. Despite offers of a bounty of nine guineas per person, Nova Scotia proved unacceptable. Black leaders were "totally disinclined" to go to the Bahamas, for fear of "putting themselves in any situation where Traffick in Slaves is carried on."[60]

The committee's representative, Henry Smeatham, a trader who had spent four years in the Gambia region, presented another plan to the Black Loyalists. Describing the blacks as "People of Colour, Refugees from America, disbanded from his Majesty's Service by Sea or Land, or otherwise distinguished objects of British humanity," Smeatham's plan included cash bounties, provisions, and other allowances for three months. The British government promised to purchase land, mark out a township, and help construct housing. Each person would receive as much land as they could cultivate. The plan mandated an eight hour work day during the week and six hours on Saturday. The British government would provide protection from slave traders. Disputes among the Black Loyalists would be settled by a judge chosen from among peers or at a town meeting. Smeatham's plan was an acknowledgment of the deep debts the British owed the Black Loyalists and the republican goals they sought. The plan emphasized government patronage for an interim period. After a brief time, blacks could construct their own democratic, self-governed society established on republican principles of small land ownership and community adjudication.[61]

Smeatham's role was cloudy, and soon Jacob Hanway and other members of the committee warned the blacks not to trust him, describing him as a "potential slave trader." The truth remains unknown because Smeatham suddenly died. The Committee took this as proof of the unhealthfulness of Africa and asked the blacks to reconsider New Brunswick. Some did accept this alternative. The rest negotiated and rejected the suggestions of Nova Scotia or the Bahamas. They disputed among themselves the wisdom of the Sierra Leone plan. The chief reason for reluctance was not the climate or disease, but the proximity of slave traders at Bance Island. In a memorable meeting on June 7, 1786, Jacob Hanway heard black pleas for assurances of liberty in Sierra Leone. Frustrated, he formed them into a circle and "harangued them, appealing to God and Common Sense of Mankind, for the Pure and benevolent Interests of the Government."[62]

Into the chasm of distrust stepped Granville Sharp. Gustavus Vasa, the famed black writer and abolitionist vouched for the venerable radical. Vasa had been the initial informant to Sharp in the infamous Zong case of 1782 when a British captain threw 130 blacks overboard, then claimed insurance for the losses. Beginning with the case of Jonathan Strong in 1765, and culminating in his powerful arguments in the famous Somerset decision of 1772, which created precedent for the abolition of slavery in England, Sharp's powerful radicalism transformed black status in England forever. His words were well known and regarded among English and American blacks.[63]

Together with black seamen, free blacks emancipated in the Somerset decision, and escaped slaves from the West Indies, the Black Loyalists in London gave close attention to a May 1786 handbill advertising passage to the Grain Coast of Africa, where "the necessaries of life may be supplied by the force of industry and moderate labour and life rendered very comfortable." Granville Sharp promised the potential settlers self-government in Sierra Leone. The Black Loyalists demanded documentary proof of British protection of their freedom and insurance that the proposal was not an evil design to resell them into slavery. To allay these fears, the English government issued parchments granting the Black Loyalists the status of free citizens of "the Colony of Sierra Leone or in the Land of Freedom." Actually these certificates were worthless, as Sierra Leone was not a British colony. Worse, the parchments placed the Loyalists under the jurisdiction of the Sierra Leone

Company and the British government. Nor did the supposed British treaty with the Temne, the largest nearby nation in Sierra Leone, conclusively allot the settlers four hundred square miles. Many of the blacks dropped out of the project before departure. Poverty among blacks escalated and the government rounded up any African-Americans found begging in London. Lists of passengers were made on board the several vessels in early 1787; these enumerations include three hundred forty-four men, women and children prepared to leave for Sierra Leone as well as officers of the fleet, their wives and children. Accompanying them were thirty white women, who had married Black Loyalists. The lists are the earliest evidence available of racial intermarriage occurring in Atlantic port cities. A human experience as old as international trade, interracial sex is rarely documented because it occurred chiefly among the poor. Chronicles of Sierra Leone history usually describe these white women as prostitutes. In fact, as Ellen Wilson has stressed, the women were either common-law wives or married to the black men. Further evidence on interracial love exists in the lists of black women married to white men; there has been no suggestion that these couples were illicit.[64]

Departure was delayed by bad weather and about fifty of the company died before leaving the shores of England. As the survivors left, Sharp provided the settlers with a letter regarding agreements with Captain Taylor of the Brig *Myro* and of his desires for their conduct en route. He appointed several men—Richard Collins, Henry Estwick, John Irwin, Thomas Peal, Alexander Saunders and Charles Tacitus—as trustees of supplies. Sharp advised the passengers to elect a seventh trustee and replacements for any who died on board. As soon as the ship left the port of London, Sharp instructed the settlers to form themselves into dozens, each electing a head-borough and an assistant head-borough to settle disputes, distribute food and supplies, and rum. All males above sixteen should form a militia, and receive arms, cutlasses, and belts "that you may land in a decent and military manner." The plan provided immense autonomy for the settlers. Governance was democratic with free elections of a black leadership.[65]

Sharp outlined in his 1786 pamphlet, *A Short Sketch of Temporary Regulations (Until Better Shall be Proposed) for the Intended Settlement on the Grain Coast of Africa near Sierra Leone*, a vision of an agrarian utopia where natural man could be civilized through reason. Sharp's republican plan for the Black Loyalists reached far back into English political history. The community would be self-governing, through a system of tithings of ten families, each of which elected a leader, the tithingman. Ten tithingmen elected a hundredor, who collectively ruled the province, and acted as the judiciary. Slavery was prohibited. In an early expression of the labor theory of value, the cost for any commodity derived from the amount of labor needed for its production, based upon an eight-hour day. Taxation was based not on money, but on contributions of sixty-two days' labour. Sharp added an element of state enterprise by planning for the government to keep thirty per cent of the land in its own hands, to be worked under the land-labor tax. In addition to these utopian proposals, Sharp envisioned the settlement as a beacon of Christianity in Africa, civilizing and christianizing Africans in one project. Black Loyalists' ready acceptance of the plan suggests the powerful currents of revolutionary republicanism flowing through the blood of the freed people in London.[66]

The Black Loyalists encountered several obstacles. Their destination, Sierra Leone, had been used by European slave traders for over two centuries.[67] Slavers occupied two islands along the Sierra Leone river, while just above the site of Granville Town in the mountains, maroons who escaped from a Danish vessel in 1788 created a Deserters' Town. Local Africans largely worked for slave traders and were often hostile to the new settlers. Friction between the free blacks and slave traders culminated when several blacks raided a store at Bance. Captured, they were initially sentenced to transportation, but were conveniently sold to a passing French trader as slaves. Indeed, the slave trade offered the largest source of employment and some settlers worked as clerks, laborers, and artisans at the factories. Deadly diseases also cut a huge swath in the Black Loyalists' population. By September, eighty-six emigrants were dead and fifteen had vanished, leaving 276 of the 377 who landed still in Granville Town. By the beginning of the following year only 130 remained as the others drifted off into the country. Finally, in a dispute between local Africans and the slave traders, Granville Town was sacked and burned. The British government showed little interest in aiding exiled Black Loyalists.[68]

The Old Settlers, as they were known, tried to communicate their troubles and determination to Sharp, but were frustrated by "the rascality of captains, as packet-bearers, who through some particular views have destroyed" at least one hundred letters. One surviving letter, dated September 3, 1788, which did make it to Sharp described the "good progress in clearing our land," and of hopes for "some tolerable good crops this season." The settlers assured Sharp of their determination to build a church, court-house, and prison. A major problem was a lack of cement for bricks. Natives charged extortionate amounts for limestone and oyster shells. A ship-captain embezzled a supply of chalk sent by Sharp. The settlers worried about nearby hostile nations and feared that the supply of small arms would only "aggravate our guilt in the sight of our adversaries." Although down to only forty able-bodied men, the settlers asked Sharp to send muskets for their defense.[69] In 1791 a relief-agent named Falconbridge arrived to help "a number of unfortunate people, both blacks and whites, . . . sent to Sierra Leone." Falconbridge found forty-six of the settlers. He learned that some of the black poor previously departed for the West Indies, others went back to England, and a few fled into the jungle. With the supplies brought by Falconbridge, the settlers cleared four acres and reestablished the colony.[70]

Despite its initial setbacks, Sierra Leone remained attractive to discontented blacks in Nova Scotia. By 1791, over one thousand Black Loyalists in Nova Scotia petitioned the government for permission to immigrate to Sierra Leone. Thomas Peters, a revolutionary war veteran, presented the petition to the English government. His brief complained of poor conditions in Nova Scotia and alluded to the plan of Thomas Clarkson and other English abolitionists to establish a self-governing colony of free blacks on the west coast of Africa. Peters traveled to London to meet with other Black Loyalists and with Granville Sharp and William Wilberforce, who were interested in the plight of black Nova Scotians. Peters also discussed emigration with Sir Henry Clinton, his old commanding officer, and found the general receptive to black complaints. Clinton even gave Peters a small contribution. The Sierra Leone Company appointed John Clarkson, younger brother of Thomas Clarkson, to promote emigration of Nova Scotian blacks. The English government combined debate over abolition of the slave trade with creation of a Sierra Leone company to handle migration of Nova Scotia and English blacks to Africa. The Black Loyalists' proposal to repatriate to Africa gained quick acceptance, placing Peters and his companions in a vanguard movement fusing African American nationalism and enlightenment liberalism.[71]

Peters' petition reflected a revolutionary republicanism born of military service. He opened his letter identifying himself as "a Free Negro and late a Sargeant in the Regiment of Guides and Pioneers serving in North America under the command of General Sir Henry Clinton." Clearly, Peters believed that as a veteran acting "on behalf of himself and others, the Black Pioneer and Loyal Black

Refugees," he was entitled to a hearing, and to the satisfaction of economic and political demands, beliefs any American republican would appreciate. A second impulse was religious republicanism. Joining Peters were such important black preachers as David George, Moses Wilkinson, John Ball, and Cato Perkins. Entire congregations including Joseph Leonard's Anglicans and the Brindley town Methodists left as did Halifax County churches led by Boston King, Hector Peters, and Catherine Abernathy. Black religious nationalists, they regarded the inevitable assimilation into white Nova Scotian sects as a dilution of their identity.[72] The third issue which would resound through African American nationalist philosophies for the next half-century was access to land. A few Nova Scotian blacks received land in comparable size to that allotted in the American South after the Civil War and Emancipation. Like their counterparts in the United States would be four generations later, most blacks in Nova Scotia remained landless. The Sierra Leone plan offered land, and the elusive political independence lacking in Nova Scotia.[73]

John Clarkson, the principal British agent for the emigration scheme, met with blacks at Birchtown. After cautioning against reports of poor climate and exaggerated stories of fertile land in Africa, Clarkson described the terms of emigration. In return for a quit-rent (property tax), the Sierra Leone Company promised each freedman twenty acres of land for himself, ten for his wife, and five for every child. Company stores would provide food to whites and blacks according to fixed rules. The civil, military, personal and commercial rights, and duties of blacks and whites would be the same. Black settlers would be protected from marauding slave traders. In the next three days 150 men, 147 women and 217 children enrolled for the voyage. Clarkson's sincerity touched the republican idealism of the Black Loyalists, who were tired of deceit, racism, and poverty in Nova Scotia.[74]

Blacks questioned Clarkson very closely whether ship captains would let them hold religious services, and how much stowage each would be allowed. Clarkson, surprised at the overwhelming black interest in the project, wanted assurances that only the most healthy blacks, with proven veterans' status would embark for Sierra Leone. He instructed that any lame, elderly single women "in short any one who cannot maintain himself or herself," be denied access.[75]

Black enthusiasm for Clarkson's plan caught the Anglican establishment and Stephen Blucke by surprise. Anglicans turned to Blucke for "responsible" leadership. Blucke reported to the Lieutenant-Governor and Commander-in-Chief of Nova Scotia, John

Parr, "to inform you that numbers of our brethren are so infatuated as to embrace the proposals of the Sierra Leone Company (which with all due submission) we conceive will be their utter annihilation." To encourage blacks to stay, Blucke suggested "a grant of a cow and 2 sheep." Blucke's signature was followed by his wife's, mother's, and fifty-six other Black Loyalists. White Nova Scotians also worried about the prospective departure of hundreds of black laborers. Stephen Skinner wrote Henry Dindal, Secretary of State for the Home Department in London, that despite universal suffering. most blacks did very well. He blamed the plans for immigration on "general delusion . . . [and a] desire for a warm climate," and accused Peters of being "flattered by imaginary happenings."[76]

The loss of black labor cut deeply into the economies of Birchtown and Shelburne. Conditions for remaining blacks varied. Most were tied to the Anglican church. The S.P.G. formed segregated schools in each black town. Stephen Blucke's empire shrank to about fifty people. In a case which paralleled earlier charges against his patron, Stephen Skinner, Blucke was charged a few years later with embezzlement and disappeared. Legend has it that he was devoured by a savage animal. Unlike Skinner, Blucke lacked the required social standing and loyal allies to see him through the crisis.[77]

Passage to Africa was neither timely nor easy and over sixty settlers died en route. By March 9, 1792, all fifteen transport vessels arrived in Sierra Leone.[78] The first year was a dying season. The Nova Scotians arrived at Sierra Leone at the approach of the rainy season with no shelter and in poor health from the voyage. In a repeat of their arrival in Nova Scotia, they had to clear a thick forest. Just before Christmas 1792, a census showed a loss of two hundred Nova Scotians. Survivors enjoyed well-made houses and gardens sprouting from seeds providentially brought in trunks from Nova Scotia.[79]

The patronizing airs and negligence of the English authorities soon angered Thomas Peters and other black leaders. The Nova Scotians were already irritated by the prospect of quit-rents for lands just recently acquired, despite Clarkson's promise that such taxes would be deferred for ten years. Worse, at a shilling per acre, the proposed quit-rents were fifty times those in other colonies. In petitions to Clarkson, Peters complained of English racism and incompetence. Such practices, Peters noted, infuriated those "who had just emerged from Slavery and who were therefore jealous of every action, nay of every look that came from White Men, who were put in authority over them." A number of Nova Scotians presented a demand that Peters be made governor. Clarkson, though far more liberal than other Englishmen, could not accept black demands for liberty and self-governance. Clarkson vetoed a proposal that twelve blacks be appointed peace officers for the settlement. Dissident blacks sent another protesting the governor's suspension of credit. The petition accepted the laws of England but not "without having any of our Color in it." Though assuring Clarkson that they "don't mean to take the law into our own hands," the petition was a sure step of greater black political autonomy. Peters' ambition was halted first by a scandal involving embezzlement of funds and then, tragically, by his early death.[80]

Peters' death did not end animosity between Black Loyalists and the colonial governors. The one trustworthy Englishman failed to return to Sierra Leone, as political pressure and health problems stalled Clarkson's departure from England. His replacements soon alienated the Nova Scotian population. Land disputes and quit-rent controversies, exacerbated by English dalliances with nearby slave-traders, brought the colony near rebellion when a French fleet nearly destroyed it in October 1794. In the aftermath, the English demanded blacks return any booty taken during the attack. Despite threats, few blacks bothered to answer the demands.[81] After the company charter plan proved unworkable, the Sierra Leone Company instituted a government by a governor and council of two members. It demanded further taxes from the Nova Scotians, controlled market prices, and licensed taverns, butchers, and other trades. Clarkson had ruled largely through persuasion. Succeeding governors were far more autocratic.[82]

C. B. Wadstrom, a Danish scientist working for the Sierra Leone Company, noticed the strongly republican tempers of the Nova Scotians. He wrote that the Nova Scotians had an "unreasonable estimation of their own merits and their inadequate sense of the obligation they owe the company, is another defect." These personality disorders "combined with the misconceptions of the more forward, concerning their rights as freemen."[83] The central pulse for this republicanism, however, came from religion. The Nova Scotians experienced a profound religious revival in Sierra Leone. Mrs. Falconbridge noticed seven religious sects, each with a preacher "who alternately preach throughout the whole night." She found the Nova Scotians to be uncommonly pious and could not recall a single night "without preachings from some quarter or other." One major effect of the revival was the splintering of

Methodist congregations into many different sects. George Thompson described how "one man gets disaffected and will begin for himself, gathering a company around him who are called after his name, then another. Thus there is Elliott's' Chapel, Jewett's Chapel." Less orthodox churches had the greatest display of emotionalism with much shouting and shaking and "finding the Lord."[84]

In Africa, black women developed leadership gained only by Rose Fortune in Nova Scotia. Settler women asserted independence in Sierra Leone by establishing themselves as market women in Freetown and on routes deep into the interior. The first three market licenses the Sierra Leone Company awarded in 1795 were to women. Mary Perth from Norfolk, Virginia, became very prosperous through trade and her association with Zachery Macauley, governor of Sierra Leone from 1796 to 1799. Later she provided meals for Church Missionary Society clergy. Both she and Sophia Smalls were able, despite severe pillaging and loss of goods purchased on credit, to survive the 1795 French attack. Nova Scotia women traded with African nations to the interior through membership in Bundu or Sande secret societies. Settler women, many of them from South Carolina, where such organizations were abundant among slaves, used the societies for entree into host cultures and to establish trade relationships. Others gained entrance through marriage. They were able to connect these networks with the international British trade out of Freetown. Their aggressive methods of obtaining such connections, despite pervasive sexism and racism in the Sierra Leone Company, speaks to their determination to become economic and cultural intermediaries.[85]

Female autonomy derived from polygamy practiced among the settlers, which blended well with local national methods. A representative from the Countess of Huntingdon remarked that "the conjugal union is little understood or regarded." Fractured families, gender imbalances, and cultural traditions allowed black women more sexual and economic freedom outside of European conceptions of nuclear families. Despite the pleas of the still-active Granville Sharp and stronger pressures from British authorities, blacks simply ignored legal prohibitions.[86]

The controversies over quitrents and the antagonism in the aftermath of the French attack reinforced the strong black nationalism born in revolutionary America and Nova Scotia. The Nova Scotians believed they were fully entitled to the rights of freeborn Englishmen. One unsympathetic government report commented on those "false and absurd notions, which the more forward among them have imbibed, concerning their rights as freemen." Despite English chauvinism, Nova Scotians created a solid block in Sierra Leone politics. The Sierra Leone Company retained the three tier representation of black tithing men and hundredors who advised the company management. Though presumably lacking power, these offices quickly became the forum for black grievances. Nova Scotians elected black representatives who recommended appointment of black judges in 1799, which the company ignored. Recalling Clarkson's promises of full equality and judicial power made, the settlers presented petitions to complain about racism in the company stores, courts and auctions. Nova Scotians battled with the company over wages, finally agreeing on two shillings six pence per day. While the Nova Scotians simmered just below the point of rebellion, English authorities anxiously awaited the arrival of Maroons, exiled from Jamaica and presently leaving a temporary home in Nova Scotia. Company officers negotiated with leaders of the Nova Scotians, essentially stalling for time. The insurgents attempted an alliance with the local Temne chief, King Tom. Before that could happen, the English made a decisive move to quell any dissent by attacking Freetown, using British soldiers from the transport ship *Asia*, and one hundred fifty newly arrived Maroons. The English abolished any representative government in Sierra Leone, silenced any incipient rebellion, and placed the young nation under royal charter. In response, the last years of the eighteenth century saw a resurgent black nationalism in religious, political, and economic spheres.[87]

African American and Black Loyalists' cultures re-embraced in 1811. Paul Cuffe of New Bedford, Massachusetts, the wealthiest African American of his generation, and a strong proponent of emigration to Africa, visited Sierra Leone. Cuffe was soon frustrated by Sierra Leone trade restrictions and shifted his attention to the Nova Scotians. Cuffe presented one visitor with a Bible, a Quaker history, and an antiwar essay. Later, Cuffe visited King George from the Bulom Shore with whom he had a theological discussion and exchange of gifts. Cuffe admired settler preachers, particularly Methodist minister Henry Warren, formerly from Philadelphia. Cuffe proposed enlargement of black trade between Sierra Leone, England and America. This was endorsed enthusiastically by the Nova Scotians, but subverted by crown officials. Eventually, the governor and other prominent whites supported Cuffe's antislavery petition while condemning him in letters as no better than a slave trader.[88]

While in Sierra Leone, Cuffe spoke with several veteran Black Loyalists. Warwick Francis recalled the savage beatings, which caused him to flee to the British lines. Cuffe discussed trade relations and emigration of free blacks with John Kizell, a Black Loyalist from South Carolina, who returned to his native Sherbro via Nova Scotia to become the leading black merchant of Freetown. Cuffe, Kizell, Francis, and others authored a petition to Parliament to support and encourage further black emigration to Sierra Leone. Later, under Cuffe's guidance, Kizell and others made up an antislavery petition. These documents, sent to England and America, indicate the strength of the black political exchanges among the Black Loyalists of Sierra Leone, Cuffe, and American blacks in New York.[89]

Cuffe was deeply inspired by his Sierra Leone experience. He returned to the United States in 1811, and enthusiastically met with black leaders in Philadelphia, New York, and Boston to promote trade with the colony. Cuffe's plan, using black capital, ships, and crews, reinstituted ties between New Yorkers, New Jerseyans, and Nova Scotians broken since 1783. He found black New York clerics, activists, and intellectuals had a solid interest in Nova Scotia. For the Nova Scotians, Cuffe was a chance to break the suffocating stranglehold British governors placed on their economic development. Cuffe shared with Peter Williams, Jr., William T. Hamilton, and other important black leaders of New York, despair about opportunity for blacks in the United States. Cuffe and the Nova Scotians were frustrated by local bureaucrats who held negative powers over the captain's ability to sell his cargoes. Even so, Cuffe's visit was the initial appearance of a black pride and identification with Africa. Economically, his trade proposals were among the earliest nationalist formulas for black self-help and autonomy.[90]

Cuffe's plans for a triangular trade between Sierre Leone, England, and New York were stymied by the War of 1812 and the antipathy of local officials towards black enterprise which might threaten their oligarchy. White liberals, especially those hoping that Cuffe would become the vanguard of free American blacks voluntarily leaving for Africa, gave the New Bedford Quaker private support. After several years of planning, diplomatic negotiations, and fund-raising, Cuffe sailed to Freetown with a cargo of tobacco, soap, candles, bar iron, and "several colored families who intend to make a settlement there." Among them was Charles Calumbine from New York who planned to return to his original home in Senegal. Upon arrival, Cuffe overcame the governor's suspicions and sold his goods, encouraging black trade and enterprise. When departing, Cuffe promised to return soon and to promote emigration to Freetown from America.[91]

The lessons of the Black Loyalists resonated well beyond the coast of Africa. The migration of thousands of blacks from New York to Nova Scotia and, later, the passage of over one thousand blacks from Nova Scotia to Sierra Leone symbolized the freedom struggles of African Americans for generations. In Nova Scotia, Black Loyalists continued their struggle, augmented by the arrival of maroons from Jamaica in 1794 and blacks loyal to Great Britain in 1812. Religious ties formed in colonial America sustained the black community in Nova Scotia until 1915. At the close of the War of 1812, several thousand blacks fled with the British forces to Nova Scotia. Among them was Richard Preston who revitalized black Baptists in Nova Scotia.[92]

Whether they remained in Nova Scotia or migrated further to Sierrra Leone, the 3,000 African Americans created, under great hardship, their own community with churches and schools. Their version of the American Revolution preceded similar events in the United States. They demonstrated that black republicanism, hardened in the crucible of the American Revolution, could create an independent nation. Eventually, their example inspired the creation of Liberia. Blacks not only won their freedom in America, but returned by choice to Africa. In the United States, the memory of the Black Loyalists may be measured not only by Paul Cuffe's exploits, but with reference to their place in black rituals of freedom. In 1827 as New York State formally abolished slavery, William Hamilton, a local black leader, alluded in his commemoration speech to those who gained freedom by "leaving the country at the close of the [Revolutionary] War," winning "a respite from slavery."[93]

Graham Russell Hodges
Colgate University
Hamilton, NY
February 20, 1995

Notes

[1] For substance of their meeting see John C. Fitzpatrick, ed. *The Writings of George Washington from the Original Manuscript Sources, 1745–1799.* 39 vols. (Washington, 1944) 26: 401–414. For a good account of this see Benjamin Quarles, *The Negro in the American Revolution* (Chapel Hill, N.C., 1960), 160–181. Fifty-six blacks were among 501 persons sailing from New York City bound for Halifax in October, 1782. For vessel bound for Halifax see its shipping manifest, October 20, 1782, Public Records Office (PRO) 30/55/52 p. 5938.

[2] Ellen Wilson, *The Loyal Blacks* (New York, 1973), 53–55. For summary of Carleton's decision see PRO 30/8/344/109–111. For dispute see Arnett G. Lindsay, "Diplomatic Relations between the United States and Great Britain Bearing on the Return of Negro Slaves, 1783–1828," *Journal of Negro History*, 5 (1920), 391–419.

[3] The Black Loyalists are an early example of the ideologies expressed in Paul Gilroy, *The Black Atlantic: Modernity and Double Consciousness* (Cambridge, 1993).

[4] For several works illustrating the halting advance of black freedom in the United States see Gary B. Nash and Jean Soderlund, *Freedom by Degrees: Emancipation in Pennsylvania and its Aftermath* (New York, 1991); Shane White, *"Somewhat More Independent" The End of Slavery in New York City, 1770–1810* (Athens, Ga., 1991) and Graham Russell Hodges, *Slavery and Freedom in the Rural North: African Americans in Monmouth County, New Jersey, 1660–1870* (Madison, 1995).

[5] James W. St. G. Walker, *The Black Loyalists: The Search for the Promised Land in Sierra Leone and Nova Scotia* (New York, 1976) 45–46, 53–54; Wilson, *The Loyal Blacks*, 81–95.

[6] For best discussions of the proclamation and events leading up to it see Quarles, *The Negro in the American Revolution*, 18–31 and Sylvia Frey, *Water From the Rock: Black Resistance in a Revolutionary Age* (Princeton, N.J., 1991), 63, 67, 114.

[7] For figure of 800 blacks see Nathaniel Greene to George Washington, July 21, 1776 in Peter Force, *American Archives*, 5th Series, (Washington, 1840), 1:486. A captured slave named Strickland informed Greene of this figure. See also *American Archives*, 1:862, 949 for intelligence about Dunmore's moves.

[8] Donald L. Robinson, *Slavery in the Structure of American Politics, 1765–1820* (New York, 1971), 54–98; F. Nwabueze Okoye, "Chattel Slavery as the Nightmare of the American Revolutionaries," *William and Mary Quarterly* 3rd ser. 37 (1980), 3–28.

[9] The best review of American use of blacks remains Quarles, *The Negro in American Revolution*, 68–111.

[10] See William H. Nelson, *The American Tory* (Oxford, UK, 1961), 111–112; Muhlenberg quote in Theodore G. Tappert and John W. Doberstein, *The*

Journals of Henry Melchior Muhlenberg, 3 vols. (Philadelphia, 1942–1958), III, 53, 105; see also "Lee Papers," in *Collections of the New-York Historical Society for 1871* (New York, 1871), 379, 410.

[11] See Graham Hodges, "Black Revolt in New York City and the Neutral Zone," in *New York in the Age of the Constitution*, eds. Paul A. Gilje and William Pencak (Cranbury, N.J., 1992), 20–48.

[12] For estimates of American losses and black services to the English see Quarles, *The Negro in the American Revolution*, 111–134; Frey, *Water from the Rock*; and Hodges, "Black Revolt."

[13] Hodges, "Black Revolt."

[14] "Memoirs of Mr. Boston King," *Methodist Magazine for March, 1798*, 109–110.

[15] *Ibid.*

[16] See James W. St. G. Walker, "Blacks as American Loyalists: The Slave's War for Independence," *Historical Reflections/Reflections Historique*, 2(1975), 51–57; P.E.H Hair, "Africanism: The Freetown Contribution," *Journal of Modern African Studies*, 4 (1967), 521–539; K.L. Little, "The Significance of the West African Creole for Africanist and Afro-American Studies," *African Affairs*, 49, no. 197 (1950), 308–319; and Akintola Wyse, *The Krio of Sierra Leone, An Interpretation* (London, 1990). For artisan republicanism see R. Sean Wilentz, *Chants Democratic New York City & the Rise of the American Working Class, 1788–1850* (New York, 1984), 61–107; For Murphy Stiel vision see Clinton Papers, vol. 170: 27, Clements Library. For entry see page 177.

[17] See Lt. General Alexander Leslie to Carleton, June 27, 1782, and James Moncrief to Henry Clinton, March 13, 1782, Moncrief Letter Book, 1780–1782, Clements Library. Intelligence given to General Nathaniel Greene refers to British use of "black dragoons" and "Ethiopian Dragoons" in South Carolina. See Green Manuscripts, November 6, 1782, Clements Library.

[18] King, "Memoirs of Mr. Boston King," 155.

[19] For payroll see PRO 30/55/47,52, 58, 63. For land grants see Carleton Papers, Document 6480, Public Archives of Nova Scotia (PANS).

[20] David Syrett, *Shipping and the American War: A Study of British Transport Organization* (London, 1970), 240.

[21] For requests see John Harbeck to Carleton, April 14, 1783, Colonial Office (CO) 50/152; Nicholas Jamieson to Lt. Governor Elliott, April 22, 1783, CO 25/93; John Willoughby, a Virginian, to Carleton, April 28, 1783 in pursuit of 300 slaves, CO 52/69 and Wilson, *Loyal Blacks*, 51–52. See also Peter D. Vroom to General Carleton, "Petition to Secure Runaway Negro," ca.1782–1783, New-Jersey Historical Society (N-JHS.) One agent, Ralph Wormley charged £48 for returning 31 slaves to Virginia. See Ralph Wormley to John Robinson, April 19, 1782, Misc. Mss., Library of Congress (LOC); "Memoirs of the Life of Boston King," 155.

[22] "Carleton Orderly Book," 138, 166 and Wilson, *Loyal Blacks*, 65. See also Reverend Dirck Romeyn to Richard Varick, July 20, 1782, Varick Papers, New-York Historical Society (N-YHS) and "Guy Carleton Orderly

Book, 1782–1783," 44–45, Frederick Mackensie Papers, Bound Volume F, Clements Library.

[23] Fitzpatrick, *Writings of Washington*, 26: 364–370. I am indebted to Daniel Meaders for this reference.

[24] "Board of Commissioners for Superintending British Embarkation," Force Manuscripts, Series 8D, Item 14, Library of Congress also available in PRO 30/55/100; for American claimants' problems see CO 30/55/70 and CO 30/55/73.

[25] For her runaway notice see *Virginia Gazette* (Purdie and Dixon), May 6, 1773. For other information see "Board of Embarkation Minutes." July 15, July 24, August 2, 7, 1783. I am indebted to Daniel Meaders for much of the information in this paragraph.

[26] "Board of Embarkation Minutes." July 15, July 24, August 2, 7, 1783.

[27] Graham Russell Hodges and Alan Edward Brown, eds. *"Pretends to be Free": Runaway Slave Advertisements from Colonial and Revolutionary New York and New Jersey* (New York, 1994).

[28] Ann Patton Malone, *Sweet Chariot: Slave Family & Household Structure in Nineteenth-Century Louisiana* (Chapel Hill, 1992).

[29] See Hodges and Brown, eds. *"Pretends to be Free,"* p. 307; Billy G. Smith and Richard Wojtowicz, eds., *"Blacks Who Stole Themselves": Advertisements for Runaways in the Pennsylvania Gazette, 1728–1790,* (Philadelphia, 1989); Freddy Lee Parker, *Running for Freedom: Slave Runaways in North Carolina, 1775–1840* (New York, 1993); Gerald W. Mullin, *Flight and Rebellion: Slave Resistance in Eighteenth-Century Virginia* (New York, 1972).

[30] See Quarles, *The Negro in the American Revolution*; Frey, *Water from the Rock*, 216–222; Hodges, "Black Revolt," and Hodges, *Black Resistance in Colonial and Revolutionary Bergen County, New Jersey* (River Edge, NJ, 1989), 18–19.

[31] For Van Sayls see page 81; for Isaac Corie, page 7.

[32] For early slavery in Nova Scotia see Robin W. Winks, *The Blacks in Canada, A History* (New Haven, 1971), 24–61 and T. Watson Smith, "The Slave in Canada," *Collections of the Nova Scotia Historical Society*, 10 (1896–1898), 1–161.

[33] For travel time to Nova Scotia see "Diary of Stephen Skinner, 1783–1787," PANS, *Report*, 1974 (Halifax, N.S., 1974), 19–34; for arrival of blacks at Birchtown see Marion Robertson, *King's Bounty: A History of Early Shelburne, Nova Scotia* (Halifax, 1973), 71, 79, 105; Evangeline B. Harvey, "The Negro Loyalists," *Nova Scotia Historical Quarterly*, 1 (1971), 182; Wilson, *The Loyal Blacks*, 73–77, 109.

[34] Robertson, *King's Bounty*, 33–35, 87–89; W.O. Raymond, "The Founding of Shelburne, Benjamin Marston at Halifax and Miramiche," *New Brunswick Historical Society Collections*, 3: 7 (1907), 228–230, 232; "State of the Provisions Sent by Reverend Mr. Brundle, 1783–1784," PANS MG 1, Box 1894, Folder 8; Wilson, *Loyal Blacks*, 82.

[35] Robertson, *King's Bounty*, 90–91; Carleton Papers, 8800, 9130, PANS; "Extracts from the General Sessions of Shelburne," PANS, MG 4, Vol. 141, April 7, 1784.

[36] "Diary and Letters of Captain Booth," March 17, 1787; John Britton, "A Description of the Harbours on the Coast of Nova Scotia from Halifax to Mahone Bay with the Estimated Exports of Fish and Lumber in 1784," Typescript, Ferguson Papers, PANS, MG 1, Box 1898, Folder 9.

[37] Walker, *Black Loyalists*, 21–23, 39; Wilson, *Loyal Blacks*, 87.

[38] For Rose Fortune see Mary Byers and Margaret McBurney, *Atlantic Hearth: Early Homes and Families of Nova Scotia* (Toronto, 1994), 185. See also "List of Negroes belonging to Citizens of Pennsylvania Carried away by the British," August 9, 1786, Records of the Supreme Executive Council, Reel 27, Pennsylvania State Archives, Harrisburg, Pennsylvania.

[39] "Extracts from the Court of Special Sessions"; Robertson, *King's Bounty*, 95–96.

[40] Walker, *Black Loyalists*, 42–49; Wilson, *Loyal Blacks*, 89–92; "Extracts from the Court of Special Sessions of Shelburne," PANS, MG 4, Vol. 141; Robertson, *King's Bounty*, 96–97, 147–149. For runaway notices see *Halifax Gazette*, September 14, 1784; December 9, 1787; *St. John Gazette*, July 15, 1784, June 29, 1786.

[41] "Diary and Letters of Captain Booth of the Royal Engineers Stationed in Shelburne, 1789," Ferguson Papers, MG 1, Box 1911, Folder 16, PANS. For Blucke commission see PANS, MG 1, Box 1894, Folder 1/9: 16. For companies of Black Pioneers see "A List of those Mustered At Shelburne, Nova Scotia in the Summer of 1784 by William Porter, Deputy Commissary of Musters," PANS, MG 64, Vol. 141.

[42] "Extracts of the General Court of Sessions of Shelburne," August 21, 1784.

[43] Stephen Skinner Ledger, 1786–1791, PANS, MG 63, #305: 9–11, 126, 162, 314; Bray Associates/Canada, August 1, 1788. For Prince William dinner see Fergusson, *Clarkson's Mission*, 191. For Blucke pew rental see "Anglican Church Records, Shelburne, Nova Scotia, Vestry Records, 1769–1868," PANS, MG 4, Vol. 141: 19.

[44] "Blucke to Associates, December 22, 1787, Dr. Bray's Associates/Canada File" Folio 4:1, Rhodes Library; *An Account of the Designs of the Associates of the late Dr. Bray with an Abstract of their Proceedings* (London, 1785), 24–27.

[45] Walker, *Black Loyalists*, 83–86; Colonel James Barton to Reverend Mr. Breynton, January 25, 1785; Barton to Reverend Wicker, December 13, 1786; Mr. Marchute to Breynton, April 17, 1785; Charles Inglis to Reverend Lydecker, November 30, 1792, all in Bray/Canada, File 1, Rhodes Library. See also *An Account of the Designs of the Associates*, 27, for roster of Leonard's students.

[46] Judith Fingard, *The Anglican Design in Loyalist Nova Scotia, 1783–1816* (London, 1972), 135–137; Walker, *Black Loyalists*, 80–84; Robertson, *King's Bounty*, 99.

[47] Walker, *Black Loyalists*, 22–23.

[48] See Gary B. Nash, *Forging Freedom: The Formation of Philadelphia's Black Community, 1720–1840* (Cambridge, 1988); and Graham Russell Hodges, *Black Itinerants of the Gospel: The Narratives of John Jea and George White* (Madison, 1993).

[49] Walker, *Black Loyalists*, 68–69; Wilson, *Loyal Blacks*, 124–128; Robertson, *King's Bounty*, 97–98; "Records of the Digby Anglican Church," PANS, MG 64, vol. 23: 7–11; Annapolis Royal, Annapolis St. Luke's Anglican Church, Baptismal Register, 1782–1786, PANS, Reel 1, Annapolis Anglican Churches; Anglican Church Vestry Records, Shelburne, Nova Scotia, 1769–1868, PANS, MG 4, vol. 141: 19, 42, *passim*. See also "Shelburne Baptism from Reverend Dr. Walters' Records," PANS, MG 4, vol. 141; Digby Township Records, MG 4, vol. 23.; Trinity Church Records, 6–16; St. Matthew's Session Records, 1769–1857, PANS, MG 4, vol. 46: 20–25.

[50] Walker, *Black Loyalists*, 68–69; Wilson, *Loyal Blacks*, 129–131.

[51] Nathan Bangs, *The Life of Reverend Freeborn Garretson . . . .* (New York, 1829), 167–168, 174, 177.

[52] See Hodges, *Black Itinerants of the Gospel.*

[53] Walker, *Black Loyalists*, 73–74; Wilson, *Loyal Blacks*, 124, 129.

[54] "Journal of Reverend William Jessop, January 1–March 11, 1788," PANS, MG 100, vol. 169, Document 27–27: 20–21.

[55] "An Account of the Life of Mr. David George, from Sierra Leone in Africa; given by himself in a Conversation with Brother Rippon and Brother Pearce of Birmingham," *The Baptist Annual Register for 1790–1793* (London, 1793), 473–484. For influence of Henry Alline see George A. Rawlyk, *Ravished by the Spirit Religious Revivals, Baptists, and Henry Alline* (Kingston, Ontario, 1984).

[56] Pearleen Oliver, *A Brief History of the Coloured Baptists of Nova Scotia, 1782–1953* (Halifax, N.S., 1953). On developments in the United States see Nash, *Forging Freedom*, 109–133 and Carol V. George, *Segregated Sabbaths, Richard Allen and the Rise of Independent Black Churches, 1760–1840* (New York, 1973), 49–116.

[57] Robertson, *King's Bounty*, 94–97.

[58] Wilks, *Blacks in Canada*, 100–107.

[59] For Black Poor receiving alms see Appendix 2.

[60] See "Minutes of the Committee in Relief of the Black Poor, July 28, 1786," PRO T/1/634/117 and T/1/658/145 for rejection of Bahamas. See "Minutes" Treasury (T)/1/145–47, for rejection of Nova Scotia.

[61] Plan of a Settlement to be Made Near Sierra Leone on the Grain Coast of Africa by Henry Smeatham, Esq. (London, 1786), PRO T/1/632/93.

[62] "Committee Reports, June 7, 1786," PRO T/1/632/105.

[63] For Sharp see Prince Hoare, *Memoirs of Granville Sharp. Esq. Composed from his own manuscripts and other authentic documents in the*

possession of his family of the African Institution, . . . (London, 1820), 33, 41–48, 52–61, 236–250; and E.C.P. Lascelles, *Granville Sharp and the Freedom of Slaves in England* (London, 1928), 17–34, 81–87. For his voluminous writings see among others *A Representation of the Injustice and Dangerous Tendency of Treating Slavery or of the Admitting the Least Claim of Private Property in the Persons of Men in England, in Four Parts* . . . . (London, 1769).

[64] See appendix 2. For sources see PRO T/1/632–643; Peter Fryer, *Staying Power, the History of Black People in Britain* (Atlantic Highlands, N.J., 1984), 96–103; R.R. Kuczynski, *Demographic Survey of the British Empire*, 3 vols. (London, 1948), I, 40–44; Wilson, *Loyal Blacks*, 3, 22, 34, 143, 148; Norton, "The Fate of Some Black Loyalists," 402–403.

[65] "Regulations Proposed for the Settlers at Sierra Leone To the Worthy Passengers on Board the Myro Brig," May 20, 1788 in Hoare, *Memoirs of Granville Sharp*, appendix xi.

[66] Philip D. Curtin, *The Image of Africa, British Ideas and Action, 1780–1850* (Madison, 1964), 60–63, 70–72, 99–102.

[67] C.B. Wadstrom, *Report to the Directors of the Sierra Leone Company* (London, 1791), 79.

[68] C.B. Wadstrom, *An Essay on Colonization Particularly Applied to the Western Coast of Africa with Some Free Thoughts on Cultivation and Commerce; Also Brief Descriptions of the Colonies Already Formed or Attempted, in Africa, including those of Sierra Leone and Bulama*, 2 vols. (London, 1794), II, 8–10. "History of Sierra Leone," *Philanthropist*, 4 (1814), 94–102. For Sharp letter see Hoare, *Memoirs of Granville Sharp*, 345. See also Wilson, *Loyal Blacks*, 158–166, 169–170; Christopher Fyfe, *A History of Sierra Leone* (London, 1962), 13–16, 22–24.

[69] "The Old Settlers at Sierra Leone, to Granville Sharp, Esq., September 3, 1788," in Hoare, *Memoirs of Granville Sharp*, 331–333. See also Christopher Fyfe, *Our Children Free and Happy: Letters from Black Settlers in Africa in the 1790s* (Edinburgh, 1991).

[70] Anna Marie Falconbridge, *Narration of Two Voyages to the River Sierra Leone during the years 1791–1792*, 2nd Edition (London, 1802), 10–11, 32–40, 63–65.

[71] See "The Honorable Memorial and Petition of Thomas Peters . . . ," CO/217/63/54, 60 and "History of Sierra Leone," 100–102; C.B. Fergusson, *Clarkson's Mission to America, 1791–1792* (Halifax, N.S., 1971), 13–15, 17; Wilks, *Blacks in Canada*, 63–75; Wilson, *Loyal Blacks*, 177–186.

[72] Walker, *Black Loyalists*, 126–128. For the text of Peters' petition see Fergusson, *Clarkson's Mission*, 31–33. Letters from the black settlers in Sierra Leone are available in Paul Edwards and David Dabydeen, *Black Writers in Britain 1760–1890* (Edinburgh, U.K., 1991), 83–99.

[73] Walker, *Black Loyalists*, 127–129.

[74] Wilson, *Loyal Blacks*, 205–208. For text of statement see Fergusson, *Clarkson's Mission*, 35–36 and *An Account of the Colony of Sierra Leone*

from Its First Establishment in 1793 Being the Substance of a Report Delivered to the Proprietors (London, 1795), 4–5.

[75] Fergusson, *Clarkson's Mission*, 71–72.

[76] "C.B. Fergusson Papers, PANS, MG 1, Box 1894, Folder 1. "Stephen Skinner to Henry Dundall, Esq., Secretary of State for the Home Department," CO 217/63, 362–366; Walker, *Black Loyalists*, 128; Wilson, *Loyal Blacks*, 208–210. For Blucke's letters see Fergusson, *Clarkson's Mission*, 40, 73, 78–79.

[77] For the rosters of students in the schools run by the Associates of Dr. Bray see Bray/Canada/ Folio 4, Rhodes Library; For Blucke, see Walker, *Black Loyalists*, 85–87; Fergusson, *Clarkson's Mission*, 191.

[78] Fergusson, *Clarkson's Mission*, 134–145, 160–165.

[79] Christopher Fyfe, *Sierra Leone Inheritance* (London, 1964), 117–119; Kuczynski, *Demographic Survey*, I, 62–69.

[80] For the details of Peters' life see "Thomas Peters: Millwright and Deliverer," in David G. Sweet and Gary B. Nash, eds. *Struggle and Survival in Colonial America* (Berkeley, 1981), 69–86.

[81] "Petition of the Settlers of the New Colony of Sierra Leone," John Clarkson Papers, 4 vols., Additional Manuscripts 41263, British Library; Falconbridge, *Narration of Two Voyages*, 141; for quit-rents see N.A. Cox-George, *Finance and Development in West Africa: The Sierra Leone Experience* (London, 1961), 39–52.

[82] Cox-George, *Finance and Development*, 39–52, 55, 76–84, 145–148.

[83] Wadstrom, *An Essay on Colonization*, 67.

[84] Falconbridge, *Narration of Two Voyages*, 201; Wadstrom, *An Essay on Colonization*, 66–67; Reverend Charles Marke, *Origin of Wesleyan Methodism in Sierra Leone* (London, 1913), 15.

[85] For development of trade ties see E. Frances White, *Sierra Leone's Settler Women Traders: Women on the Afro-European Frontier* (Ann Arbor, 1987), 5, 12–20; for South Carolinian membership in secret societies see Margaret Washington Creel, *"A Peculiar People": Slave Religion and Community-Culture Among the Gullahs* (New York, 1988), 46–50, 60–64, 181–182, 288–290.

[86] Falconbridge, *Narration of Two Voyages*, 77; Fyfe, *History of Sierra Leone*, 88–89; White, *Sierra Leone's Settler Women*, 23–25, 33.

[87] *An Account*, 76–82, 87–89. Walker, *Black Loyalists*, 228–234; Wilson, *Loyal Blacks*, 321–327; Fyfe, *History of Sierra Leone*, 84–86; Mavis C. Campbell, *The Maroons of Jamaica, 1655–1796* (Trenton, 1990), 256–257.

[88] *Philanthropist*, vol. 2: 32–44. For Cuffe see Lamont D. Thomas, *Rise to be a People, A Biography of Paul Cuffe* (Urbana, Il., 1986), 52–55.

[89] "Sufferings Seen Among Slaves in America," February 18, 1812, Paul Cuffe Papers, New Bedford Public Library. For Kizell see Thomas, *Paul*

Cuffe, 52–56 and Floyd J. Miller, *The Search for a Black Nationality, Black Emigration and Colonization, 1787–1863* (Urbana, Il., 1975), 21–31.

[90] Thomas, *Paul Cuffe*, 66–71.

[91] Thomas, *Paul Cuffe*, 100–105; Miller, *Search for a Black Nationality*, 40–41.

[92] Byers and McBurney, *Atlantic Hearth*, 81–83.

[93] William Hamilton, "Extract from an ORATION, Delivered in the African Church, in the City of New York on the Fourth of July, 1827, in Commemoration of the ABOLITION OF DOMESTIC SLAVERY, in this State," quoted in Howard Rock and Paul Gilje, *Keepers of the Revolution: New Yorkers at Work in the Early Republic* (Ithaca, 1992), 242.

A Note on the Text

The Black Loyalist Directory is derived from a list compiled under orders from Sir Guy Carleton, Commander-in-Chief of His Majesty's Armies for North America in 1783. Susan Hawkes Cook created the initial transcript from the American version, which Egbert Benson, William Smith and Daniel Parker sent to George Washington on January 18, 1784. This copy, created by the commissioners over several months, is on deposit in the National Archives Papers of the Continental Congress: Miscellaneous Papers: Papers Relating to Specific States (folios 21, 25, 26, 29, 30, 44, 47 and 52). It is generally available on microfilm as Record Group 360, *Records of the Continental and Confederation Congresses and the Constitutional Convention*, specifically Microcopy 247, *Papers of the Continental Congress, 1774–1789*, Reel 66 and Microcopy 332, *Miscellaneous Papers of the Continental Congress, 1774–1789*, Reel 7.[1]

Subsequently, Graham Hodges compared the commissioner's copy with the British Headquarters Papers version in the New York Public Library. The New York Public Library copy is a photostat of the original rolls now located at the Public Record Office, Kew Gardens, London.[2] The commissioner's and the British Headquarters Papers versions are fundamentally the same, with slight variations in order, as indicated in the transcript. Because the American version is more widely available, we have used it as the final model for this transcript. Important differences are noted in the text.

In each version, the list is divided into three books. Book 3 is rendered in paragraph form, while the records in the first two books appear originally in nine column format. Paragraph format has been used entirely for this transcription. In the original, the first two columns indicate the name and commander of the vessel and destination. The next three columns show name, age, and description of the "Negro." Descriptions are restricted to adjectives including healthy, worn out, stout, thin, ordinary; occasionally pock marks, cuts and blindness are mentioned. Though called for in Carleton's orders, occupations are rarely mentioned. The two columns following are names and residence of claimant, though most are left blank. This transcription places those names in parentheses. The last column, "Remarks," includes name and location of former owner or if free born. Where ditto marks were used in any of the columns, the wording intended by ditto has been enclosed by brackets.

As was customary at that time, many given names were abbreviated; this transcription, for the convenience of the reader, expands the abbreviated given or forename, i.e. Charles for Chas., Daniel for Danl, Thomas for Thos. etc. Every effort has been made to preserve the original spelling with the exception of expanded names as noted above. The reader will thus find many names and places not spelled as they are today and many variant spellings. For instance, the name Franswa today is more commonly spelled Francois, but will appear in the index as Franswa, as it appeared on the original ledger.

Present day Charleston, South Carolina, was often abbreviated and spelled in many different ways. The uniform spelling, Charlestown, as it was known then, has been used. No other attempt has been made to use a preferred spelling as was done in *Index: The Papers of the Continental Congress, 1774–1789*, compiled by John P. Butler.

Editorial comments are in italics within brackets so that [*Remarks blank*] indicates there was nothing in the appropriate column. At the conclusion of some lists is a lengthy paragraph beginning, "in pursuance of two Orders . . . " giving the number of travellers on preceding lists. Emphasis has been added to these numbers by using bold type.

Exact interpretation of the original spelling is not always perfect. Terminal t's are often not crossed, giving the appearance of the letter l. The lower case letters m and w, u and n present problems. Upper case F may not be crossed so appears to be T. These are just a few of the difficulties encountered in such a transcription.

We have abbreviated names of regiments and certificates of freedom only when called for in the original. The abbreviation for General Birch's Certificate is GBC; for General Musgrave's Certificate, GMC.

Susan Hawkes Cook
Graham Russell Hodges

Notes

1 A small portion of these lists has previously appeared in print. See "An Inspection Roll of Negroes Bound for Nova Scotia," ed. with introduction by Debra Lynn Newman, abstracts by Marcia Eisenberg, *The Journal of Afro-American Historical and Genealogical Society* 1: 2, 72–79.

2 British Headquarters Papers, Document 10427, Manuscript Room, New York Public Library. Another photocopy is available in the United States at the Guy Carleton Papers, Colonial Williamsburg Library. The original version is known as "Book of Negroes," and is found in British Headquarters Papers, PRO 30/55/100.

Introduction to the 2021 Edition

Since publication of *The Black Loyalist Directory* in 1996, the chief component, *The Book of Negroes*, has become one of the most cited of American Revolutionary primary sources. This new edition salutes *The Book of Negroes* by using the original title of this famous accounting of Black freedom. On the surface, *The Book of Negroes* is a laconic, ledger-style enumeration of 3,000 self-emancipated and free Blacks who departed as part of the British evacuation of Loyalists from New York City in the summer and fall of 1783 for Nova Scotia, England, Germany, and other parts of the world. Created under orders from Sir Guy Carleton (Lord Dorchester), Commander-in-Chief of British forces in North America, to placate an angry George Washington, Commander-in-Chief of the Continental Army (USA), who regarded the Black Loyalists as fugitive slaves, *The Book of Negroes* is, as Alan Gilbert has observed, a "roll of honor." Such a term is apt because it both reveals the immense courage of self-emancipated Black Americans and free people and serves as a testament to the fact that the English honored the promises that the British army made during the Revolutionary War, which exchanged protection of Black freedom for military service.[1]

The Book of Negroes references "GBCs," or General Birch Certificates, which were "passports" that allowed Black Loyalists passage on the ships leaving New York harbor. Over three thousand were issued to free men, women, and children. Of those, 1,336 were issued to men; 914, or 30 percent, were issued to women. Over 450 people migrated as a family unit. Young people predominated, but there were people as old as ninety-three. In contrast, there were more infants than older children, an indication of the hopes and aspirations of Black Loyalists uniting as families in occupied New York City. Women with children were common, a participation not generally seen among self-emancipated people but one that occurs frequently in wartime.[2]

At a minimum, the three thousand Black Loyalists represented a sizable portion of Revolutionary War refugees from slavery and accounted for the largest single group of Black self-emancipators from slavery before the Civil War.[3] Reappearance of *The Book of Negroes* comes at a propitious time. Scholars once considered African American participation to be marginal to American Revolutionary War history. It is now understood to be integral. This powerful shift in the historiography of the American Revolution was already advanced in 1996. The purpose of this new introduction is not to revise the old version, which retains its original strength, but to update it with new insights and directions

Scholarship employing *The Book of Negroes* has expanded dramatically in a number of ways. First, scholars, academic and popular, use *The Book of Negroes* to connect Black roles in the American Revolution with the long African American struggle to gain freedom. Often, Black Loyalism is regarded as a key knot in the long rope of Black American resistance to slavery leading up to the Civil War and the massive escape of so-called contrabands. *The Book of Negroes* is an invaluable source for genealogists looking for Revolutionary Period relatives and veterans.[4]

Second, studying *The Book of Negroes* allows an expanded understanding of the importance of Black Loyalism. Maya Jasanoff has labeled their wartime experience as the "Spirit of 1783." Black Loyalism reveals an evolving understanding of the Black American search for citizenship, political representation, and power in the Atlantic world. Key to this were the differing perceptions of the Patriots who saw the Black Loyalists as escaped property and the English who bestowed them with an emerging vision of citizenship. Eliga Gould expands upon this yawning perceptual gap. When Sir Guy Carleton agreed to provide General George Washington with a list of Blacks embarking from New York City to Nova Scotia and other parts of the world and to investigate American claims of recent escapes from slave owners, he recognized the validity of Patriot property ownership over human beings. Carleton was surely aware that he was exposing the Crown government to legal actions for American losses, claims that lasted into the 1820s. Carleton, influenced by recommendations by General Alexander Leslie of Black courage and valor in the South Carolina campaign, ordered certificates confirming British protection of Black freedom. These "General Birch Certificates," in Gould's words, "heralded a new government-level commitment to emancipation." Couched in terms of national honor and the public faith in the religion of a Christian, Carleton's determination to protect the Black Loyalists referenced "a higher law of humanity." Gould contends that Carleton was expanding upon the Somerset decision of 1774 that disallowed a British master's slave ownership on the grounds that slavery was not legal in Britain. Accordingly, occupied New York City and then Canada became "free soil." Carleton's actions, designed in part to embarrass the Americans, earned the British the reputation as the best friends of Black aspirants for freedom. I have argued elsewhere that American Blacks held this notion long before.[5]

Third, understanding Black Loyalism adds greater insight into Canadian history. Tracing the Black Loyalist past has become a cottage industry in Canada with titles about several provinces. Black Loyalism has become a core part of Canadian national history.[6] In part, this is because of the immense pride in and popularity of Lawrence Hill's Commonwealth Prize–winning novel, *The Book of Negroes*. Hill employed *The Book of Negroes* as the central device for his novel, published first in 2007, reprinted in several editions and languages, and converted into a televised mini-series on BET in 2015. The mini-series and coverage of the original *Book of Negroes* are now staples of Afro-Canadian historical observances.[7]

Fourth, Black Loyalism affected disputes that surfaced in diplomatic relations between Great Britain and its former American colonies, now the United States. This history indicates how, during the Revolutionary and Early National Eras, self-emancipated African Americans were powerfully affecting American politics. At the conclusion of the Revolutionary War, discontented Patriot memories of Black Loyalists roiled American political attitudes toward the British. Throughout the 1780s and during the Constitutional years, Americans expressed bitterness at what they regarded as British theft of their property. Americans raised the loss of thousands of former enslaved people in negotiations. As Gould notes, John Adams described the flight of enslaved people to the British lines in Virginia and South Carolina as comparable to the burning of American ports, the deadly confinement of American prisoners of war in British prison hulks, and the theft of Benjamin Franklin's library. As minister to England, Adams raised the issue of compensation constantly. Jefferson argued to his London creditors that they should help pay for the losses of his bond people before he took care of his consumer debts.[8]

While Adams fretted about the British position, John Jay, a leading New York lawyer, founder of the New York Manumission Society, and later the first U.S. Supreme Court Justice, strived to clarify the controversy. Jay, the son of a leading Huguenot slave master, and father and uncle of important nineteenth-century anti-slavery advocates, argued in a detailed report to Congress in 1786 that there were three classes of escaped slaves. The first, captured as booty by the British and carried away before the war ended, had been legitimately emancipated; the Americans were not eligible for compensation for them. The second class included those who remained with their owners inside British lines and therefore could not be "carried away." Nor could the third, encompassing those who had escaped from their masters and were still inside British lines but in American territory when the war ended. Most, if not all those evacuated in 1783, fell into this category. The British had violated the treaty by taking them and owed Patriots restitution. However, Jay argued, angering slaveholders, the treaty was immoral because it called for the re-enslavement of people already freed. The safest recourse for the Americans, he contended, was to cease demanding return of the escaped former slaves and accept monetary compensation from the British. Though upset with Jay, Southerners reluctantly accepted his logic and pushed for cash payments.[9]

Even in 1795, during George Washington's second term as president, the compensation issue occupied much debate during the negotiations that led to the Jay Treaty. When John Jay, now President George Washington's special minister to Britain, broached the plan for compensation, the British Foreign Secretary, Lord Grenville, referred to such payments as "odious" as they would break faith with people who were by then legally British subjects. Americans retorted that the British still recognized slavery in their colonies and were at fault for its presence in the United States. That point went nowhere and eventually Jay concluded that insistence upon it would detract from the real concerns of removal of British troops from key forts along the Great Lakes and Northwest and reopening the West Indies trade. Though slave master politicians howled at this omission, Jay would not budge and Washington signed the treaty later that year.[10]

Alexander Hamilton, a fellow member of the New York Manumission Society and now the former Treasurer of the United States, but a deeply influential political voice, created a potent memo defending the treaty. Hamilton argued that although the British had been infamous in "seducing away our Negroes during the war, re-enslaving them would be even more infamous." As James Oakes brilliantly argues, Hamilton claimed to be speaking according to the Law of Nations. Written during a time, as Eliga Gould shows, when the United States was desperate for status among nations, Hamilton's viewpoint was highly political. It also introduced an extraordinary argument, that there was "no property in man." Slaves were not like land, which had to be returned. As human beings, they had a desire to be free and escape from bondage. Britain did not even have the power to take away the freedom the nation had granted to the former enslaved people. For Americans to insist upon re-enslavement was indeed odious. Though James Madison led the opposition to Hamilton's memo, he avoided direct attack on it and argued for arbitration. By 1796, most American leaders were taking Carleton's position about national honor, even as they sought compensation.[11] Initially considered a sell-out, the treaty had enormous success in opening up trade and the Northwest territories for white American land exploitation.

Northern political figures carried Hamilton's reasoning further. James Hillhouse of Connecticut added that the 1783 treaty clause requiring return of self-emancipated enslaved people violated natural law and that the British had no legitimate right to return people who had been emancipated. Moreover, the Black Loyalists (though he did not use that term) had escaped to a country where there was no slavery and so therefore the British and their Nova Scotia subjects had to refuse to give them up. As there was no racial exception to principles of fundamental human equality, Canada had become free soil. Unsurprisingly, Southern plantation owners objected, but the arguments of Hamilton and Hillhouse made antislavery political in the early Republic.[12]

This dispute carried into the War of 1812 era when the British navy welcomed nearly 5,000 enslaved Black Virginians onboard and carried them off to Nova Scotia. Once again, Americans and British quarreled during treaty-making about compensation for losses to slave masters. Ultimately the two nations invited the Czar of Russia to arbitrate. That monarch awarded some damages to the Americans but generally upheld the British position. The Americans received £250,000 as a sop from the British. What came out of this decades-long dispute were concepts of "no property in man," the legitimacy of military emancipation for enslaved people, and a powerful linkage of military service with citizenship.[13]

Fifth, the British government's invitation to enslaved Blacks during the American Revolution to leave their masters for freedom inside its military forces expands the history and definition of abolitionism, the Underground Railroad, and black migration for a better life. The history of Black Loyalist self-emancipation, supported by Carleton's recognition of their rights, reaffirms Manisha Sinha's observation that Black escapes from enslavement are the core of the abolitionist movement. Further, as indicated in the original introduction to this book, Black Loyalists shaped a unique, freedom-seeking politics, the extent of which scholars are just now understanding. The strong presence of women among the Black Loyalists, more than a third of the total, is an early example of Black female politics, recently illuminated by Martha Jones.[14]

Generally, the Underground Railroad is viewed as resulting from the actions of local, benevolent individuals or families. In this case, a British colonial official and, later, chief military officers extended promises of freedom and succor in a rough exchange for some kind of service. *The Book of Negroes* offers the most extensive list of female self-emancipation. Historians generally regard Black flight from slavery as the action of young adult males. However, *The Book of Negroes* lists many Black women who escaped their masters or came as free people to join the British effort. Their actions give rise to a number of questions about wartime and the Underground Railroad. What was the importance of the invitation by a recognized, state military force on the decisions of Black men and women to leave their enslavers? How important was the succor that the British military offered to Black women escaping from slavery with their children? Was the possibility of a legal marriage in New York City, where Anglican and Methodist churches performed services for Black couples, an attraction? How important was the Black enclave on Manhattan Island to the formation of Black community, church, and political organization?[15]

Sixth, examination of the people enrolled in *The Book of Negroes* demonstrates the significant opportunity for wartime flight afforded to Black women and their children. As Karen Cook-Bell has brilliantly uncovered, enslaved and free Black women seized upon the proximity of the British lines to secure new or enlarged freedoms, find paid work, meet partners with whom they could build families recognized by English law and religious ritual, and, in the case of Rose Fortune, become community leaders and entrepreneurs. While Black women rarely were more than a small fraction of Black fugitives from slavery during times of peace, the Revolutionary tumult created opportunities for flight. Black women seized upon them.[16]

Last, *The Book of Negroes* has global dimensions. While the majority of Blacks leaving New York City in 1783 traveled to Nova Scotia, a number went to Great Britain, Germany, and other parts of the world. Cassandra Pybus has found that Black Loyalists ventured as far as India and Australia while Roger Buckley uncovered units of Black Loyalists who enlisted in the imperial British army and fought in India and the West Indies. As scholars expand the story of runaways to encompass the world, *The Book of Negroes* offers good evidence of how enslaved American people gained their freedom by leaving for distant parts of the globe.[17]

These brief comments indicate that *The Book of Negroes* is a living document whose importance spreads across a number of historical fields and in popular memory. This new edition will, we hope, spark even more ventures into the history of Black Loyalism and resistance to slavery.

Notes

1   Alan Gilbert, *Black Patriots and Loyalists: Fighting for Emancipation in the War of Independence* (Chicago: University of Chicago Press, 2013), 196; Patrick Rael, *Eighty-Eight Years: The Long Death of Slavery in the United States, 1777–1865* (Athens: University of Georgia Press, 2015), 50–61. Karen Cook-Bell, *Running for Freedom: Enslaved Women and Their Remarkable Fight for Freedom in Revolutionary America* (New York: Cambridge University Press, 2021).

2   Gilbert, *Black Patriots*, 201–4.

3   Cassandra Pybus, "Jefferson's Faulty Math: The Question of Slave Defections in the American Revolution," *The William and Mary Quarterly* 62, no. 2, Third Series (April 2005): 243–64.

4   Simon Schama, *Rough Crossings: Britain, The Slaves and the American Revolution* (London: BBC Books, 2005); Robert G. Parkinson, *The Common Cause: Creating Race and Nation in the American Revolution* (Chapel Hill: University of North Carolina Press for the Omohundro Institute of Early American History and Culture, 2016), 551–71; Alan Taylor, *The Internal Enemy: Slavery and War in Virginia, 1772–1832* (New York: Norton, 2013); Philip D. Morgan and Andrew Jackson O'Shaughnessy, "Arming Slaves in the American Revolution," in *Arming Slaves from Classical Times to the Modern Age*, ed. Christopher Leslie Brown and Philip D. Morgan (New Haven: Yale University Press, 2006), 180–208; Graham Russell Hodges, *Root & Branch: African Americans in New York and East Jersey, 1613–1863* (Chapel Hill: University of North Carolina Press, 1999), chapter 5.

5   Maya Jasanoff, *Liberty's Exiles: American Loyalists in the Revolutionary World* (New York: Knopf, 2011); Eliga H. Gould, *Among the Powers of the Earth: The American Revolution and the Making of a New World Empire* (Cambridge: Harvard University Press, 2012), 153–55; John W. Pulis, ed., *Moving On: Black Loyalists in the Afro-Atlantic World* (New York: Garland Publishing, 1999); Hodges, *Root and Branch*.

6   For an excellent survey of this literature, see Harvey Amani Whitfield, "The African Diaspora in Atlantic Canada: History, Historians, and Historiography," *Acadiensis* 46, no. 1 (2017), 213–32. For local Canadian studies, see Ruth Holmes Whitehead, *Black Loyalists: Southern Settlers of Nova Scotia's First Free Black Communities* (Halifax: Nimbus Publishing, 2013); Steven Davidson and Peter Zwicker, *Birchtown and the Black Loyalist Experience: From 1775 to the Present* (Halifax: Formac, 2019); Steven Davidson, *Black Loyalists in New Brunswick: The Lives of Eight African Americans in Colonial New Brunswick 1783–1834* (Halifax: Formac, 2020); Mary Louise Clifford, *From Slavery to Freetown: Black Loyalists After the American Revolution* (Jefferson, N.C.: McFarland, 2006).

7   Lawrence Hill, *The Book of Negroes* (Toronto: HarperCollins, 2005); first published in the United States as *Someone Knows My Name: A Novel* (New York: Norton, 2007); title reverted to original in subsequent editions. See BlackLoyalist.com and https://www.bac-lac.gc.ca for guides to sites.

8   Gould, *Among the Powers of the Earth*, 162–66; Don E. Fehrenbacher, *The Slaveholding Republic: An Account of the United States Government's Relations to Slavery* (New York: Oxford University Press, 2001), 92–94.

9   James Oakes, *The Scorpion's Sting: Antislavery and the Coming of the Civil War* (New York: Norton, 2014), 113–15. For an opposing view that the Americans prevailed, see Benedict Ostdiek and John Fabian Witt, "The Czar and the Slaves: Two Puzzles in the History of International Arbitration," *American Journal of International Law* 113, no. 3 (July 2019): 535–67.

10   Oakes, *Scorpion's Sting*, 117–18.

11   Oakes, *Scorpion's Sting*, 115–22; Gould, *Among the Powers of the Earth*, 150–53.

12   Oakes, *Scorpion's Sting*, 128–32.

13   Oakes, *Scorpion's Sting*, 130–45; Rael, *Eighty-Eight Years*, 160.

14   Manisha Sinha, *The Slave's Cause: A History of Abolitionism* (New Haven: Yale University Press, 2016), 1; Christopher James Bonner, *Remaking the Republic: Black Politics and the Creation of American Citizenship* (Philadelphia: University of Pennsylvania Press, 2020); Martha S. Jones, *Vanguard: How Black Women Broke Barriers, Won the Vote, and Insisted on Equality for All* (New York: Basic Books, 2020).

15   Steven Hahn, *The Political Worlds of Slavery and Freedom* (Cambridge: Harvard University Press, 2009); Ira Berlin, *The Long Emancipation: The Demise of Slavery in the United States* (Cambridge: Harvard University Press, 2015); Sinha, *The Slave's Cause*, 52.

16   Cook-Bell, *Running for Freedom*.

17   Marcus Rediker et al., eds., *A Global History of Runaways: Workers, Mobility, and Capitalism, 1600–1850* (Oakland: University of California Press, 2019); Cassandra Pybus, *Epic Journeys of Freedom: Runaway Slaves of the American Revolution and Their Global Quest for Liberty* (Boston: Beacon Press, 2006); Roger N. Buckley, *Slaves in Red Coats: The British West India Regiments, 1795–1815* (New Haven: Yale University Press, 1979); Aline Helg, *Slave No More: Self-Liberation in the Americas* (Chapel Hill: University of North Carolina Press, 2019).

Classroom Use for *The Book of Negroes*

Using *The Book of Negroes* in the classroom has become much easier and more fruitful since the first edition appeared in 1996. Since then, the internet has spawned websites and search engines that can lead students to remarkable discoveries. The simplest way to recover life experiences of the self-emancipated or their enslavers is through a family search engine such as Ancestry.com or Genealogy.com or by examining newspaper databases such as Proquest, Newspapers.com, and Readex. Linking Black Loyalist names through these massive databases can lead to remarkable discoveries of personal vital records, family records, and descendants. A great source for fugitive slave advertisements that includes some of the figures in this book is https://app.freedomonthemove.org/educators. The records of former masters often reveal much about the past homes and lives of the self-emancipated. Students interested in reading the narratives of Black Loyalists Boston King, John Marrant, and Thomas Peters can find these and others at https://docsouth.unc.edu/neh.

The Book of Negroes is a natural resource for genealogists and historians of family history. In addition to the sites listed at the end of this document, researchers should consult the home page of the Afro-American Historical and Genealogical Society at https://www.aahgs.org. Other useful genealogical sources include https://www.americanancestors.org/education/learning-resources/read/african-american-research; https://www.blackpast.org/african-american-history/african-american-history/genealogy/ and https://www.familysearch.org/wiki/en/African_American_Genealogy.

Teachers familiar with the *New York Times 1619* project can profitably use *The Book of Negroes*. The compilation of self-emancipated Blacks is a clear example of what Jarvis R. Givens has called "fugitive pedagogy," or the construction of an alternative and competing history of the struggle for freedom and against racial oppression. One of the most controversial claims of the project regards whether the American Patriots fought the Revolution to defend slavery. The fact that at least 15,000 enslaved Blacks, and likely far more, escaped from their masters to join with the British forces during the Revolution had a profound impact. A number of the former masters listed in *The Book of Negroes* were influential Patriots with political and economic importance through the Constitutional Era. Thomas Jefferson, in particular, was very bitter about the loss of his perceived human property during the Revolution when over thirty bond people escaped from his plantations. Classroom discussion may focus on the effects that these escapes would have on these masters/politicians as they devised the new nation's government, especially the Constitution. Consider as well, the response of the British Commander-in-Chief for North America, Sir Guy Carleton, to General George Washington's objection to the news that many Black Loyalists had already embarked from New York City to Nova Scotia and would continue to do so. Carleton's words are worth discussing. Washington could not abide by any return of self-emancipated Blacks as that would be "inconsistent with prior Engagements binding the National Honor, which must be kept with all Colours." Discuss whether the General Birch Certificates given out to Black passengers were passports and thereby amounted to recognition of British citizenship.[1] Students can study the exchange between General George Washington and Sir Guy Carleton. Visit https://founders.archives.gov/documents/Washington/99-01-02-11217 and https://docsouth.unc.edu/csr/index.html/document/csr16-0620 for documents. Following that, students can discuss the continued controversy over Black Loyalists between Americans and the British in the 1790s and beyond. Discuss concepts of "No Property in Man" and "Free Soil."

Black participation in the American War for Independence may have been the largest slave revolt before the Civil War. Were the Black Loyalists revolutionaries in every sense of the word? Did they have ideologies similar to the Patriots? What did they seek for themselves? What were their conceptions of freedom and nationality? Were they "imaging" a nation as were the Patriots? Was there continuity between the roles for Blacks in

---

1   Quoted in Maya Jasanoff, *Liberty's Exiles: American Loyalists in the Revolutionary World* (New York: Knopf, 2011), 89; Jarvis R. Givens, *Fugitive Pedagogy: Carter G. Woodson and the Art of Black Teaching* (Cambridge: Harvard University Press, 2021).

the American Revolution with the key participation of Blacks later in the Union Army of the Civil War.

As discussed in the new introduction, the choice that Black Loyalists made to side with the British meant exile from what became, after 1783, the United States. They made that decision decisively. Maya Jasanoff calls it the Spirit of 1783. Compare with students the laws regarding slavery and Black rights in the 1780s in the United States and Canada. While the northeastern United States was moving toward gradual emancipation, Blacks in Canada had somewhat more freedom, though few of them enjoyed the hard winters of Nova Scotia and the remote towns to which the British government assigned them.

Much can be found about Black Loyalists in their new home, Canada. Ancestry.com links *The Book of Negroes* to various land records in Nova Scotia. Harry Washington, for example, who escaped from bondage under George Washington in 1775, was one of many listed in *The Book of Negroes* and Nova Scotia Land Petitions. For example, students can also pursue family records. John and Rose Gosman of Connecticut and Rhode Island met in occupied New York City, then left for Nova Scotia. Their son, John, was born in Birchtown in 1789. The family then moved to York County, New Brunswick. The younger John married Nancy. The couple had six children, all of whom spent their lives in New Brunswick. In the late twentieth century, the family produced Measha Brueggergosman, one of Canada's most famous opera singers.

Students may be familiar with the general facts and parameters of the Atlantic slave trade. Few, however, will be familiar with the return diaspora made in the late 1780s when the Black Poor of London, England, and many of the Black Loyalists in Nova Scotia opted to leave their present homes for an uncertain future in Sierra Leone on the west coast of Africa. This locale, over which the British government had limited power, was often far from the ancestral homes of the Black Loyalists. It was on the same continent, but distant in language and other forms of culture. Discuss with your students the meaning of this return diaspora.

Students wishing to find *The Book of Negroes* online can do so at these sites:

> https://www.bac-lac.gc.ca/eng/discover/military-heritage/loyalists/
>   book-of-negroes/Pages/introduction.aspx#d
> https://novascotia.ca/archives/africanns/BN.asp
> http://blackloyalist.com/cdc/documents/official/book_of_negroes.htm
> https://www.ancestry.com/search/collections/61530/

Suggested Readings

As noted in the Introduction, scholars have studied Black Loyalism and *The Book of Negroes* attentively since the first appearance of this list in 1996. Among the fullest treatments are Alan Gilbert, *Black Patriots and Loyalists: Fighting for Emancipation in the War of Independence* (Chicago: University of Chicago Press, 2012); Patrick Rael, *Eighty-Eight Years: The Long Death of Slavery in the United States, 1777–1865* (Athens: University of Georgia Press, 2015); Graham Russell Hodges, *Root & Branch: African Americans in New York and East Jersey, 1613–1863* (Chapel Hill: University of North Carolina Press, 1999), chapter 5; Maya Jasanoff, *Liberty's Exiles: American Loyalists in the Revolutionary World* (New York: Knopf, 2011); Eliga H. Gould, *Among the Powers of the Earth: The American Revolution and the Making of a New World Empire* (Cambridge: Harvard University Press, 2012), 153–55; and John W. Pulis, ed., *Moving On: Black Loyalists in the Afro-Atlantic World* (New York: Garland Publishing, 1999). Karen Cook-Bell has added important insights on women's participation in Revolutionary Era enslaved flight in her book *Running from Bondage: Enslaved Women and Their Remarkable Fight for Freedom in Revolutionary America* (New York: Cambridge University Press, 2021). James Oakes wonderfully expounds upon the international and internal politics stemming from Sir Guy Carleton's 1783 decision not to return Black Loyalists to their American masters in his book *The Scorpion's Sting: Anti-Slavery and the Coming of the Civil War* (New York: Norton, 2014) and expands upon this theme in *The Crooked Path to Abolition: Abraham Lincoln and the Antislavery Constitution* (New York: Norton, 2021). For the study of abolitionism with important arguments about the American Revolution, see Manisha Sinha, *The Slave's Cause: A History of Abolition* (New Haven: Yale University Press, 2016).

Harvey Amani Whitfield has written several books and articles that provide the fullest exploration of the Black Loyalists in Canada, including "The African Diaspora in Atlantic Canada: History, Historians, and Historiography," *Acadiensis* 46, no. 1 (2017): 213–32; and *Blacks on the Border: The Black Refugees in British North America, 1815–1860* (Lebanon, N.H.: University Press of New England, 2006). The experience of Black Loyalism in North America and throughout the world is explored in Cassandra Pybus, *Epic Journeys of Freedom: Runaway Slaves of the American Revolution and Their Global Quest for Liberty* (Boston: Beacon Press, 2006). For a global context of the Black Loyalists with other escaped bond people, see Marcus Rediker et al., eds., *A Global History of Runaways: Workers, Mobility, and Capitalism, 1600–1850* (Oakland: University of California Press, 2019).

For Lawrence Hill's fictional masterwork, see *The Book of Negroes* (Toronto: HarperCollins, 2005), first published in the United States as *Someone Knows My Name: A Novel* (New York: Norton, 2007); title reverted to original in subsequent editions. See BlackLoyalist.com and https://www.bac-lac.gc.ca for guides to sites.

THE BLACK LOYALIST DIRECTORY

Inspection Roll

of

Negroes

Book No. 1

[New York City
Book No. 1
April 23–September 13, 1783]

**Ship *Spring*
bound for St. John's**

George Black, 35, (Lt. Col. Isaac Allen). Freed by Lawrence Hartshorne as certified.

Ann Black, 25, ([Lt. Col. Isaac Allen]). [Freed by Lawrence Hartshorne as certified.]

Reuben, 7, ([Lt. Col. Isaac Allen]). [Freed by Lawrence Hartshorne as certified.]

Sukey, 5, ([Lt. Col. Isaac Allen]). [Freed by Lawrence Hartshorne as certified.]

**Ship *Aurora*
bound for St. John's**

Billy Williams, 35, healthy stout man, (Richard Browne). Formerly lived with Mr. Moore of Reedy Island, Carolina, from whence he came with the 71st Regiment about 3 years ago.

Rose Richard, 20, healthy young woman, (Thomas Richard). Property of Thomas Richard, a refugee from Philadelphia.

Daniel Barber, 70, worn out, (James Moore). Says he was made free by Mr. Austin Moore of little York nigh 20 years ago.

Sarah Farmer, 23, healthy young woman, (Mrs. Sharp).

Free negress indented to Mrs. Sharp for one year.

Barbarry Allen, 22, healthy stout wench, (Humphry Winters). Property of Humphrey Winters of New York from Virginia.

Elizabeth Black, 24, mulatto from Madagascar, (Mr. Buskirk). Free, indented when nine years of age to Mrs. Courtland.

Bob Stafford, 20, stout healthy negro, (Mr. Sharp). Taken from Mr. Wilkinson in Virginia by a party from the Royal Navy about four years ago.

Harry Covenhoven, 24, [stout healthy negro], (Mr. Buskirk). Came in two years ago from Mr. Covenhoven in Jersey.

John Vans, 39, healthy, blind of his right eye, (Mr. Buskirk, Jr.). Taken in Pennsylvania by a party of the British Army about 6 1/2 years ago; lived there with Sam Barber who he says had eight months before given him his freedom.

Anthony Haln, 27, stout negro, (Nicholas Beckle). His own property willed to him by his father.

Joyce, 12, healthy negress, (James Moore). Lived with James Moore for 6 years; her father died in the King's service.

Simson McGuire, 23, stout healthy negro man, (John Buskirk). Came in to General Arnold in Virginia from Benjamin Hill.

Bristol Cobbwine, 14, stout negro boy, (Richard Browne). Came from Woodbury, Charlestown, South Carolina, with Major Grant of the King's American regiment about 4 years ago.

Paul, 19, [stout] mulatto, ([Richard Browne]). [Came from Woodbury, Charlestown, South Carolina, with Major Grant of the King's American regiment.]

**Ship *Ariel*
bound for St. John's
Richardson**

Sam Brothers, 25, stout negro man, (Thomas Harrison). Certificate from General Birch, formerly lived with Willis Wilkinson in Virginia.

Betsy his wife, 2 children, 32, 14 & 12, stout & healthy, ([Thomas Harrison]). [Certificate from General Birch, formerly lived with Willis Wilkinson in Virginia.]

Susanna Jarvis, 22, stout healthy negress, (John Brown). Indented to J. J. Browne. Says she was made free about nine years ago when Mr. Blowfield died.

Dinah Mitchel, 30, [stout healthy negress] with a child in her arms, (Matthew Stewart). Left Charlestown from whence she was ordered by Dr. Humphry of the York Volunteers then the property of Mitchel.

Frank her son, 10, fine boy, ([Matthew Stewart]). [Left Charlestown from whence he was ordered by Dr. Humphry of the York Volunteers then the property of Mitchel.]

Joseph, 20, stout lad, sawyer & cooper, (Capt. Richardson of the *Ariel*). Formerly the property of Col. DeVois whom he left at the taking of Savanna.

Clara, 20, stout wench, ([Capt. Richardson of the *Ariel*]). [Formerly the property of Col. DeBois whom he left at the taking of Savanna.]

**Ship *Spencer*
bound for St. John's
Ballantine**

Sarah Fox, 21, stout healthy wench, (John Bettle). Purchased her freedom of Mr. Lowell of Antigua as per his certificate.

John Lynch, 18, [stout healthy] lad, (Andrew Ritchse). Certificate from General Birch, formerly the property of Mr. Lynch of South Carolina.

Jacob Lynch, 42, stout, blind right eye, ([Andrew Ritchse]). [Certificate from General Birch, formerly the property of Mr. Lynch of South Carolina.]

Phebe Lynch, 42, stout little woman, (James Ritchse). [Certificate from General Birch, formerly the property of Mr. Lynch of South Carolina.]

Isaac Corie, 27, stout man, (Col. Gilbert). Formerly the property of William Mott of Great Neck, Long Island, a Quaker who gave him his freedom.

Hagar Corie, 22, [stout] wench, small child 18 mo. old, ([Col. Gilbert]). [Formerly the property of] Joseph Hewlett of Great Neck, Long Island.

Ship *Peggy*
bound for Port Roseway
Jacob Wilson

Josiah Smith, 42, stout sayer & labourer, (Malcom Morrison). Formerly the property of William Smith of Portsmouth, Virginia; left it about six years ago.

Richard Stanley, 39, stout man, (Col. Thomson). Certificate from General Birch, formerly the property of Mr. Stoddart of Jamaica who he says at the time of his death made him free.

Paul Coffin, 29, stout labourer, (Major Coffin, Fanning's reg't.). Property of Major Coffin purchased from Mr. Greentree.

Harry, 23, stout labourer, ([Major Coffin, Fanning's reg't.]). [Property of Major Coffin purchased from Mr. Greentree.]

Phebe, 21, stout wench, ([Major Coffin, Fanning's reg't.]). [Property of Major Coffin purchased from Mr. Greentree.]

Fortune, 35, stout man, (Col. Winslow). Certificate from General Birch, formerly the property of Isaac Warner of Philadelphia.

Letitie, 26, stout wench, (Col. Winslow). [Certificate from General Birch], freed by Mr. Deane of Jamaica, Long Island.

Peter, 10, stout boy, (Col. Winslow). [Certificate from General Birch, freed by Mr. Deane of Jamaica, Long Island.]

William, 22, stout man, (Col. Winslow). [Certificate from General Birch], freeborn in Mont Serrat.

Ceasor & a boy 9 years old, 30, stout man, (Peter Ryerson). Property of Peter Ryerson with whom he is going to Nova Scotia.

Abraham &, 21, stout man, (Mr. Edwards). [Property of] Gideon White but allowed to go with Mr. Edwards to Nova Scotia.

Hannah his wife, 22, stout wench, ([Mr. Edwards]). Free born on Staten Island both of them having General Birch's Certificate.

Joe and, 36, stout man, labourer, (Lt. Reed Delancey's brigade). [His own property.]

Mary his wife & boy, 26, stout wench, ([Lt. Reed Delancey's brigade]). [His own property.]

Abraham, 19, stout lad, (John Cutler). Came from Virginia with Lieut. Col. Pennington of the Guards, formerly the property of Peter Rose.

Parthenia Stanly, 35, stout wench & small boy, (Col. Winslow). Free as per Certificate of her late Mrs. Mott.

George, 13, stout boy, (Capt. Philips). His own property.

George, 18, stout lad, (Peter Ryerson). Formerly lived with Dennis Hagan in South Carolina to whom he was indented for 20 years; brought from thence by Capt. Gore, 33d Reg't.

**Ship *Camel*
bound for St. John's
Tinker**

Henry, 47, stout man, (Charles Richards). Formerly the property of Thomas Marren of Old Fairfield whom he left on account of the proclamation of Sir W. W. Howe.

Kate & girl 6 years, 40, stout wench, ([Charles Richards]). [Formerly the property of Thomas Marron of Old Fairfield whom he left on account of the proclamation of Sir W. W. Howe.]

Almin, 32, stout healthy man, (James Richards). Formerly the property of Williams at Tappan in New Jersey, came in on Sir William Howe's proclamation.

Isaac, 17, stout boy, (Joseph Scribner). Property purchased from Ebenezer Scribner of Setockett, Long Island.

Eleanor Hicks, 13, stout wench born at Rockaway, (Johnson Kearstead). Free, but indented for five years to Johnston Kearstead.

**Ship *Mars*
bound for St. John's
Grayson**

Venus & 2 small children, 25, [stout wench], (Jolly

Longshore). Free, indented to him for two years.

Peggy Lynch, 18, [stout wench], (William Cross). Formerly the property of Mr. Lynch at Charleston, certificate from General Birch.

Samuel Ives, 44, stout man, (Capt. Grayson). Sold to Captain Grayson by Jonathan Eilbeck of New York who it does not appear had any right to sell him as he was the property of Capt. Talbot of Virginia from whence he was brought by the troops 5 years ago and had a pass from Lt. Clinton which Mr. Eilbeck destroyed.

Joe, 27, [stout man], (Caleb Mallory). His property as per bill of sale produced.

Henry Lyon, 36, stout fellow, (Capt. James Grayson). Formerly to Andrew Lyon, Horseneck, New England; left him three years past.

Phebe Lyon, 40, ordinary wench, ([Capt. James Grayson]). Formerly to James Lyon, Horseneck, New England; left him three years past.

Phillis Lyon, 5, ([Capt. James Grayson]). [Formerly to James Lyon, Horseneck, New England; left him three years past.]

Simon White, 32, likely lad, M, (on his own bottom). Born free, Redding, Connecticut.

Lamb Hewell, 65, nearly worn out, M, ([on his own bottom]). [Born free], South Carolina.

Darkas & child, 28, nearly worn out, M, ([on his own bottom]). [Born free, South Carolina.]

Catharine, 66, worn out, M, ([on his own bottom]). [Born free], Norwalk, Connecticut.

Moses, 4, fine boy, M, ([on his own bottom]). [Born free, Norwalk, Connecticut.]

Dempse Slaughter, 35, stout fellow, (Jolly Longshore). Says he was born free, that he lived for some time with Dempsee Walls, Norfolk, Virginia.

Joseph Collins, 30, stout fellow. Dr. VanBuren of Hackensack, New Jersey, claimant. (John Buskirk). Formerly slave to John Kipp, New York Island, sold by Kipp to Dr. VanBuren, Hackensack, New Jersey, whom he left four years past.

Joseph Phillips, 22, stout fellow, (Capt. Grayson). [Formerly slave] to Phil Hawkins, Jamaica, West Indies; left him about 8 years past.

Betsey Collins, 30, stout wench, (John Buskirk).

[Formerly slave] to Nicholas Terhune, Hackensack, New Jersey; left him about four years past.

Ship *Lady's Adventure* bound for St. John's Capt. Robt. Gibson

Nathaniel Lindsay, 20, stout man, (Cornet Lechmore, KAD). Free born in the Grenades. General Birch's Certificate.

Edward Lloyd, 19, [stout man], (Trumpeter, KAD). Formerly the property of Ebenezer Cowley of Fairfield who gave him his freedom.

John Stewart, 19, [stout man], (Lt. Stewart, KAD). General Birch's certificate says he was born free but formerly lived with John Williamson, Charleston, South Carolina.

Peter Moses, 27, [stout man], (Pioneer, KAD). Formerly the property of General Balford of Hampton, Virginia, says that at his death got his freedom about 8 years ago.

Stephen Samson, 22, [stout man], (Cornet Reynolds, KAD). General Birch's Certificate; formerly the property of John Whitman of Charlestown, South Carolina who just before he died at New York about 4 1/2 years ago

gave him his freedom in presence of William Bryant.

James Watson, 30, stout man, (Cornet Nicholson, KAD). Formerly the property of Mr. Colb at Cheerwas, South Carolina, General Birch's Certificate.

Dick Jackson, 21, [stout man], (Trumpeter, [KAD]). Formerly the property of Col. Lloyd of Maryland, free as certified by General Birch.

Joseph Kelley, 25, [stout] mulatto, (Pioneer, [KAD]). Free agreeable to General Birch's Certificate, till 21 years of age lived at Sam Hopkins's of Satocket.

Edmund Hill, 21, [stout] man, ([Pioneer, KAD]). General Birch's Certificate to be free, formerly the property of Lewis Adams of Somerset County, New Jersey.

Andrew Hilton, 22, [stout] mulatto, ([Pioneer, KAD]). Free by General Birch's Certificate, says he was born in the family of Basil Brooks, Benedict County, Maryland; his mother an Indian.

Charles Allen, 25, [stout], M, between an Indian & Span., ([Pioneer, KAD]). Free by General Birch's Certificate, says he lived with Mathew Hobbs of Sussex County, Maryland, untill 25.

William Hanson, 22, [stout], (Capt. Fulton, [KAD]). Free by General Birch's Certificate, formerly lived with Mr. Hanson in Maryland from whom he was taken by an armed boat about a year ago.

Gabriel Dickenson, 22, [stout], (Pioneer, [KAD]). Free by General Birch's Certificate. Free born at North Castle, New York Government.

Charles Terrill, 21, [stout], (Trumpeter, [KAD]). Free by General Birch's Certificate; formerly the property of Mr. John Murphy, Richmond, Virginia.

John Frederick, 21 1/2, [stout], ([Trumpeter, KAD]). Free by General Birch's Certificate; formerly the property of Lord Baltimore who gave him his freedom.

Pompey Brown, 21, [stout], (Maj. Murray, [KAD]). General Birch's Certificate Proclamation. Formerly the property of Richard Stevens, Back Society, New Jersey.

Joseph Williams, 23, [stout], (Pioneer, [KAD]). General Birch's Certificate Proclamation. Free, formerly the property of John Walker, North Carolina.

Will Higginson, 23, [stout], (Cornet Nicollson, [KAD]). General Birch's Certificate

Proclamation. Formerly the property of Capt. Billings of [*blank*].

Abraham Marrian, 25, [stout], (Lt. Tarbell, [KAD]). General Birch's Certificate Proclamation. Formerly the property of General Marion.

Scipio Jenkins, 16, stout boy, (Cornet Freeman, [KAD]). General Birch's Certificate Proclamation. Formerly the property of Benjamin Jenkins, Charlestown, South Carolina.

James Jenkins, 23, [stout] man, (Lt. Davidson, [KAD]). [General Birch's Certificate Proclamation. Formerly the property of Benjamin Jenkins, Charlestown, South Carolina.]

Joseph Stewart, 15, stout boy, (Capt. Stewart, [KAD]). General Birch's Certificate Proclamation. Formerly the property of Crawford, Middletown, Jersey.

Henry Cruden, 13, [stout boy], (Col. Thomson, [KAD]). Given to Col. Thomson by Col. Cruden.

Hester Walton, 28, stout, blind of an eye, (Cornet Nicolson, [KAD]). Formerly Mr. Colb's, South Carolina; left him 4 years ago. General Birch's Certificate.

George Greenard, 19, stout mulatto, (Capt. Fulton, [KAD]). Formerly served Mr.

Greenard at Charlestown; left it with Sir Henry Clinton's Army. GBC.

Hector Micuro, 23, [stout mulatto], (Trumpeter [KAD]). Formerly servant to Mr. Pyate at Charlestown; left it with Col. Thompson. GBC.

Daniel Green, 20, [stout] black, ([Trumpeter, KAD]). Given free by Captain Williams, Master of a Transport in England. GBC.

William Dixon, 18, [stout black], (Lt. Jones, [KAD]). Formerly slave to Mr. Glenn near Charlestown; left that five years ago. GBC.

Silvia Bailley, 26, thin wench, black, (Major Murray, [KAD]). Formerly servant to Thomas Heartley, Georgia; sent from thence by Col. Cruger. GBC.

Nancy Bailley, 9, [thin wench, black], ([Major Murray, KAD]). [Formerly servant to Thomas Heartley, Georgia; sent from thence by Col. Cruger.]

Joe Bailley, 7, [thin wench, black], ([Major Murray, KAD]). [Formerly servant to Thomas Heartley, Georgia, sent from thence by Col. Cruger.]

Thomas Morgan, 21, lame of the left arm, (Lt. Jones, [KAD]). Formerly slave to Mr. Theophilas Morgan,

Killingsworth, Connecticut; left him one year ago. GBC.

Israel Crawford, 27, stout, blind of the right eye, (Lt. Tomlinson, [KAD]). Formerly servant to John Griffin at Campden. Left him two years ago. GBC.

James Anthony, 20, stout, (Capt. Fulton, [KAD]). Formerly slave to John Smith, Statia, who left the negro & went to England & the latter afterwards joined the army 6 yrs. ago. GBC.

Samuel Edmond, 38, remarkably tall & stout, (Lt. Jones, [KAD]). Served Liven Ballad, Nancook town, to the years of 21. GBC.

Jeremy Dyer, 20, tall and stout, (Cornet Parks, [KAD]). Formerly slave to Samuel Dyer, Rhode Island; left him with the troops four years ago.

George Roberts, 30, stout, (Capt. Humble, Ship *Adventure*). Free born, totally ignorant of the place of his birth. GBC.

Hannah Roberts, 30, healthy, ([Capt. Humble, Ship *Adventure*]). Free born at Bermuda. [GBC]

Clarisa Roberts, 6, healthy, ([Capt. Humble, Ship *Adventure*]). Born free.

Sam Everly, 30, stout and tall, (Major Murray, KAD). Free man, formerly slave to Mr. Thomas Everley at Charlestown.

Judith Everly, 18, squat, stout wench, Guinea born ([Major Murray, KAD]). Formerly slave to Mr. Everly.

Joyce Moses, 20, healthy mulatto wench, (R. A. Dragoon). Says she was born free in the West Indies.

Tilley Moses, 12, [healthy mulatto wench], ([R. A. Dragoon]). Born free in Virginia.

Elsia Doughty, 19, stout mulatto, half Indian, ([R. A. Dragoon]). Free born and served Ben Doughty at Flushing, 18 years.

Sally Terrell, 22, [stout mulatto, half Indian], ([R. A. Dragoon]). Formerly slave to Mr. Graham, Jamaica, West Indies.

Lucy Letchmore, 22, [stout], black, ([R. A. Dragoon]). Formerly slave to Mr. Barker, South Carolina; came to New York about 8 years ago with Captain Lawson, bridge master.

Keatie Dyer, 25, stout mulatto wench, (Cornet Reynolds, KAD). Formerly servant to Mr. Dyer, Rhode Island, and left

that place with the troops six years ago.

Bella Jenkins, 24, [stout mulatto wench], (Cornet Freeman, [KAD]). Formerly slave to Mr. Wigfall, Charlestown; left in the year 1780. G. B. Certificate.

Grand Dutchess of Russia bound for St. John's Stephen Holman, Master

[*Name, age, description are blank*], (Colonel Tyng). Slave received from Capt. Tyng in Jamaica.

Bill Tyng, 16, stout black, ([Colonel Tyng]). Slave received from Mrs. Ross.

John Tyng, 19, stout black, ([Colonel Tyng]). Slave bred in his service.

Dinah Tyng, 20, low wench, ([Colonel Tyng]). [Slave bred in his service.]

Juliet Tyng, 5, mulatto, ([Colonel Tyng]). [Slave bred in his service.]

Lewis Carter, 20, mustee, ([Colonel Tyng]). Formerly servant to Archibald Gilbert, Virginia; left his service about 4 years ago and came with the troops to New York.

Effie Douglas, 24, mulatto, ([Colonel Tyng]). Free woman.

John Banter, 2, [mulatto] boy,
([Colonel Tyng]). [Free] man.

Thomas Banter, 24, stout
black, ([Colonel Tyng]).
Formerly slave to Albert
Banter, Paramus, New Jersey;
left him about six years ago.
GBC.

Moses Simson, 20, [stout
black], (George Leonard, Esq.).
[Formerly slave] to William
Sheppard, Virginia; left him
about five years ago and came
to New York with the troops.
GBC.

Lieut. Berry, 42, [stout black],
([George Leonard, Esq.]).
[Formerly slave] to James
Berry, Frederick town,
Virginia; left him about six
years ago. GBC.

Ishmael Colley, 23, [stout
black], ([George Leonard,
Esq.]). [Formerly slave] to
Ebenezer Colley, Connecticut,
town Fairfield; left him about
six years ago. GBC.

Sarah Caesor, 25, squat
wench, ([George Leonard,
Esq.]). Free, formerly slave to
Jonathan Vallantine, Hamstead
Plains, made her free at his
death.

Lucey Lykes, 24, [squat
wench], ([George Leonard,
Esq.]). Formerly slave to John
Woodward, New Jersey, taken
from thence about six years

ago by Capt. Robinson,
commanding a galley. GBC.

George Kent, 30, tall stout
fellow, ([George Leonard,
Esq.]). [Formerly slave] to Mr.
Lockart, Antigua. GBC.

Joseph Talbot, 28, stout
[fellow], (James Sutter).
[Formerly slave] to Job
McPherson, Charlestown; left
him about 7 years ago, came
to New York with General
Patterson. GBC.

Nancy Talbot, 21, health
seemingly sound, ([James
Sutter]). [Formerly slave] to
Daniel Strooger of
Charlestown; left him about
four years ago, came to New
York with [General Patterson].
GBC.

Ship *Polly*
bound for Port Roseway
John Browne

Simon Gairway, 26, stout man,
(William Johnson). Served
Jenkin Philips, Pennsylvania,
21 years when he got his
freedom; left him about four
years ago. GBC.

Jack Smith, 31, tall stout man,
(John McNeal). Formerly slave
to Jacomiah Smith of
Elizabeth town who he left
about five years ago.

William Williams, 25, middle
sized man, (William Johnson).

[Formerly slave] to Sam Williams of Pennsylvania; left him about three years ago. GBC.

Jacob Lawson, 30, stout man, (Mr. Dewit). [Formerly slave] to Col. Lawson of Princess Ann, Virginia. GBC.

Ruth his wife, [*age not listed*], ([Mr. Dewit]). [Formerly slave] to Henry Corneck, Virginia; left him about 6 years ago.

Luke Brian, 25, stout man, (William Johnson). Says he was born free in the family of Mr. Warrington, Seabrook, Connecticut; left him two years ago.

Harry Gray, 30, [stout man], (John Hoke). Formerly slave to Benjamin Churchwell of Rappahannock, Virginia; left him six years ago.

Abby his wife, 28, stout wench, 3 scars in her face, ([John Hoke]). [Formerly slave] to Captain Tennant, Norfolk, Virginia; [left him six years ago]. GBC.

Sam Dickinson, 24, stout tall man, (Robert French). [Formerly slave] to Thomas Hunt, Philips's Manor, in the year 1776 taken in arms by Capt. Daniel Kipp.

Thomas Foster, 28, [stout], scar in his forehead, (Francis Hunter). [Formerly slave] to John Harbeck of New York. His

master left him there in the year 76 since which he has served & done duty in the Black Company.

Jack Gordon, 40, stout, middle size, blemish left eye, (John Miller). [Formerly slave] to Benjamin Gordon, Charlestown, who he says gave him his freedom about 4 years ago.

Fanny, 33, stout wench, 3 scars in each cheek, (James Fraser). [Formerly slave] to Mr. Cunningham who died in England where she got her freedom 6 years ago. GBC.

Eleanor Foster, 34, thin wench, (Francis Hunter). Appears to be free to the satisfaction of Mr. Parker.

George Lacy, 42, stout man marked with small pox, (John Finch). Born free in the family of Mr. Churchill in Virginia with whom he served until 30 years of age. GBC.

Fanny his wife, 33, stout mulatto wench, (John Finch). Born free, her mother being a white woman; served 31 years with George McCall, Rappahannock, Virginia. GBC.

Kate her daughter, 16, [stout mulatto wench], ([John Finch]). Free.

Guinea, 21, stout, cut in his right eye, Guinea born, (John Miller). Formerly slave to

Captain Brew who brought him from Jamaica in the West Indies who he says gave him his freedom. GBC.

Harry Squash, 22, stout middle sized, (Mr. Lynch). Property of Mr. Lynch, purchased from Captain Huddleston, Royal Artillery.

Deborah his wife, 20, stout wench, thick lips, pock marked, ([Mr. Lynch]). Formerly slave to General Washington, came away about 4 years ago. GBC.

Sam Bayard, 45, stout tall man, (Matthew Tankard). [Formerly slave] to Peter Bayard, New Jersey, came off about 5 years ago. GBC.

London, **Frigate bound for Port Roseway Hugh Watts, Master**

George May, 34, stout fellow, (James Dowell). [Formerly slave] to Mr. Radlow, Jamaica, West Indies; came to New York about 9 years ago in a transport.

William Mannan, 27, thin lathy fellow, (Richard White). [Formerly slave] to George Sobriskey at Oldbridge, Jersey, about 7 years ago.

Henry McGrigger, 24, stout fellow, (Alpheus Palmer). [Formerly slave] to Thomas

Haywood, Charlestown; joined the British troops under the command of General Provost on its march near Charlestown.

Peter Randall, 23, [stout fellow], (William Cassels). [Formerly slave] to James Field in Petersburg, Virginia, whom he left 4 years ago & came to New York.

Robert Blew, 30, stout fellow, (Richard White). Formerly a servant to Captain Gills who left him with Parson Turner which parson he left 4 years ago & joined the British troops at Norfolk in Consequence of Proclamation.

Sippio Simmons, 26, stout lad, ([Richard White]). Given to General Provost by General Haldin and on the General's death left him free.

Jacob Miles, 36, [stout] fellow, (James Dowell). Came with the Troops from Philadelphia to New York; says he was born free at Dover, Pennsylvania.

William Fortune, 40, stout man, (Mr. Ray). Formerly slave to John Morgan at Harrington, New Jersey, came in on the strength of General Howe's proclamation 6 years past. GBC.

Samuel Wyllie, 30, [stout man], ([Mr. Ray]). [Formerly slave] to Edward Davis at Savannah; left the said place with General Clark and the troops. GBC.

Gad Saunders, 25, [stout man], (George Rapalje). [Formerly slave] to David Gilbert, New Haven, Connecticut; left him 4 years ago. Deserter from the Continental army.

Judith [Saunders], 25, [stout] wench, better half Indian ([George Rapalje]). Born free at Stonington in the home of Thomas Williams, Connecticut.

Simsa Herring, 25, stout fellow, (Charles Oliver Bruff). Formerly slave to Daniel Herring near Tappan, New Jersey; left him 4 1/2 years ago on the strength of the proclamation.

Thomas Ogden, 29, stout, scar on the point of left eye, (on his own bottom). [Formerly slave] to Stephen Baldwin, New Jersey; left him 4 1/2 years ago in consequence of Proclamation.

Ben Broughton, 38, passable, (Alpheus Palmer). [Formerly slave] to Thomas Hoggat, Norfolk, Virginia; left him about 4 years ago in [consequence of Proclamation].

Thomas Smith, 25, stout, brickmaker, (Charles Oliver Bruff). [Formerly slave] to Sparrows Maybee, Tappan, New Jersey; left him about 5 years ago [in consequence of Proclamation].

William Bogert, 20, stout make, ([Charles Oliver Bruff]). [Formerly slave] to John Bogart, Tappan, [New Jersey; left him about 5 years ago in consequence of Proclamation].

William Syrrus, 30, [stout make], (Alpheus Palmer). [Formerly slave] to Joseph Smith, Charlestown, taken at the siege of Charlestown on his way from the Enemy Camp.

Samuel Martin, 16, [stout make], (on his own bottom). [Formerly slave] to Stephen Baldwin in N. Ark mountains in the Jerseys; left his master 4 1/2 years past by proclamation.

Richard Lautten, 41, [stout make], (James Dowell). Free born in New Castle County, Pennsylvania, at his father's house.

Thomas Browne, 40, [stout make], 3 long scars each cheek, (George Rapalje). Formerly slave to Ahasmerus Merselis near Hackensack, New Jersey; left him 4 1/2 years past by proclamation.

William Dunk, 32, stout fellow, (Charles Oliver Bruff). [Formerly slave] to John Blavalt, Tappan, New Jersey; [left him 4 1/2 years past by proclamation].

Dick Richards, 22, [stout fellow], (William Cassels). [Formerly slave] to John Wriden, Isle of White, Virginia; [left him 4 1/2 years past by proclamation].

Joseph, 32, [stout fellow], (James Dowell). [Formerly slave] to Capt. Cunningham, Jamaica, West Indies, who left him free at his death.

Isaac, 21, squat stout mulatto, (William Cassels). [Formerly slave] to John Henderson, Williamsburgh, Virginia; brought off by his parents 5 years ago by proclamation.

John Simonsbury, 43, healthy, (Alpheus Palmer). [Formerly slave] to Charles Collins, Fredericksburgh, Dutchess County; left him four years past by [proclamation].

Isaac Connor, 49, ailing man, (John Wilson). [Formerly slave] to Charles Connors, Norfolk, Virginia; left him 4 years past by [proclamation].

James Perrow, 38, squat little man, (Charles Oliver Bruff). Left free by Alexander Blaes, Raritan landing, New Jersey.

Tom Knight, 38, [squat little man], (Joseph Inglish). Left Antigua about four years ago. Steven Clarkely.

Moses Palmer, 18, stout, Ben Palmer of Frogs Neck, claimant. Goes with the son.

Elizabeth Williams, 36, small wench, (Kenneth Renck). Free.

Hana Palmer, 15, stout wench, Ben Palmer of Frogs Neck, claimant. Goes with Ben Palmer's son.

Susanna Herring, 22, [stout wench], (Charles O. Bruff). Formerly slave to Daniel Herring, Tappan, New Jersey; left him 4 1/2 years past by proclamation.

Mary Brown, 38, small [wench], (George Rapalje). [Formerly slave] to Daniel Vancepes, Bergen, New Jersey; left him six years past by [proclamation].

Mary Richards, 22, [small wench], (William Carson). [Formerly slave] to Thomas Fleming, John's Island, South Carolina; left him 3 years past by [proclamation].

Dinah Blavelt, 20, stout wench, 1 child named Jack 1 year old, (Charles O. Bruff). [Formerly slave] to Mr. Blauvelt, Tappan, New Jersey; left him 4 1/2 years past by [proclamation].

Sarah Bunyan, 27, stout wench, ([Charles O. Bruff]). [Formerly slave] to Gerrit Smith, Cacyte, New Jersey; left him 4 1/2 years past by [proclamation].

Sara Graham, 24, [stout wench], (James Dowell). Says

she came free as a servant to Mr. Graham from Antigua about 2 years ago. Mr Graham went to England last fall.

Moriah, 26, weakly wench, (Alpheus Palmer). Formerly slave to John Smith, Charlestown; left him at the siege of that place.

Dinah McGrigger, 24, stout wench, mulatto, ([Alpheus Palmer]). [Formerly slave] to John Dale on John's Island, South Carolina; left him 5 years past by proclamation.

Preniah Perry, 21, [stout wench, mulatto], (Richard White). Free as appears by a bill of sale signed by Stephen Crane to John Munnall, 15 Oct. 177__.

Phillis Blew, 24, stout short wench, ([Richard White]). Formerly slave to Captain Archie, Norfolk, Virginia; left him about 4 years past.

Phillis Sparrow, 28, [stout] sizeable [wench], mulatto, (Charles O. Bruff). [Formerly slave] to Charles Suydam, Brunswick, New Jersey; left him 7 years past by proclamation.

Nannis Sparrow, 11.

Sukey [Sparrow], 9.

John [Sparrow], 3.

Charles Francis, 20, stout mulatto, (Charles O. Bruff).

Formerly slave to David Smith, Tappan, New Jersey; left him 4 1/2 years past by proclamation.

Jeremy, 4, mulatto, (Thomas Whiting). Free as appears by a Bill of Sale dated March 1781, signed by William Wade to William Carman.

Samuel Gullet, 32, stout fellow, black, (Hugh Hays). Formerly slave to William Deshee, Wooster County, Virginia; left him 5 years past.

Hester Singleton, 30, stout, flat, square wench, M, ([Hugh Hays]). [Formerly slave] to John Singleton, Wanda River, South Carolina; [left him] 5 years past.

Catharine, 17, [stout wench]. James Dowell, claimant. Free born in the family of James Dewitt at Albany.

Nancy, 20, slim made black wench, (William Cassells). Formerly slave to Mr. Dove, Georgia; left him at the Siege of Savannah.

Phillis, 34, stout wench, (John Wilson). [Formerly slave] to Andrew Stewart, Crane Island, Virginia; left him 4 years ago.

Nan, 12, stout girl, ([John Wilson]). [Formerly slave] to Charles Connor, [Crane Island, Virginia; left him 4 years ago].

Nancy, 25, stout wench, (Benjamin Palmer). [Formerly slave] to John Wigfall, Charlestown, South Carolina; left him 3 years ago.

Nancy Broughton, 24, remarkably stout & lusty, scars right arm, (Alpheus Palmer). [Formerly slave] to Thermer Hogwood, Princess Ann County, Virginia; left him 4 years ago.

Little Dale
bound for Halifax
Ketrick, Master

Barbara Ogden, 35, stout wench, (on her own Bottom). [Formerly slave] to Stephen Baldwin, Paramus, New Jersey; left him 4 years ago.

Peter, 15, (Capt. Pitcairn, 82 Regt.). [Formerly slave] to John Munn, Charlestown, South Carolina; left him 2 years past by proclamation.

Ship *Ann*
bound for Port Roseway
Joseph Clark, Master

James Robertson, 49, thin, pilot by order, (Capt. Mowat). [Formerly slave] to Captain Paul Layon, Portsmouth, Virginia; left him 4 years ago, employed as a pilot.

Betsey Robertson, 46, thin wench, ([Capt. Mowat]). [Formerly slave to Captain Paul Layon, Portsmouth, Virginia]; left him with her husband.

James Robertson, 2 1/2, small boy, ([Capt. Mowat]).

James Jackson, 50, thin, goes as pilot, ([Capt. Mowat]). [Formerly slave] to late Robert Tucker, Norfolk, Virginia; left him with Lord Dunmore when he left that country & was employed as a pilot.

Judith Jackson, 24, thin wench, mulatto, ([Capt. Mowat]). Says she served her time to John Bell at Cape Fear and left that with the army of Sir H. Clinton in 1776.

Harry Jackson, 8, good L boy, ([Capt. Mowat]).

Charles Fox, 33, stout fellow, (John Anderson). Formerly slave to John Fox, Gloster, Virginia; left him about five years ago by proclamation. GBC.

Rachel Fox, 42, thin weakly wench, ([John Anderson]). [Formerly slave] to James Moorfield, late of Norfolk, Virginia; came from thence with Lord Dunmore. GBC.

London Jackson, 32, stout fellow, pilot by order (Capt. Mowat). [Formerly slave] to William Ballad, Hampton,

Virginia; left him two years past.

Sebro Jackson, 25, thin wench, mulatto ([Capt. Mowat]). [Formerly slave] to Luke Sheets, New York, who left him there in the year 1782; sent on board the *Thetis*.

Zolpher Jackson, 1/2. [Formerly slave to Luke Sheets, New York, who left him there in the year 1782; sent on board the *Thetis*.]

Nelly Jackson, 33, stout wench. [Formerly slave] to Hampstead Bailie, Hampton, Virginia; left him two years past.

Nancy Walker, 21, likely wench, M, (on her own bottom). [Formerly slave] to Col. Cornel, Hampton, Virginia; left him two years past.

James Collin, 43, ordinary man, pilot by order (Capt. Mowat). [Formerly slave] to John Williams, Norfolk, Virginia; taken by Gen. Arnold at Petersburgh 3 years past.

Dick Leich, 28, [ordinary man, pilot by order], ([Capt. Mowat]). Manney Goddin, Nansemond, Virginia; taken prisoner about 5 years past by the *St. Alban* Man of War.

Ruth Leich, 20, stout wench, ([Capt. Mowat]). Formerly

slave to Col. Conel, Virginia; left him two years past.

Grace Leich, 17, likely wench, ([Capt. Mowat]). [Formerly slave to Col. Conel, Virginia; left him two years past.]

Jacob Wanton, 35, ordinary man, (James Cotton). [Formerly slave] to Latham Thurston, Rhode Island; left him with the troops 4 years past by proclamation.

Thomas Hicks, 15, fine boy, M, (John Norstrandt). Born free at Rockaway.

Thomas Terhune, 19, [fine boy], (Paul Speed). Formerly slave to Samuel Terhune, Hackensack; left him 2 1/2 years past.

Dinah Terhune, 16, thin girl, ([Paul Speed]). [Formerly slave] to Edward Bruce, New York; both the property of Paul Speed as appears by Bill of Sale presented at the inspection.

Prince Few, 26, thin mulatto, (Robert McCulloch). Free born, Pearson town, Connecticut.

Judah Few, 35, stout M wench, child 5 yrs. old, ([Robert McCulloch]). [Free born], James Way's, English Kills, Newtown, Long Island.

Abigail, 35, [stout child] 4 mo., (Thomas Statia). Formerly

slave to White at Brunswick, New Jersey; left him five years ago.

John Pell, 28, stout man, pock marked, (William Hill). Free as appears by a Certificate of General Birch to whom he was given by Sir Henry Clinton; says he left Charlestown about 5 years ago.

John Pell, 14, stout mulatto boy, ([William Hill]). Son to the above mentioned person.

Judah Pell, 25, S. B. wench, child 5 yrs. old, ([William Hill]). Formerly slave to Dr. Ramsey, Norfolk, Virginia; left him about five years ago.

Casar Nicholls, 22, stout black man, ([William Hill]). [Formerly slave] to Dr. Van Wyck at Fishkills; left him 3 1/2 years ago. GBC.

Peter Warner, 30, [stout], cut above his left eye, ([William Hill]). [Formerly slave] to Michael Mount, Monmouth, New Jersey; left him 5 years ago. GBC.

Effie Warner, 33, stout wench & boy 2 yrs. old, ([William Hill]). [Formerly slave] to John Matthews, Princess Ann, Virginia; left him 5 years ago. GBC.

Dick Gray, 25, stout fellow, ([William Hill]). Free; says he served untill he was 21 years of age with John Lee, Westfield, Massachusetts.

Harry, 23, [stout]. John Anderson of Port Roseway, claimant. (John Anderson). Purchased as per Bill of Sale from Medcalf Eden, New York; born on Staten Island.

William, 14, fine boy. [John Anderson of Port Roseway, claimant.] ([John Anderson]). Purchased from Hugh Dunn, New York; born nigh Stoney Point. Formerly the property of Edison, taken with a Guard of the Enemy by a party from the Garrison, 1779.

**Ship *Ann*
bound for Port Roseway
Joseph Clark, Master**

Joe Gold, 30, stout black, (Robert Turnbull). Formerly slave to Daniel Descan, about 14 miles from Charlestown, South Carolina; left him 4 years ago. GBC.

Betsey his wife, 33, [stout] mulatto wench, ([Robert Turnbull]). [Formerly slave] to Mrs. Harriet Crook, Savannah, Georgia; left that place 5 years ago.

Sukey her daughter, 12, thin [mulatto] girl, ([Robert Turnbull]). [Formerly slave to Mrs. Harriet Crook, Savannah, Georgia; left that place 5 years ago.]

Ship *Esther*
bound for Port Roseway
Robert Gill, Master

Thomas Scutcheon, 20, stout fellow, (Engineer Department). [Formerly slave] to Solomon Wilson, Virginia; left him 5 years ago. GBC.

Rachel [Scutcheon], 14, likely girl, mulatto, ([Engineer Department]). [Formerly slave] to [Solomon Wilson, Virginia; left him 5 years ago]. [GBC]

Jack Browne, 48, stout old man, ([Engineer Department]). [Formerly slave] to Mr. Pertrie, Georgia; left him when Savannah was taken. GBC.

Dinah Browne, 33, stout wench, M., ([Engineer Department]). [Formerly slave] to [Mr. Pertrie, Georgia; left him when Savannah was taken]. [GBC]

Acky Dickson, 25, sound sizeable man, ([Engineer Department]). [Formerly slave] to Matt Godray near Norfolk, Virginia; left him 5 years past. [GBC]

Clara Dickson, 24, sound able wench, mulatto, ([Engineer Department]). [Formerly slave] to Mr. Quinby, North Carolina; left him about 7 years past. [GBC]

Andrew Johnson, 25, short stout fellow, 1/2 M ([Engineer Department]). [Formerly slave] to Thomas Fowler, Ashley River, South Carolina; left him 4 years past. [GBC]

Jenny Johnson, 21, short [stout] wench, 1/2 M ([Engineer Department]). [Formerly slave to Thomas Fowler, Ashley River, South Carolina; left him 4 years past. GBC.]

Jenny Reynolds, 25, thin looking wench, ([Engineer Department]). [Formerly slave] to Cornelius Van Horne, Jersey; left him 6 years past. [GBC]

Ned Godfrey, 42, thin fellow, ([Engineer Department]). [Formerly slave] to Col. Godfrey, Norfolk, Virginia; left him 4 years past. [GBC]

Elizabeth Godfrey, 30, short and stout, ([Engineer Department]). [Formerly slave to Col. Godfrey, Norfolk, Virginia; left him 4 years past. GBC.]

Jeffry Godfrey, 17, likely boy, ([Engineer Department]). [Formerly slave to Col.

Godfrey, Norfolk, Virginia; left him 4 years past. GBC.]

Betsey Godfrey, 1 1/2, ([Engineer Department]).

Abigail Godfrey, 75, nearly worn out, ([Engineer Department]). [Formerly slave to Col. Godfrey, Norfolk, Virginia; left him 4 years past. GBC.]

Nero Simmon, 45, stout fellow, ([Engineer Department]). [Formerly slave] to Mr. Cal Voise, South Carolina; left him at the Siege of Charlestown. [GBC]

Cudja, 40, ordinary [fellow], ([Engineer Department]). [Formerly slave] to Mr. Franswa; left him when Charlestown was taken. [GBC]

Nancy Sears, 43, [ordinary] wench, ([Engineer Department]). Appears by sundry papers to be a free wench.

August Isaac, 25, [ordinary] lad, ([Engineer Department]). Formerly slave to Isaac Rippen, Charlestown; left him about 4 years past. [GBC]

Joseph Dickson, 25, stout lad, ([Engineer Department]). Formerly an apprentice to late Col. Hutchins of Norfolk, Virginia; left Virginia with Lord Dunmore. GBC.

John Prison, 24, stout black, ([Engineer Department]). Formerly slave to Thomas Bridges, Charlestown, South Carolina, who he says died at five fathom hole 3 1/2 years ago. GBC.

Cathrine his wife, 19, stout wench, ([Engineer Department]). Free born, bound with widow Field at fresh meadows, Long Island, untill 18 years of age. GBC.

Brass Watson, 30, [stout] fellow scar left forehead, ([Engineer Department]). Formerly slave to John Day, Charlestown; left him about 4 years ago. GBC.

Nancy his wife, 30, [stout] wench, 2 small children ([Engineer Department]). [Formerly slave] to Patt Quince, Wilmington, North Carolina; left him about 7 years ago. [GBC]

Stephen Peters, 20, squat stout fellow, ([Engineer Department]). [Formerly slave] to John Day, Charlestown, South Carolina; left him about 4 years ago. [GBC]

Bristol, 40, [squat], scar over right eye, 3 marks between his eyes, ([Engineer Department]). [Formerly slave] to Kal Rivers, [Charlestown, South Carolina; left him about 4 years ago]. [GBC]

Peter Prentice, 32, [squat], scar on right wrist, ([Engineer Department]). [Formerly slave] to John Southern, Williamsburg, Virginia; left him 3 years ago. [GBC]

Samuel Mason, 25, stout, pockmarked, scar in forehead, ([Engineer Department]). [Formerly slave] to Col. Allen, Caven Point, James river; [left him 3 years ago]. [GBC]

Polly his wife, 26, stout wench, [scar in forehead], ([Engineer Department]). [Formerly slave] to Dick Sharp, Richmond, Virginia; [left him 3 years ago]. [GBC]

John Bullet, 35, stout, ([Engineer Department]). [Formerly slave] to Nathan Lagree, Wando River; [left him 3 years ago]. [GBC]

Sall his wife, 26, stout squat wench, small child, ([Engineer Department]). [Formerly slave to Nathan Lagree, Wando River; left him 3 years ago. GBC.]

Lewis Moore, 50, stout fellow, ([Engineer Department]). [Formerly slave] to Mr. Moore, Hampton County, Virginia; [left him 3 years ago]. [GBC]

John Lewis, 26, [stout] yellow, ([Engineer Department]). [Formerly slave] to Carter, Western Shore, Virginia; left him 6 years ago. [GBC]

Job Allen, 27, [stout] black, scar in forehead, ([Engineer Department]). [Formerly slave] to David Wilson, Eastern Shore, Maryland; left him 4 [years ago]. [GBC]

Polly his wife, 27, [stout] yellow wench, 2 small children, ([Engineer Department]). Free born, Burlington, New Jersey; left it 7 years ago. [GBC]

Emanuel, 26, [stout] Black. Lt. Col. Moncrief, claimant, ([Engineer Department]). Property of Lieutenant Col. Moncrief. [GBC]

Isabella & small child, 29, stout black wench, ([Engineer Department]). Free born in the island of Jamaica; wife to Emanuel.

**Ship *Apollo*
bound for Port Roseway
John Adamson, Master**

Joseph Fowler, 41, stout man, (Robert Whiten). Formerly slave to Mr. Fowler, Savannah; left it about three years ago. [GBC]

Mary Fowler, 9, ([Robert Whiten]). [Formerly slave to Mr. Fowler, Savannah; left it about three years ago. GBC.]

Cato Boden, 28, stout fellow, (Capt. Lounz). Formerly an inhabitant on John's Island, say they were born free, that the woman was employed as servant to Major Trail.

Peg Boden, 23, stout short wench, ([Capt. Lounz]). Man employed as carpenter in the Artillery. GBC.

Nathaniel Black, 50, ordinary fellow, (Capt. Lounz). Formerly slave to John Nesbit, Strasburg ferry, Charlestown; left him 5 years past. GBC.

Effy Black, 25, stout wench, ([Capt. Lounz]). [Formerly slave to John Nesbit, Strasburg ferry, Charlestown; left him 5 years past. GBC.]

Nathaniel Black, 1 1/2, ([Capt. Lounz]).

Prince Wigsal, 25, short and stout, (Richard Whittin). Formerly slave to Mr. Wigfall, Charlestown; left him at the Siege of that place. GBC.

Rose Morgan, 15, [short and stout]. Free as appears by a Bill of Sale produced.

Jac Lawrence, 23, ordinary man, (John Talbot). Formerly slave to John Lawrence, Isle of Wight, Virginia; left him about 4 years ago.

John Jarvis, 34, [ordinary man], (Robert Campbell). Says he was free born on John's Island, South Carolina.

Brig *Kingston*
bound for Port Roseway
John Atkinson, Master

Moses Laston, 24, [ordinary] mulatto, (John Davis). Formerly slave to Thomas Jacob, Virginia; left him about 5 years past.

Robert Brown, 26, stout lad, (John Browne).

Towerhill Hall, 32, ordinary fellow, (Thomas Ball). Formerly slave to Elihu Hall, Nottingham township, Pennsylvania; left him 6 1/2 years past.

Frank Crumline, 30, short and stout, (George Patten). [Formerly slave] to Harry Crumline, Santee, South Carolina; left him 5 years past.

Chloe Crumline, 45, old & worn out, ([George Patten]). [Formerly slave to Harry Crumline, Santee, South Carolina; left him 5 years past.]

Mingo [Crumline], 7, fine boy, ([George Patten]). [Formerly slave to Harry Crumline, Santee, South Carolina; left him 5 years past.]

Ned Lawson, 22, stout fellow, (Timothy Pruett). [Formerly slave] to Lawson, Princess Ann, Virginia; left him 6 years past.

Patty Johnson, 17, stout wench, M, ([Timothy Pruett]). Says she was free born at Portsmouth in Virginia.

Adam Bush, 24, stout fellow, M, (Reed). Formerly slave to Mr. Bush, Princess Ann, Virginia; left him on the strength of General Howe's proclamation about 6 years past.

Charity Bush, 26, low wench, M, ([Reed]). [Formerly slave to Mr. Bush, Princess Ann, Virginia; left him on the strength of General Howe's proclamation about 6 years past.]

Sampson [Bush], 40, ordinary man. Richard Birmingham claimant, Port Roseway. Property of Birmingham by Bill of Sale produced.

Ship *Stafford*
bound for Port Roseway
Robert Watson, Master

Jack Spencer, 34, stout fellow, M.

Robert Willet, 53, worn out, half Indian, (Robert Spencer). Perfectly free.

John Dempse, 27, stout man, 1/2 mulatto, (Charles Hart). Formerly slave to David Mead, Nansemond, Virginia; left him 4 years past. GBC.

Mary Collins, 28, stout wench, (David Phillips). The property of said David Phillips.

Hanna Collins, 2, mulatto, ([David Phillips]). [The property of said David Phillips.]

Ship *Jane*
bound for Port Roseway
Frederick Laingeh

Tom Davis, 25, stout make, (John King). Says he served with Phil Tygner, Cumberland County, Virginia. Says he is no slave; left his master 5 years past.

Becca Teggen, 14, [stout make], ([John King]). His slave as appears by a Bill of Sale produced.

Ship *Venus*
bound for Port Roseway
John Martin

Charles Rinn, 32, tall & stout. Mary Rinn of Port Roseway, claimant. Property of Mary Rinn as appears by written authority.

Billy Rinn, 40, ordinary fellow. [Mary Rinn of Port Roseway, claimant. Property of Mary Rinn as appears by written authority.]

Carsy Rinn, 28, [ordinary] wench. [Mary Rinn of Port

Roseway, claimant. Property of Mary Rinn as appears by written authority.]

Phillis Rinn, 32, stout & short. [Mary Rinn of Port Roseway, claimant. Property of Mary Rinn as appears by written authority.]

Anthony Jones, 40, stout fellow. [Mary Rinn of Port Roseway, claimant.] Formerly slave to Mrs. Marianna Jones; left to Mrs. Rinn by Marianna Jones as appears by Copy of a Will produced.

Sentry & child, 28, stout wench. [Mary Rinn of Port Roseway, claimant. Formerly slave to Mrs. Marianna Jones; left to Mrs. Rinn by Marianna Jones as appears by Copy of a Will produced.]

Fanny, 22, sick wench. [Mary Rinn of Port Roseway, claimant. Formerly slave to Mrs. Marianna Jones; left to Mrs. Rinn by Marianna Jones as appears by Copy of a Will produced.]

**Ship *Three Sisters*
bound for Port Roseway
John Wardell**

Pompey Fleet, 26, short & stout, (Alexander Robertson). [Formerly slave] to Thomas Fleet, Boston; left him at the evacuation of Boston. GBC.

Sukey Coleman, 21, slight make, ([Alexander Robertson]). [Formerly slave] to Mr. Teaboult, Philadelphia; left at the evacuation of Philadelphia. GBC.

Sam Fleet, 5, small boy, ([Alexander Robertson]).

Mary Ann, 23, very small, (John Clirby). Formerly slave to Thomas Cooper, Santee, South Carolina; left him at the Siege of Charlestown. GBC.

Foreman Pleasant, 15, slight made wench, (John McInzie). Says she was born free in New York in the house of the late John McAdam.

Sam Morris, 40, stout, carpenter by trade, (Alexander Robertson). Says she was born free in the family of Mr. Ponthien, Charlestown, South Carolina.

Betsey Morris, 38, stout wench, ([Alexander Robertson]). Formerly slave to William Gibbs, Charlestown, South Carolina; left him six years ago.

Cuff Warwick, 28, stout fellow, ([Alexander Robertson]). [Formerly slave] to Dr. Cuthbert nigh Savannah in Georgia; left him [six years ago]. GBC.

Lydia his wife, 20, stout squat wench, ([Alexander Robertson]). [Formerly slave to

Dr. Cuthbert nigh Savannah in Georgia; left him six years ago. GBC.]

Jim, 10, a stout boy, John McAlpine of Port Roseway, claimant, (John McAlpine). Property of John McAlpine purchased from D. Peters, Hampstead, South Long Island.

**Ship *Blacket*
bound for Port Roseway
John Roxby, Master**

Thomas Bacchus, 28, stout made, (Alexander Robertson). Formerly slave to Captain Williams, Charlestown; left him 5 1/2 years past. GBC.

Jenny Bacchus, 33, low wench, ([Alexander Robertson]). [Formerly slave] to Mrs. Stanyard, John's Island; left her before the Siege of Charlestown. GBC.

Flora Bacchus, 11, ([Alexander Robertson]). General Birch's Certificate.

Mary Bacchus, 4, ([Alexander Robertson]). [General Birch's Certificate.]

William Bacchus, 1, ([Alexander Robertson]). [General Birch's Certificate.]

Jacob Howard, 26, stout fellow, M, ([Alexander Robertson]). Formerly slave to J. Howard, North Carolina; left him about 4 years past. GBC.

Peggy Summer, 21, stout black wench, ([Alexander Robertson]). [Formerly slave] to Luke Sumner, North Carolina; [left him about 4 years past]. [GBC]

Sarah Howard, 1, ([Alexander Robertson]).

Charles Dixon, 47, stout make, carpenter, (William McLeod). [Formerly slave] to Willis Wilkinson, Nansemond, Virginia; left him about 4 years past.

Dolly Dixon, 41, sizeable wench, mulatto, ([William McLeod]). [Formerly slave to Willis Wilkinson, Nansemond, Virginia; left him about 4 years past.]

Myles Dixon, 15, stout boy, [mulatto], ([William McLeod]). [Formerly slave to Willis Wilkinson, Nansemond, Virginia; left him about 4 years past.]

Luke Dixon, 13, [stout boy, mulatto], ([William McLeod]). [Formerly slave to Willis Wilkinson, Nansemond, Virginia; left him about 4 years past.]

Dick Dixon, 12, [stout boy, mulatto], ([William McLeod]). [Formerly slave to Willis Wilkinson, Nansemond,

Virginia; left him about 4 years past.]

Sophia Dixon, 10, [stout] wench, [mulatto], ([William McLeod]). [Formerly slave to Willis Wilkinson, Nansemond, Virginia; left him about 4 years past.]

Sally Dixon, 4, [stout] wench, mulatto, ([William McLeod]). [Formerly slave to Willis Wilkinson, Nansemond, Virginia; left him about 4 years past.]

Henry Beach, 30, low lad, (George Betty). Formerly slave to Daniel Beach, Newark, Jersey; left him about 5 years past.

Robert Freeman, 27, stout fellow, mulatto, (Thomas Powers). Says he was born free. Served his time to Gabriel Philips, powder maker at the Walkill near Goshen.

Jonathan Monday, 19, [stout fellow, mulatto], ([Thomas Powers]). Says he was born free at Mont Serrat; came to New York in Mr. Goodriches Privateer.

William Simmons, 19, [stout fellow, mulatto], (Joshua Hill). Formerly slave to Mr. Simmons, Charlestown; left his master who was killed at the Siege of Savannah.

Shadrick Jones, 23, [stout fellow], black, (William McLeod). [Formerly slave] to Thomas Winter, Chester, Cumberland County, Virginia; left him about 6 years past.

Francis Bruff, 18, [stout fellow], black, (Andrew Barclay). Born at Grenada, West Indies, from whence he was taken by General Arnold about 12 years past, that he left the General at Quebec & is now free.

Silva Shepherd, 25, sizeable mulatto wench, (Lieut. Dan McLeod). Formerly slave to Israel Shepherd, Nansemond, Virginia; left him about 4 years past.

Peggy Jones, 1, ([Lieut. Dan McLeod]).

William Smith, 33, stout mulatto carpenter, (James Robinson). Free born nigh Tabs Creek, Lancaster County, Virginia.

Silas Bright, 31, [stout mulatto], ([James Robinson]). Formerly slave to Griffin Pierte, Greatbridge, Virginia; left him about 7 years ago. GBC.

Robert Jenkins, 31, stout black fellow, ([James Robinson]). Free as per manumission produced signed by Jacob Varse of Charlestown, South Carolina, dated 5 June 70, his former name appears to have been Samuel.

Sarah Browne, 20, stout wench, ([James Robinson]). Says she was born free at Charlestown, lived since a child at Hackensack, New Jersey.

Sukey, 25, [stout wench], ([James Robinson]). Formerly slave to John Hudson, Virginia (Norfolk); left him about 7 years ago. GBC.

John Prior, 26, stout fellow, ([James Robinson]). Says he was free born in Jamaica, served as cooper on board the *Lyon* frigate from which he shows a discharge signed by D. Barns, Purser.

Nancy Mumford, 21, stout wench, ([James Robinson]). Free as per Bill of Sale of her mother from Mrs. Mumford, Rhode Island, to her father Bristol.

Adam Jones, 26, stout black fellow, (Andrew Barclay). Says he was born free on the Estate of Thomas Vandexter, Goldmine, Virginia; left that place about 6 years ago.

Francis Bruff, 18, [stout Black fellow], a cooper, ([Andrew Barclay]). Born free in the Grenadas, W. Indies, says he was engaged till 21 years of age to Gen. Arnold.

Charles, ([Andrew Barclay]). Came from Jamaica, can't understand him.

Joe Ramsey, 31, [stout black fellow, a cooper], (John McLeod). Formerly slave to James Jarridar, Indian Land, South Carolina; left him 5 years ago. GBC.

Peggy his wife, 31, sickly wench, ([John McLeod]). [Formerly slave to James Jarridar, Indian Land, South Carolina; left him 5 years ago. GBC.]

Richard Ball, 20, stout fellow, ([John McLeod]). [Formerly slave] to Captain McCulloch of the Legion who died at Camden & left him free.

Peter Richards, 33, [stout fellow], cut on his left thumb, (Lt. McLeod, Legion). [Formerly slave] to James Jarvis, Cowsatrachy, who he says gave him his freedom at his death about 8 years ago. GBC.

Bella his wife, 30, stout wench, black, ([Lt. McLeod, Legion]). [Formerly slave to James Jarvis, Cowsatrachy]; left him at the same time but was not made free. [GBC]

Libby, their daughter, 16, fine [wench], black, ([Lt. McLeod, Legion]). [Formerly slave to James Jarvis, Cowsatrachy; left him at the same time but was not made free. GBC.]

John Richards, 15, stout boy, their son, ([Lt. McLeod,

Legion]). [Formerly slave to James Jarvis, Cowsatrachy; left him at the same time but was not made free. GBC.]

John Gray, 28, stout fellow, (James Rees). [Formerly slave] to Captain Howard Harrand, Williamsburgh, Virginia, who put him in the Army from whence he deserted.

Mary Bella, 29, stout wench, B 1/2 M, (James Smithers). Slave to Captain Graham, Royal Americans, who left her in New York 4 years ago.

Esther Smith, 14, fine wench, B, (George Bentley). Formerly slave to John Smith of Frog's Point, taken from him about 6 years ago.

**Ship *Nero*
bound for Port Roseway
George Burnett**

Peter Donnel, 29, ordinary fellow, M. James Driscoll of Port Roseway, claimant. His property as appears by Bill of Sale produced.

Nancy Van Horne, 26, stout made wench, [James Driscoll of Port Roseway, claimant]. [His property as appears by Bill of Sale produced.]

**Ship *Elizabeth*
bound for Port Poseway
Hodgson**

John Jones, 40, slow, well sized man, M, (George Low). Formerly slave to Richard Jones, Williamsburg, Virginia; left that with Lord Dunmore in 1776. GBC.

Lucretia Jones, 27, likely wench, M, ([George Low]). Says she is free; left Philadelphia with the Troops. GBC.

Charlotte Jones, 3, ([George Low]).

William Wells, 30, stout fine fellow, ([George Low]). Formerly slave to Captain John George Wills, Mulberry Island, Virginia; left him with Lord Dunmore, 1775. GBC.

Mary Wells, 35, stout wench, ([George Low]). [Formerly slave] to Jo. Hutchins, Norfolk, Virginia; left him in 1775 with Lord Dunmore.

William Francis, 30, fine stout fellow, (Robert Merrit). [Formerly slave] to John Van Wyck, N. Castle Province of New York; left him with Gen. Clinton in 1777.

Rose Yeates, 30, fine wench, M, ([Robert Merrit]). Says she was free born in North Castle, that her mother was free; left N. Castle in 1777.

Billy Francis, 3, ([Robert Merrit]).

Dick Van Wart, 30, stout made fellow, M, ([Robert Merrit]). Formerly slave to John Van Wart, Tarrytown, New York province; left him 7 years past. GBC.

Charles Francis, 27, [stout made fellow], B, ([Robert Merrit]). [Formerly slave] to John Myers, Philips's manor; left him about 7 years past. [GBC]

Thomas Francis, 36, [stout made fellow], B, ([Robert Merrit]). [Formerly slave] to Isaac Vermilla, [Philips's manor]; left him about 6 years past. [GBC]

Robert James, 26, [stout made fellow], M, (William Chetwine). Says he was born free in Kent in Virginia, joined the British fleet in Chesapeake in 1777. [GBC]

Rebecca Williams, 25, likely wench, 1/4 M, ([William Chetwine]). Formerly slave to Frank Molden, Maryland, joined Lord Howe's fleet in 1777.

Rachel James, 9, 1/4 M, ([William Chetwine]). [Formerly slave to Frank Molden, Maryland.]

James James, 3/4, 1/4 M, ([William Chetwine]).

Jack Dunlap, 9, fine boy, black. Lowerhele of Port Roseway, claimant. His property as appears by a Bill of Sale produced.

Jenny Bruce, 15, fine girl, 3/4 white, (William Wilson). These three persons appear to be the property of William Wilson, they having fallen to him in consequence of a marriage settlement between him and Elizabeth Nansberg, Virginia.

Betsey Bruce, 13, [fine girl], 3/4 white, ([William Wilson]).

Hilley Ivey, 12, [fine girl], black, ([William Wilson]).

Jacob, 20, stout fellow, B, ([William Wilson]). Lately the property of Daniel Jenkins at Eddestow, purchased by William Wilson as appears by the receipt of William Donglish, DMCCVA at Savannah, 4 June 79.

Sarah Gordon, 28, tall limber wench, B, (Owen Roberts). Formerly slave to George Ancram in Charlestown; left him with Lord William Campbell in 1775.

Jasper Gordon, 7, fine boy, B, ([Owen Roberts]).

Lucy Lydacre, 24, snug little wench, 1/4 M, (John Kingston). [Formerly slave] to William Lydacre, Jersey; left him in the year 1776 by Proclamation.

Fanny Lydacre, 3, (John Kingston).

**Ship *Grace*
bound for Port Roseway
William Oxley, Master**

Peter Martin, 12, fine boy, M, (Robert Martin). Formerly slave to P. Field, Chesterfield, Virginia; left him 3 years past. Indented to said Martin as appears by an indenture produced till 18 years of age.

Wallace, 21, short & stout, 1/2 M, (Hemus White). [Formerly slave] to William Smith, Savannah; left him about 7 years past, certified to be free by Col. Bocebeck.

Nancy Hill, 22, [short], well made, 1/2 M, 1 child, ([Hemus White]). [Formerly slave to William Smith, Savannah; left him about 7 years past, certified to be free by Col. Bocebeck.]

Jack Tucker, 18, stout lad, (John Stewart). [Formerly slave] to Capt. Smith, N. Port, Glasgow, taken in the ship *Cato* belonging to Capt. Smith of Newport & Glasgow.

Samuel Albert, 20, [stout lad], M, (Samuel Mann). [Formerly slave] to Samuel Tin at Hackensack, New Jersey; says

he was made free by the death of his master 7 years ago.

Billy Williams, 23, stout fellow, (Hugh Eagle). [Formerly slave] to Col. Isaac Haynes, Charlestown, South Carolina, GBC. Proclamation.

Rose Jackson, 22, stout wench, ([Hugh Eagle]). [Formerly slave to Col. Isaac Haynes, Charlestown, South Carolina, GBC. Proclamation.]

Anthony Piggot, 47, stout man, (John Stewart). Says he was born free at Massanacchus nigh Hackensack, Jersey; left it 9 years ago.

Sarah Piggot, 36, stout wench, ([John Stewart]). [Says she was born free at Massanacchus nigh Hackensack, Jersey; left it 9 years ago.]

John [Piggot], their son, 18, stout fellow, B, ([John Stewart]). [Says he was born free at Massanacchus nigh Hackensack, Jersey; left it 9 years ago.]

Casar [Piggot, their son], 9, fine boy, ([John Stewart]). [Says he was born free.]

Isaac James, 22, stout fellow, B, blind left eye, (Hugh Eagle). Formerly slave to George Wilson of Boston, taken about 3 years when his master was killed.

Ship *Hope*
bound for St. John's River
Robert Peacock, Master

Cato Cannon, 40, short stout fellow, (Samuel Ketcham). [Formerly slave] to John Cannon, Norwalk, New England; left him about 6 years ago.

Phillis Ketchin, 44, old & worn wench. John Ketchin of St. John's River, claimant. Clearly his property.

Frank Fairweather, 10, fine boy. Thomas Fairweather of [St. John's River], claimant. [Clearly his property.]

Jack Hide, 50, almost past his labour, (John Kitchin). Formerly slave to Joseph Hyde, Fairfield, New England; left him 6 years past. GBC.

Dick, 38, stout fellow, (Capt. Peacocke). [Formerly slave] to John Jones, Savannah; left him 5 years past, indented for 7 years with said Captain.

Ship *Sovereign*
bound for St. John's River
William Stewart, Master

Cornelius Moss, 30, [stout fellow], likely, (Capt. Ed Ellison). [Formerly slave] to Daniel Moore, Woodbridge, New Jersey; left him 7 years ago. GBC.

Thomas Brinkerhoof, 34, very short ordinary man, (James Petters). [Formerly slave] to Cornelius Boggard near Hackensack, New Jersey; left him 5 years past. GBC.

Peter Bean, 32, likely fellow, (James Travess). [Formerly slave] to David Davis, White Plains; left him two years past, says he has since been sold by his master to said Travess.

Anthony Gilman, 46, stout short fellow, (Hilliard). [Formerly slave] to Major Gillman, Plasto, New England; left him about 3 years past.

George Black, 40, stout fellow, (Jere Ketcham). [Formerly slave] to Josiah Portress, Petersburg, Virginia; left him 4 years past. GBC.

Betsey Black, 35, ordinary wench, ([Jere Ketcham]). [Formerly slave to Josiah Portress, Petersburg, Virginia; left him 4 years past. GBC.]

William Black, 14, fine boy, ([Jere Ketcham]). [Formerly slave to Josiah Portress, Petersburg, Virginia; left him 4 years past. GBC.]

Sam, 30, stout black, (James Sayre). [Formerly slave] to Henry Bracy, Great Bridge, Virginia; left him about 2 years ago. GBC.

Luke Spencer, 25, [stout], (Dr. Stevens). [Formerly slave] to

Oliver Spencer, Elizabeth town, New Jersey; left him 6 years ago.

Abigail his wife, 26, stout wench, small child, ([Dr. Stevens]). Served her time out with Joseph Graham of Boston.

Bill Piggot, 28, stout fellow, (George Harding). Formerly slave to Gabriel Jones, Augusta County, Virginia; left him eight years ago.

Pompey Chase, 28, [stout fellow], Reuben Chase of River St. John's, claimant, (Reuben Chase). Property of Reuben Chase as per Bill of Sale from Jacob Sharpe of Boston.

John Voice, 36, [stout fellow], B, (Captain Stewart St. Louis). Free born at Fonta Bell, Barbadoes.

Dian, 20, stout, squat wench small child, (George Harding). Formerly slave to John Scull, Philadelphia; left him 4 years ago.

**Ship *Ann & Elizabeth*
bound for Port Roseway
Ben Fowler, Master**

Peter Johnson, 35, stout fellow, (Stephen Shakespeare). Says he got his freedom from Silvester Brinoly, Quaker, New Jersey; that he has lived in New York these 6 years past. GBC.

Judith Johnson, 27, ordinary wench, ([Stephen Shakespeare]). Formerly slave to Gerrit Langston, Shrewsbury; left him 3 years past. GBC.

Thomas Danvers, 45, [ordinary] fellow, (Archibald Clarke). [Formerly slave] to Thomas Brown, Savannah; left him 5 years past. GBC.

Sarah Cross, 34, stout squat wench, M, ([Archibald Clarke]). Says she was born free at Tappan, served her time to James Rickman, New York Island.

Harry Spencell, 38, slender fellow, (Stephen Hairran). Formerly slave to B. Benson, New York Island; that Benson left him on the Landing of the British troops on New York Island.

John Dunham, 25, [slender fellow], (Nathaniel Hannah). [Formerly slave] to James Dunham of Augusta; left him 5 years past. GBC.

Jack Smith, 25, [slender fellow], (Edward Hannah). [Formerly slave] to William Smith, Charlestown; left him about 5 years past. GBC.

Venus, 28, [slender] wench, ([Edward Hannah]). [Formerly slave to William Smith,

Charlestown; left him about 5 years past.]

Samuel Drayton, 40, stout fellow, ([Edward Hannah]). [Formerly slave] to Mrs. Drayton near Charlestown; left her before the Siege of Charlestown.

Cath Drayton, 40, ordinary wench, ([Edward Hannah]). [Formerly slave to Mrs. Drayton near Charlestown; left her before the Siege of Charlestown.]

Dinah Edmonds, 34, [ordinary wench], (Stephen Shakespeare). [Formerly slave] to Mr. Edmonds, Charlestown; left him 5 years past.

Thomas Edmonds, 5, small boy, ([Stephen Shakespeare]). [Formerly slave to Mr. Edmonds, Charlestown; left him 5 years past.]

John Rogers, 29, stout fellow, (Andrew Gibson). [Formerly slave to] Captain Rogers, Brig *Dispatch*, who went to England and left him free.

Henry Maxfield, 33, [stout fellow], (Alexander Watson). Free born in Mr. Philips's house of Philips's Manor. GBC.

Hannah his wife, 23, stout wench, 2 small children, ([Alexander Watson]). [Free born] in John Predun, Closters, New Jersey.

Bill Browne, 24, stout fellow, (Nicholas Browne). Formerly slave to Jacob Arnold, Morristown, New Jersey; left him three years ago.

Dinah his wife, 23, lusty, squat wench, B, small child ([Nicholas Browne]). Born free, her mother an Indian; served her time with Edmund Palmer who lived & was hanged at Fishkill for being Tory.

Tom, 40, sickly man, (Thomas Hartley). Formerly slave to Henry Smith, Charlestown, South Carolina, who died soon after it was taken by the British; left no heirs.

Nancy his wife, 40, thin wench, ([Thomas Hartley]). [Formerly slave] to Widow Lott of [Charlestown] who she says gave her free before she died 11 years ago.

Charles, 21, stout, B, ([Thomas Hartley]). [Formerly slave] to Charles Elliot of [Charlestown] who died about 4 1/2 years ago.

Prince Fraction, 25, [stout], blind left eye, Edward Trigler of Port Roseway, claimant (Edward Trigler). Property of Edward Trigler, purchased from James Stokes of New York.

———————————

**Ship *Montague*
bound for Port Roseway
Robert Wilson, Master**

Will Woodhouse, 48, tall &
worn out, (James Rose).
Formerly slave to William
Woodhouse, Princess Ann,
Virginia; left Virginia 6 years
past by proclamation.

Jenny Perrill, 45, stout wench,
1 child a year old, ([James
Rose]). Served with Captain
Perrill, N. Town, Virginia; left
him 6 years past, no slave.

Benjamin Phillips, 40, tall
slim fellow, (Robert Fox).
Formerly servant to George
Phillips, Middletown,
Connecticut; left him six years
past by proclamation.

Rachel, 28, stout wench. Isaac
Enslow of Port Roseway,
claimant. Clearly proved his
property.

David, 8, fine boy. [Isaac
Enslow of Port Roseway,
claimant. Clearly proved his
property.]

Polly Pompey, 9, fine wench,
(Robert Fox).

Minnus, 19, remarkable fine
wench, (Sarah Nunn). Says she
is free; was born at Fresh
Meadows, Long Island, near
the House of Mr. Skidmore.

**Ship *Providence*
bound for Port Roseway
John Richee**

Nero McCulloch, 22, stout
short fellow, (Stephen
Shakespeare). Formerly slave
to General Thomas Scribbins,
Georgia; left him 5 years past.
GBC.

Patty Shewbrick, 20, likely
wench, M, a boy 10 mo. old,
([Stephen Shakespeare]).
[Formerly slave] to Thomas
Shubrick, Charlestown; left
him 5 years past by
Proclamation. GBC.

London Bloy, 40, ordinary
fellow, M, (Jesse Lear).
[Formerly slave] to Lemuel
Yestown, Newtown, Virginia;
left him 4 years past. GBC.

Abigail Richardson, 38, stout
wench, ([Jesse Lear]).
[Formerly slave] to Mr.
Richardson, Norfolk, Virginia;
[left him 4 years past]. [GBC]

Catharine [Richardson], 9, fine
girl, ([Jesse Lear]). [Formerly
slave to Mr. Richardson,
Norfolk, Virginia; left him 4
years past. GBC.]

James Ramsey, 20, stout lad,
(on his own bottom). [Formerly
slave] to Murphey Godfrey,
Norfolk, Virginia; left 5 years
past. [GBC]

Hana Hazard, 36, likely
wench, (Andrew Hoggarth).

Born free to a certainty at Rhode Island.

Ben Hazard, 11, fine boy, ([Andrew Hoggarth]). [Born free to a certainty at Rhode Island.]

David Jones, 40, ordinary fellow, (Stephen Shakespeare). Formerly slave to Lawrence Lownse, Ketchatche, South Carolina; left him about 4 years past. GBC.

Cato Ramsey, 45, slim fellow, ([Stephen Shakespeare]). [Formerly slave] to Dr. John Ramsey, Norfolk, Virginia; left him 7 years past. GBC.

China Godfrey, 35, ordinary wench, ([Stephen Shakespeare]). [Formerly slave] to Col. Godfrey, Norfolk, Virginia; left him 4 years past. GBC.

Nelly Ramsey, 15, fine girl, ([Stephen Shakespeare]). [Formerly slave] to Lawrence Lounse as above. [*David Jones*], GBC.

Betsey Ramsey, 10, [fine girl], ([Stephen Shakespeare]). [Formerly slave to Lawrence Lounse as above.] [*David Jones*] [GBC]

Thomas Ellis, 25, stout little fellow, ([Stephen Shakespeare]). [Formerly slave] to Ellis Remain, Hackensack, New Jersey; left him 3 years past. GBC.

Dinah Ellis, 25, very little wench, ([Stephen Shakespeare]). [Formerly slave to Ellis Remain, Hackensack, New Jersey; left him 3 years past. GBC.]

Samuel Ellis, 5, fine boy, ([Stephen Shakespeare]). [Formerly slave to Ellis Remain, Hackensack, New Jersey; left him 3 years past. GBC.]

Lucy Ellis, 3, fine girl, ([Stephen Shakespeare]).

Fonlove Jackson, 25, likely wench, M, (on her own bottom). Free wench born at Rhode Island.

Dinah Jackson, 9, fine girl, ([on her own bottom]). [Free wench born at Rhode Island.]

Ned Jackson, 6, fine boy, ([on his own bottom]). [Free boy born at Rhode Island.]

Francis, 50, stout man of his age, B, (Fredrick Myers). Made free by Mr. John Rosser to whom he belonged as appears by Certificate dated at Savannah, Georgia, 22d June 1772.

Sylvia, 30, stout wench, B, ([Fredrick Myers]). [Made free by Mr. John Rosser to whom he belonged as appears by Certificate dated at Savannah, Georgia, 22d June 1772.]

Ben, 12, fine boy, B, ([Fredrick Myers]). [Made free by Mr. John Rosser to whom he belonged as appears by Certificate dated at Savannah, Georgia, 22d June 1772.]

Anthony Loyal, 36, stout man, M, (Daniel Grandon). Born free at Monmouth, New Jersey, served his time with William Wykoff, Monmouth County. GBC.

Hagar his wife, 35, stout wench, ([Daniel Grandon]). Formerly slave to David Forman, Monmouth, New Jersey; left him 5 years ago. [GBC]

Abner Cromwell, 16, stout lad, ([Daniel Grandon]). [Formerly slave] to Lewis Thomas, Duplin County, North Carolina; left him 3 years ago. [GBC]

James Campbell, 22, stout fellow, (Stephen Shakespeare). Says he was born free in the family of Thomas Ford, Charlestown, South Carolina.

Bill, 26, [stout fellow]. William Black of Port Roseway, claimant. (William Black). Property of William Black.

Luke Johnson, 18, [stout fellow], (Stephen Shakespeare). Formerly slave to Charles Casoner, Norfolk, Virginia; left him 5 years ago.

John Dick, 25, [stout fellow], (Capt. Richie). Born in Kingston, Jamaica; free, indented to John Ritchie.

Henry Williams, 23, [stout fellow], ([Capt. Richie]). Born free at Bridge town, Barbadoes.

Ship *Mary*
bound for Port Roseway
Francis Roughbottom

Anthony Davis, 29, stout fellow, (Joseph Veasey). Formerly slave to Mark Davis on the Delaware; left him about 3 years past. GBC.

Wynie Hempstead, 18, stout wench & a child 2 mo. old, ([Joseph Veasey]). [Formerly slave] to William Hempstead, Pancatant, Virginia; came to New York with Lord Dunmore. GBC.

Thomas Patrick, 42, stout fellow, (Hugh Fraser). [Formerly slave] to Captain Colbert, Norfolk, Virginia; left him 5 years past. GBC.

Phebe Patrick, 29, [stout] wench, ([Hugh Fraser]). [Formerly slave] to Mrs. Taylor, [Norfolk, Virginia; left him 5 years past]. [GBC]

Ichabod Cornwall, 23, slim weakly fellow, (Joseph Pimken). [Formerly slave] to Nat Dungey, New Milford,

Connecticut; left him 4 years past. GBC.

Frances Cornwall, 21, stout square built wench, ([Joseph Pimken]). [Formerly slave to Nat Dungey, New Milford, Connecticut; left him 4 years past. GBC.]

Samuel Warner, 36, ordinary fellow, (Phil Ackland). Formerly slave to William Warner, Warwick, Rhode Island; left him about 6 years past. GBC.

Sally Hays, 46, very thin wench, 1 child 2 years old (Daniel Lafferty). Served her time to Thomas Cassidy, Potomack river, Virginia; left him 6 years past.

Sally Taylor, 35, square made wench, (Phil Ackland). Formerly slave to Col. Ruscow, Warwick, Virginia; left him 5 years past.

Samuel Whitting, 25, likely fellow, M, (Andrew Calder). Born free on Picken Creek, served his time to John Gordon there; left that about 6 years past.

Lucy Whitting, 36, stout wench, M, ([Andrew Calder]). [Born free] in Potomack, Virginia, served some time with Aaron Mozley; left him 6 years past.

John Smith, 49, ordinary fellow, (James Graham).

Formerly belonged to John Carter, Barbadoes; left that place 3 years past.

Scipio Buxton, 26, stout [fellow], (Richard Williams). Formerly slave to Mr. Buxton, Nansemond, Virginia; left him 5 years past.

Thomas Plumb, 42, [stout fellow], M, carpenter, (Andrew Ross). Born free, Little York, Virginia.

Zaccheus Curle, 30, [stout fellow], B, (Peter Parker). Formerly slave to Mr. Curle, Hampton, Virginia; left him 4 years.

George Butler, 23, [stout fellow], M, (John Mitchell). Born free at Hallets Cove, Long Island.

Sukey Butler, 23, stout wench, M, ([John Mitchell]). [Born free], served 18 years with Abner Shadwell, East end, Long Island.

Frank Peters, 20, stout fellow, B, (George Scot). Formerly slave to Woodward Flowers, Monk's Corner, South Carolina; left him 4 years ago.

Nancy Peters, 20, stout wench, B, ([George Scot]). [Formerly slave to Woodward Flowers, Monk's Corner, South Carolina; left him 4 years ago.]

Joe, 26, stout fellow, B, (Peter Parker). [Formerly slave] to

William Bennet, Hampton, Virginia; left him 3 years ago.

Hannah his wife, 21, stout wench, B, 2 small children, ([Peter Parker]). [Formerly slave] to Ned Cooper, [Hampton, Virginia; left him 3 years ago].

William Ashe, 38, stout fellow, B, (John Davis). [Formerly slave] to Cato Ashe, Charlestown, South Carolina; left him 8 years ago.

Mary Ashe his wife, 38, stout wench, B, ([John Davis]). [Formerly slave] to James Gerrido, Indian Land, South Carolina; [left him] 8 years ago.

Esther their daughter, 10, fine girl, B, ([John Davis]). [Formerly slave] to Cato Ashe, Charlestown, South Carolina.

Sam Cuthbert, 30, stout fellow, B, (James Moffat). [Formerly slave] to Joseph Cuthbert, Savannah, Georgia; left him 4 years ago.

John Cuthbert, 26, [stout fellow], B, ([James Moffat]). [Formerly slave to Joseph Cuthbert, Savannah, Georgia; left him 4 years ago.]

Lucinda his wife, 23, stout wench, 2 small children, B, ([James Moffat]). [Formerly slave to Joseph Cuthbert, Savannah, Georgia; left him 4 years ago.]

Dinah, 20, stout black wench, (Joseph Pinchon). [Formerly slave] to Beggert Butler, Leedstown, Virginia; left him 3 years ago.

Sally, 18, [stout] squat, B, (Peter Robinson). [Formerly slave] to John Hall, Charlestown, South Carolina; [left him 3 years ago].

Sarah Fillifitas, 14, fine girl, B, 1/2 Mul. ([Peter Robinson]). Born free at Philadelphia from whence she came with Peter Robinson 5 years ago.

London, 19, stout fellow, B, ([Peter Robinson]). Formerly slave to John Slinne, Charlestown, South Carolina; left him 5 years ago.

Primus, 19, stout [fellow], B. George Thomas of H. A. Dragoons, claimant. (George Thomas). Purchased from Mr. George Thomas from John Woodberry's attorney Thomas Portell as appears by record dated Charlestown, South Carolina, 2d December 1782.

Hannah, 14, fine girl, [George Thomas of H. A. Dragoons, claimant]. ([George Thomas]). [Purchased from Mr. George Thomas from John Woodberry's attorney Thomas Portell as appears by record dated Charlestown, South Carolina, 2d December 1782.]

Charlotte Plumb, 13, [fine girl], M. Daughter & property of Thomas Plumb above mentioned.

Baker & Atlee
bound for Port Roseway
Erasmus Roberts, Master

Robert Winter, 26, stout fellow, (Thomas McManus). Formerly served with Mr. Roberts in Jamaica, West Indies; left it 2 years past. GBC.

Winey VanSant, 45, very ordinary fellow, (Timothy Mahan). Formerly slave to John Van Sant, Bergen County, New Jersey; left him 6 years past. [GBC]

Betty Tynes, 30, ordinary wench, 1 child is month old, ([Timothy Mahan]). [Formerly slave] to Timothy Tynes, James River, Virginia; left him 3 years past. [GBC]

Henry Kipp, 23, stout fellow, (Alexander Frazer). [Formerly slave] to Abraham Kipp, Hackensack, New Jersey; left him 6 years past. [GBC]

August Griggs, 18, stout lad, (Thomas Jennia). [Formerly slave] to Samuel Griggs, Georgia; left him at the Siege of Savannah. [GBC]

Richard Dixon, 21, [stout lad], (Daniel Barry). [Formerly slave] to John Patterson, [Georgia]; left him at the taking of Savannah. [GBC]

Prince Princes, 53, stout man, (John Moore). [Formerly slave] to Abraham Peers, Second river, New Jersey; left him 3 years ago about 2 years since he sold him to James Stokes from whom he bought himself & paid £45.

Margaret his wife, 40, [stout] wench, M, ([John Moore]). Born free in the family of John Hull, Bergen, New Jersey; left it 3 years ago.

Nicholas their son, 11, fine boy, ([John Moore]). [Born free in the family of John Hull, Bergen, New Jersey; left it 3 years ago.]

Elizabeth their daughter, 20, stout B wench with small child, ([John Moore]). [Born free in the family of John Hull, Bergen, New Jersey; left it 3 years ago.]

Sam Van Norstrant, 28, stout fellow, M, ([John Moore]). Property of Stoffle Van Nostrant, Acquackenack, New Jersey; left him 4 years ago.

Isaac Anderson, 30, [stout fellow], B, carpenter, (Orchbert Nesbit). Born free in the family of Robert Lindsay, Charlestown, South Carolina; left it 7 years ago.

Sarah his wife, 20, [stout]
wench, B, ([Orchbert Nesbit]).
Formerly slave to Harry Smith,
Charlestown, South Carolina,
who died about 5 years ago.

Sloop *Beaver*
bound for Port Roseway
Peter Parker, Master

Casar Handell, 34, stout
fellow, (Peter Lynch).
[Formerly slave] to Mr.
Handell, Georgia; left him
when Savannah was taken by
the British troops. GBC.

Joseph Skinner, 35, stout
fellow, (Peter Lynch).
Formerly servant to Thomas
Skinner, Refugee from Amboy;
appears to be the property of
Peter Lynch.

Tinnia Lynch, 25, [stout]
Wench, ([Peter Lynch]).
[Formerly servant to Thomas
Skinner, Refugee from Amboy;
appears to be the property of
Peter Lynch.]

Sally Lynch, 6, fine girl,
([Peter Lynch]). [Formerly
servant to Thomas Skinner,
Refugee from Amboy; appears
to be the property of Peter
Lynch.]

Sloop *Katy*
bound for Port Roseway
Peter Lawrence, Master

William Robertson, 36, stout
fellow, (Alexander Ross).
[Formerly servant] to Mark
Roberts, Rappahannock,
Virginia; left him 6 years past.

Brig *Ranger*
bound for Annapolis Royal
James Philips

Anthony Philips, 23, stout,
(Capt. Philips). Captain
Philips' property clearly.

Charles Demce, 23, [stout]
mulatto, (Lt. Tardeal). Born
free; lived with William Ford,
Flushing, Long Island.

Hester Ruggles, 7, fine wench,
(General Ruggles). The
General's property.

Jeffery Ruggles, 6, fine boy
([General Ruggles]). [The
General's property.]

Prince, 19, stout B. Richard
Ruggles of Annapolis,
claimant. (Richard Ruggles).
Property of Richard Ruggles.

Robert Williams, 23, [stout],
(General Ruggles). Free born
at Shrewsbury, New Jersey.

John Coslin, 25, [stout], M,
([General Ruggles]). [Free
born] at North Hampshire,
Virginia; parents free.

William, 6, fine boy, B.
William Chandler of
[Annapolis], claimant.
(William Chandler). Property
of William Chandler as per
Bill of Sale produced.

Violett, 11, [fine] girl, B. John
McKown of [Annapolis],
claimant. (John McKown).
[Property] of William
McKown, born in his father-in-
law's family.

Sloop *Delight*
bound for River St. John's
Ben Benssis, Master

Jupiter King, 24, stout fellow,
(James Peters). Formerly slave
to Col. King, Williamsburgh,
Virginia; left him 3 years past.
GBC.

Tom Wallace, 22, stout lad,
(Mr. McMullan). Formerly
lived with Mr. Wallace, New
Providence, West Indies, free.
[GBC]

Jack Cooper, 25, slim make,
(Simonons, Esq.). [Formerly
lived] with Ged Cooper, Santa
Croix, West Indies.

John Clayton, 26, stout make,
(Capt. Bell). Lived with John
Clayton, Rappahannock river,
Virginia; left him 8 years past.

Ship *Apollo*
bound for Port Roseway
John Adams

John Kassery, 22, stout black
fellow, (James Fergusson).
Formerly slave to Thomas
Haywood, Savannah, Georgia;
left him 1st April, 1779.

Dublin Fowler, 14, stout boy,
scar over his nose, (Richard
Wheaton). [Formerly slave] to
Mr. Brisbane, [Savannah,
Georgia; left him] 5 years ago.
GBCP.

Lotche Slaide, 46, stout
fellow, scar on forehead,
(Abner Ellison). [Formerly
slave] to John Slaide,
Swansey, Massachusetts; [left
him] 6 years ago. [GBCP]

Freelove his wife, 49, stout
wench, ([Abner Ellison]).
[Formerly slave] to George
Chace, Freetown,
[Massachusetts; left him 6
years ago]. [GBCP]

Roger their son, 14, fine boy,
([Abner Ellison]). [Formerly
slave] to Jonathan Slade,
Swanzey, [Massachusetts; left
him 6 years ago]. [GBCP]

Jack Rogers, 50, stout man,
(John Libby). Left free by his
master, James Rogers,
Newport, Rhode Island, who
died 5 years before the war.

St. Louis, 60, thin, ([John
Libby]). French free negroe.

Jacob Wigfall, 36, [thin], (Richard Wheaton). Formerly the property of Mr. Joseph Wigfall, Charlestown, South Carolina; left him in the year 1779. GBCP.

Silvia his wife, 36, stout squat wench, ([Richard Wheaton]). [Formerly the property of Mr. Joseph Wigfall, Charlestown, South Carolina; left him in the year 1779. GBCP.]

Ishmael Warren, 25, stout fellow, (William Campbell). Formerly slave to Joseph Warren, Charlestown, South Carolina; [left him in the year 1779]. [GBCP]

James Wright, 21, remarkably stout, (Archibald Campbell). [Formerly slave] to Stephen Wright, Norfolk, Virginia; [left him] 5 years ago. [GBCP]

Charles Jenkins, 19, stout lad, (William Campbell). [Formerly slave] to Thomas Jenkins, Savannah, Georgia; [left him] 6 years ago. [GBCP]

**Brig Kingston
bound for Port Roseway
John Atkinson, Master**

Joe Robinson, 25, stout fellow, (Alexander Murray). Formerly property to Campbell, Charlestown, South Carolina who he says left him free about 5 years ago.

Absolom Dickson, 31, [stout fellow], mulatto, (Richard Jolly). [Formerly slave] to Solomon Sheppard, Nansemond County, Virginia; left him 4 years ago.

Peggy & small boy, 20, [stout] wench, ([Richard Jolly]). [Formerly slave] to James Jolly, Norfolk County, Virginia; [left him 4 years ago].

Sabinah, 70, ([Richard Jolly]). [Formerly slave to James Jolly, Norfolk County, Virginia; left him 4 years ago.]

Benjamin Sheppard, 20, stout fellow, ([Richard Jolly]). [Formerly slave] to Solomon Sheppard, Nansemond County, Virginia; [left him 4 years ago].

Nancy Collins, 19, [stout] wench, (Mrs. Jean Batt). Says she was born free on the Estate of Robert Collins, 12 miles from Charlestown, South Carolina; left that place 5 years ago.

Phillis Lloyd, 19, [stout wench], (George Patton). Formerly slave to Thomas Lloyd, Charlestown, South Carolina; left him 5 years ago.

Affy Lloyd her mother, 36, [stout wench], ([George Patton]). [Formerly slave to Thomas Lloyd, Charlestown, South Carolina; left him 5 years ago.]

Jack Thomson, 24, stout fellow, (Matt Grimmill). Formerly belonged to a Mr. Thompson who was killed at Fort Moultrie, South Carolina; left Charlestown 3 years ago.

Patty Stokes, 19, [stout] wench ([Matt Grimmill]). Free as appears by Certificate from A. Stokes of Savannah dated 20 June 1782.

Stephen Ficklin, 22, stout fellow, cut in arm & scar between his eyes, (Whiteford Smith). Born at John Fickins, Indian Lands, South Carolina; has been free nigh 9 years as appears by Certificate dated 17 July 1774.

Ship *Stafford*
bound for Port Roseway
Capt. Watson

Amanda Courtney, 16, stout wench. Courtney Taylor of Port Roseway, claimant. (Courtney). Purchased from Captain Irving of Charlestown.

Marianna, 29, [stout wench]. [Courtney Taylor of Port Roseway, claimant.] ([Courtney]). [Purchased] from John Reed of New York.

John Thomas, 28 1/2, stout fellow. [Courtney Taylor of Port Roseway, claimant.] ([Courtney]). Served with Phonix Fisher, Duck Creek, Delaware, till 21 years of age when he says he got his freedom.

Cato Linus, 34, [stout fellow], (Charles Kart). Born free at Kingston, Jamaica; came here with Captain Jackson of the *Aurora* 7 years ago.

Friends
bound for Halifax
John Wilson, Master

John Williams, 47, stout, (Lt. Tyers). Formerly the slave of Charles Elliot, Charlestown, South Carolina; left him about 4 years ago. GBCP.

Lucretia, 29, stout wench, ([Lt. Tyers]). [Formerly] the property of Parson ___, John's Island, South Carolina, who at his death left her free. GBC.

Thomas London, 36, stout fellow, cooper, ([Lt. Tyers]). Formerly the property of John Wilson, Charlestown, [South Carolina]; left him 4 years ago. GBCP.

Mary, 55, stout wench, (Lt. Fyer, Engineers). Formerly the slave of William Butler, Indian Land, South Carolina, who when she was young at his death left her free.

Amoretta, 50, [stout wench]. Charles Morris of Halifax, claimant. (Charles Morris). Property of Charles Morris as per Bill of Sale from Elijah

Ladson, Charlestown, South Carolina.

Solomon, 12, fine boy. Charles Morris of Halifax, claimant. (Charles Morris). [Property of Charles Morris as per Bill of Sale] from Jeremiah Savage, [Charlestown, South Carolina].

Benjamin, 21, stout fellow. Mr. Coulson of N. Castle upon Tyne, claimant. (Ship *Friends*). [Property] of William Coulson purchased from the Widow Callighan, [Charlestown, South Carolina].

Frank Gibb, 9, fine boy. Robert Gibb of New York, claimant. (Robert Gibbs). [Property] of Robert Gibbs, born in his house in New York.

Betsy Willoughby, 21, stout wench, 2 small children, (Royal Artillery). Formerly slave to Nathaniel Nightingale, Blue mountains, Virginia; left him 6 years ago. GBCP.

The Brothers
bound for River St. Johns
William Walker

Fortune, 30, stout fellow, scar on his lip, (Benjamin Myers). [Formerly slave] to Mr. Wilkinson, Savannah, Georgia; left him 5 years ago.

Sam, 23, [stout fellow], cooper, (Archibald Montgomery). [Formerly slave]

to John Dobbins, Black river, South Carolina; [left him] 4 [years ago].

Cornelius McIntire, 28, [stout fellow], Miller, (Sam Wiggan). Free, served till 21 years of age with John Schenck, Brunswick Landing. GBCP.

Lissey his wife, 24, stout wench, ([Sam Wiggan]). Formerly slave to Cornelius Lowe, Brunswick Landing who died in Spring 78 when she left that place.

Bill McIntire, 6, fine boy, ([Sam Wiggan]). Son to the above.

Charles Goodman, 11, [fine boy]. Isaac Goodman of St. John's, claimant. (Isaac Goodman). Property of Isaac Goodman.

Ship *Montague*
bound for Port Roseway
Robert Wilson

John Dunn, 45, stout, B, (Simon Fraser). Formerly slave to John Dunn, Boundbrook, New Jersey; left him in 1778.

Dinah & little boy, 40, stout wench, ([Simon Fraser]). [Formerly slave] to Mrs. Saunders in New York who gave her freedom 4 years ago.

James Lindsey, 21, stout, B, (Isaac Enslow). [Formerly]

property of Neal Gilles of the Ship *Dutchess of Hamilton* from London who gave him his freedom in the year 1778.

David Saunders, 27, [stout], pockmarked, (Benjamin Grosvenor). Born on the Estate of John Inman in Cape Fear, North Carolina. Capt. Lindsay of the *Pearl* Frigate gave him his freedom.

Nancy Davids, 25, stout wench, 3 small children, ([Benjamin Grosvenor]). Formerly slave to Robert Daniel, [Cape Fear, North Carolina]; left him in the year 1776.

Jerry Pero, 30, stout, B, (Caspar Grassman). Says he was born free on the Estate of John Myers, Savannah, Le Mar, Jamaica.

**Schooner *Nancy*
bound for Port Roseway
Joseph Duffey**

John Daniel, 31, stout B fellow, (Joseph Durffey). Free born in New Providence. GBCP.

Jacob Somerset, 21, [stout B fellow], ([Joseph Durffey]). Formerly slave to William Somerset, Charlestown, South Carolina; left him 5 years ago. GBCP.

John Gibbons, 43, [stout B fellow], ([Joseph Durffey]). [Formerly slave] to Joseph Gibbons, Savannah, Georgia; [left him] 5 years ago. [GBCP]

**Schooner *Eagle*
bound for Port Roseway
John Gardner**

Simon, 12, fine boy, B, John Jakeway of Port Roseway, claimant. (John Jakeways). Property of John Jakeways as per Receipt produced.

Scipio, 25, stout fellow, B, (John Goddard). Formerly slave to Joseph Dupont, Savannah, Georgia; left him 6 years ago.

Boston, 30, [stout fellow], B. William Briggs of [Port Roseway], claimant. (William Briggs). Property of William Briggs.

Effy & small child, 23, stout B wench, (John Goddard). Formerly slave to J. Dupont, Savannah, Georgia; left him about 6 years ago.

**Schooner *Sally*
bound for Port Roseway
John Prim**

Silas, 31, stout B fellow, (John Keriche). [Formerly slave] to William Pettitt, Bucks County,

Pennsylvania; left him about 5 years ago.

Sam, 26, [stout B fellow]. Joseph Holmes of [Port Roseway], claimant. (Joseph Holmes). Property of Joseph Holmes.

Jack, 23, [stout B fellow]. [Joseph Holmes of Port Roseway, claimant. (Joseph Holmes). Property of Joseph Holmes.]

Sloop *Greg*
bound for Port Roseway
John Ernast

Francis, 23, [stout B fellow], (James Robinson). Formerly slave to Luby Turpin, Hawiskak, James River, Virginia. GBC.

Joe Williams, 40, [stout B fellow], ([James Robinson]). [Formerly slave] to Thomas Smith of Jamaica Island who died at Charlestown 10 years ago. GBC.

John Smith, 29, [stout B fellow], (Ben Wood). Free he says, lived with Thomas Fergusson, Charlestown; left it 3 years ago. [GBC]

George Weeks, 25, [stout B fellow], ([Ben Wood]). Formerly slave to George With, Elizabeth City, Virginia; left it 4 years ago. [GBC] Will O'Neale, 25, [stout fellow], mulatto, (James Robinson). Free.

Ship *Union*
bound for St. John's
Con Wilson

Tom Hide, 27, (Tyler Dibble). Formerly slave to John Hyde, Fairfield, Connecticut; left him 5 years ago. GBC.

Sukey, 9, [stout] mulatto, ([Tyler Dibble]). Free born; indented servant to Tyler Dibble.

In pursuance of an order from His Excellency Sir Guy Carleton, K. B., General and Commander in Chief of His Majesty's Forces from Nova Scotia to West Florida inclusive, Dated Head Quarters, New York, 15th April 1783. We whose names are herewith subscribed do Certify that We have carefully inspected the before mentioned Vessels and Negroes on the 23d, 24th, 25th, 26th & 27th days of April 1783 which Negroes amount in number to **Three hundred and eighty two men, two hundred and thirty women and forty eight children** whom we have particularly described and to the best of our judgement believe to be all that were on board these vessels. And that in those vessels we did not find any Archives, public papers, Deeds, Records or property of any kind belonging to the Citizens of the United States of America, altho every enquiry was made for that purpose in presence of Messrs. Parker and Hopkins who attended at the whole of the above Inspection as witnesses on the part of the said United States of America. We also certify that We with these two persons were on board and examined every Vessel then bound to Nova Scotia excepting one Sloop and one Schooner which went off without being examined altho ordered not to do it but with which orders they would not comply. We however sent a Message to Captain Mowatt of His Majesty's Ship *La Sophia* conveying the Fleet desiring him to bring back to this Place such Negroes or American Property as should be found in those vessels on their arrival in Nova Scotia.

[*Signed*] Daniel Parker, witness; T. Gilfillan; William Armstrong

Tree Briton
bound for Port Roseway
Jacob Hays, Master

Leven Johnson, 31, stout fellow, M, (Sturges Perry). Formerly slave to Captain Thomas Bell, Philadelphia; left him at the Evacuation of said city, Gen. Birch's Certificate.

Margaret Johnson, 43, stout wench, M, ([Sturges Perry]). Free as appears by a Bill of Sale.

Thomas Johnson, 40, stout fellow, B, (Donald Ross). Formerly slave to Burgess Smith, Lancaster County; left him 4 years past and came to New York. GBC.

Sarah Johnson, 22, squat wench, quadroon, ([Donald Ross]). [Formerly slave to Burgess Smith], Lancaster County; left him with the above Thomas Johnson her husband. GBC.

Colin Johnson, 4, M, ([Donald Ross]).

Eisha Johnson, 11, M, ([Donald Ross]).

Patty Johnson, 9 months, M, ([Donald Ross]).

Abraham Thomas, 20, stout lad, B, ([Donald Ross]). Formerly slave to Lemuel Willet, Fredricksburg, Dutchess County; says he was born free in the town of West Chester. GBC.

William Pitt, 32, [stout], B, (Robert McQuay). Formerly slave to John Pitt, Nansemond, Virginia; left him & joined the army commanded by General Matthews in the Chesapeak 4 Yrs. past. GBC.

Jemima Bull, 26, slender wench, B, (Donald Ross). [Formerly slave] to Mr. Bull, Rhode Island; left him with the British troops in 1779. GBC.

Philip Bull, 13, fine boy, B, ([Donald Ross]). [Formerly slave to Mr. Bull, Rhode Island; left him with the British troops in 1779.]

Millia Bull, 6, fine wench, M, ([Donald Ross]). [Formerly slave to Mr. Bull, Rhode Island; left him with the British troops in 1779.]

Cazar Bull, 1.

Isaac Wilson, 22, stout fellow, B, (Hampton Moore). Formerly servant to John Peters near Hamstead, Long Island; says he was born free.

James Barclett, 59, ordinary fellow, M, (Henry King). Formerly slave to Col. John Washington, Potomack, Virginia; left him about 5 years past. GBC.

Kate Barclett, 45, ordinary wench, B, ([Henry King]). [Formerly slave] to Allen Mozley, Stafford County, Virginia; left him with her husband James Barclett as above. GBC.

Nancy Jackson, 11, B, (Alexander McDonald). Formerly servant to Mrs. Maitland, Long Island.

Joe Williams, 27, stout fellow, (James Robinson). Formerly servant to Benjamin McVeaugh at Franckfort nigh Philadelphia; left him 6 years past. GBC.

Billy Knowland, 18, [stout fellow], (John Christie). [Formerly] slave to George Knowland, Nansemond, Virginia; left him 3 yrs. past. GBC.

John Williams, 30, [stout fellow], (Donald McRimen). [Formerly slave] to Godolphin Moore nigh Augusta in Georgia; left him 5 years past. GBC.

Mary, 25, stout squat wench, ([Donald McRimen]). [Formerly slave to Godolphin Moore nigh Augusta in Georgia; left him 5 years past. GBC.]

Samuel Edwards, 36, stout fellow, middle sized, (John Christie). Says he is free and lived as a hired servant with Mr. Dickenson of Philadelphia.

Betsey Fountain, 21, stout wench, (John Cowling). Formerly slave to William Hascomb of Northumberland County, Virginia; left him 7 years past. GBC.

Isaac Wilkins, 15, stout boy. Thomas Cropper of Accomack County, Virginia, claimant. ([John Cowling]). [Formerly slave] to John Wilkins, Northampton County Virginia; left him 4 years past. GBC.

Josiah Berry, 30, stout fellow, (Moses Pitcher). [Formerly slave] to James Barclay, Accomack in Virginia; left him 2 years past. [GBC]

Tabitha Berry, 24, stout squat wench, ([Moses Pitcher]). [Formerly slave] to Ralph Justice, [Accomack in Virginia; left him 2 years past]. [GBC]

Jack Richards, 28, stout fellow, (Sturges Perry). [Formerly slave] to Nancy Preston, Trenton, New Jersey; left her 6 years past. [GBC]

James Johnson, 34, [stout fellow], (Moses Pitcher). [Formerly slave] to William Herbert, Norfolk, Virginia; left him 7 years past. [GBC]

Isaac Blackston, 23, [stout fellow], shoemaker, ([Moses Pitcher]). Says he was free born at Northampton, Virginia; served his time with John Cob.

Pompey Linden, 27, [stout fellow], cuts in each cheek, (Josiah Dursey). Formerly slave to Josias Lyndon, Rhode Island; left him 4 years past. GBC.

Moses Watson, 25, [stout fellow], (Moses Pitcher). [Formerly slave] to Michael King, Nansemond, Virginia; left him 4 years past. [GBC]

Henry Jackson, 35, [stout fellow], (Alexander McDonald). [Formerly slave] to John Guy, Cherrystone, Virginia; left him 6 years ago. [GBC]

Will Jackson, 22, [stout fellow], ([Alexander McDonald]). [Formerly slave] to William Williamson of the Indian Land, South Carolina; left him 4 years ago. GBC.

Cato Perkins, 44, [stout fellow], ([Alexander McDonald]). [Formerly slave] to John Perkins of Charlestown, South Carolina; left him 5 years ago. [GBC]

Symmetry bound for St. Johns Francis Maxwell

Tom Henry, 19, stout lad, (Robert Griffith). [Formerly slave] to L. Warring, Cypures, South Carolina; left him after the Siege of Charlestown. [GBC]

Cuff Fairchild, 55, ordinary fellow, B, (Ben Stanton). [Formerly slave] to George Fairchild, Stratford, Connecticut; left him 4 years past. [GBC]

Cuff Potter, 53, [ordinary fellow], M, (on his own bottom). [Formerly slave] to Ralph Potter, Rhode Island; left him in the year 1779 with the British troops. GBC.

Tom Hoggart, 22, [ordinary fellow], B, (Josiah Brownell). [Formerly slave] to Thomas Hoggart, Norfolk, Virginia; left him 4 years past. GBC.

York Oliphant, 16, fine lad, B, (Samuel Conklin). [Formerly slave] to Dr. Oliphant, Charlestown; left him at the Surrender of that Garrison in the year '80. GBC.

Bacchus Samson, 19, stout fellow, B, (Robert Napier). Formerly slave to Miss Smith & Samson, South Carolina; since Smith died & Sampson gone to England Consigned Mr. Napier as appears by an ___ writing.

Jack Griffith, 8, B, (Robert Griffith). Proved to be Robert Griffith's property as appears by a Bill of Sale produced.

Jack Josephson, 17, fine boy, B, ([Robert Griffith]). Formerly slave to Henry Raddick, Norfolk, Virginia; left him about 5 years past. GBC.

John Reid, 45, ordinary fellow, M, (on his own bottom). Says he was born free in Maryland.

Prudence Cornwell, 32, [ordinary] wench, M, ([on her own bottom]). [Says she was born free in Maryland.]

Jack [Cornwell], 2, ([on his own bottom]). Born free.

Two Sisters
bound for St. John's
John Brown

London Derry, 30, stout fellow, B, (Amos Moss). Formerly slave to Gabriel W. Ludlow, City of New York, now at nine Partners; left him two years past. GBC.

William Fortune, 25, [stout fellow], B, (Capt. Browne). Says he was born free in the Island of Grenadas.

Moses Browne, 20, [stout fellow], B, ([Capt. Browne]). Freeman, a seaman aboard the ship.

James, 25, stout squat fellow, B, ([Capt. Browne]). Formerly slave to David Hicks of Georgia, deceased; left Savannah when evacuated by the British Troops, Cook on board the Ship.

Jack Buckley, 50, ordinary fellow, B, (Joseph Heit). [Formerly slave] to Jonathan Buckley, Fairfield, Connecticut; left him at the time Fairfield was burnt. GBC.

Darcas Buckley, 45, [ordinary] wench. Property of Dr. Farque of Fairfield as aforesaid; left him as above.

Prince Buckley, 5. [Property of Dr. Farque of Fairfield as aforesaid; left him as above.]

Generous Friends
**bound for St. John's
Thomas Huntley, Master**

Andrew Creamer, 60, old & worn out, B, ([Bethaser Creamer]). [Property of Bethaser Creamer, now a passenger on board the Ship.]

Ben Creamer, 28, ordinary fellow, B, ([Bethaser Creamer]). [Property of Bethaser Creamer, now a passenger on board the Ship.]

Mary Creamer, 20, stout wench, M, ([Bethaser Creamer]). [Property of Bethaser Creamer, now a passenger on board the Ship.]

Sarah Creamer, 4, ([Bethaser Creamer]). [Property of Bethaser Creamer, now a passenger on board the Ship.]

James Ruffin, 25, stout fellow, B, (Lieut. Smithe). Says he was born free in Virginia.

Isabella, 26, stout wench, M, (Charles Looseley). Formerly slave to Resolved Waldron of Brooklyn; left him about 5 years past. GBC.

Isabella, 5, M, ([Charles Looseley]). [Formerly slave to Resolved Waldron of Brooklyn; left him about 5 years past. GBC.]

John Patterson, 15, fine boy, M, ([Charles Looseley]). Says he was born free, is now indented to Mr. Loosley.

Jack Loosely, 28, stout fellow, B, ([Charles Looseley]). Appears to be the property of Mr. Loosely.

Robert Lee, 28, [stout fellow], B, (Andrew Cornwall). Formerly slave to Thomas Edwards, 15 miles from little York, Virginia; left him about 18 months past. GBC.

David Bricker, 18, [stout fellow], B, (Robert Tungate). [Formerly slave] to Robert White of Accomack, Virginia; left him about 4 years past.

Thetis
**bound for Fort Cumberland
Robert Gordon**

Prince Williams, 17, [stout fellow], B, (Capt. Fred Williams). Property of said Williams, now a passenger.

Sill Williams, 15, stout wench, B, ([Capt. Fred Williams]). [Property of said Williams, now a passenger.]

Harry Totten, 12, fine boy, B, (Joseph Totten). Property of said Joseph Totten, [now a passenger].

Peter Totten, 28, stout lad, B, (James Totten). [Property] of said James Totten, [now a passenger].

Nicholas & Jane
bound for Fort Cumberland
John Allison, Master

Lydia Purdie, 15, stout wench, B, (Gabriel Purdie). [Property] of said Purdie, [now a passenger].

Israel Merrit, 25, stout fellow, B, (Capt. Kipp). [Property] of said Captain Kipp, [now a passenger].

Dinah Knepp, 29, [stout] wench, (Captain Knepp). [Property] of said Captain Knepp, [now a passenger].

Allice Knepp, 6, ([Captain Knepp]). [Property of said Captain Knepp, now a passenger.]

Job Knepp, 1, ([Captain Knepp]). [Property of said Captain Knepp, now a passenger.]

Amity's Production
bound for St. John's
Thomas Reid, Master

William Stepney, 24, stout fellow, B, (on his own bottom). Born free at St. Augustine.

George State, 25, [stout fellow], M, ([on his own bottom]). [Born free] at New York.

Mary State, 21, half Indian, (on her own bottom). [Born free] on Long Island.

Job State, 24, stout fellow, M, (on his own bottom). [Born free] at New York.

William Holchapan, 40, [stout fellow], M, ([on his own bottom]). [Born free] and baptised in the year 1779 in the Parish of St. Paul's, London.

William & Mary
bound for Annapolis Royal
Moses Brewer

Frank Symons, 45, ordinary fellow, B, (Thomas Grigg). Formerly slave to Edward Simmons, Charlestown, South Carolina; left him about the time that Charlestown was besieging. GBC.

Mellia Marrant, 30, squat wench, B, ([Thomas Grigg]). Formerly the property of John Marrant near Santee, Carolina;

left him at the Siege of Charlestown. [GBC]

Amelia [Marrant], 6, B, ([Thomas Grigg]). Child of Mellia Marrant.

Ben [Marrant], 4, B, ([Thomas Grigg]). [Child of Mellia Marrant.]

Cuffie Bush, 50, ordinary fellow, B, (James Heughston). Formerly slave to William Bush, Horseneck, Connecticut; left him about 5 years past. GBC.

Glasgow Grigg, 26, stout fellow, M, ([James Heughston]). Formerly the property of John Grigg, [Horseneck, Connecticut]; left him 3 years past. [GBC]

Charles Ferrel, 13, blind of one eye, fine boy, ([James Heughston]). Formerly slave of Thomas Ferrill, Stone ferry, South Carolina; left him with the troops from Charlestown. GBC.

Judith Glasgow, 22, slim wench, M, ([James Heughston]). Declared free. GBC.

Hannah [Glasgow], 6, M, ([James Heughston]). Child of Judith Glasgow.

Richard [Glasgow], 1 1/2, M, ([James Heughston]). [Child of Judith Glasgow.]

John London, 20, stout fellow, M, (Capt. Hill). Formerly servant to Mr. Fowler & says he was born of a free mother. GBC.

Peter Newbold, 30, [stout fellow], B, ([Capt. Hill]). It appears from the Commandant's Certificate that he was formerly the property of Chris Newbold of Mansfield in New Jersey. GBC.

Casar Speffen, 42, ordinary fellow, B, (Susannah Buskirk). Formerly slave to John Lawrence, Clarendon, (Province) (State in the original) of New York; left him in the year 1777. GBC.

Thames
bound for St. John's River
Abraham Ingram, Master

Richard Cole, 35, stout fellow, (Anthony Rice). [Formerly slave] to William Cole, Northumberland County, Virginia; left him 5 years ago. GBC.

Mary Braveboy, 44, [stout] wench, ([Anthony Rice]). She declares she is free and produces GBC to that purpose.

Mima, 26, [stout wench]. John Cook of St. John's, claimant. (John Cook). Who says he bought her 13 years ago.

Jenny, 12, likely girl. Henry Rayden of [St. John's], claimant. (Henry Rayden). Who bought her of Ethan Sickles & produced a Bill of Sale.

Sarah & infant, 30, short wench. Jasper Buckel of [St. John's], claimant. (Jasper Buckel). Who bought her of John Tabor Kempe and produced a Bill of Sale.

**Brig *Tartar*
bound for St. John's River
Andrew Yates**

Joshua, 22, stout fellow, scar in forehead, (John Demill). Slave to Doctor Smith of Long Island, father-in-law to Dr. Demill.

Harry Bourdet, 18, [stout fellow]. Oliver Bourdett of St. John's, claimant. (Oliver Bourdett). Property of Oliver Bourdett, born in his father's house.

Casar, 16, stout lad. [Oliver Bourdett of St. John's, claimant.] ([Oliver Bourdett]). [Property of Oliver Bourdett]; purchased from John Warmington who brought him from the West Indies.

Charles Cambridge, 27, very stout, blacksmith, M, (Joel Holmes). Says he was born free in Worcester County,

Maryland; served his time with Joseph Ducheel.

Mary, 39, little woman, (Nicholas Howell). Formerly slave to Mrs. Mott, Somersett County, Virginia; left her 6 years ago.

Betty & infant, 20, stout wench. Conrad Hendricks of St. John's claimant. (Conrad Hendricks). Property of Conrad Hendricks per Bill of Sale produced.

**Brig *Hopewell*
bound for St. John's River
William Proutt**

Nelly Cooper, 11, likely girl, (Joseph Barret). Formerly the property of Mr. Cooper of Virginia; left it with her parents 2 1/2 years ago.

Silvia, 16, [likely girl], M. James Ettridge of St. John's, claimant. (James Etteridge). Property of James Ettridge per Bill of Sale produced.

James, 13, [likely boy], M. [James Ettridge of St. John's, claimant.] ([James Etteridge]). [Property of James Ettridge per Bill of Sale produced.]

Tom, 12, [likely boy]. Robert Letson of [St. John's], claimant. (Robert Letson). Property of Robert Letson per Bill of Sale produced.

Little Dale
bound for St. John's River
Richard Helsick

London, 68, worn out, a cooper, Thomas Bosworth of [St. John's], claimant. (Thomas Bosworth). [Property] of Thomas Bosworth who purchased him 16 years ago.

Jacob, 12, likely boy. Donn VanDyne of [St. John's], claimant. (Donn VanDyne). [Property] of Donn VanDyne in whose family he was born.

Jude, 14, short wench. [Donn VanDyne of St. John's, claimant.] ([Donn VanDyne]). [Property of Donn VanDyne in whose family she was born.]

York, 23, stout fellow, (Richard Vanderborough). Formerly slave to Leonard Van Klock at Poughkeepsie; left him 5 years ago.

Sarah & 2 children, 25, short mulatto wench, ([Richard Vanderborough]). Says she was born free in Philip's Manor, lived with Isaac Vermille.

Jack, 15, stout boy, (Christopher Benson, Junr.). Formerly slave to Capt. Pearson, King's Creek, Virginia; brought away about 2 years ago by Capt. Kid, New York, Commanding a privateer.

Bridgewater
bound for St. John's River
Daniel Adnitt

Joe, 12, fine boy. Joseph O. Forrester of St. John's, claimant. (Joseph O. Forrester). Property of Captain Forrester who the boy says purchased him.

Jack, 38, stout fellow, M. Nathaniel Dickenson of [St. John's], claimant. (Nathaniel Dickenson). [Property] of Nathaniel Dickenson, sold to him by John Day.

Betty, 20, stout wench. [Nathaniel Dickenson of St. John's, claimant.] ([Nathaniel Dickenson]). [Property of Nathaniel Dickenson], purchased from Jennings of New York.

Sukey, 4, fine girl. [Nathaniel Dickenson of St. John's, claimant.] ([Nathaniel Dickenson]). [Property of Nathaniel Dickenson], present from the Rev. Mr. Badger.

Daniel Cary, 22, stout fellow, (William Bogle). Formerly slave to Richard Wyatt Carlyne in Virginia; left him 4 years ago. GBC.

Jack Coley & 3 children, 34, [stout fellow], ([John White]). [Formerly slave] to David Coley, Fairfield, Connecticut; left him 6 years ago. [GBC]

Dinah, 24, stout wench, ([John White]). Free, purchased her freedom from Joseph Handford of Fairfield, Connecticut.

Cuffie, 40, stout fellow, (Enoch Garish). Formerly slave to Hernet Farmier, 2 Mile Square, New York province; left him 7 years ago.

Jemima & 2 children, 18, stout wench, ([Enoch Garish]). Free, served her time with Ebenezer Beman of Long Island.

John Wilkins, 26, stout fellow, scar on his chin, (Peter Toner). Formerly slave of John Thomas, Harrison's purchase, W. Chester; left him 7 years ago.

Dolly, 24, stout squat wench, (James Morrel). [Formerly slave] of Robert Troup, Portsmouth, Virginia; left him 7 years ago. GBC.

Robert Lawson, 34, stout fellow, ([James Morrel]). [Formerly slave] of John Gordon, Fairfield, Virginia; left him 6 years ago. [GBC]

Philip, 40, [stout fellow], low sized, (Dr. Clarke). [Formerly slave] of William Dandridge, James River, Virginia; left him 3 years ago. [GBC]

Ann, 15, fine wench, (John McPherson). [Formerly slave] of Thomas Vinters, Virginia.

Molly, 15, stout low wench, pock marked, (Alexander Stuart). [Formerly slave] of Richard Brookes, Gwyn's Island, Virginia; left him 9 Months.

Adam, 11, fine boy. John Cochran of St. John's, claimant. (John Cochran). Free born, bound to John Cochran until 21 years of age.

Dutchess of Gordon
bound for St. John's River
James Holmes, Master

Sam, 34, stout fellow, (Hugh Quig). Formerly slave to John Grimes of Norfolk, Virginia; left him 4 years ago. GBC.

Sarah & 5 children, 26, short wench, ([Hugh Quig]). [Formerly slave] to Edmund Bruce of Norfolk, Virginia; left him 4 years ago. [GBC]

Jack White, 40, short fellow, ([Hugh Quig]). [Formerly slave] to John White of [Norfolk, Virginia; left him 4 years ago]. [GBC]

Casar Closs, 36, stout fellow, (Samuel Nicklin). [Formerly slave] to Bowes Reed of Burlington, New Jersey; left him 2 years ago. [GBC]

In pursuance of two orders from His Excellency Sir Guy Carleton K. B. General and Commander in Chief of His Majesty's Forces from Nova Scotia to West Florida inclusive, both dated Head Quarters, New York, the one 15 April 1783 and the other 2d May, We whose names are hereunto subscribed do certify that we did carefully inspect the aforegoing Vessels on the 13th June 1783 and that on board the said vessels we found the negroes mentioned in the foregoing List amounting to **sixty eight men, twenty seven women and fifty one children** and to the best of our Judgement believe them to be all the negroes on board the said vessels and we enquired of the Master of each Vessel whether he had any Records, Deeds, Archives or papers or other property of the Citizens of the United States on board and to each Enquiry We were answered in the negative. And we further certify that We furnished each master of a Vessel with a Certified List of the Negroes on board the Vessell and informed him that he would not be permitted to Land in Nova Scotia any other Negroes than those contained on the List and that if any other negroes were found on board the Vessel he would be severely punished and that We informed the Agent for the Transports of this matter and desired him to use means for returning back to this place all negroes not mentioned in the List.

[*Signed*] Present at the above Inspection on the Part of the United States: Egbert Benson; W. S. Smith, Lieut. Col.; Nathaniel Philips, M.D.; Daniel Parker;T. Gilfillan, DQM Gen.; Wilbar Cook, Capt. 27 Reg't.; William Armstrong; Samuel Jones, Secretary.

25 June 1783

**Sloop *Lydia*
bound for Annapolis Royal
Jacob Getcheus, Master**

Thomas Tait, 23, stout fellow, almost white, (Major Brown, NYV). Free born at Petersburgh in Virginia. Indented to serve till 21 years of age to John Graham of Petersburgh; left him 5 years.

Hagar Thomson, 22, stout wench, ([Major Brown, NYV]). [Free born] at Newark, New Jersey.

Kassey Aitken, 19, stout lad, ([Major Brown, NYV]). Formerly slave to Joseph Allen of Newark, New Jersey; left him in November 1776.

Henry Bruens, 45, stout fellow, ([Major Brown, NYV]). [Formerly slave] to Eliza Bruen of Newark who died about 2 years ago & at his death gave him his freedom.

Peter Huams, 50, [stout fellow], ([Major Brown, NYV]). [Formerly slave] to Solomon Bostick of New Milford, New Jersey; left him in November 1776.

Eli Atken, 14, stout boy, ([Major Brown, NYV]). [Formerly slave] to Joseph Allen of Newark, New Jersey; left him in November 1776.

Hagar Bruen, 44, stout wench, ([Major Brown, NYV]). [Formerly slave to Joseph Allen of Newark, New Jersey; left him in November 1776.]

James Johnson, 15, stout lad, (Jacob Getcheus). [Formerly slave] to Tyna Hudson of Hannaryha, James River, Virginia, from whence he was brought by Lt. Rogers, Royal Artillery, about 2 years ago who hired him to Mr. Prior of the Engineers department who has since hired him to this sloop.

Sloop *3 Friends*
bound for River St. John's
John Stewart, Master

Tom Gunn, 43, stout, pock marked, (Sam Wilson). [Formerly slave] to Enos Gunn of Waterbury, Connecticut.

Richard Merrick, 32, stout likely fellow, ([Sam Wilson]). [Formerly slave] to Samuel Merrick of Springfield, Massachusetts, who gave him his freedom & produced a Certificate dated 4 November 74, signed by Merrick, Philips & Dr. White.

Elizabeth Merrick, 27, stout wench, M, (Luther Hatheway). Born free; served her time with Lambert Woodward of Newtown, Long Island.

William Johnson, 21, stout likely fellow, (Lt. Richard Holland). Formerly slave to John Chapman of Princess Ann County, Virginia; left him 4 years.

Hannah and, 16, stout wench, ([Lt. Richard Holland]). Born free in Cow Neck, Long Island, lived with Caleb Merrill till within this last year.

Sally her child, 8 mo.

Sloop *Lydia*
bound for Annapolis Royal
Jacob Getcheus

Charles, 10, fine boy. Sam Stretch of River St. John's, claimant. (Sam Stretch). Property of Samuel Stretch as per Bill of Sale produced.

Brutus Junius, 42, stout fellow, (John Bridgewater). Formerly slave to James Devaux in the province of Georgia; joined the British troops upon their landing there in 1778. GBC.

Amey Junius, 35, stout wench, ([John Bridgewater]). [Formerly slave to James Devaux in the province of Georgia; joined the British troops upon their landing there in 1778. GBC.]

Grace her infant, 7 mo.

Cato, 25, stout fellow. John Bridgewater of Annapolis

Royal, claimant. (John Bridgewater). Property of John Bridgewater who bought him 18 years ago out of a Guinea Ship at New York.

Bristol, 35, [stout fellow]. Isaac Brown of [Annapolis Royal], claimant. (Isaac Brown) Property of Dr. Isaac Brown whose father bought him at One Year Old.

In pursuance of two Orders from His Excellency Sir Guy Carleton, K.B., General & Commander in Chief of His Majesty's Forces from Nova Scotia to West Florida inclusive, both dated Head Quarters, New York, the one 15th April 1783 and the other 22 May, We whose names are hereunto subscribed Do Certify that we did carefully inspect the aforegoing Vessels on the 25th June 1783 and that on board the said Vessels we found the Negroes mention'd in the aforegoing Lists amounting to **ten men, five women and five children** and to the best of our Judgement believe them to be all the negroes on board the said Vessels and we enquired of the Master of each Vessel whether he had any Records, deeds, or Archives or papers or other property of the Citizens of the United States on board and to each enquiry we were answered in the negative and We further Certify that We furnished each Master of a Vessel with a Certified List of the Negroes on board the Vessel and informed him that he would not be permitted to Land in Nova Scotia any other negroes than those contain'd in the list and that if any other negroes were found on board the Vessel, he would be severely punish'd and that we informed the Agent for the Transports of the matter and desired him to use means for returning back to this Place all Negroes not mentioned in the lists.

[*Signed*]: Present at the above Inspection on Behalf of the United States: Daniel Parker; Samuel Jones, Sec'y.; Wilbar Cook, Capt. 37 Regiment; P. Armstrong, DJQM Gen.

July 8, 1783

Ann
bound for St. John's River
John Clark, Master

Pompey Wanton, 25, squat fellow, B, (John Burgis). Formerly slave to Stephen Wanton, Rhode Island; left him at the Evacuation of said place. GBC.

Peter Stogdon, 23, stout [fellow], M, (James Scot). [Formerly slave] to Robert Stogdon, Princetown; left him about 3 years past. [GBC]

Jacob Smith, 20, [stout fellow], B. Thomas Cropper of Accomack, Eastern Shore, Virginia, claimant. ([James Scot]). [Formerly slave] to Reuben Waterhouse near Horntown Eastern Shore, Virginia; left him summer 82 & joined Capt. Kid in his whaleboat in the Chesepeake. GBC.

Dinah Simmons, 40, stout wench, M, (Peter FitzSimmons). Mr. Fitzsimmons property as appears by a Bill of Sale produced.

Sylvia Smith, 14, likely [wench], B, (Robert Chillar). Formerly slave to Smith, Norfolk, Virginia; left him 4 years past & joined the Troops at New York. GBC.

Grace
bound for St. John's River
William Oaxley, Master

Reuben Upkins, 24, squat fellow, B, (Thomas Walsh). [Formerly slave] to Isaac Furbs, Nansemum, Virginia; left him 4 years past & joined the Troops in the Chesapeake. GBC.

Lydia Tomkins, 34, likely wench, M, (Daniel Fowler). [Formerly slave] to Elnathan Hunt, Philipse Manor, New York province; left by her master in 1776. GBC.

Sam Tomkins, 2, M, ([Daniel Fowler]).

Lord Townshend
bound for [St. John's River]
James Hogg, Master

David Riddle, 28, stout fellow, B, (Thomas Woolverton). Formerly slave to Joseph Griffiths, Newcastle County, Pennsylvania; left him in 1777 & joined the troops at the Head of Elk.

Ben Riddle, 7, M, ([Thomas Woolverton]). [Formerly slave to Joseph Griffiths, Newcastle County, Pennsylvania; left him in 1777 & joined the troops at the Head of Elk.]

Nancy Howard, 23, neat wench, B, (James Hogg). [Formerly slave] to Bland

Stewart, Dorchester, South Carolina, who left him in the year 1779 when she joined the British troops. GBC.

John Casor, 3 months old, B.

John Howard, 26, stout fellow, B, (James Hogg). Formerly slave to William Mallery, Norfolk, Virginia; left him & joined the troops with Lord Dunmore in 1776.

Commerce
bound for St. John's River
Richard Strong

Scipio Bazely, 30, [stout fellow], B, (Rev. John Beardsley). Property of the Rev. John Beardsley.

Peter Beardsley, 24, [stout fellow], M, ([Rev. John Beardsley]). [Property of the Rev. John Beardsley.]

Anthony Jarvis, 34, ordinary fellow, M, (Daniel Sickles). Daniel Sickles' property as appears by a Bill of Sale.

Betsey Jarvis, 2, M, ([Daniel Sickles]). Free born.

Joseph
bound for St. John's River
Martin Stout

Isaac Berry, 36, ordinary fellow, B, (Capt. Drummond). Formerly slave to F. Parker,

Eastern Shore, Virginia; left him & went on board the *Otter* sloop in the year 1776. GBC.

Hagar Britain, 41, [ordinary] wench, B, ([Capt. Drummond]). Mr. Drummond's property, Bill of Sale produced.

Apollo
bound for Port Roseway
John Adamson

Thomas Rogers, 40, [ordinary] fellow, B, (Lewis Palmer). Formerly slave to Thomas Wollerd, Chester County, Pennsylvania; left him about 5 years ago.

Cara Wilkins, 27, stout wench, M, ([Lewis Palmer]). [Formerly slave] to John Wilkinson, New Jersey; left him in the year 1776.

Jupiter Wise, 25, [stout] fellow, B, (Henry Hotchinson). Certified to be free by the Commandant.

Sealia Bowden, 27, ordinary wench, M, (Atkinson). Formerly slave to Solomon Dean, Norfolk, Virginia; left him in the year 1776. GBC.

Sally Bowden, 27, ordinary wench, B.

Dempsey Bowden, 2 months, M.

Mars
bound for Port Roseway

Dinah Haynes, 45, ordinary
wench, B, (James Cummins).
Formerly slave to Thomas
Hammond, Suffolk town,
Virginia; left him in the year
1779. GBC.

Cloe Haynes, 8, B.

Nancy Haynes, 1/2, B.

Esther
bound for Port Roseway
Robert Gill, Master

Sarah Jackson, 23, ordinary
wench, B, (Alexander
McDonald). Formerly slave to
Thomas Hanley, Georgetown,
South Carolina; left him 1780
after the Siege of Charlestown.
GBC.

Hannah Jackson, 2, B,
([Alexander McDonald]). Born
within the British lines.

Mary Ann, 25, ordinary wench,
B, ([Alexander McDonald]).
Formerly slave to John
Rutledge, Shore river, South
Carolina; left him before the
Siege of Charlestown & joined
the British troops. GBC.

Elizabeth, 6, B, ([Alexander
McDonald]). [Formerly slave
to John Rutledge, Shore river,
South Carolina; left him before
the Siege of Charlestown &
joined the British troops.]

Nancy, 3 months, B,
([Alexander McDonald]). Born
within the British lines.

Charles Harbert, 50, nearly
worn out, M. [*Remarks blank.*]

Rose Harbert, 45, ordinary
wench, M. [*Remarks blank.*]

Hanna Harbert, 40, B.
[*Remarks blank.*]

Jenny Harbert, 9, B. Mr.
Harbert's property, brought
with him from Virginia at the
time Lord Dunmore left that
Country.

David Harbert, 5, B. T. Martin
Harbert of Port Roseway,
claimant. [*Remarks blank.*]

Isaac Harbert, 11, M. [*Remarks
blank.*]

London Harbert, 30, B.
[*Remarks blank.*]

Venus Harbert, 16, M.
[*Remarks blank.*]

Kimme Williams, 18, stout
wench, M, (J. Martin Harbert).
Says she was born free & that
she served her time to Isaac
Kimme in New York &
Certified free by General
Birch.

Elizabeth
bound for St. John's River
John Watson, Master

George Goddin, 22, squat
fellow, B, (James Reed).

Formerly slave to Eliza Goddin, Nansemond, Virginia; left him 3 years past & came to New York with General Arnold. GBC.

Penny Channell, 22, ordinary wench, B, ([James Reed]). [Formerly slave] to Thomas Channel, [Nansemond, Virginia; left him 3 years past] & joined General Arnold. [GBC]

Abraham Channell, 1, M. Born within the British lines.

Abraham Dalton, 18, likely boy, B, (Charles McPherson). Formerly slave to David Dalton, North Castle; left him about 4 years past. GBC.

Jenny Cole, 36, ordinary wench, B, ([Charles McPherson]). [Formerly slave to David Dalton, North Castle; left him about 4 years past. GBC.]

Henry Cole, 33, [ordinary] fellow, B, ([Charles McPherson]). [Formerly slave] to James Gosbeck, Esopus, New Jersey; left him in the year 1777. [GBC]

Fanny Mosely, 27, strong ugly wench, B, (James Baxter). [Formerly slave] to William Moseley, Rhode Island; left him 4 years past & joined the British troops.

Tommy Mosely, 1, B. Born within the British Lines.

8th July 1783

Ann
bound for St. John's River
Joseph Clark

Harry Myers, 21, stout fellow, (John Jenkins). Formerly slave to John Middleworth of Rariton, New Jersey; left him in the year 1777 when the troops left the Jerseys. GBC.

George Williams, 27, [stout fellow], (John Cooke). [Formerly slave] to Widow Ward of Richmond, Virginia; left her 4 years ago. GBC.

Polly Williams, 20, stout wench, ([John Cooke]). Formerly lived with Parker Quince of Cape Fear in North Carolina; left him 7 years ago, produced GBC that she is free.

Lord Townshend
bound for [St. John's River]
James Hogg

Anna, 27, [stout wench], (Thomas Wolverton). Formerly slave to Edmund Warde of East Chester in the province of New York; left him near 7 years ago.

Sukey her daughter, 11 mo., likely child, ([Thomas

Wolverton]). Born since Anna left E. Warde.

Sovereign
bound for [St. John's River]
William Stewart

Peter Wearin, 21, stout fellow, (John Menzies). Formerly slave to Thomas Wearin of Charlestown, South Carolina; left him 2 years ago. GBC.

Kezzia, 16, likely wench. Thomas Bean of River St. John's, claimant. (Thomas Bean). The property of Thomas Bean, he having produced a regular Bill of Sale.

Jack, 18, likely boy, (William Stuart). Formerly slave to [*blank*] Barnes of Santee Province of South Carolina; left him 3 years ago.

Commerce
bound for [St. John's River]
Richard Strong

Adam, 24, stout fellow, (Caspar DeDalmack). [Formerly slave] to Dr. Casey of John's Island, [Province of South Carolina]; left him 2 years ago. GBC.

Hercules, 21, [stout fellow], ([Caspar DeDalmack]). [Formerly slave] to Thomas Wilton of Charlestown, South Carolina; left him 4 years ago.

Sally, 20, stout wench, ([Caspar DeDalmack]). [Formerly slave] to Ben Garret of Charlestown, [South Carolina; left him 4 years ago].

Jacob, 12, likely boy, (Rev. Mr. Beardsley). [Formerly slave] to Thomas Harboard of Portsmouth, Virginia; left him 4 years ago.

Dinah, 35, sickly wench. Rev. Mr. Beardsley of River St. John's, claimant. ([Rev. Mr. Beardsley]). Says she is his own property having always been in the Family.

Brig *Joseph*
bound for [St. John's River]
Martin Stokes

Henry Perry, 20, stout fellow, (Donald Drummond). Formerly slave to Nicholas Perry of Nansemond County, Virginia; left him 4 years ago. GBC.

Betty, 26, likely wench. Edward Beattie of River St. John's, claimant. (Edward Beattie). His property having produced a regular Bill of Sale.

Sarah, 11 mo., fine child. [Edward Beattie of River St. John's, claimant.] ([Edward Beattie]). Born since Edward Beattie bought Betty.

Jack, 4, [fine] boy. [Edward Beattie of River St. John's, claimant.] ([Edward Beattie]).

[Born since Edward Beattie bought Betty.]

**William
bound for [St. John's River]
Edward Major**

Andrew West, 24, very stout fellow, (William Wright). Formerly the property of James West of Shrewsbury, New Jersey; left him 4 years ago. GBC.

Flora Nerna, 48, stout wench, ([William Wright]). [Formerly the property] of Mr. Kingsland of Barbadoes Neck, New Jersey; left him 3 years ago. GBC.

Michael Wilkins, 15, stout boy, M, ([William Wright]). [Formerly the property] of John Thomas of the White Plains, New York province; left him 5 years ago.[GBC]

Apollo
**bound for Port Roseway
John Adamson**

Edward Jackson, 14, [stout boy], (Edward Green). Produced a Certificate from Benjamin James that he is free.

James Jackson, 12, [stout boy], ([Edward Green]). [Produced a Certificate from Benjamin James] that he is free, both

indented to Edward Green till they are 21 to learn the trade of Shoemaker.

Henry Carter, 24, stout fellow, ([Edward Green]). Formerly slave to William Elliot of Middlesex, Virginia; left him 3 years ago. GBC.

Dinah, 26, stout wench, M. Robert Wilkins of Port Roseway, claimant. (Robert Wilkins). His property having produced a Bill of Sale.

---

3 Sisters
**bound for River St. John's
John Wardell**

No negroes on board or property of the United States.

Mars
**bound for Port Roseway
James Grayson**

Anna, 20, [stout wench], M. John Speir of [Port Roseway], claimant. (John Speir). His property having produced a Bill of Sale.

Prince Augustus, 50, feeble old fellow, (Isaac Hildrith). Formerly slave to John Simon of Boston, New England; left him upon the Evacuation of the Town.

Thomas Britton, 30, stout fellow, ([Isaac Hildrith]).

Produces a Certificate from General Birch of his being free.

Richard Betts, 22, [stout fellow], (Archibald Anderson). Formerly slave to Thomas Betts of Chesterfield County, Virginia; left him 3 years ago. GBC.

Silas Bright, 25, [stout fellow], M, (James McKee). [Formerly slave] to Gilfin Post of Norfolk, Virginia; left him 6 years ago. GBC.

Tony Haines, 45, [stout fellow], (James Cornet). [Formerly slave] to William Haines of [Norfolk, Virginia]; left him 8 years ago. [GBC]

Sukey, 9, fine girl, (Thomas Wood). Says she is his own property having purchased her in Savannah.

Samuel Ivey, 44, stout fellow. James Grayson of Whitehaven, England, claimant. (James Grayson). His property having produced a Bill of Sale.

Montague
bound for River St. John's
Robert Wilson

John Potter, 25, stout fellow, (Tim Whitmore). Formerly slave to Robert Potter of Rhode Island; left him 5 years ago. GBC.

Lucy Potter, 24, [stout] wench, ([Tim Whitmore]). [Formerly slave] to Isaac Acker of White Plains, province of New York; left him 6 years ago. GBC.

Tom Mills, 15, [stout] boy, (Jesse Lamorce). [Formerly slave] to Joseph Mills of Suffolk, Virginia; left him 2 years ago. GBC.

Ben Grey, 50, [stout] fellow, (Robert Wilson). [Formerly slave] to Peter Lusam of Georgetown, South Carolina; left him 2 years ago. GBC.

Aurora
bound for [River St. John's]
Jackson

Thomas Brown, 26, [stout fellow], (John Henderson). This Negroe came from the Island of Jamaica about 3 months ago & has bound himself to John Henderson for 4 years.

Esther
bound for Port Roseway
Robert Gill

John Postell, 22, sickly fellow, ([Alexander McDonald]). Formerly slave to Andrew Postell of Cochchanties, South Carolina; left him 5 years ago. GBC.

Robert Postell, 12, fine boy, M, (Alexander McDonald).

[Formerly slave to Andrew Postell of Cochchanties, South Carolina; left him 5 years ago. GBC.]

Cesar Williams, 41, stout fellow, (Alexander Grant). Says he was born free and produces Gen. Birch's Certificate of his being free.

Thomas Jackson, 40, feeble old fellow, (Alexander McDonald). [Says he was born free and produces Gen. Birch's Certificate of his being free.]

John Upham, 62, [feeble], ([Alexander McDonald]). Produces a Certificate from John Upham of the Island of Barbadoes of his being free.

Hagar Upham, 42, [feeble], ([Alexander McDonald]). [Produces a Certificate from John Upham of the Island of Barbadoes of his being free.]

Nancy Williams, 29, stout wench, (Alexander Grant). Says she is free and produces General Birch's Certificate.

Fanny her daughter, 5 mo., fine child, ([Alexander Grant]). Goes with her mother.

Lucy Bloom, 40, stout wench, (James Dunn). Formerly slave to Michael Bloom of Charlestown, South Carolina; left him 3 years ago.

Dinah, 13, likely girl, ([James Dunn]). [Formerly slave to Michael Bloom of Charlestown, South Carolina]; goes with her mother Lucy.

Ben, 11, fine boy, M. James Dunn of Port Roseway, claimant. ([James Dunn]). Was born & brought up in the family of James Dunn.

Robert Pleasant, 30, stout fellow, (Alexander Grant). Formerly slave to Thomas Pleasant of 4 Mile Creek in Virginia; left him 7 years ago. GBC.

Elizabeth
**bound for River St. John's
John Watson**

Abraham Mifflin, 42, [stout fellow], (John Boggs). Formerly the property of Charles Mifflin of Philadelphia; came in with his widow who married Capt. Roberts. GBC.

Nancy, 40, stout wench. John Boggs of River St. John's, claimant. ([John Boggs]). Says she is his property having purchased her 11 years ago.

David, 7, an idiot. [John Boggs of River St. John's, claimant.] ([John Boggs]). Born in the family of John Boggs.

Walley Waring, 23, stout fellow, ([John Boggs]). Formerly slave to Joseph Waring of Stono, South

Carolina; left him 3 years ago. GBC.

Toney, 10, fine boy, (Dugal McPherson). Indented to Dugal McPherson for 7 years by his own consent.

Prince Royal, 26, stout fellow (Nathan Horton). Formerly the property of John Tollman of Charlestown, South Carolina, left him 3 years ago. GBC.

In Pursuance of two orders from His Excellency, Sir Guy Carleton, K.B., General & Commander in Chief of His Majesty's forces from Nova Scotia to West Florida inclusive, both dated Head Quarters, New York, the one 15 April 1783 and the other 22 May, We whose names are hereunto Subscribed Do Certify that we did carefully inspect the aforegoing Vessels on the eight day of July 1783 and that on board the said Vessels we found the Negroes mentioned in the aforegoing List amounting to **forty four men, twenty nine Women and thirty two Children** and to the best of our Judgement believe them to be all the Negroes on board the said Vessels and we enquired of the Master of each Vessel whether he had any records, deeds or Archives or papers or other property of the Citizens of the United States on board and to each Enquiry we were answered in the negative, and we further Certify that we furnished each Master of a Vessel with a Certified list of the negroes on board the vessel and informed him that he would not be permitted to Land in Nova Scotia any other Negroes than those contained in the List and that if any other negroes were found on board the Vessel, he would be severely punished and that we informed the Agent for the Transports of this matter and desired him to use means for returning back to this place all negroes not mentioned in the list.

[*Signed*]: W. S. Smith, Colonel; Samuel Jones, Secretary; Wilbar Cook, Capt. 37th Reg't; Nathaniel Phillips; T. Gilfillan.

10 July 1783

Townshend
bound for River St. John's
J. Hog

Thomas Lydecker, 32, stout fellow, (John Mercereau). Formerly the property of Garret Lydecker of Hackensack, New Jersey; left him 6 years ago. GBC.

Mars
bound for Port Roseway
James Grayson

Willis Herbert, 30, [stout fellow], (James Miller). [Formerly the property] of William Herbert of Norfolk, Virginia; [left him] 4 [years ago]. GBC.

Jonas Bracey, 25, [stout fellow], ([James Miller]). [Formerly the property] of Thomas Bracey of [Norfolk, Virginia; left him] 2 [years ago]. GBC.

Aurora
bound for River St. John's
Thomas Jackson

Peter Cox, 24, [stout fellow], (Thomas Rogers). [Formerly the property] of John Lloyd of Stamford, Connecticut; left him 3 [years ago]. GBC.

Ned Morris, 36, [stout fellow], ([Thomas Rogers]). [Formerly the property] of Gideon Wakeman of Fairfield, Connecticut; [left him] 6 [years ago]. [GBC]

Charity Morris, 28, stout wench, ([Thomas Rogers]). She lived with Jonathan Mills on Long Island till she was 18. Says she was born free, produces Gen. Birch's Certificate to that purpose.

Isaac, 9, fine boy, ([Thomas Rogers]). Son of Charity Morris.

Edward, 5, [fine boy], ([Thomas Rogers]). [Son of Charity Morris.]

Mary Ann, 3, fine girl, ([Thomas Rogers]). Daughter of [Charity Morris].

Unus Deaton, 27, quadroon, sickly, ([Thomas Rogers]). Formerly lived with William Bush of Horseneck, Connecticut; says she is free. Produces Gen. Birch's Certificate to that purpose.

Mary
bound for Quebec
Matthew Peacock

George Flanders, 23, stout fellow, B, (Agent Chipcot). Formerly slave to Thomas Irwin at St. Augustine; left him about 18 months past.

Phillis Duet, 46, ordinary wench, B, (Matthew Peacock). Says she was born free; that she lived as servant with James Duet at Pedee, South Carolina; that she left him about 3 years past.

Judith Duett, 8, likely girl, B, ([Matthew Peacock]). [Says she was born free; that she lived as servant with James Duet at Pedee, South Carolina; that she left him about 3 years past.]

Camel
bound for Quebec
William Tinker

Abigail Orser, 14, likely wench, B. Joseph Orser of Quebec, claimant. Appears to be said Orser's property.

Oliver Orser, 11, [likely] boy. [Joseph Orser of Quebec, claimant. Appears to be said Orser's property.]

Blackett
bound for Quebec
John Roxby

Nicholas Clouse, 40, stout fellow, M, (Alexander White). Formerly slave of William Nockle of Tappan, New Jersey; left him 3 1/2 years ago. GBC.

Lena Clouse, 40, stout wench, [M], ([Alexander White]).

[Formerly slave] to Cornelius Tollman of [Tappan, New Jersey; left him] 3 1/2 [years ago]. GBC.

Nancy Hill, 27, likely girl, [M], (Robert Cockrill). Says she is free and produces General Birch's Certificate to show it.

Elsee Boon, 28, stout wench, ([Robert Cockrill]). Formerly the property of Samuel Boon of Charlestown, South Carolina; left him 4 1/2 years ago. GBC.

Dick Boon, 50, stout fellow, (Jane Croser). [Formerly the property of Samuel Boon of Charlestown, South Carolina; left him 4 1/2 years ago.] GBC.

Celia Boon, 30, likely wench, ([Jane Croser]). [Formerly the property of Samuel Boon of Charlestown, South Carolina; left him 4 1/2 years ago.] GBC.

Rosetta, 30, stout wench. David Whitehill of Quebec, claimant. (David Whitehill). His property having produced a Bill of Sale.

Hope
bound for Quebec
R. Peacock

Lucia, 37, stout wench, (William Dempsey). Says she was born free & that she left Charlestown in the year 1781.

Baker & Atlee
bound for Quebec
Roberts

Tampier, 50, ordinary fellow,
(Peter Dollyer). Formerly the
property of John Pell, Paramus,
New Jersey; left him about 5
years past.

Mary, 11, likely girl, (Thomas
Darling). The property of
Thomas Darling.

Union
bound for Québec
Consill Wilson

Jack Harrison, 60, ordinary
fellow, (William Campbell).
Formerly the property of Mr.
Charleson, South Carolina; left
him when Charlestown was
taken. GBC.

Charity Umberston, 22,
ordinary wench, (Samuel
Umberston). Samuel
Umberston's property proved
by Bill of Sale.

---

16 July 1783

Frigate *London*
bound for Bremer Lee
Hugh Watts

Jeffery, 10, likely boy, (Hugh
Watts). Says that he lived with
Daniel Smith at Secaucus in
New Jersey; that his father
brought him to New York; that

his mother was born free; that
both of them are gone to Nova
Scotia.

Antelope Gordon
bound for Bremer Lee

Dan, 7, [likely boy]. Kloproth
Lt. Anhalt Zerbel of East
Friesland, claimant. (Kloproth).
Produces a receipt from John
Oakes of Oyster Bay of having
bought him for seven guineas,
who insures him his property.

George Bishick, 26, stout
fellow. He is Cook on board the
ship. Left Virginia 6 years ago.
Says he was born free and
brought off by a party of
marines of the *Otter* Sloop.

New Blessings
bound for Portsmouth
Thomas Craven

The mate declared there was
not any Negroes or American
property of any kind on board.

Ocean
bound for Bremer Lee
George Willis

[The mate declared there was
not any Negroes or American
property of any kind on board.]

Trident
bound for Bremer Lee
Robert Gallilee

Tom, 26, stout fellow, (Major Weidersheim). Says he ran away from John Pickhall of the Island of Jamaica 4 years ago; that he saw his master since in Canada who did not claim him.

Judith, 16, stout wench, ([Major Weidersheim]). She says she was born free and indented for 7 years to Mr. Wright of Philby in Canada with whom she served her time.

Toby, 23, stout fellow. He says he was the property of Capt. Ezekiel Pope of the American Militia who was killed in the ___ of Guilford & that he was taken prisoner. Says he wishes to go home in the ship being hired by the Month.

Dick, 25, [stout fellow]. Robert Gallilee of Whitby, claimant. (Robert Gallilee). He says he was purchased by Robert Gallilee at Kingston in the Island of Jamaica.

———————————

His Majesty's Solitaire
bound for Portsmouth
Moyston, Esq.

No Negroes or American Property of any Kind.

———————————

In Pursuance of two orders from His Excellency, Sir Guy Carleton, K.B., General & Commander in Chief of His Majesty's forces from Nova Scotia to West Florida inclusive, both dated Head Quarters, New York, the one 15 April 1783 and the other 22 May, We whose Names are hereunto subscribed Do Certify that We did carefully Inspect the aforegoing Vessels on the 10th and 16th July 1783 and that on board the said Vessels We found the negroes mentioned in the aforegoing List amounting to **fourteen men, Eleven Women and nine children** and to the best of our Judgement believe them to be all the negroes on board the said Vessels and we enquired of the Master of each vessel whether he had any Records, deeds, or Archives or other papers the property of the Atorney of the United States on board and to each inquiry we were answered in the negative. And We further Certify that we furnished each master of a Vessel with a Certified List of the Negroes on board the Vessel and informed him that he would not be permitted to land any other negroes than those contained in the List and that if any other negroes were found on board the Vessel he would be severely punished and that We informed the Agent for the

Transports of this matter and desired him to use means for returning back to this place all Negroes not mentioned in the Lists.

[*Signed*]: W. S. Smith; Samuel Jones, Secretary; Wilbar Cook, Captain, 37th Regiment; T. Gilfillan, DQM Gen.

29 July 1783

Sally
bound for River St. John's
William Bell

John Primus, 22, stout fellow, (William Bell). Says he was born free & produces a Certificate dated 29 July 82 from Robert Ballingall, Commissioner of Claims at Charlestown; he is hired as a Sailor on board.

James, 26, [stout fellow], ([William Bell]). Formerly the property of Mr. Smith of Savannah, Georgia; left him 3 years ago. He is hired as a Sailor.

Nancy
bound for Halifax
Robert Bruce

Ursula Fortune, 24, stout wench, (Capt. Frazer Guideste). Says she was born free, served her time with Mr. Benjamin Hubbert nigh Fredericksburg, Virginia.

Simon, 12, fine boy, ([Capt. Frazer Guideste]). Formerly slave to Cyrus Griffin, Esq., Virginia; left him in the year 1780.

Jeff, 9, [fine boy]. John Fox of Halifax, claimant. (John Fox). Property of John Fox, purchased by his brother who gave him to him.

Andrew Moore, 23, stout man, ([John Fox]). Formerly slave to James Ray nigh Augusta, Georgia; left him 4 years ago.

William Allen, 23, [stout man], (Robert Bruce). Says he was born free at St. Kitts; Cook of the *Nancy*.

Spencer
bound for River St. John's
A. Valentine

Lucinda, 25, stout mulatto wench. Manuel Housterman of River St. John's, claimant. (M. Housterman). She is wife to Manuel Housterman.

Hesperus
bound for [River St. John's]
Samuel Clark

Tom, 23, stout man, (Samuel Clarke). Formerly the property

of Cary Kelly of New York who died about 2 years ago; he says he gave him his freedom.

Jim, 14, stout boy. Sam Clarke of the *Hesperus*, claimant. ([Samuel Clarke]). Property of Samuel Clarke as per Bill of Sale produced.

Sally, 23, stout wench, ([Samuel Clarke]). Formerly the property of Captain Philips who brought her from Guinea to Savannah where he died & left her free.

Fishburn
bound for [River St. John's]
Joseph Gill

James Langford, 21, stout fellow, (William Nutter). Formerly the property of Capt. Langford of Dorset County, Maryland; left him 2 years ago. GBC.

Gabriel Philcox, 22, [stout fellow], (Henry Ellis). Formerly the property of Francis Melden, Cecil County, Maryland; left him 5 years ago. GBC.

Stach, 17, stout wench. Gabriel Fowler of River St. John's, claimant. (Gabriel Fowler). His property by Bill of Sale produced.

Joe, 9 mo., likely child. Gabriel Fowler of River St.

John's, claimant. ([Gabriel Fowler]). Son to Stach.

Fortune, 12, likely boy, (William Gray). The boy says he was taken from William Churchill's house of Virginia by a Capt. Dempsey who commanded a privateer 3 years ago.

Richard Fowler, 25, stout fellow, (Gabriel Fowler). Formerly the property of Ben Conway, Eastern Shore, Virginia; he was taken by a privateer 4 years ago & brought into New York. GBC.

Mary
bound for [River St. John's]
Francis Rowbottom

No Negroes or property of any kind belonging to the United States.

Brig *Kingston*
bound for Port Roseway
John Atkinson

George Peters, 23, stout fellow, (James Duncan). Formerly slave to Christian Jenkins of Indian Land, South Carolina, who died before the war; left the Estate 5 years ago.

Thomas Channell, 24, [stout fellow], (Duncan Cameron). Formerly the property of Dr.

John Channell, Savannah, Georgia; left him 5 years ago.

Benjamin Dunn, 21, [stout fellow], frost bit in the feet, (Alexander Munns). [Formerly the property] of William Hoyt, Charlestown, South Carolina; [left him] 4 [years ago].

Jack Sweley, 12, stout boy, (Robert Lavender). Born free in the Island of Jamaica; apprentice to Robert Lavender.

Clarissa Channill, 20, stout wench, (Duncan Cameron). Formerly the property of Mrs. Delahant of Charlestown, South Carolina; left her 7 years ago.

Jenny Parker, 30, [stout wench], (William Morris). [Formerly the property] of Thomas Parker of Boston; left him in 1776.

Peggy
bound for River St. John's
Jacob Wilson

William Faucet, 25, stout fellow, (Richard Walker). [Formerly the property] of David Faucitt of Sinepuxent, Maryland; left him 3 years ago. GBC.

Jeremiah Cole, 20, [stout fellow], (Thomas Mallard). [Formerly the property] of Elizabeth Cole of Northumberland County,

Virginia; left her 5 years ago. GBC.

Thomas Fountain, 44, [stout fellow], ([Thomas Mallard]). [Formerly the property] of Edward Cole of [Northumberland County, Virginia]; left him 7 years ago. GBC.

Peter Parker, 40, [stout fellow] with one arm, ([Thomas Mallard]). Formerly the property of Thomas Parker of Providence, Rhode Island, whom he says gave him his freedom & produces Gen. Birch's Certificate.

Jenny, 22, stout wench, ([Thomas Mallard]). She says she was the property of Walter Lyon of Princess Ann County, Virginia; that she left him 6 years ago.

Jenny, 14, likely mulatto girl. Thomas Mallard of River St. John's, claimant. (Thomas Mallard). His property having produced a Bill of Sale.

Pomp Willet, 36, stout fellow, (Robert Hicks). Formerly the property of Sarah Willet of West Chester County who died in 1776 when he came into the British Lines. GBC.

Nancy Willet, 23, stout wench, ([Robert Hicks]). [Formerly the property of Sarah Willet of West Chester County who died in 1776 when he came into the British Lines. GBC.]

John, 8, likely boy, ([Robert Hicks]). [Formerly the property of Sarah Willet of West Chester County who died in 1776 when he came into the British Lines. GBC.]

Lilley, 5, likely girl, ([Robert Hicks]). Born within the British Lines, daughter to Nancy Willet.

Pompey Ravo, 40, stout fellow, ([Robert Hicks]). [Formerly the property] of Gabriel Ravo of Perrysburgh, South Carolina; left him 4 years ago. GBC.

Charles Stiephon, 18, stout lad, (Richard Walker). [Formerly the property] of William Samuel of Charlestown, South Carolina; left him 3 years ago. GBC.

Mary Anne, 43, stout wench. Bartholomew Coxeter of River St. John's, claimant. (Bartholomew Coxeter). The property of him.

Rebecca, 12, likely girl. [Bartholomew Coxeter of River St. John's, claimant.] ([Bartholomew Coxeter]). Daughter to Mary Anna.

Binah Jones, 36, stout wench, (Richard Walker). She says she is a free woman & lived one year with Mr. Rogers of Charlestown, South Carolina & left it upon the Evacuation.

Stafford
bound for Port Roseway
Robert Watson

Bill Williams, 19, stout lad, (Donald McLeod). Formerly the property of John Frazer of White Bluff of Georgia; left him 4 years ago. GBC.

Peter Johnson, 18, [stout lad], (Donald McCrimmond). [Formerly the property] of William Johnson of Wilmington, North Carolina; [left him] 2 [years ago]. GBC.

John Ranger, 24, stout fellow ([Donald McCrimmond]). The property of James Wright by Certificate from David Matthews, Mayor of New York.

William Williams, 23, [stout fellow], (Donald McLeod). Formerly the property of Col. Warrington of North Carolina; left him 3 years ago. GBC.

---

31 July 1783

L'Abondance
bound for Port Roseway
Lt. Philips

John Green, 35, stout fellow. Formerly the property of Ralph Faulkner of Petersburgh,

Virginia; left him 4 years ago. GBC.

David Shepherd, 15, likely boy. [Formerly the property] of William Shepherd, Nansemond, [Virginia; left him] 4 [years ago]. [GBC]

Cathern Van Sayl, 26, stout wench. [Formerly the property] of John Vanderveer of Monmouth, New Jersey; [left him] 5 [years ago]. [GBC]

Mary Van Sayl, 5, likely girl. [Formerly the property of John Vanderveer of Monmouth, New Jersey; left him 5 years ago. GBC.]

Peter Van Sayl, 2 months, healthy child. Daughter to Catharine Vansayl & born within the British Lines.

Cornelius Van Sayl, 30, stout fellow. Formerly the property of John Lloyd of Monmouth, New Jersey; left him 5 years ago. GBC.

Rose Bond, 21, stout wench. [Formerly the property] of Andrew Stuart of Crane Island, Virginia; [left him] 4 [years ago]. [GBC]

Dick Bond, 18 months, likely child. Daughter to Rose Bond & born within the British Lines. [GBC]

Kate Mosely, 12, [likely] girl. Formerly the property of Andrew Stuart of Crane Island,

Virginia; left him 4 years ago. [GBC]

Dick Wilkinson, 10, fine boy. [Formerly the property] of John Bond of Nancymond, Virginia; [left him] 4 [years ago]. [GBC]

Charles Ford, 28, stout fellow. [Formerly the property] of William Hodges of Norfolk County, Virginia; [left him] 6 [years ago]. [GBC]

Hannah Ford, 30, stout wench. [Formerly the property] of Joseph Jolly of [Norfolk County, Virginia; left him] 6 [years ago]. [GBC]

Keziah Ford, 2, fine child. Daughter to Hannah Ford & born within the British lines.

Joseph Elliot, 30. Formerly the property of John Elliot, Gloucester County, Virginia; left him 6 years ago. GBC.

Nancy Elliot, 26, stout wench. [Formerly the property] of Edward Mozley of Norfolk County, Virginia; [left him] 5 [years ago]. [GBC]

Margaret Wallus, 27, [stout wench]. She says she is free & produces Gen. Birch's Certificate. She came from Virginia four years ago.

Judith Wallis, 2 weeks, healthy infant. Daughter to Margaret Willus; born within the British lines.

Jenny Bush, 11, likely girl. [Daughter to Margaret Willus] and came from Virginia with her mother who says she is free born.

James Connor, 25, stout fellow. Formerly the property of Charles Connor of Norfolk County, Virginia; left him four years ago. GBC.

Teresa Connor, 24, stout wench. [Formerly the property] of Richard Jordan of the Isle of White County; [left him four years ago]. GBC.

Betsey Connor, 18 months, likely child. Daughter to Teresa Connor and born within the British lines.

Jane Connor, 6, likely girl. Formerly the property of Charles Connor of Norfolk County, Virginia; left him 4 years ago. GBC.

Sally Godfrey, 36, sickly wench. [Formerly the property] of Joseph Simmons of [Norfolk County, Virginia; left him] 6 [years ago]. [GBC]

John Godfrey, 13, stout boy. [Formerly the property of Joseph Simmons of Norfolk County, Virginia; left him 6 years ago. GBC.]

Jacob Godfrey, 10, [stout boy]. [Formerly the property of Joseph Simmons of Norfolk County, Virginia; left him 6 years ago. GBC.]

Kate Godfrey, 15, likely girl. [Formerly the property of Joseph Simmons of Norfolk County, Virginia; left him 6 years ago. GBC.]

Judith Bush, 50, feeble wench. [Formerly the property] of Samuel Bush, Norfolk County, Virginia; left him 6 years ago. [GBC]

Elizabeth Hutchins, 23, stout mulatto wench. She says she was born free & produces GBC & says she came from Swansea, New England, 4 years ago.

Jane Hill, 60, feeble wench. Formerly the property of Willis Reddick of Suffolk County, Virginia; left him 5 years ago. GBC.

Patience Euinge, 16, stout girl. [Formerly the property] of Barnaby Carney of Norfolk County, Virginia; [left him] 4 [years ago]. [GBC]

Sarah McDonald, 17, [stout girl]. [Formerly the property] of James Goddin of Nansemond, Virginia; [left him] 4 [years ago]. [GBC]

Ishmael Moseley, 26, stout fellow. [Formerly the property] of James Carraway of Norfolk County, Virginia; [left him] 5 [years ago]. [GBC]

John Jackson, 33, [stout fellow]. [Formerly the property] of William Malcombe of the

Province of New York; [left him] 6 [years ago]. [GBC]

Samuel Johnson, 27, [stout fellow]. [Formerly the property] of Willis Hargrove of Nansemond, Virginia; [left him] 4 [years ago]. [GBC]

Patty Johnson, 27, stout wench. Thomas Copper of Accomak, Eastern Shore Virginia, claimant. Formerly the property of George Parker of the Eastern Shore, Virginia; left him 4 years ago. [GBC]

Harry Williams, 35, stout fellow. [Formerly the property] of John Gray of Bladen County, North Carolina; [left him] 4 [years ago]. [GBC]

Norfolk, Virginia, 30, [stout fellow]. Formerly the property of Philip Carberry of Norfolk County, Virginia; left him 5 years ago. [GBC]

John White, 30, [stout fellow]. Formerly the property of Thomas Ben of Nansemond, Virginia; [left him] 4 [years ago]. [GBC]

Silvia White, 24, stout wench. [Formerly the property] of Lambert Newton of Princess Ann County, Virginia; [left him] 5 [years ago]. [GBC]

Prima Johnston, 60, feeble fellow. [Formerly the property] of William Currier of Cecil County, Maryland; [left him] 6 [years ago]. [GBC]

Nancy Johnston, 45, stout wench. [Formerly the property] of John Randall of Prince George County, Virginia; [left him] 4 [years ago]. [GBC]

Dominick Yellow, 17, [stout] fellow, M. [Formerly the property] of Anthony Ball of Northumberland County, Virginia; [left him] 2 [years ago]. [GBC]

Rose Williams, 28, stout wench. She says she is free & produces GBC & says she came from Rhode Island 6 years ago.

Harry Williams, 1, sickly child. Son to Rose Williams and born within the British Lines.

Polly Carey, 26, stout wench. Formerly the property of Humphrey Gwin of Gloucester County, Virginia; left him 7 years ago. GBC.

Charlotte Cary, 15 months, healthy child, M. Daughter to Polly Carey and born within the British lines.

Jenny Carey, 4, fine child, [M]. [Daughter to Polly Carey and born within the British lines.]

Nancy McKay, 20, stout wench. Formerly the property of Francis Ballard of Hampton, Virginia; left him 3 years ago. GBC.

Esther Langley, 23, [stout wench], M. [Formerly the property] of Johnson Langley of Norfolk Co., Virginia; [left him] 3 [years ago]. GBC.

Priscilla Gordon, 19, [stout wench]. [Formerly the property] of Willis Wilkinson of Nansemond Co., Virginia; [left him] 4 [years ago]. [GBC]

Mary, 11 months, healthy child. Daughter to Priscilla Gordon and born within the British Lines.

Daniel Moore, 26, stout fellow. Formerly the property of John Moore of Wilmington, North Carolina; left him 7 years ago. GBC.

Tinah Moore, 31, stout wench. [Formerly the property] of Elizabeth Porter of Portsmouth, Virginia; left her 7 years ago. [GBC]

Elizabeth Moore, 6, fine child. Daughter to Tinah Moore and born within the British lines.

Sarah Goddin, 45, feeble wench. Formerly the property of Grizzy Cooper of Nansemond, Virginia; left her 2 years ago. [GBC]

Celia Goddin, 9, likely girl. [Formerly the property of Grizzy Cooper of Nansemond, Virginia; left her 2 years ago. GBC.]

Cyrus Speir, 40, stout fellow. [Formerly the property] of Cyrus Speir of Cross creek, No. Carolina; left him 7 [years ago]. [GBC]

Judith Speir, 30, stout wench, M. [Formerly the property] of George Parker of Nansemond, Virginia; [left him] 4 [years ago]. [GBC]

Patty Speir, 18 months, healthy child, M. Daughter to Judith Speir and born within the British lines.

Frank Speir, 9, fine boy. Formerly the property of George Parker of Nansemond, Virginia; left him 4 years ago.

Jane Robert, 26, stout wench. [Formerly the property] of George Bar of [Nansemond, Virginia; left him] 6 [years ago]. [GBC]

Simon Robert, 6 months, sickly child. Daughter to Jane Robert and born within the British lines.

Grace Thomson, 24, stout wench. Formerly the property of Edward Thewston of Norfolk County, Virginia; left him 4 years ago. GBC.

Isabella Thomson, 14, likely girl. [Formerly the property of Edward Thewston of Norfolk County, Virginia; left him 4 years ago. GBC.]

Lydia Thomson, 9, [likely girl].
[Formerly the property of
Edward Thewston of Norfolk
County, Virginia; left him 4
years ago. GBC.]

Mary Perth, 43, stout wench.
[Formerly the property] of John
Willoughby of Norfolk,
Virginia; left him 7 years ago.
[GBC]

Zilpah Cevils, 15, likely girl.
[Formerly the property of John
Willoughby of Norfolk,
Virginia; left him 7 years ago.
GBC.]

Hannah Cevils, 10, [likely
girl]. [Formerly the property of
John Willoughby of Norfolk,
Virginia; left him 7 years ago.
GBC.]

Patience Freeman, 18, [likely
girl]. [Formerly the property of
John Willoughby of Norfolk,
Virginia; left him 7 years ago.
GBC.]

Mary Williams, 40, feeble
wench. [Formerly the property]
of Rollins Lawrence of
Charlestown, South Carolina;
left him 5 years ago. [GBC]

Violet Snowball, 34, stout
wench. [Formerly the property]
of Richard Murray of Princess
Ann County, Virginia; [left
him] 7 [years ago]. [GBC]

Nathaniel Snowball, 12, fine
boy. [Formerly the property of
Richard Murray of Princess

Ann County, Virginia; left him
7 years ago. GBC.]

Mary Snowball, 3 months,
healthy child. Property of
Violet Snowball and born
within the British lines.

China Sparrow, 13, stout girl.
Formerly the property of
Richard Sparrow of Princess
Ann County, Virginia; left him
4 years ago. [GBC]

Anna Cheese, 30, stout wench.
[Formerly the property] of
William Glover of Prince
George County, Virginia; [left
him] 3 [years ago]. [GBC]

William Cheese, 45, stout
fellow. [Formerly the property]
of Benjamin Harrison,
Province of Virginia; [left him]
3 [years ago]. [GBC]

Binah Jackson, 28, stout
wench. [Formerly the property]
of Thomas Waring of
Charlestown, South Carolina;
[left him] 5 [years ago]. [GBC]

Thomas Jackson, 30, stout
fellow. [Formerly the property]
of Stephen Shrewsbury of
[Charlestown, South Carolina;
left him] 4 [years ago]. [GBC]

Betsey August, 27, stout
wench. [Formerly the property]
of Thomas Bowman, Indian
Land, [South Carolina; left
him] 4 [years ago]. [GBC]

Violet King, 35, [stout wench].
[Formerly the property] of Col.

Young of Wilmington, North Carolina; [left him] 3 [years ago]. [GBC]

Boston King, 23, stout fellow. [Formerly the property] of Richard Waring of Charlestown, South Carolina; [left him] 4 [years ago]. [GBC]

Elizabeth Thomson, 28, stout wench. [Formerly the property] of George Ingrim of Northumberland County, Virginia; [left him] 6 [years ago]. [GBC]

Grace Thomson, 2, healthy child. Daughter to Elizabeth Thomson and born within the British Lines.

Betty Thomson, 4 months, [healthy child]. [Daughter to Elizabeth Thomson and born within the British Lines.]

Charles Thompson, 33, stout fellow. Formerly the property of John Ustus of Northumberland County, Virginia; left him 7 years ago. GBC.

Chloe Walker, 30, stout wench. [Formerly the property] of James McKay of Norfolk, Virginia; [left him] 7 [years ago]. [GBC]

Samuel Walker, 13, fine boy. [Formerly the property of James McKay of Norfolk, Virginia; left him] 7 [years ago]. [GBC]

Lydia Walker, 7, fine girl. [Formerly the property of James McKay of Norfolk, Virginia; left him] 7 [years ago]. [GBC]

Duskey York, 24, stout fellow. [Formerly the property] of Nathaniel Degree of Charlestown, South Carolina; [left him] 4 [years ago]. [GBC]

Betsey York, 24, stout wench. [Formerly the property] of John Boden of the Eastern Shore, Virginia; [left him] 5 [years ago]. [GBC]

Sally York, 18 months, sickly child. Daughter to Betsey York and born within the British lines.

Richard Swan, 23, stout fellow. Formerly the property of John Willoughby of Norfolk, Virginia; left him 7 years ago. GBC.

Sally Dennis, 20, stout wench. [Formerly the property] of Lucas Burrell of Williamsburgh, Virginia; [left him] 2 [years ago]. [GBC]

John Dennis, 19 months, likely child, M. Son to Sally Dennis and born within the British lines.

Tobia Peterkin, 22, stout fellow. Formerly the property of William Wilder of Somerset County, Maryland; left him 3 years ago. GBC.

Harry Harrington, 40, [stout fellow]. [Formerly the property] of Litrop Blake of Charlestown, South Carolina; [left him] 5 [years ago]. [GBC]

Sally Harrington, 35, stout wench. [Formerly the property] of Smith McKenzie of Savannah, Georgia; [left him] 5 [years ago]. [GBC]

George Talbot, 36, stout fellow. [Formerly the property] of Solomon Talbot of Norfolk, Virginia; [left him] 5 [years ago]. [GBC]

Susannah Talbot, 37, stout wench. [Formerly the property] of Bayley Guy of [Norfolk, Virginia; left him] 4 [years ago]. [GBC]

James Talbot, 13, fine boy. [Formerly the property] of Thomas Ball of [Norfolk, Virginia; left him] 4 [years ago]. [GBC]

James Hallstead, 65, feeble fellow. [Formerly the property] of Samuel Hallstead of Norfolk County, Virginia; [left him] 7 [years ago]. [GBC]

Sally Hallstead, 60, feeble wench. [Formerly the property] of Edward Mosely of Princess Ann County, Virginia; [left him] 7 [years ago]. [GBC]

George Snail, 10, fine boy. [Formerly the property of Edward Mosely of Princess

Ann County, Virginia; left him] 7 [years ago]. [GBC]

Jane Milligan, 20, stout wench. [Formerly the property] of James Johnson of Savannah, Georgia; [left him] 2 [years ago]. [GBC]

Maria Milligan, 9 months, healthy child. Daughter to Jane Milligan and born within the British lines.

Abby Brown, 30, stout wench. Formerly the property of John Willoughby of Norfolk County, Virginia; left him 7 years ago. GBC.

William Patrick, 12, fine boy. [Formerly the property of John Willoughby of Norfolk County, Virginia; left him 7 years ago. GBC.]

Dinah Brown, 3, sickly child. Daughter to Abby Brown & born within the British lines.

Venus Miller, 24, stout wench. Formerly the property of John Whitten of Norfolk County, Virginia; [left him] 4 [years ago]. [GBC]

Betsey Herbert, 26, [stout wench]. [Formerly the property] of Robert Barron of [Norfolk County Virginia; left him] 3 [years ago]. [GBC]

Jenny Herbert, 6, fine child. [Formerly the property of Robert Barron of Norfolk

County, Virginia; left him] 3 [years ago]. [GBC]

Lancaster Herbert, 10, fine boy. [Formerly the property of Robert Barron of Norfolk County, Virginia; left him] 3 [years ago]. [GBC]

Peter Herbert, 28, stout fellow. [Formerly the property] of John Whitten of [Norfolk County, Virginia; left him] 3 [years ago]. [GBC]

Rose Stewart, 25, stout wench. [Formerly the property] of Thomas Brown of Portsmouth, Virginia; [left him] 4 [years ago]. [GBC]

Mary White, 21, [stout wench]. She says she was born free and produces General Birch's Certificate. She came from Virginia 3 years ago.

Jane Parks, 65, feeble wench. Formerly the property of Jonathan Parks of Norfolk, Virginia; left him 7 years ago. GBC.

Francis Jones, 42, stout fellow. [Formerly the property] of Thomas Mocock of Charles city, [Virginia; left him] 3 [years ago]. [GBC]

Philip Gordon, 23, [stout fellow]. [Formerly the property] of George Gordon of Nansemond, [Virginia; left him] 3 [years ago]. [GBC]

Priscilla Gordon, 20, stout wench. [Formerly the property] of Willis Wilkinson of Charlestown, South Carolina; [left him] 5 [years ago]. [GBC]

Stephen Blucke, 31, stout fellow. Says he was born free in the Island of Barbadoes and produces General Birch's Certificate.

Margaret Blucke, 40, stout wench. Says she was born free in Mrs. Coventry's family in New York & bought her freedom 14 years ago. GBC.

Isabel Gibbons, 20, likely girl. Margaret Blucke purchased her of Mrs. Coventry's daughter and gave her freedom. [GBC]

Benjamin Hevelin, 50, stout fellow. Formerly the property of John Hevlin of Elizabeth town, New Jersey; left him 7 years ago. [GBC]

Nancy Brown, 13, stout girl. [Formerly the property] of Matthew Phips of Norfolk, Virginia; [left him] 6 [years ago]. [GBC]

Peter Johnson, 30, stout fellow. [Formerly the property] of Robert Morris of Philadelphia; [left him] 6 [years ago]. [GBC]

Betsey Johnson, 32, stout wench. She produces a Certificate of freedom from Margaret Ogilvie her former mistress.

Peter Johnson, 4, fine child.
[She produces a Certificate of
freedom from Margaret Ogilvie
her former mistress.]

Sukey Johnson, 2, [fine child].
[She produces a Certificate of
freedom from Margaret Ogilvie
her former mistress.]

York Lawrence, 30, stout
fellow. Formerly the property
of Catharine Lawrence of
Albany province of New York;
left her 6 years ago. GBC.

Dinah Lawrence, 26, likely
wench. [Formerly the property]
of Peter Shanerhorn of New
York; left him 6 years ago.
[GBC]

Betsey Lawrence, 3, fine child.
Daughter to Dinah Lawrence
and born within the British
lines.

Gabriel Lawrance, 18 months,
[fine child]. Son to [Dinah
Lawrence and born within the
British lines].

Marshal Johns, 32, stout
fellow. Formerly the property
of John Fullerton of
Philadelphia; left him 5 years
ago. GBC.

Clinton
**bound for Annapolis &
St. John's
Lt. Trounce**

Stepney Hancock, 36, stout
fellow. Formerly the property
of William Hancock of
Norfolk, Virginia; left him 7
years ago. GBC.

Benjamin Bush, 47, [stout
fellow]. [Formerly the property]
of Samuel Bush of [Norfolk,
Virginia; left him] 7 [years
ago]. [GBC]

Frank Patrick, 28, [stout
fellow]. [Formerly the property]
of Richard Brown of [Norfolk,
Virginia; left him] 4 [years
ago]. [GBC]

Anthony Randall, 53, feeble
fellow. [Formerly the property]
of Solomon Shepherd of
Nansemond, Virginia; [left
him] 5 [years ago]. [GBC]

Isaac White, 27, stout fellow.
[Formerly the property] of
Theodric Bland of George
County, [Virginia; left him] 4
[years ago]. [GBC]

Anthony Stevens, 47, [stout
fellow]. [Formerly the property]
of Peter Connoway of
Lancaster, [Virginia; left him]
7 [years ago]. [GBC]

Dick Richard, 30, [stout
fellow]. [Formerly the property]
of Peter Willis of Little York,

[Virginia; left him] 5 [years ago]. [GBC]

Job Christeen, 60, feeble fellow. [Formerly the property] of Walker Connaway of Northumberland County, Virginia; [left him] 6 [years ago]. [GBC]

John Sparrow, 40, [feeble fellow]. [Formerly the property] of Peter Sparrow of Norfolk, Virginia; [left him] 5 [years ago]. [GBC]

James Nickins, 35, stout fellow. [Formerly the property] of John Clayton of Lancaster County, Virginia; [left him] 7 [years ago]. [GBC]

Thomas Stevens, 13, likely boy. [Formerly the property] of Peter Pew of Tappan, New Jersey; [left him] 5 [years ago]. [GBC]

Moses Jessup, 48, feeble fellow. [Formerly the property] of William Lee of Northumberland County, Virginia; [left him] 2 [years ago]. [GBC]

William Keeling, 40, [feeble fellow]. [Formerly the property] of Grumbelly Keeling of the East Shore, Virginia; [left him] 6 [years ago]. [GBC]

Samuel Hunter, 36, [feeble fellow]. [Formerly the property] of James Hunter, Norfolk County, Virginia; [left him] 5 [years ago]. [GBC]

Robert Fleming, 30, stout fellow. [Formerly the property] of John Holloway of Petersburgh, Virginia; [left him] 4 [years ago]. [GBC]

Harry Moore, 38, feeble fellow. [Formerly the property] of James Moore of Norfolk, Virginia; [left him] 7 [years ago]. [GBC]

Bristol Mitchel, 57, [feeble fellow]. [Formerly the property] of Joseph Mitchell of Norfolk, Virginia; [left him] 7 [years ago]. [GBC]

Andrew Randall, 22, stout fellow. [Formerly the property] of Henry Burgess of Nansemond, Virginia; [left him] 6 [years ago]. [GBC]

Dorothy Bush, 36, stout wench. She says her master Andrew Sproule gave her freedom before he died which was 7 years ago. [GBC]

Barbara Hancock, 20, [stout wench]. Formerly the property of Samuel Bush of Norfolk County, Virginia; left him 7 years ago. [GBC]

Robert Bray Hancock, 6, fine boy. Son to Barbara Hancock and born within the British lines.

Nancy Randall, 49, stout wench. Formerly the property of Thomas Newton of Norfolk County, Virginia; left him 5 years ago. [GBC]

Adam Randall, 9, fine boy.
[Formerly the property of
Thomas Newton of Norfolk
County, Virginia; left him 5
years ago. GBC.]

Nancy Sparrow, 45, feeble
wench. [Formerly the property]
of Robert Barns of Norfolk,
Virginia; [left him] 5 [years
ago]. [GBC]

Nancy Johnson, 26, stout
[wench]. [Formerly the
property] of John Whitten of
Norfolk County, Virginia; [left
him] 7 [years ago]. [GBC]

Andrew Johnson, 15 months,
likely child. Son to Nancy
Johnson and born within the
British lines.

Pindar Keeling, 29, stout
wench. Formerly the property
of Willis Ball of Norfolk
County, Virginia; left him 5
years ago. [GBC]

Hannah Moore, 50, feeble
[wench]. [Formerly the
property] of John Perry of
Fairfield, Virginia; [left him] 7
[years ago]. [GBC]

Jenny Hunter, 25, stout
[wench]. [Formerly the
property] of John Sobrisky of
Hackensack, New Jersey; [left
him] 6 [years ago]. [GBC]

Phebe Randall, 21, [stout
wench]. [Formerly the property]
of Betsey Jones of Suffolk
County, Virginia; [left her] 5
[years ago]. [GBC]

Thomas McLeod, 3, fine child,
M. Son to Phebe Randall and
born within the British lines.

Sarah Stephens, 35, stout
wench. Formerly the property
of Peter Pew of Tappan, New
Jersey; left him 4 years ago.
[GBC]

Moses Stephens, 3 months,
healthy child. Son to Sarah
Stevens and born within the
British lines.

Judith Christeen, 60, feeble
wench. She says that Charles
Lee set her free nine years ago
and produces General Birch's
Certificate.

Peggy Richards, 33, stout
[wench]. Formerly the property
of John Loveat of Princess Ann
County, Virginia; left him 7
years ago. GBC.

Esther Richards, 11, fine child.
[Formerly the property of John
Loveat of Princess Ann
County, Virginia; left him 7
years ago. GBC.]

Richard Richards, 3, [fine
child]. Son to Peggy Richards
and born within the British
lines.

James Richards, 2, [fine child].
[Son to Peggy Richards and
born within the British lines.]

Jane Halladay, 22, stout
wench. Formerly the property
of Benjamin Guy of Norfolk

County, Virginia; left him 5 years ago. GBC.

Peter Halladay, 18 months, healthy child. Son to Jane Halladay and born within the British lines.

Elizabeth White, 25, stout wench. Formerly the property of John Perrin of Gloucester County, Virginia; [left him] 5 [years ago]. GBC.

Hannah Fleming, 28, [stout wench]. [Formerly the property] of David McClaurin of Norfolk, Virginia; [left him] 7 [years ago]. [GBC]

Susannah Wynah, 25, [stout wench]. [Formerly the property] of William Hancock of Princess Ann County, Virginia; [left him] 3 [years ago]. [GBC]

John Gordon, 26, stout fellow. [Formerly the property] of Benjamin Ball of Dorset County, Maryland; [left him] 6 [years ago]. [GBC]

John Babus, 21, [stout fellow]. [Formerly the property] of David Mead of Suffolk County, Virginia; [left him] 4 [years ago]. [GBC]

Abraham Saunders, 17, likely boy, M. Says that William Connor, his master, set him free when he was born & produces General Birch's Certificate.

John Gustus, 19, stout fellow. Formerly the property of John Tasswell of Williamsburg, Virginia; left him 4 years ago. GBC.

Christopher Hallstead, 50, feeble fellow. [Formerly the property] of Philomel Halstead of Rye, Connecticut; [left him] 6 [years ago]. [GBC]

Isaac Mead, 40, stout fellow. [Formerly the property] of David Mead of Nansemond, Virginia; [left him] 4 [years ago]. [GBC]

Peter Warren, 23, [stout fellow]. [Formerly the property] of Peter Warren of Northampton County, Virginia; [left him] 5 [years ago]. [GBC]

Mingo Jordan, 19, [stout fellow]. [Formerly the property] of Richard Jordan of Isle of Wight county, Virginia; [left him] 4 [years ago]. [GBC]

Henry Reddick, 24, [stout fellow]. [Formerly the property] of Lambert Reddick of Suffolk county, Virginia; [left him] 4 [years ago]. [GBC]

Bill Williams, 37, [stout fellow]. [Formerly the property of] William Causins of Amelia county, Virginia; [left him] 4 [years ago]. [GBC]

Henry Warren, 26, [stout fellow]. [Formerly the property] of [*blank*] Eastern Shore,

Virginia; [left him] 4 [years ago]. [GBC]

Andrew Casey, 26, likely lad. [Formerly the property] of David Mead of Nansemond, Virginia; [left him] 5 [years ago]. [GBC]

Benjamin Nelis, 24, stout fellow. [Formerly the property] of Andrew McKay of Isle of Wight county, Virginia; [left him] 4 [years ago]. [GBC]

George Scarbery, 25, [stout fellow]. Thomas Cropper of Accomack, Virginia, claimant. [Formerly the property] of George Abbot of Accomack county, Virginia; [left him] 6 [years ago]. [GBC]

Samuel Tomkin, 23, [stout fellow]. [Formerly the property] of Richard Tomkin of Little York, Virginia; [left him] 7 [years ago]. [GBC]

Robert Johnson, 21, [stout fellow]. [Formerly the property] of John Alexander of Strafford, Virginia; [left him] 6 [years ago]. [GBC]

Joseph Reddick, 12, fine boy. [Formerly the property] of John Tatum of Craney Island, Virginia; [left him] 4 [years ago]. [GBC]

Wynce Gordon, 28, stout wench. [Formerly the property] of Richard Jordan of Isle of Wight county, Virginia; [left him] 5 [years ago]. [GBC]

Phillis Gordon, 20, likely wench. [Formerly the property] of Anthony Walker of Tanners Creek, Virginia; [left him] 5 [years ago]. [GBC]

Nancy, 28, stout wench. [Formerly the property] of Charles Conner of Norfolk, Virginia; [left him] 7 [years ago]. [GBC]

James, 6, fine boy. Son to Nancy and born within the British lines.

Polly, 3, fine child. Daughter to [Nancy] and [born within the British lines].

Betsey, 18 months, [fine child]. [Daughter to Nancy and born within the British lines.]

Phillis Halstead, 35, stout wench. Formerly the property of Benjamin Drake of East Chester County, New York; left him 5 years ago. GBC.

Peggy Halstead, 2, fine child. Daughter to Phillis Halstead and born within the British lines.

Betty Mead, 30, stout wench. Formerly the property of David Mead of Nansemond, Virginia; left him 4 years ago. GBC.

Nanny Mead, 10, fine girl. [Formerly the property of David Mead of Nansemond, Virginia; left him 4 years ago. GBC.]

Pleasant Reddick, 29, stout wench. [Formerly the property] of John Tatum of Crane Island, Virginia; [left him] 5 [years ago]. [GBC]

Elsey Reddick, 7, fine girl. [Formerly the property of John Tatum of Crane Island, Virginia; left him 5 years ago. GBC.]

Agnes Reddick, 5 months, fine child. Daughter to Pleasant Reddick and born within the British lines.

Betsey Williams, 40, stout wench. Formerly the property of John Jordan of Nansemond, Virginia; left him 5 years ago. GBC.

Polly Williams, 3, fine girl. Daughter to Betsey Williams & born within the British lines.

Betsey William, 2, [fine] child. [Daughter to Betsey Williams & born within the British lines.]

Judith Warren, 30, stout wench. Formerly the property of Peter Warren of the Eastern Shore, Virginia; left him 5 years ago.

Nancy Babus, 15, stout girl. [Formerly the property] of Saul Shepperd of Nansemond, Virginia; [left him] 5 [years ago]. [GBC]

Jane Nelis, 30, stout wench. [Formerly the property] of John

Hirst of Norfolk, Virginia; [left him] 7 [years ago]. [GBC]

Jonathan Nelis, 4, fine child. Son to Jane Nelis and born within the British lines.

Sally Nelis, 2, [fine child]. Daughter to [Jane Nelis] and [born within the British lines].

Sarah Scarberry, 26, stout wench. Formerly the property of Judith Burton of Nansemond, Virginia; left her 4 years ago. GBC.

Betsey Scarberry, 3, fine girl. Daughter to Sarah Scarberry & born within the British lines.

Peter Scarberry, 8 months, fine child. Son to [Sarah Scarberry & born within the British lines].

Judith Johnson, 18, stout wench. Formerly the property of Samuel Elliot of Norfolk, Virginia; left him 5 years ago. GBC.

Dinah Griffin, 23, [stout wench]. She produces a Certificate from her late master ___ Bagout of New York of having purchased her freedom as also that for her daughter Sal.

Sal Griffin, 1, fine child. Daughter to Dinah Griffin.

William McKnight, 30, stout fellow. Says he is free and that he lived 18 years with John

Hammond of Scamping, New Jersey, and produces GBC.

Nancy Johnson, 44, stout wench. Formerly the property of John Baynes of Norfolk, Virginia; left him five years ago. GBC.

Hannah Johnson, 13, stout girl. [Formerly the property of John Baynes of Norfolk, Virginia; left him five years ago. GBC.]

Luke Johnson, 12, fine boy. Formerly the property of John Baynes of Norfolk, Virginia; left him 5 years ago. GBC.

Fanny Johnson, 7, fine girl. [Formerly the property of John Baynes of Norfolk, Virginia; left him 5 years ago. GBC.]

Chloe Johnson, 18, [fine girl]. [Formerly the property] of George Robinson of Crane Island; [left him] 3 [years ago]. [GBC]

Nanny Johnson, 6, [fine girl]. [Formerly the property of George Robinson of Crane Island; left him 3 years ago. GBC.]

Miles Jordan, 28, stout fellow. [Formerly the property] of Richard Jordan of the Isle of Wight County, Virginia; left him 5 years ago. GBC.

David Tankard, 28, [stout fellow]. [Formerly the property] of Stephen Tankard of Norfolk,

Virginia; [left him] 6 [years ago]. [GBC]

Esther, 60, feeble wench. [Formerly the property] of Miles Wilkinson of [Norfolk, Virginia; left him] 3 [years ago].

Seelah, 17, likely wench. [Formerly the property of Miles Wilkinson of Norfolk, Virginia; left him 3 years ago.]

Edward Godfrey, 17, [likely] lad. [Formerly the property] of Matthew Godfrey of Norfolk, Virginia; [left him] 5 [years ago].

Thomas Bing, 26, [likely lad]. [Formerly the property] of John Miles of Salt Ketches, South Carolina; [left him] 5 [years ago].

Robert Bing, 22, [likely lad]. [Formerly the property] of John Watters of Charlestown, [South Carolina; left him] 5 [years ago].

Valentine Godfrey, 22, [likely lad]. [Formerly the property] of Matthew Godfrey of Norfolk, Virginia; [left him] 5 [years ago].

Bristol Storm, 40, stout fellow. [Formerly the property] of Garrett Storms of Fishkill, New York; [left him] 3 [years ago].

Bob Johnson, 18, [stout fellow]. [Formerly the property] of William Hunter of Princess

Ann, Virginia; [left him] 2 [years ago].

Jack Colhoun, 15, [stout] lad. [Formerly the property] of Samuel Colhoun of Nansemond, Virginia; [left him] 5 [years ago].

Thomas Tucker, 40, stout fellow, Blind of an Eye. [Formerly the property] of Tom Tucker of Providence; [left him] 8 [years ago].

Walter Hammer, 23, [stout fellow]. [Formerly the property] of William Parker of Accomack, Virginia; [left him] 4 [years ago].

William Seaman, 23, [stout fellow]. Thomas Cropper of Eastern Shore of Virginia, claimant. [Formerly the property] of George Gilchrist of Eastern Shore, Virginia; [left him] 5 [years ago].

Lewis Kirby, 29, [stout fellow]. [Formerly the property] of John Kirby, little York, Virginia; [left him] 3 [years ago].

John Jackson, 26, [stout fellow]. [Formerly the property] of Anthony Walk, Princess Ann, Virginia; [left him] 3 [years ago].

Henry Mitchell, 23, [stout fellow]. [Formerly the property] of John Mitchell of Charlestown, South Carolina; [left him] 4 [years ago].

Bristol Godfrey, 22, [stout fellow]. [Formerly the property] of Matthew Godfrey, Norfolk, Virginia; [left him] 5 [years ago].

Daphne Shields, 25, likely wench. [Formerly the property] of David Shields, Nansemond, [Virginia; left him] 5 [years ago].

Hannah Kirby, 25, [likely wench]. [Formerly the property] of Robert Bruff of Hampton, [Virginia; left him] 3 [years ago].

Kitty Godfrey, 22, [likely wench]. [Formerly the property] of Captain Hullet, Charlestown, South Carolina; [left him] 3 [years ago].

Lydia Friend, 21, [likely wench]. [Formerly the property] of Widow Friend, James River, Virginia; [left her] 3 [years ago].

Hannah Bing, 35, [likely wench], one child 7 months. [Formerly the property] of William Jordan of Salt Ketchers, South Carolina; [left him] 5 [years ago].

Phillis Mitchel, 22, [likely wench], one child 6 months. [Formerly the property] of John Mitchell of Charlestown; [left him] 4 [years ago].

Fortune Dixon, 20, likely lad. [Formerly the property] of Josiah Riddick of Nansemond,

Virginia; [left him] 4 [years ago].

Henry Floyd, 28, [likely lad]. [Formerly the property] of William Floyd of Long Island; [left him] 7 [years ago].

James Liverpool, 40, stout fellow. [Formerly the property] of Christopher Coduise of Brooklin, New York; [left him] 7 [years ago].

Jacob Bummele, 35, [stout fellow]. [Formerly the property] of Benjamin Chew of Cecil County, Virginia; [left him] 4 [years ago].

John Shepherd, 30, [stout fellow]. [Formerly the property] of William Shepherd of Nansemond, [Virginia; left him] 5 [years ago].

Dempsey Buxton, 23, [stout fellow]. [Formerly the property] of James Buxton of [Nansemond, Virginia; left him] 5 [years ago].

Jacob Adams, 26, [stout fellow]. Says he was born free, Little York, Virginia; [left] 6 [years ago].

Samuel Hutchins, 26, [stout fellow]. Formerly the property of William Harden, Indian Land, South Carolina; [left] him 8 [years ago].

Ben Elliot, 69, ordinary fellow. [Formerly the property] of Joseph Elliot, Savannah,

Georgia; [left him] 2 [years ago].

John Cox, 31, stout fellow. [Formerly the property] of Eleazer Goddin, Maroneck, New York; [left him] 7 [years ago].

Joe Stone, 24, [stout fellow]. [Formerly the property] of Ben Stone, Charlestown, South Carolina; [left him] 5 [years ago].

Andrew Cole, 26, [stout fellow]. [Formerly the property] of Ben Cole, Marroneck, New York; [left him] 4 [years ago].

Joshua Thomson, 21, [stout fellow]. [Formerly the property] of Thomas Fisher of Smith's Neck, Virginia; [left him] 5 [years ago].

Richard Henry, 23, [stout fellow]. [Formerly the property] of John Broden, Eastern Shore, Virginia; [left him] 5 [years ago].

Samuel Sampson, 20, [stout fellow]. [Formerly the property] of Edward Welch, Charlestown, South Carolina; [left him] 4 [years ago].

Daniel Herring, 35, [stout fellow]. [Formerly the property] of Daniel Herring of Isle of Wight, Virginia; [left him] 4 [years ago].

George White, 63, worn out. West Indies.

Henry Elliot, 46, [worn out]. Formerly the property of Joseph Elliot, Weremay, South Carolina; [left him] 2 [years ago].

Jane Shepherd, 40, stout wench. [Formerly the property] of Nathaniel Buxton, Suffolk County, Virginia; [left him] 5 [years ago].

Fanny Floyd, 26, [stout wench]. [Formerly the property] of Abraham Ketteltas of Long Island; [left him] 7 [years ago].

Sarah Hutchins, 21, stout wench, 1 child 7 months. Formerly the property of William Harding, Indian Land, South Carolina; left him 5 years ago.

Mary Coles, 23, [stout wench]. Says she was free born, Musquito Cove, Long Island.

Sally Williams, 36, [stout wench]. Formerly the property of Doctor Gardiner, Charlestown; [left him] 5 [years ago].

Nelly Cox, 33, [stout wench], 2 children, 4 years and the other 6 months. [Formerly the property] of Paul Burtis, Long Island.

John Holland, 29, stout fellow. [Formerly the property] of Henry Holland, New York; [left him] 5 [years ago].

Henry Biverowdt, 26, [stout fellow]. Born free, St. Croix.

Samuel Jarvis, 60, worn out. Free man.

John Prime, 39, stout fellow. Formerly the property of Valentine Ling, Pond Pond, South Carolina; left him 6 years ago.

John Williams, 26, [stout fellow]. [Formerly the property] of John Williams, Charlestown; [left him] 5 [years ago].

Harry Wait, 63, [stout fellow]. [Formerly the property] of Isaac Wait, John's Island, South Carolina; [left him] 5 [years ago].

Samuel Farmer, 41, [stout fellow]. [Formerly the property] of William Nagle, Chester, New Jersey; [left him] 6 [years ago].

Francis Griffin, 45, [stout fellow]. [Formerly the property] of John Duryea.

Adam Way, 80, worn out. [Formerly the property] of General Broadstreet, Albany.

Harry Middleton, 50, [worn out]. [Formerly the property] of Harry Middleton, Charlestown; [left him] 5 [years ago].

Robert James, 39, stout fellow. [Formerly the property] of Jacobus Lowe, Esopus, New York, [left him] 7 [years ago].

Aaron James, 12, fine boy. [Formerly the property] of William Kingsland, Barbadoes Neck; [left him] 4 [years ago].

Sampson Miles, 12, [fine boy]. [Formerly the property] of John Miles, Indian Land, South Carolina; [left him] 4 [years ago].

Princessa, 30, stout wench. [Formerly the property] of Valentine Ling of Point Ponds, [left] 5 [years ago].

Mary Miles, 46, [stout wench]. [Formerly the property] of John Miles, Indian Land, South Carolina; [left him] 4 [years ago].

Miley Wilkins, 30, [stout wench]. [Formerly the property] of John Wilkins, Savannah, Georgia; [left him] 5 [years ago].

Jingo Johnson, 16, fine lad. [Formerly the property] of Colonel Bird, Rappahannock, Virginia; [left him] 4 [years ago].

Sally Farmer, 56, stout of her age. [Formerly the property] of Barin Norgall, Tappan, New Jersey; [left him] 6 [years ago].

Catharine Livingston, 50, [stout of her age]. [Formerly the property] of Robert Livingston of Livingston Manor; [left him] 8 [years ago].

Phillis Crutchley, 30, stout wench with a child 5 years old. [Formerly the property] of William Crutchley deceased, of New York.

Jane James, 40, [stout wench]. [Formerly the property] of William Kingsland, Barbadoes Neck, New Jersey; [left him] 4 [years ago].

Mary Biverout [*under her name appears "a Davis"*], 28, [stout wench]. Says she was born free at Savannah in Georgia.

Lizzy Williams, 20, [stout wench], 1 child 3 weeks old. Formerly the property of John Williams, Port Royall, North Carolina; [left him] 4 [years ago].

Mary Tomkins, 23, [stout wench]. [Formerly the property] of Capt. Tomkins of Little York, Virginia; [left him] 7 [years ago].

Amy Wait, 33, [stout wench]. [Formerly the property] of Israel Wait, John's Island, South Carolina; [left him] 5 [years ago].

Chressy Wait, 16, [stout wench]. [Formerly the property of Israel Wait, John's Island, South Carolina; left him 5 years ago.]

Phillis Scot, 75, worn out. [Formerly the property] of John Harbords, Southern branch,

Virginia; [left him] 6 [years ago].

Sarah Middleton, 25, stout wench, with a child 6 months old. [Formerly the property] of Harry Middleton, Charlestown, South Carolina; [left him] 6 [years ago].

Samuel Flemming, 20, stout fellow. Born free, lived with James Morgan, Valley Forge; [left him] 5 [years ago].

Robert Johnson, 24, [stout fellow]. [Formerly the property] of Richard Van Meter, Monmouth, New Jersey; [left him] 4 [years ago].

James Jackson, 24, [stout fellow]. [Formerly the property] of Richard Sweepston of Mecklenburgh, Virginia; [left him] 5 [years ago].

Robert Roberts, 26, [stout fellow]. [Formerly the property] of Josiah Pandarves of Horse Shoe, New Jersey; [left him] 6 [years ago].

Peter Scot, 24, [stout fellow]. [Formerly the property of Josiah Pandarves of Horse Shoe, New Jersey; left him 5 years ago.]

Christopher Plummitty, 22, [stout fellow]. [Formerly the property] of Benjamin Temple of King William County, Virginia; [left him] 4 [years ago].

Jonah Hewelett, 23, [stout fellow]. [Formerly the property] of William Johnson, Savannah, Georgia; [left him] 5 [years ago].

John James, 21, [stout fellow]. [Formerly the property] of John James of Chesterfield County, Virginia; [left him] 5 [years ago].

Eleanor Fleming, 21, stout wench with a son 4 years old. [Formerly the property] of William Pugsley of Phillipse Manor, NYP [*New York Province*]; [left him] 6 [years ago].

Rachel Johnson, 24, stout wench with a boy 3 1/2 years old. Says she was born free at Shrewsbury, New Jersey; [left] 4 [years ago].

Peggy Jackson, 22, stout wench with 3 children, 8 years, 5 and 4 months. [Formerly the property] of William Egerson, Norfolk, Virginia; [left him] 5 [years ago].

Richard Wheeler, 30, stout man. Purchased his freedom from Caleb Wheeler, New Jersey; [left him] 7 [years ago].

Henry Van Ryper, 34, [stout man]. [Formerly the property] of Abraham VanRyper of Acquackanung; [left him] 5 [years ago].

Abraham Smith, 35, [stout man]. [Formerly the property] of John Jones of Philadelphia; [left him] 5 [years ago].

John Francis, 30, stout man. Formerly the property of Daniel Birch, Newark, New Jersey; left him 3 years ago.

Jenny Francis, 36, stout wench with 3 children, 5, 4, & 1 1/2 years of age. [Formerly the property of Daniel Birch, Newark, New Jersey; left him 3 years ago.]

John Strong, 25, tall thin man. [Formerly the property] of Col. Kindle, Cherrystone, Virginia; left him 5 years ago.

John Smith, 27, stout fellow. [Formerly the property] of William Kirkham of New Cumberland, Virginia; left him 7 years ago.

Randel Stewart, 45, [stout fellow]. [Formerly the property] of Andrew Stewart of Norfolk, Virginia; left him 5 years ago.

Samuel Thomas, 24, [stout fellow]. [Formerly the property] of Lewis Cakrean of Montreal, Canada; left him 6 years ago.

Mathew Anthony, 29, [stout fellow]. [Formerly the property] of Francis More of Philadelphia; left him 2 years ago.

Thomas Malby, 35, [stout fellow]. [Formerly the property] of John Cockburn of [Philadelphia]; left him 5 [years ago].

John Richards, 52, [stout fellow]. [Formerly the property] of Roger Kingsland of Barbadoes Neck; left him 4 [years ago].

Philip Woodley, 36, [stout fellow]. Free by certificate from Samuel Schumaker, late of Philadelphia.

Robert Smallwood, 42, [stout fellow]. Formerly the property of Robert Ruffean, King William County, Virginia; left him 7 [years ago].

Frank Marshal, 33, [stout fellow]. [Formerly the property] of Abraham Odell of Philipse Manor; left him 6 [years ago].

Daniel Stewart, 16, fine boy. [Formerly the property] of Andrew Stuart of Norfolk, Virginia; left him 5 [years ago].

John Maxwell, 25, stout fellow. [Formerly the property] of Francis Tybout of Newark, New Jersey; left him 7 [years ago].

James Hogwood, 27, [stout fellow]. [Formerly the property] of Simon Hogwood, Norfolk, Virginia; left him 4 [years ago].

John Cald, 36, [stout fellow]. [Formerly the property] of John Cockburn of Philadelphia; left him 5 [years ago].

Anthony Dimry, 18, [stout fellow]. [Formerly the property] of David Denny of English Neighbourhood; left him 5 [years ago].

Casar Kingsland, 16, fine boy. [Formerly the property] of John Seep, Aquackanung, New Jersey; left him 4 [years ago].

Thomas Nason, 25, stout fellow, flat nose. [Formerly the property] of Thomas Codbert of Philadelphia; left him 5 [years ago].

James Richards, 20, [stout fellow]. [Formerly the property] of John Richards, Barbadoes Neck; left him 7 [years ago].

William Homes, 26, [stout fellow]. [Formerly the property] of Robert Morris of Philadelphia; left him 5 [years ago].

Nathaniel Wandry, 23, [stout fellow]. [Formerly the property] of James Stewart, Newcastle, Pennsylvania; left him 5 [years ago].

John Savage, 31, [stout fellow], M. Born free, served untill 21 years of age with Henry James, Virginia.

Tamar Stewart, 26, stout wench, 3 small children. Formerly the property of Andrew Stewart of Norfolk, Virginia; left him 5 [years ago].

Polly Richards, 22, [stout wench]. [Formerly the property] of John Sipe of Acquackanung; left him 4 1/2 [years ago].

Chloe Wandry, 18, [stout wench]. [Formerly the property] of Andrew Stewart of Norfolk, Virginia; left him 5 [years ago].

Jenny Coddamus, 24, [stout wench], 2 small boys. [Formerly the property] of Pat Garrison of Stotterdam, New Jersey; left him 3 [years ago].

Tilla Mosely, 16, [stout wench]. [Formerly the property] of Colonel Mosely of Newtown, Virginia; left him 6 [years ago].

Nelly Smallwood, 22, [stout wench]. [Formerly the property] of Anthony Walker of Cape Ann, [Virginia]; left him 7 [years ago].

Jane Marshall, 23, [stout wench], 2 children 11 years & 1 month old. [Formerly the property] of Elthen Hunt, Philipse manor; left him 7 [years ago].

Mary Savage, 24, [stout wench]. [Formerly the property] of Ellis Harkham, Northumberland County, Virginia; left him 6 [years ago].

Susanna Vanryper, 24, [stout wench]. [Formerly the property] of John Sipe, Acquackanung, New Jersey; left him 4 [years ago].

Dinah Strong, 20, [stout wench] with a son 8 years of age. [Formerly the property] of John Covenhoven, [Acquackanung, New Jersey]; left him 3 1/2 [years ago].

Mary Vanryper, 24, [stout wench] with a son 1 year old. [Formerly the property] of Jacob Vanryper of [Acquackanung, New Jersey]; left him 5 [years ago].

Livsa Sally, 20, [stout wench]. [Formerly the property] of John Lashley of [Acquackanung, New Jersey]; left him 6 [years ago].

Betsey Holmes, 18, [stout wench] with 2 children 3 & 1 years of age. Says she was born free.

Sarah Flee, 21, [stout wench]. [Says she was born free.]

Rachel Dye, 22, [stout wench]. Formerly the property of Derrick Dye, Pracaness, New Jersey; left him 3 [years ago].

Sukey Smith, 25, [stout wench]. [Formerly the property] of Major Smith of Gloucester, Virginia; left him 7 [years ago].

Dinah Kingsland, 33, [stout wench], a girl 12 years of age. [Formerly the property] of John Sype of Acquackanung, New Jersey; left him 4 [years ago].

Patty Mosely, 18, [stout wench] with a child 2 months old. [Formerly the property] of

Edward Mosely of Princess Ann County, Virginia; left him 7 [years ago].

---

31 July 1783

L'Abondance
bound for Port Roseway
Lt. Phillips, Commander

Peter Vansuyl, 32, stout fellow. Late the property of Gabriel Woodman of Tom's River, New Jersey; left him 5 years ago. GBC.

Charles Bailey, 19, [stout fellow]. [Late the property] of Barney Bailey, Southampton, Virginia; left him 3 [years ago]. [GBC]

Ned Cox, 19, [stout fellow]. [Late the property] of Philip Grimes, Rappahannock, [Virginia]; left him 4 [years ago]. [GBC]

Tommy Post, 33, [stout fellow]. [Late the property] of John Post, Stotterdam, New Jersey; left him 6 [years ago]. [GBC]

Sarah Edwards, 23, stout wench with 2 small children. [Late the property] of Mrs. Col. Carleton; left by her in New York. [GBC]

David Edwards, 27, stout fellow. Born free at Boston, lived as coachman with Sir William Pepperel. [GBC]

Robert Keeling 26, [stout fellow]. [Late the property] of Captain Keeling of Nansemond, Virginia; left him 4 [years ago]. [GBC]

Anny Keeling, 26, stout wench with 1 small child. [Late the property] of Thomas Halliday of [Nansemond, Virginia]; left him 4 [years ago]. [GBC]

Edmond Bell, 33, stout fellow. [Late the property] of John Bell of Sussex County, Maryland; left him 1 1/2 [years ago]. [GBC]

Jane Bell, 26, stout wench with a daughter 8 years old. [Late the property of John Bell of Sussex County, Maryland; left him 1 1/2 years ago. GBC.]

Alice Tankard, 20, [stout wench] with a daughter 5 years old. [Late the property] of Scarborough Tankard, Norfolk, Virginia; left him 5 [years ago]. [GBC]

Sarah Jones, 33, stout wench. [Late the property] of Richard Stevens, Port Royal, South Carolina; left him 4 [years ago]. [GBC]

Dennis Ford, 29, [stout] man. [Late the property] of John Hodges, Norfolk, Virginia; left him 5 [years ago]. [GBC]

Patience Ford, 24, [stout] wench. [Late the property] of Matthew Baxton, [Norfolk,

Virginia]; left him 5 [years ago]. [GBC]

Thomas Shepperd, 55, [stout man]. [Late the property] of Joseph Shepperd, [Norfolk, Virginia]; left him 5 [years ago]. [GBC]

Lucy Shepperd, 45, [stout] wench. [Late the property] of Robert Barrett, [Norfolk, Virginia]; left him 5 [years ago]. [GBC]

Maria, 10, fine girl. [Late the property of Robert Barrett, Norfolk, Virginia; left him 5 years ago. GBC.]

Rachel Bell, 16, fine wench. [Late the property] of John Bell, Sussex County, Maryland; left him 1 [year ago].

Luke Wilson, 28, stout man. [Late the property] of James Parker, Norfolk County, Virginia; left him 7 [years ago].

Dolly Wilson, 45, stout wench. [Late the property] of Henry Singleton, [Norfolk County, Virginia]; left him 7 [years ago].

Isaac Bush, 35, stout fellow. [Late the property] of Matthew Phrip, [Norfolk County, Virginia]; left him 5 [years ago].

Lucy Bush, 35, stout wench with a boy 5 years old. [Late the property] of William

Warner nigh Philadelphia; left him 5 [years ago].

James Jones, 42, stout fellow. [Late the property] of Benjamin Jones of the Island of Bermuda; taken & brought in here 7 [years ago].

William Jordan, 32, [stout fellow]. [Late the property] of Richard Jordan of the Isle of Wight, Virginia; left him 5 [years ago].

Anny Jordan, 26, stout wench with a boy 3 years old. [Late the property of Richard Jordan of the Isle of Wight, Virginia; left him 5 years ago.]

Clara Campbell, 23, [stout wench] with a boy 3 months old. Says she was born free, Norfolk, Virginia.

Adam Fall, 27, stout fellow. [Late the property] of Edward Fenwick, St. Mary's, Maryland; left him 4 [years ago].

Dorothy Fall, 22, stout wench with a boy 1 year old. [Late the property] of William White of Nansemond, Virginia; left him 4 [years ago].

Thomas Shields, 63, worn out. [Late the property] of William Shields, Norfolk, Virginia; left him 5 [years ago].

Margaret, 65, [worn out]. [Late the property] of John Whitten,

Southern branch, Virginia; left him 5 [years ago].

Thomas Pool her grandson, 15, fine boy. [Late the property] of Robert Barrett, [Southern branch, Virginia]; left him 1 year ago.

Joseph Tramell, 24, stout fellow. [Late the property] of Henry Jones, Northampton County, Virginia; left him 5 [years ago].

Silvie Tramell, 22, stout wench. [Late the property] of Andrew Stewart of Princess Ann County, Virginia; left him 5 [years ago].

Daniel Proffitt, 24, stout fellow. [Late the property] of Joseph Jolly, Norfolk County, Virginia; left him 7 [years ago].

John Jackson, 23, [stout fellow]. [Late the property] of Mrs. Jemma Whittfield, Isle of Wight [County, Virginia]; left her 5 [years ago].

John Johnson, 24, [stout fellow]. [Late the property] of William Wade, Sussex County, Maryland; left him 2 [years ago].

Hester Johnson, 26. [Late the property] of John Bell, [Sussex County, Maryland]; left him 2 [years ago].

John Townsend, 21, [stout fellow]. [Late the property] of Daniel Sturgis of

Pennsylvania; left him 2 [years ago].

John Martin, 30, [stout fellow], stutters. [Late the property] of John Wyatt, Norfolk County, Virginia; left him 4 [years ago].

Thomas Carey, 50, [stout fellow]. [Late the property] of William Reed, Blackwater, [Virginia]; left him 7 [years ago].

Lydia Carey, 45, stout wench. [Late the property] of Joseph Jolly, Norfolk County, Virginia; left him 4 [years ago].

Samuel Cranney, 20, stout fellow. [Late the property] of Edward Wise of Great Patowmack river, Virginia; left him 4 [years ago].

Jeffery Burgis, 35, [stout fellow]. [Late the property] of Nathaniel Burges, Norfolk County, [Virginia]; left him 4 [years ago].

Molly Burgis, 24, stout wench, M. [Late the property] of Nathaniel Batt, Buttermilk bay, Massachusetts; left him 4 [years ago].

James Young, 30, stout fellow. [Late the property] of John Phillips, Norfolk County, Virginia; left him 6 [years ago].

Susannah Smith, 40, stout wench with a child 4 years old. [Late the property] of William Hodges, [Norfolk County, Virginia]; left him 6 [years ago].

Rose Smith, 12, fine girl. Formerly the property of William Hodges, Norfolk County, Virginia; left him 6 [years ago].

Eunis Smith, 10, [fine girl]. [Formerly the property of William Hodges, Norfolk County, Virginia; left him 6 years ago.]

James Smith, 50, worn out. [Formerly the property] of William Bayley, [Norfolk County, Virginia]; left him 6 [years ago].

Saunders Smith, 22, stout fellow. [Formerly the property] of William Hodges, Western branch, [Virginia]; left him 6 [years ago].

Luke Smith, 18, [stout fellow]. [Formerly the property of William Hodges, Western branch, Virginia; left him 6 years ago.]

Anthony Trewell, 26, [stout fellow]. [Formerly the property] of John Trewell, Sussex County, Delaware; left him 1 [years ago].

Thomas Basset, 39, [stout fellow]. Born free at Petersburgh, Virginia; left 2 [years ago].

George Bayley, 22, [stout fellow]. [Formerly the property]

of Matthew Phrip, Norfolk, [Virginia]; left him 4 [years ago].

George Shields, 19, [stout fellow]. [Formerly the property] of William Nixon, [Norfolk, Virginia]; left him 3 [years ago].

Jenny Toney, 52, worn out. [Formerly the property] of Daniel Underwood, Connecticut, Rhode Island; free by Bill of Sale.

Judy Weedon, 14, fine girl. Free as per Bill of Sale.

Sarah Bell, 19, stout wench. [Formerly the property] of John Bell of Suffolk County, Virginia; left him 2 [years ago].

Moses Murray, 30, stout fellow. [Formerly the property] of James Murder, Norfolk [County, Virginia]; left him 4 [years ago].

Kitty Murray, 30, stout wench with a girl 10 years old. [Formerly the property] of William Sheppard, Nansemond, [Virginia]; left him 4 [years ago].

Unis Caldwell, 19, [stout wench], M. [Formerly the property] of Ozel Kimberly of Newhaven, New England; left him 4 [years ago].

Jenny Rogers, 30, stout wench with 2 children 9 & 6 years old. [Formerly the property] of

David Pursell of Portsmouth, Virginia; left him 4 [years ago].

Kessiah Sheppard, 18, stout wench. [Formerly the property] of Saul Sheppard, Norfolk, [Virginia]; left him 4 [years ago].

Dinah Conner, 19, [stout wench]. [Formerly the property] of Charles Conner, Crane Island, [Virginia]; left him 5 [years ago].

Baggerty Rogers, 45, stout fellow. [Formerly the property] of Nicholas Gautter, Norfolk County, [Virginia]; left him 4 [years ago].

Kingston Hutchins, 29, [stout fellow]. [Formerly the property] of John Hutchins, [Norfolk County, Virginia]; left him 5 [years ago].

James Morris, 28, [stout fellow]. [Formerly the property] of Phil Lord, Grimes, Middlesex County, Virginia; left him 5 [years ago].

Robert Nickinson, 54, worn out. [Formerly the property] of Capt. Joseph Nickinson of Norfolk, [Virginia]; left him 4 [years ago].

Nat Taskew, 23, stout fellow. [Formerly the property] of Charles Graham, lower Marlborough, Maryland; left him 3 [years ago].

Thomas Hawkins, 28, [stout fellow]. [Formerly the property] of Richard Nottingham, Northampton, Virginia; left him 7 [years ago].

William Moses, 18, stout lad. [Formerly the property] of Peter Birdny, [Northampton, Virginia]; left him 4 [years ago].

Joseph Westcott, 60, worn out. [Formerly the property] of Wright Westcott, Norfolk, [Virginia]; left him 5 [years ago].

Dick Profitt, 57, [worn out]. [Formerly the property] of Harry Brown, Portsmouth, [Virginia]; left him 7 [years ago].

Sharp Westcott, 12, fine boy. [Formerly the property] of George Isdale, Elizabeth, [Virginia]; left him 5 [years ago].

John Paul, 48, worn out. [Formerly the property] of Wilson Curt, Northampton, [Virginia]; left him 5 [years ago].

Joseph Glair, 50, [worn out]. [Formerly the property] of John Blair, Eastern shore, [Virginia]; left him 5 [years ago].

Jack Taylor, 27, stout fellow. [Formerly the property] of Widow Taylor, Norfolk, [Virginia]; left her 4 [years ago].

Michael Thomas, 18, [stout fellow]. [Formerly the property] of Charles Thomas, James river, [Virginia]; left him 3 [years ago].

Samuel Brown, 17, [stout fellow]. [Formerly the property] of Richard Garret, Beaufort, South Carolina; left him 3 [years ago].

Adam Veters, 30, [stout fellow]. [Formerly the property] of Sovereign Ayres, Northampton, Virginia; left him 4 [years ago].

John McKay, 40, [stout fellow]. [Formerly the property of Sovereign Ayres, Northampton, Virginia; left him 4 years ago.]

John Ivory, 35, [stout fellow]. [Formerly the property] of Thomas Newton, Norfolk, [Virginia]; left him 3 [years ago].

Toney Christian, 40, [stout fellow]. [Formerly the property] of Michael Christian, Northampton, [Virginia]; left him 4 [years ago].

Nel Richards, 19, [stout fellow]. [Formerly the property] of Mr. McNeill of the Island of Jamaica; left him 4 [years ago].

Amos Carrey, 45, [stout fellow]. [Formerly the property] of Mrs. Col. Carey of Newport; left her 7 [years ago].

James Knapp, 12, fine boy. [Formerly the property] of Andrew Sproule, Portsmouth, Virginia; left him 7 [years ago].

Joseph Haynes, 28, stout fellow. [Formerly the property] of Peter Boder, Eastern Shore, Virginia; left him 4 [years ago].

Dick Lawrence, 35, [stout fellow]. [Formerly the property] of John Laurence of Isle of Wight who gave him his freedom 4 [years ago].

Abby Paul, 45, stout wench & son 7 years old. [Formerly the property] of Wright Westcott, Norfolk, Virginia; left him 5 [years ago].

Sally Haynes, 25, [stout wench]. [Formerly the property] of Peter Boden, Eastern Shore, Virginia; left him 4 [years ago].

Rose, 40, [stout wench]. [Formerly the property] of Nicholas Ryall of Elsabeth, Virginia; left him 5 [years ago].

Lucy Morris, 26, [stout wench] & child 8 months old. [Formerly the property] of Lambert Lightfort, Isle of Wight, [Virginia]; left him 4 [years ago].

Dinah Weeks, 35, [stout wench]. [Formerly the property] of Robert Bruce of New York who she says gave her her freedom 6 months ago.

Dinah Laurence, 30, [stout wench]. [Formerly the property] of John Murphy, Isle of Wight, Virginia; left him 5 years ago.

Priscilla Ivory, 45, [stout wench]. [Formerly the property] of Robert Gordon of Nansemond, [Virginia]; left him 4 [years ago].

Patty Nickinson, 40, [stout wench]. Says she served 21 years with James Tinnibald of Willoughby bay, Virginia; left him 5 [years ago].

Venus Profit, 50, ordinary wench. Formerly the property of Mr. Knapp of Gosport, Virginia; left him 7 years ago.

Hannah Jackson, 12, fine girl. [Formerly the property] of William Holt of Williamsburgh, Virginia; left him 4 [years ago].

Hannah Jackson, 33, stout wench. [Formerly the property of William Holt of Williamsburgh, Virginia; left him 4 years ago.]

Becky Seabrook, 27, [stout wench]. [Formerly the property] of John Seabrook of Charlestown, South Carolina; left him 5 [years ago].

Molly Wescot, 36, stout wench with 2 fine girls, 12 & 8 years old. [Formerly the property] of George Izzard, Norfolk, Virginia; left him 5 [years ago].

Hannah Blair, 25, stout wench with 2 fine sons, 4 & 2 years old. [Formerly the property] of Jacob Hancock, Eastern Shore, Virginia; left him 7 [years ago].

Nancy Peters, 50, [stout wench]. [Formerly the property] of Thomas Phipps of Charlestown, South Carolina; left him 4 [years ago].

Rachel Herbert, 24, [stout wench] with 1 girl 3 weeks old. [Formerly the property] of Melsey Wilkinson, Nansemond, Virginia; left him 4 [years ago].

Peter Weeks, 45, stout fellow. Says he was born free at Northampton on the estate of Major John Robins; left him 5 [years ago].

Samuel Moore, 26, [stout fellow]. [Formerly the property] of Skinker More at Lokers folly, North Carolina; left him 7 [years ago].

Thomas Evans, 40, [stout fellow]. [Formerly the property] of Andrew Evans of Charlestown, South Carolina; left him 7 [years ago].

James Legree, 48, [stout fellow]. [Formerly the property] of Thomas Lagree of [Charlestown, South Carolina]; left him 5 [years ago].

Dublin Gordon, 31, [stout fellow]. [Formerly the property] of Patrick Haynes of [Charlestown, South Carolina]; left him 7 [years ago].

Abby Moore, 30, stout wench with 3 children 6 years, 3 years, one 9 months. [Formerly the property] of Philip Dickinson of Philadelphia; left him 7 [years ago]. GBC.

Amos Thomas, 55, ordinary fellow. Says he was born free. GBC.

John Banbury, 38, stout fellow. [Formerly the property] of Arthur Middleton of Charlestown, South Carolina; left him 7 [years ago].

Bellah Miles, 44, stout wench. [Formerly the property] of Philip Dickinson of Philadelphia; left him 7 [years ago].

Sukey Leffers, 39, small wench with 2 children 6 years & 2 years old. [Formerly the property] of John Townsend of Marneck, County of Westchester; left him 6 [years ago].

Grace, 36, ordinary wench & daughter 10 months. [Formerly the property] of Charles Dawson of Charlestown, South Carolina; left him 6 [years ago].

Sally Miles, 18, fine wench. [Formerly the property] of Philip Dickinson of Philadelphia; left him 6 [years ago].

Patience Wilkison, 60, worn out. [Formerly the property] of Miles Wilkinson of Nansemond, Virginia; left him 4 [years ago].

Juno Thomas, 40, worn out. [Formerly the property] of Daniel Johnson of Savannah, Georgia; left him 6 [years ago].

Flora Rutledge, 40, ordinary wench. [Formerly the property] of Gov. Rutledge of Charlestown, South Carolina; left him 7 [years ago].

Pompey Rutledge, 44, stout fellow. [Formerly the property of Gov. Rutledge of Charlestown, South Carolina; left him 7 years ago.]

John Thomas, 40, [stout fellow]. [Formerly the property] of Henry Long, Cape Fear, North Carolina; left him 6 [years ago].

Charlotte Hammond, 22, small wench. [Formerly the property] of John Hammond of Ashley River, South Carolina; left him 7 [years ago].

Venus Lagree, 32, stout wench with her son 7 years old. [Formerly the property] of Mallaby Rivers of Charlestown, [South Carolina]; left him 6 [years ago].

Lucy Banbury, 40, [stout wench]. [Formerly the property] of Arthur Middleton of [Charlestown, South Carolina]; left him 6 [years ago].

Judith Evans, 30, [stout wench]. [Formerly the property] of George Ben, Nansemond, Virginia; left him 6 [years ago].

Sarah Evans, 16, [stout wench]. [Formerly the property of George Ben, Nansemond, Virginia; left him 6 years ago.]

Jane Roberts, 23, [stout wench]. [Formerly the property] of John Cottarge of Charlestown; left him 4 [years ago].

Peggy Campbell, 38, [stout wench] & son 8 years old. [Formerly the property] of James Rogers, Norfolk, Virginia; left him 7 [years ago].

Silvia Gordon, 30, [stout wench]. [Formerly the property] of Mallaby Rivers of James Island, South Carolina; left him 4 [years ago].

Tom Cain, 30, stout fellow. [Formerly the property] of John Thomas, a black freeman, Charlestown, South Carolina; left him 4 [years ago].

Nancy Moody, 14, fine girl. [Formerly the property] of Henry Moody of Williamsburgh, Virginia; left him 5 [years ago].

Harry Washington, 43, [fine] fellow. [Formerly the property] of General Washington; left him 7 [years ago].

Moses Campbell, 25, [fine fellow]. [Formerly the property] of James Campbell of Wilmington, North Carolina; left him 7 [years ago].

Rob Robinson, 23, [fine fellow]. [Formerly the property] of John Hearns of James Island, South Carolina; left him 6 [years ago].

Moses Wilkinson, 36, blind & lame. [Formerly the property] of Miles Wilkinson of Nancymond, Virginia; left him 7 [years ago].

Abraham Cry, 40, stout fellow. [Formerly the property] of John Ward of Charlestown, South Carolina; left him 7 [years ago].

Sillah Cain, 40, [stout] wench. [Formerly the property of John Ward of Charlestown, South Carolina; left him 7 years ago.]

William Smith, 40, ordinary fellow. [Formerly the property] of Jacob Hemmings of [Charlestown, South Carolina]; left him 4 [years ago].

Titus Milliner, 30, stout fellow. [Formerly the property] of Peter Farmer of Brunswick, New Jersey; left him 5 [years ago].

James Gibson, 23, [stout fellow]. [Formerly the property]

of William Sparrow of Norfolk, Virginia; left him 2 [years ago].

James Campbell, 44, [stout fellow]. [Formerly the property] of Mallaby Rivers of Savannah, Georgia; left him 6 [years ago].

Hannah Miller, 21, stout wench & child 1 year old. [Formerly the property] of Colonel Carnel of Hampton, Virginia; left him 4 [years ago].

Abigail Newton, 40, [stout wench & child 1 year old]. [Formerly the property] of Lambert Newtown of Norfolk, [Virginia]; left him 6 [years ago].

Lydia Newton, 14, [stout wench]. [Formerly the property of Lambert Newtown of Norfolk, Virginia; left him 6 years ago.]

Francis Jones, 46, stout fellow. Formerly the property of William Logan of Charlestown; left him 6 years ago.

Cesar Jones, 35, [stout fellow]. [Formerly the property] of Caleb Davis of Newark, New Jersey; left him 6 [years ago].

Jupiter Grosvenor, 55, [stout fellow]. [Formerly the property] of Samuel Grosvenor of New Jersey who he says gave him his freedom in 76.

Thomas Whitten, 23, [stout fellow]. [Formerly the property] of John Whitten of Portsmouth, Virginia; left him 5 [years ago].

Harry Fruen, 35, [stout fellow]. [Formerly the property] of Thomas Sheppard of Charlestown, South Carolina; left him 7 [years ago].

John Sharp, 67, worn out. [Formerly the property] of A. Hay of Haverstraw, New Jersey; left him 4 1/2 [years ago].

Catharine, 30, stout wench. [Formerly the property] of Dr. Van Solinger of Philadelphia; left him in New York about 5 [years ago].

Elizabeth Thomas, 52, [stout wench] & a girl 8 years old. [Formerly the property] of John Aston from whom her husband bought her freedom.

John Thomas, 58, stout man. Says he was left free at the death of William McAdam of New York.

Peter Pharo, 35, [stout man]. [Formerly the property] of Abraham Duryee of Millstone, New Jersey; left him 6 [years ago].

Richard Miller, 27, [stout man]. [Formerly the property] of Charles Ingram of Northumberland, Virginia; left him 7 [years ago].

Daniel Sepkins, 54, [stout man]. [Formerly the property] of Mr. Hogworth, 2nd River New Jersey; left him 7 [years ago].

Betty Patterson, 35, stout wench with 2 boys 9 and 5 years old. [Formerly the property] of Garret Hopper of Paramus, New Jersey; left him 5 [years ago].

Henry Walker, 60, stout man of his age. [Formerly the property] of William Nicholson of Norfolk, Virginia; left him 7 [years ago].

Tobias Walker his son, 13, fine lad. [Formerly the property] of John Chapman of Princess Ann County, Virginia; left him 3 [years ago].

Thomas Patterson, 45, worn out. [Formerly the property] of Garret Akerman of Paramus, New Jersey; left him 5 [years ago].

James Sharpe, 48, stout man. Free, says that about 14 [years ago] he lived with Mr. Childs of New York.

Jonathan Glasgow, 39, [stout man]. [Formerly the property] of William Curle, Hampton, Virginia; left him 3 [years ago].

Pamela Glasgow, 30, stout wench with a girl 8 years old. [Formerly the property] of James Barrow, [Hampton,

Virginia]; left him 3 [years ago].

Susannah Rivers, 30, [stout wench]. [Formerly the property] of Thomas Fitt, Indian Lands, South Carolina; left him 4 [years ago].

Patty Gibson, 23, stout wench with 2 children 3 & 1 years old. Says she was born free at Norfolk, Virginia.

Joseph Brown, 30, stout fellow. [Formerly the property] of Matthew Phrip, [Norfolk, Virginia]; left him 3 [years ago].

Toney Wilkin, 40, [stout fellow]. [Formerly the property] of John Wilkinson, Indian Lands, South Carolina; left him 4 [years ago].

James Thompson, 25, [stout fellow]. [Formerly the property] of Edward Cooper, Hampton, Virginia; left him 3 [years ago].

Sikes Rivers, 40, [stout fellow]. [Formerly the property] of John Shemby, Savannah, Georgia; left him 6 [years ago].

William Davis, 26, [stout fellow]. [Formerly the property] of Francis Land, Norfolk, Virginia; left him 6 [years ago].

Abram Quince, 30, [stout fellow]. [Formerly the property] of Richard Quince, Wilmington, North Carolina; left him 4 [years ago].

Anna Davis, 24, stout wench with 2 girls 7 & 4 years of age. [Formerly the property] of John Biddle, Norfolk, Virginia; left him 4 [years ago].

Olive Saunders, 25, [stout wench] with a boy 2 years of age. [Formerly the property] of Charles Connor of Crane Island, Virginia; left him 5 [years ago].

Thomas Saunders, 30, stout man. [Formerly the property] of John Baynes, [Crane Island, Virginia]; left him 5 [years ago].

Sarah Wilkins, 23, stout wench. [Formerly the property] of John Wilkins, Indian Lands, [Virginia]; left him 5 [years ago].

Patty Saunders, 18, [stout wench]. [Formerly the property] of George Robertson, Crane Island, [Virginia]; left him 4 [years ago].

James Langleyn, 28, stout fellow. [Formerly the property] of George Bibbin, Norfolk, [Virginia]; left him 4 [years ago].

Patience Wilkinson, 30, stout wench with a girl 3 years of age. [Formerly the property] of Willis Wilkinson, Nansemond, [Virginia]; left him 4 [years ago].

Violet Collet, 22, [stout wench] with a girl 3 weeks old.

[Formerly the property of Willis Wilkinson, Nansemond, Virginia; left him 4 years ago.]

Edie Gordon, 23, [stout wench]. [Formerly the property] of Christoper Gordon, Western branch, [Virginia]; left him 4 [years ago].

Savinah Miles, 25, [stout wench]. [Formerly the property] of John Miles, Indian Land, [Virginia]; left him 5 [years ago].

Venus Miles, 14, stout wench. [Formerly the property of John Miles, Indian Land, Virginia; left him 5 years ago.]

Jane Thompson, 23, stout wench with a girl 6 years old. [Formerly the property] of William Ham of Northampton County, [Virginia]; left him 3 [years ago].

Hagar Miles, 22, [stout wench]. [Formerly the property] of John Miles of Askakoo, South Carolina; left him 4 [years ago].

Betsy Wilson, 27, [stout wench] with 2 children 5 & 1 years of age. Says she is free, lived with Mrs. Randsberry of Norfolk, Virginia, who died in New York.

Billy Williams, 36, stout fellow. [Formerly the property] of Charles Middleton of Savannah, Georgia; left him 5 [years ago].

Hector Peters, 20, [stout fellow]. Says he was born free at Charlestown, South Carolina; left that place 4 [years ago].

Henry Minton, 16, [stout fellow]. [Formerly the property] of Henry Middleton, Senior, Charlestown, South Carolina; left him 5 [years ago].

Henry Cook, 37, [stout fellow]. [Formerly the property] of Thomas Newton, Norfolk, Virginia; left him 7 [years ago].

James Walker, 25, [stout fellow]. [Formerly the property] of Col. Mosely, Newtown, Virginia; left him 5 [years ago].

Thomas Miller, 25, [stout fellow]. [Formerly the property] of John Whillax, Norfolk, [Virginia]; left him 5 [years ago].

Ephraim Jerret, 29, [stout fellow]. Says he was born free in New York; lived with Peter Earl, ship carpenter.

Nathaniel Snowball, 39, [stout fellow]. [Formerly the property] of Mrs. Shrewstin, Norfolk, Virginia; left her 7 [years ago].

Marmory Brown, 58, [stout fellow]. [Formerly the property] of Derrick Van Ryper, Bergen, New Jersey; left him 7 [years ago].

Patty Brown, 55, ordinary wench. [Formerly the property]

of Harry Cooper, [Bergen, New Jersey]; left him 7 [years ago].

Casar Perth, 37, stout fellow. Formerly the property of Hardy Waller, Norfolk, Virginia; left him 4 years ago.

Mary Brow, 69, worn out. [Formerly the property] of Cornelius Van Ryper, Bergen, New Jersey; left him 7 [years ago].

Samuel Whitten, 39, stout fellow. [Formerly the property] of John Whitten, Norfolk, Virginia; left him 5 [years ago].

Betsey, 60, worn out & a fine boy 7 years old. [Formerly the property] of Mr. Davis, West Indies.

Britton Murry, 28, stout fellow. [Formerly the property] of Isaac Murray, Princess Ann, Virginia; left him 5 [years ago].

Hannah Whitten, 30, stout wench with 5 children 8, 7, 6, 5, & 1 years old. [Formerly the property] of William Smith, Norfolk, Virginia; left him 5 [years ago].

Peggy Crumwell, 50, [stout wench]. [Formerly the property] of Melsey Wilkinson, Nansemond, Virginia; left him 4 [years ago].

Dorcas Crumwell, 14, [stout wench]. [Formerly the property of Molsey Wilkinson,

Nansemond, Virginia; left him 4 years ago.]

James Young, 35, stout fellow. [Formerly the property] of Willis Nickinson, Norfolk, [Virginia]; left him 5 [years ago].

Laker Jordan, 36, [stout fellow]. [Formerly the property] of George Jordan, Nansemond, [Virginia]; left him 5 [years ago].

Joshua Jordan, 14, stout fellow. [Formerly the property] of Willis Wilkinson, Nansemond, [Virginia]; left him 5 [years ago].

Nancy Whitten, 32, stout wench with a boy 14 months old. [Formerly the property] of John Reed, Portsmouth, [Virginia]; left him 7 [years ago].

Harry Whitten, 10, fine boy. [Formerly the property of John Reed, Portsmouth, Virginia]; left him 7 [years ago].

Dempse Sullivan, 27, stout fellow. [Formerly the property] of Henry Best, Elizabeth County, [Virginia]; left him 4 [years ago].

Casar McKenzie, 32, [stout fellow]. [Formerly the property] of John McKensie of Charlestown, South Carolina; left him 5 [years ago].

James Moses, 17, [stout fellow]. [Formerly the property] of Leddleton Ayres, Northampton, Virginia; left him 1 [years ago].

Katy Reddick, 22, stout wench with a girl 5 months old. [Formerly the property] of Thomas West, Bellingsport, New Jersey; left him 5 [years ago].

Joan Murray, 24, stout wench with 2 children 4 & 2 years old. [Formerly the property] of Thomas Cheeseman, Gloster County, Virginia; left him 7 [years ago].

Daniel Archer, 32, stout fellow. [Formerly the property] of Thomas Archer of Little York, [Virginia]; left him 4 [years ago].

Jane Thompson, 70, worn out, with a grandchild 5 years old. Says she was born free; lived with Col. Tucker, Norfolk, Virginia; left him 6 [years ago].

Kate Mason, 21, stout wench, mulatto. [Says she was born free]; lived in Charlestown.

Hannah Jackson, 40, [stout wench]. [Formerly the property] of Thomas Newton, Norfolk, Virginia; left him 7 [years ago].

Bob Jackson, 12, [stout] fellow. [Formerly the property of Thomas Newton, Norfolk, Virginia]; left him 7 [years ago].

James Newcombe, 27, stout fellow. Says he was born free on the estate of Arnet Ellison, Somerset County, Maryland; left him 7 [years ago].

Jane Pearce, 23, stout wench with 2 children 8 years & 7 months. [Formerly the property] of Thomas Pearce, Nansemond, Virginia; left him 5 [years ago].

**Frigate *Cyclops*
bound for Port Roseway
Capt. Christian**

Abram Myers, 20, stout lad. (Mr. Burke, purser of *Cyclops*). [Formerly the property] of Mr. Thomas Blackwell, Black river, [Virginia]; left him 6 [years ago].

***Grand Dutchess of Russia*
bound for Annapolis Royal
Holman, Master**

Abraham Hammond, 40, stout, M. (Mr. Nat Hubbard). [Formerly the property] of John Lloyd, Stamford, Connecticut. GBC.

Andrew Bush, 25, [stout]. (Mr. Nat Hubbard). [Formerly the property] of William Bush, Horseneck, [Connecticut]; left him 5 [years ago]. [GBC]

Michael Cox, 26, [stout]. (Mr. Nat Hubbard). [Formerly the

property] of John Lloyd, Stamford, [Connecticut]; left him 5 [years ago]. [GBC]

Rachel, 39, stout wench with 3 children 10, 6 & 2 years old. (Mr. Nat Hubbard). [Formerly the property] of Nathaniel Hubbard as per Bill of Sale produced from Nathaniel Williams, Huntingdon, Long Island.

Jack, 21, stout lad. (Mr. Nat Chandler). [Formerly the property] of Albert Bonta, Hackensack, New Jersey; left him in 1776. [GBC]

Cyrus, 50, stout man. (Major Bayard). [Formerly the property] of Mr. William Bayard of New York, father to Major Bayard.

Nell, 18, stout wench with a mulatto child 7 months old. (Major Bayard). [Formerly the property of Mr. William Bayard of New York, father to Major Bayard.]

Phillis, 46, [stout wench]. (Reverend Mr. Sayre). [Formerly the property] of the Reverend Mr. Sayre.

Rosanna, 27, [stout wench]. (Reverend Mr. Sayre). [Formerly the property of the Reverend Mr. Sayre.]

Will, 23, stout fellow. (Mr. D. Seabury). [Formerly the property] of David Seaburry.

In Pursuance of two orders from His Excellency Sir Guy Carleton, K.B., General and Commander in Chief of His Majesty's Forces from Nova Scotia to West Florida inclusive, both dated Head Quarters, New York, the one 15th April, the other the 22d May 1783, We whose names are hereunto subscribed Do Certify that We did carefully inspect the aforegoing Vessels on the Twenty ninth and Thirty first days of July 1783 and that on board the said Vessels we found the negroes mentioned in the aforegoing List amounting to **Two Hundred and eighty seven men, two hundred thirty seven women and one hundred and ninety six children** and to the best of our Judgement believe them to be all the negroes on board the said Vessels and we inquired of the master of each Vessel whether he had any other property of the Citizens of the United States on board and to each inquiry we were answered in the negative. And We further Certify that we furnish'd each master of a Vessel with a Certified List of the negroes on board the Vessel and inform'd him that he would not be permitted to Land in Nova Scotia any other negroes than those contain'd in the List and that if any other negroes were found on board the Vessel he would be severely punish'd and that We inform'd the Agent for the Transports of this matter and desired him to use means for returning back to this place all negroes not mentioned in the Lists.

[*Signed*]: Wilbar Cook, Captain of the 37th Regt.; W. S. Smith; Samuel Jones, Secretary; P. Armstrong, DQM Gen.

August 1783

Sybil
bound for The Downs
Lt. Fitzgerald

Samuel Edmonds, 27, stout fellow, goes as a passenger. Formerly the property of John Smith of Accomack, Virginia; left him one year ago. GBC.

Hind
bound for Spithead & Germany
Lt. Brison

David, 10, likely boy, residence of claimant, Germany. (M. Gen. Kosporth) The boy goes with the General who got him at Philadelphia; the boy can give no account with whom he formerly lived.

Peter, 27, stout fellow, residence of claimant, Germany. (Kineschmidt) The negro lived with Stephen Townsend of Charlestown, South Carolina that near 2 years ago married Mr.

Townsend's daughter when his master gave him to her.

Ladies Adventure
bound for [Spithead & Germany]
Humble, Master

Samuel Banmord, 30, [stout fellow], (Knyphanson). Formerly the property of Jeremiah Brewer of Brooklyn, Long Island; left him 7 years ago. GBC.

David Devonshire, 21, [stout fellow], ([Knyphanson]). [Formerly the property] of Mr. John Hamilton of South Carolina; left him & returned to Augustine.

Hero
bound for Spithead & Germany
G. Burnet

Peter, 21, [stout fellow], (Major S. DeBose). [Formerly the property] of John Giles of

Suffolk County, Virginia; left
him 3 years ago.

Polly
**bound for [Spithead &
Germany]**
John Broome

John, 15, likely boy. Q.M.
Hunter of Germany, claimant.
(Q.M. Hunter, reg. Knoblauch).
[Formerly the property] of the
Quartermaster who bought him
of Benjamin Carpenter of
Jamaica, Long Island.

George, 30, [stout fellow],
(Waggoner reg., [Knoblauch]).
[Formerly the property] of
Thomas Middleton of
Charlestown, South Carolina;
[left him] 4 [years ago].

George, 26, [stout fellow],
(Drummer reg., [Knoblauch]).
[Formerly the property] of
Thomas Bean of Savannah,
Georgia; [left him] 4 [years
ago].

George, 23, [stout fellow],
(Drummer reg.). [Formerly the
property] of James Hartley of
[Savannah, Georgia; left him]
4 [years ago].

Francis Stewart, 30, [stout
fellow], ([Drummer reg.]).
[Formerly the property] of John
Williamson of the Indian
Lands, South Carolina; [left
him] 4 [years ago].

July, 20, [stout fellow],
([Drummer reg.]). [Formerly
the property] of John Lewis
Burgoyne of [the Indian Lands,
South Carolina; left him] 4
[years ago].

Mingo, 18, [stout fellow].
[Formerly the property] of John
Williamson of [the Indian
Lands, South Carolina; left
him] 4 [years ago].

Hannah, 32, stout wench, (Col.
Risbeck). [Formerly the
property] of [John Williamson]
and wife to Francis Stewart.

Peggy, 20, [stout wench],
([Col. Risbeck]). [Formerly the
property] of [John Williamson]
and daughter to [Francis
Stewart].

Christiana, 15, [stout wench],
([Col. Risbeck]). [Formerly the
property] of [John Williamson
and daughter to Francis
Stewart].

Kitty, 22, [stout wench], ([Col.
Risbeck]). [Formerly the
property] of George Huge of
Stono, South Carolina; left him
4 years ago.

Sarah, 4, fine child, ([Col.
Risbeck]). Daughter to Kitty
and born within the British
lines.

Lucy, 1, [fine child], ([Col.
Risbeck]). [Daughter to Kitty
and born within the British
lines.]

Sally, 24, stout wench, ([Col. Risbeck]). [Formerly the property] of Matthew Roach of Savannah, Georgia; left him 4 years ago.

Rose, 23, [stout wench], (Elish Hendrick). [Formerly the property] of John Williamson of the Indian Lands, South Carolina; [left him] 4 [years ago].

Peter, 2, fine child, ([Elish Hendrick]). Daughter to Rose and born within the British lines.

Bob, 30, stout fellow, (Provost Master). [Formerly the property] of Middleton of South Carolina; left him 4 years ago.

Ann & Elizabeth
bound for [Spithead & Germany]
Ben Fowler

George Barnes, 47, feeble fellow, goes as Cook to the Ship. Says he is a free man; produces a Certificate dated 1770 from John Davis of Newport, Rhode Island, Justice of the Peace.

Rachel, 7, fine child. Daughter to George Barnes.

Rebecca
bound for [Spithead & Germany]
John Wallow

Cornwallis, 25, stout fellow, (Knoblauch). [Formerly the property] of John Keayton of Indian Lands, South Carolina; left him 6 years ago.

Toby, 25, [stout fellow], ([Knoblauch]). [Formerly the property] of John Lewis Burgoyne, [Indian Lands, South Carolina; left him] 6 [years ago].

George, 20, [stout fellow], ([Knoblauch]). [Formerly the property] of John Fox, Savannah, Georgia; [left him] 6 [years ago].

York, 30, [stout fellow], ([Knoblauch]). [Formerly the property] of William Logan of Charlestown, South Carolina; [left him] 4 [years ago].

Nancy, 25, stout wench with 1 child 4 years old. Wife to the above.

George, 27, stout squat fellow. [Formerly the property] of William Stoutenburg of Charlestown, South Carolina; [left him] 4 [years ago].

Will, 19, [stout squat fellow]. Sailor on board *Rebecca*, claimant. Left Virginia; can't inform us the name of the person he lived with.

Anthony Ricks, 45, stout fellow. Sailor on board *Rebecca*, claimant. West India negro.

John, 25, [stout fellow], (Knoblauch). [Formerly the property] of Henry Middleton, Charlestown, South Carolina; left him 4 years ago.

Betsy, 28, stout wench, (Major Gable). [Formerly the property] of Owen Adam of Tinker's Creek, [South Carolina; left him] 4 [years ago].

Bess, 20, [stout wench], ([Major Gable]). [Formerly the property] of Benjamin Garret of Charlestown, [South Carolina; left him] 4 [years ago].

Jeanis, 19, [stout wench], (Capt. Pitcher). [Formerly the property] of Miss McFarlane, Savannah, Georgia; left him 2 [years ago].

Enterprise
bound for [Spithead & Germany]
T. Graham

George Andrews, 22, stout fellow, (Ens. Seeble, reg. Dilforth). [Formerly the property] of William Curl of Northampton, Virginia; left him 3 [years ago].

Elizabeth
bound for [Spithead &

Germany]
Michael Hodson

Michael, 18, [stout] lad. Property of Lieut. Fleck, reg. of Angellells; purchased from Fleck of Philadelphia.

Lucifer
Fireship bound for Spithead Patton, Esq.

James Iron, 28, stout fellow. Lt. Fleck, claimant. [Formerly the property] of Robert Hamilton of Buckingham County, Virginia; left him 15 months ago.

Harry Dean, 16, stout lad, (sailor on board). [Formerly the property] of Benjamin Dean of Salem, Massachusetts; [left him] 10 [months ago].

14 Aug 1783

Aurora
bound for Germany
C. Saunders

James Joseph, 15, [stout lad], ([sailor on board]). Says he was born free at the Head of Elk; left it with his father 6 years ago. He is indented to the ship 7 years and has been 4 on board.

Polydore, 15, likely boy, (Robert Milliner). [Formerly the property] of John Palmer of

Charlestown, South Carolina; left him 3 years ago.

William & Mary
bound for [Germany]
M. Bauer

Rosannah Mott, 26, stout wench, (Lt. Carter agent). [Formerly the property] of Jacob Mott of [Charlestown, South Carolina; left him] 3 [years ago]. GBC.

Roy Britton
bound for [Germany]
James Dunn

Ben, 20, stout fellow, (Col. Schuler, reg. Dilforth). [Formerly the property] of Rowland Lownds [of Charlestown, South Carolina; left him] 3 [years ago].

Volcano fireship
bound for Spithead
Walter, Esq.

Bill Searum, 17, stout, (Prince Hereditaire). [Formerly the property] of Dr. James Searum [of Charlestown, South Carolina; left him] 3 [years ago]. GBC.

George Glocestor, 15, likely boy, (Lt. Col. der Tuck). [Formerly the property] of William Tugle of Gloucester,

Virginia; left him 2 [years ago]. [GBC]

Sam Taylor, 17, stout lad, (sailor on board). [Formerly the property] of Thomas Edwards of Northumberland County, Virginia; left him 1 [year ago].

James Davis, 35, stout fellow, ([sailor on board]). West India Negro.

Minerva
bound for [Spithead]
John Hall

Casar, 14, [stout fellow]. John Watson of Yorkshire, claimant. (John Watson). Who says he brought him up.

Jane, 16, likely girl. [John Watson] of [Yorkshire], claimant. ([John Watson]). [Who says he brought her up.]

Milford
bound for Germany
John Moy

London, 24, stout fellow, (Knoblauch). Formerly the property of James Tiller of Charlestown, South Carolina; left him 4 years ago.

Juno, 24, stout fellow, (Knoblauch). [Formerly the property] of Burgoyne of Perrysburgh, Georgia; left him 4 [years ago].

Peter, 26, stout fellow,
(Knoblauch). [Formerly the
property] of George Roberts of
Masters Bluff, South Carolina;
left him 4 [years ago].

Hannah, 26, stout wench,
(Knoblauch). [Formerly the
property] of Thomas
Humphries, James Island,
South Carolina; left him 4
[years ago].

George, 2, fine child. Son to
Hannah & born within the
British lines.

---

21 Aug. 1783

Nautilus
bound for Abaco
Kildare Williamson, Master

Joe Grant, 19, stout fellow,
(John Shoemaker). Born free at
Bristol in Barbadoes.

James Snow, 25, [stout fellow],
p[ock] marked, (Capt. Patrick
Kennedy). [Formerly the
property] of John Elwin from
Jamaica who died at
Charlestown about 15 years
ago. GBC.

Anthony Townass, 40, [stout
fellow], (William Lerner).
[Formerly the property] of
Henry Townass of Middletown
of New Jersey; left him 4 years
ago. [GBC]

Isaac Bush, 28, [stout fellow],
(Isaiah Low). [Formerly the

property] of Lincey Opey of
Cherry point, Potowmack river,
Virginia. [GBC]

Charles Hazell, 57, [stout
fellow], blind right eye,
(William Goldthwait). Says he
was born free at New London.
[GBC]

Joseph Cox, 40, [stout fellow],
cooper by trade, (Patrick
Kennedy). [Formerly the
property] of John Bybank,
Totowa, New Jersey; left him 2
years ago. [GBC]

Flora Bush, 26, thin wench,
(Isaiah Low). [Formerly the
property] of Patrick Symons,
Cherry point, Virginia; left him
2 [years ago]. [GBC]

Sally Jones, 25, stout wench,
M, (Capt. Patrick Kennedy).
[Formerly the property] of
James Jones of Charlestown,
South Carolina; left him 3
[years ago]. [GBC]

Joseph Paul, 30, stout low
man, ([Capt. Patrick
Kennedy]). Free having
purchased his freedom from
Lawrence Cartwright of New
York. [GBC]

Susannah Paul, 30, stout
wench, mulatto, 3 children 13,
5 & 2 years old, ([Capt.
Patrick Kennedy]). [Free
having purchased her freedom
of] William Brown of [New
York]. [GBC]

Ichabod Wilkins, 25, stout man, ([Capt. Patrick Kennedy]). [Formerly the property] of John Thomas of White Plains, New York province; left him 7 years ago. [GBC]

Phillis Wilkins, 31, [stout] wench, M, ([Capt. Patrick Kennedy]). Born free on Long Island. [GBC]

Ned Price, 40, [stout] little man, ([Capt. Patrick Kennedy]). [Formerly the property] of Joshua Buntin of Crosswick, New Jersey, who he says gave him his freedom in 1776. [GBC]

Kate, 19, [stout] little wench, ([Capt. Patrick Kennedy]). Born free at Jericho on Long Island; served 10 years with John Duryee. [GBC]

Charles Johnson, 49, stout man of his age, (Thomas Cartwright). [Formerly the property] of George Biscoe, St. Mary's County, Maryland; left him 4 1/2 years ago. [GBC]

Nancy Dixon, 30, sick at present with a girl her daughter, 6 years old ([Thomas Cartwright]). [Formerly the property] of John Dixon of Williamsburgh, Virginia; left him 3 [years ago]. [GBC]

Jack Jordan, 55, stout little man, (John Job). [Formerly the property] of Robert Jordan,

Norfolk, Virginia; left him 7 [years ago]. [GBC]

Venus Jordan, 64, stout little wench ([John Job]). [Formerly the property] of Capt. Wingfield of Boston, New England; left him 7 [years ago]. [GBC]

Timothy Snowball, 37, stout fellow, M, (Capt. Kennedy). [Formerly the property] of Cornelius Colbert, Norfolk, Virginia; left him 7 [years ago]. [GBC]

Peter Johnson, 25, stout fellow, scar on his forehead, (William Smith). [Formerly the property] of Daniel Sera, Savannah, Georgia. [GBC]

Cuffy Lucas, 38, [stout fellow], (Humphrey Massenburgh). [Formerly the property] of Ann Lukes, Eastern Shore, Virginia; left 2 [years ago]. [GBC]

Isabella, 40, [stout] wench, ([Humphrey Massenburgh]). [Formerly the property] of Charles Mifflin of Philadelphia; left him 5 [years ago]. [GBC]

Thomas Miller, 20, stout fellow, (Isaac Punderson). [Formerly the property] of John Whitten of Portsmouth, Virginia; left him 4 [years ago]. [GBC]

Jack, 25, [stout fellow], (John Longley). [Formerly the property] of John Longley purchased from Sarah Ayoner as per Bill of Sale produced.

Robert Johnson, 49, [stout fellow], (Thomas Cartwright). [Formerly the property] of George Biscoe of St. Mary's County, Maryland; left him 4 1/2 years ago. [GBC]

Hannah Johnson, 40, stout wench, ([Thomas Cartwright]). [Formerly the property] of Simon Hallyar, Hampton, Virginia; left him 4 [years ago]. [GBC]

Benjamin Harris, 29, stout tall fellow, ([Thomas Cartwright]). [Formerly the property] of Caleb Herman, St. Mary's County, Maryland; left him 5 [years ago]. [GBC]

Hesther Scot, 25, stout M wench, (Matthew Arnold). Free as per Gov. Bull's Certificate.

Tom, 64, stout fellow, (Charles Whitehead). Free; made his escape from Cape Francois.

Lucas, 30, [stout fellow], (Joseph Pilgrim). [Formerly the property] of Benedict Burgoyne, Savannah, Georgia; left him 6 [years ago].

Hercules, 16, [stout fellow], very flat nose, ([Joseph Pilgrim]). [Formerly the property] of Isaac Harleston who was killed at the Eutaws of Irish town, South Carolina, 6 [years ago].

Nancy, 60, stout wench, ([Joseph Pilgrim]). [Formerly the property] of Colonel Cole of Swynyard, James river; left him 8 [years ago].

Tom, 10, [stout] thin man, (Robert Smith). [Formerly the property] of Mr. Ulon of Norfolk who was killed.

Adam, 11 1/2, stout boy, scar on forehead, (Richard Warner). [Formerly the property] of Richard Warner.

Rose, 20, fine girl, (John Shoemaker). [Formerly the property] of John Shoemaker who purchased her from Vandewater, Bedford, Long Island.

----

22 Aug. 1783

William
**transport bound for Abbaco
John Cook, Master**

George, 25, stout fellow, (Patrick Kennedy). Came from Jamaica where he says he was born free. [GBC]

Sharp, 36, [stout fellow], ([Patrick Kennedy]). [Formerly the property] of John Cooke of Charlestown; left him 4 years ago.

Joe Elliot, 26, [stout fellow], (J. Heid). [Formerly the property] of George Elliot,

Charlestown, South Carolina; left 3 [years ago]. [GBC]

James Nash, 28, [stout fellow], ([J. Heid]). [Formerly the property] of John Ash near Stono, [South Carolina]. [GBC]

Diana, 22, stout wench & child 10 months old ([J. Heid]). [Formerly the property] of Mrs. Cross, Charlestown, [South Carolina]; left 4 [years ago]. [GBC]

Daphne Rivers, 35, [stout wench], (Elias Davis). [Formerly the property] of Samuel Fulton, [Charlestown, South Carolina]; left 4 [years ago]. [GBC]

William Kinty, 27, stout fellow, (Cornelius Blanchard). [Formerly the property] of William Petery of St. John, [South Carolina]; left 5 [years ago].

John Jackson, 26, [stout fellow], (Alexander Dean). Says he is free; lived with Tom Hutchinson, Charlestown, South Carolina; left him 5 years ago.

James Kain, 37, [stout fellow], (Joseph Moore). [Formerly the property] of John Houston, Savannah, Georgia; left 4 years ago.

Kate Johnson, 11, stout wench, ([Joseph Moore]). [Formerly the property] of Andrew

Johnson, Charlestown, South Carolina; left 2 [years ago].

Jack Johnson, 11, fine boy, ([Joseph Moore]). [Formerly the property] of [Andrew Johnson, Charlestown, South Carolina; left 2 years ago].

Esther Moore, 16, [fine] girl, (Joseph Moore). [Formerly the property] of Joseph Moore.

Joseph Scot, 40, stout fellow, (Alexander Dean). Says he is free, lived in Charlestown, carpenter.

Primus Fortune, 30, stout fellow (Alexander Dean). Formerly the property of Isaac Warner of Philadelphia; left him 4 years ago.

Maurice Williams, 35, stout fellow, ([Alexander Dean]). [Formerly the property] of Robert Miles of Savannah, South Carolina; left him 5 [years ago].

Sally Beariman, 25, fine wench, ([Alexander Dean]). [Formerly the property] of Thomas Beauman of Beaufort, [South Carolina]; left him 4 [years ago].

Juba, 30, stout fellow, ([Alexander Dean]). [Formerly the property] of Alexander Dean by Bill of Sale produced.

Carolina, 10, fine boy, ([Alexander Dean]). [Formerly

the property of Alexander Dean by Bill of Sale produced.]

Rebecca, 22, stout wench with a child 1 year old, ([Alexander Dean]). [Formerly the property] of Joseph Bradford of Charlestown, South Carolina; left him 4 [years ago].

Paris, 50, stout fellow, (John Wallis Barclay). [Formerly the property] of John Willis Barclay by Bill of Sale.

Venus, 33, stout wench with 4 children 11, 8, 4 & 2 years old, ([John Wallis Barclay]). [Formerly the property] of [John Willis Barclay] by [Bill of Sale].

George Taylor, 28, stout fellow, (George Antill). Says he is free.

Hannah Taylor, 22, [stout] wench with a child 6 months old, ([George Antill]). [Formerly the property] of Timothy Burges of Portsmouth, Virginia; left him 4 [years ago].

Lettice London, 29, [stout wench], ([George Antill]). [Formerly the property] of George Webb of Norfolk, Virginia; left him 6 [years ago].

Henry Jackson, 25, [stout] fellow, ([George Antill]). [Formerly the property] of Thomas Gold of Richmond, [Virginia]; left him 4 [years ago]. GBC.

Peggy, 21, stout wench, 1 child 8 months ([George Antill]). [Formerly the property] of Jesse Barlow of Portsmouth, [Virginia]; left him 5 [years ago].

Jane Williams, 60, ordinary wench, ([George Antill]). [Formerly the property] of Matthew Burgis of [Portsmouth, Virginia]; left him 5 [years ago].

Isaac Wickfall, 45, [ordinary] fellow ([George Antill]). [Formerly the property] of Joseph Wickfall, Waubam, South Carolina; left him 4 [years ago].

Susanna Pavell, 34, [ordinary] wench with a boy 5 years old, (John Jordan). [Formerly the property] of Capt. Dickson who she says left her free.

Isaac Murray, 16, fine boy, (Cornelius Blanchard). Certificate of Freedom from Gabriel Marygault.

Luce, 11, [fine] girl, (John Hutchins). Property of said Hutchins by Bill of Sale.

Nancy, 24, fine wench, 2 children 4 & 2 years old, (Blanchard). Property of said Blanchard.

Patty, 21, fine wench, 1 child 6 months old, (William McDonald). [Formerly the property] of General Howe of the Continental Army; left him 4 years ago.

Bob Powell, 32, stout fellow, (John Jordan). [Formerly the property] of John Powell of Charlestown; left him 3 [years ago].

Tom Tanyard, 31, [stout fellow], ([John Jordan]). [Formerly the property] of James Tanyard, Stono, South Carolina; left him 4 [years ago].

Betsey, 28, idiot, (Mrs. Barclay). Says she is free.

James Dickson, 24, stout fellow, (William McDonald). Says he was left free by Capt. Benjamin Dixon of Charlestown when he died 5 years ago.

Fortune, 23, [stout fellow], (Cornelius Blanchard). [Formerly the property] of Thomas Haywood of Charlestown; left him 6 years ago.

Thomas Griswell, 23, [stout fellow], (John Jones). [Formerly the property] of Hector Criswell of Georgetown, South Carolina; left him 5 [years ago].

James Brown, 23, [stout fellow], (George Wilbank). Born free at Salem Township, New Jersey; served untill 21 with Abraham Hewlins.

Peter Brown, 35, [stout fellow], (John Davis). [Formerly the property] of James Bruce, Annapolis, Maryland; left him 6 [years ago].

Ned Johnson, 31, [stout fellow], carpenter, (George Wilbank). Says he was born free at Bermuda; served his apprenticeship with John Morrell.

Bridget Wanton, 22, stout little woman and small girl 5 years old, (John Davis). [Formerly the property] of Colonel Joseph Wanton of Rhode Island who at his death left him free.

William Willis, 39, stout husky man, (John Cameron). [Formerly the property] of Joseph Pinto of New York who gave him his freedom about 10 years ago.

Hester Willis, 26, stout wench, ([John Cameron]). [Formerly the property of Joseph Pinto of New York who gave him his freedom about 10 years ago.]

In Pursuance of two Orders from His Excellency Sir Guy Carleton K.B. General & Commander in Chief of His Majesty's forces from Nova Scotia to West Florida inclusive both dated Head

Quarters New York the one 15th April and the other the 22d May 1783, We whose names are hereunto Subscribed Do Certify that We did carefully Inspect the aforegoing Vessels on the 13th, 14th, 21st & 22d days of August 1783 and that on board the said Vessels We found the Negroes mentioned in the aforegoing list amounting to **eighty men thirty nine women and thirty five children** and to the best of our Judgement believe them to be all the negroes on board the said Vessels and We Enquired of the Master of each Vessel whether he has any Records, deeds or Archives or papers or other property of the Citizens of the United States on board and to each enquiry we were answered in the negative and We further Certify that We furnished each Master of a Vessel with a Certified List of the negroes on board the Vessel and informed him that he would not be permitted to land any other Negroes than those contained in the list and that if any other negroes were found on board the vessel he would be severely punished and that we informed the Agent for the transports of this matter and desired him to use means for returning back to this place all Negroes not mentioned on the list.

[*Signed*] W. L. Smith, Col.; Samuel Jones, Secretary; Nathaniel Philips, N.B.; William Armstrong, DQM Gen.

Commerce
bound for St. John's
Richard Strong

Joe Freeman, 22, ordinary fellow, B, (Capt. Swift, Pennsylvania Loyalist). Says he was born at St. Kitts; that he came to New York in a privateer.

Jack Brinkerhoff, 26, [ordinary fellow], (Lt. Cooper). Mr. Cooper's property.

Bridgewater
bound for [St. John's]
Daniel Addinot

Fortune Logan, 24, [ordinary fellow].

Isaac York, 27, [ordinary fellow].

Eagle
bound for [St. John's]
John Blane

Lucy, 16, stout wench, mulatto, (Albert Vanshant). His own property.

Dorothy, 5, black, (Widow Conley). Her own property.

**Ship *Berwick*
bound for England
Capt. Prideaux**

John Humphries, 22, stout fellow. Capt. Prideaux of Ship *Brunswick*, claimant. (Capt. Prideaux). Formerly slave to Mr. Clarkson of Philadelphia; was captured in South Carolina.

Casar Jones, 18, ordinary fellow. [Capt. Prideaux of Ship *Brunswick*, claimant.] (Capt. Prideaux). Purchased by Capt. Prideaux at St. Eustatius in the West Indies.

---

6 Sept. 1783

Grace
**bound for Quebec
William Oxley**

Jenny Miller, 38, [ordinary] wench, M, (Alexander Hare). Hares own property.

Hannah Harris, 30, [ordinary wench], mustee, goes on her own bottom. Freeborn.

Polly Harris, 4 months.

Betsey Graham, 13, likely girl, B, (John Graham). Graham's property.

Margaret Matthews, 26, stout wench, [B], (Stephen Delancey). Formerly slave to John Smith of Connecticut & late of New York government who left her at New York after New York was taken.

Peter Matthews, 27, ordinary fellow, ([Stephen Delancey]). Free as appears by a discharge from Major Stephenson dated in London in 1780.

Betsey, 16, [ordinary] wench, ([Stephen Delancey]). Slave to Guy Johnson.

John Martine, 22, [ordinary] fellow, (Capt. McDonald). Formerly slave to Mr. Delanse of Charlestown; left him immediately after that town was taken in the year 1780.

---

3 Sisters
**bound for [Quebec]
John Wardell**

Cuff Van Alstine, 16, stout lad, (Major Van Alstine). Major Van Alstine's own property.

Ben Johnson, 11, fine boy, (John Johnston). Mr. Johnston's own property.

Simon Helenbeck, 19, likely lad, (Casper Hellenbeck, Esq.). Mr. Hellenbeck's property.

Cato Huggenel, 44, ordinary fellow, (Daniel Huggenell). Formerly slave to William

Carson of South Carolina; left him after the Siege of Charlestown. GBC.

Pusie, 30, ordinary wench, (Peter Van Alstyne). Appears to be Peter Van Alstyne's property.

Child, 1 1/2, ([Peter Van Alstyne]). [Appears to be Peter Van Alstyne's property.]

York, 11, ordinary boy, (John Huyck). Proved to be John Huych's property.

---

18 September

Duke of Richmond bound for St. John's

Jack, 40, stout fellow, (Q.M. Jones). Formerly slave to John Colvill of 96 in South Carolina; said to be purchased from him by Q.M. James. Witnessed by Ens. Banks of this corps.

Hannah Jarvis, 26, fine wench, M, (Capt. Thatcher). Purchased from Stephen Biddle of Staten Island by the captain.

Edward Christie, 27, very short fellow, (Dr. Carle, 1 Bat., N.J. Vols.). Formerly slave to William Smith, Susquehanna ferry; left him about 6 years ago & joined the British troops at the Head of Elk.

Frank Addie, 14, good looking boy, (Lt. Haddin, [1 Bat., N.J. Vols.]). [Formerly slave] to Molton Wilkinson of Charlestown, South Carolina; left in the year 1780 after the Siege.

Thomas Williams, 30, stout fellow, (Lt. Britain, [1 Bat., N.J. Vols.]). Certified by William Walton, Esq., Magistrate of P., to have availed himself of Sir William Howe's proclamation; was formerly slave to Mr. Tomkins, Northampton County, Virginia.

Vaughan Covenhoven, 19, likely boy, (Capt. Coggle, [1 Bat., N.J. Vols.]). Formerly slave to Peter Covenhoven, Middletown, New Jersey; captured by Col. Hyde's detachment in 1779 & afterwards purchased by Capt. Coggle.

Plato, 18, [likely boy], (Capt. Barbaree, 2nd [Bat., N.J. Vols.]). Born in the Captain's family.

John January, 7, small boy, (Ensign Banks, [2nd Bat., N.J. Vols.]). His own property.

John Sygh, 18, likely rascal, (Capt. Lee, [2nd Bat., N.J. Vols.]). Formerly slave to John Murick of Charlestown, South Carolina; left him about four years ago.

Sunbury, 26, stout fellow,
(Capt. Thatcher, [2nd Bat, N.J.
Vols.]). [Formerly slave] to
John Jones, Savannah; left said
master and joined the British
troops before the Siege of
Savannah.

Mars
Peter Jackson

Peter Jackson, 24, [stout
fellow], M, (Dr. Smith, Brit.
Legion). [Formerly slave] to
Peter VanRyker of Bergen
County, New Jersey; joined the
British troops on York Island in
1776.

Samuel Williams, 16, stout
lad, (Lt. Davids, [Brit.
Legion]). [Formerly slave] to
Richard Subsion, Charlestown,
South Carolina; left him in the
year 1780 & joined the British
on John's Island.

James Webb, 18, stout fellow
(Capt. Vernon, [Brit. Legion]).
[Formerly slave] to Mr. John
Webb, Halifax, North
Carolina; left him early in
1781.

Richard Richardson, 30,
ordinary fellow & lame, (Ens.
Stanley, [Brit. Legion]).
[Formerly slave] to Isaac
Woodruff, Elizabeth town,
New Jersey; left him 4 years
ago.

Ann
bound for St. John's
Clark

Elizabeth Mitchell, 13, stout
girl, (Lt. Clows, Guides &
Pioneers). Says she was born
free near Charlestown, South
Carolina; joined the Army in
1780.

Dick Vincent, 10, [stout] boy,
(Ens. Vincent). Formerly slave
to Charles Vincent, East
Chester, grandfather to the
Ensign who has delivered the
boy to the said Ensign.

Duke Richmond
bound for St. John's

Lydia Williams, 17, stout
wench, (Lt. Britton). Certified
by William Walton, Esq.,
Magistrate of Police to have
availed herself of Sir William
Howe's proclamation; was
formerly slave to William
Timkins, Northampton County,
Virginia.

Elizabeth
bound for St. John's
Watson, Master

Jerry Miller, 22, stout made,
(Trumpeter, Am. Legion).
Formerly slave to Charles
Harrison, Prince George,
Virginia; joined the army in

1781. Mustered in the regiment.

Simon Johnson, 16, likely lad, ([Trumpeter, Am. Legion]). [Formerly slave] to John Cooper, Williamsburgh, Virginia; joined the army with General Arnold in 1781.

Melinda, 11, likely girl. Major Monzies of St. John's, claimant. (Major Monzies). Born & bred in the Major's family.

Primus, 11, likely boy. [Major Monzies of St. John's, claimant.] ([Major Monzies]). [Born & bred in the Major's family.]

Chloe, 19, likely wench, (Lieut. Ambruse). [Formerly slave] to Mrs. Boykin, Charlestown, South Carolina; left him in 1780 & joined the army on John's Island.

Susannah, 7 months, M, ([Lieut. Ambruse]).

George, 17, stout likely boy, M, (Trump. Am. Legion). [Formerly slave] to Col. Carter, Virginia; joined General Arnold in 1781.

London, 17, [stout] black, ([Trump. Am. Legion]). [Formerly slave] to Robert Pleasant, Virginia; [joined General Arnold in 1781].

Nathaniel, 16, likely boy, M, (Lieut. Bull, A.L.). [Formerly slave] to Col. Bannister, [Virginia; joined General Arnold in 1781].

James, 16, [likely boy], B, (Capt. Frink, A.L.). [Formerly slave] to Mrs. Cuyler who gave him to her daughter Mrs. Frink.

Diana, 7, likely girl, ([Capt. Frink, A.L.]). Who bought her from Mrs. Beadle, Staten Island.

King George
bound for [St. John's]

Andrew, 9, likely boy, (Lt. Cox, K.A. reg't.). Who brought him a child from North Carolina after picking him up in a wood by Lieut. Cox.

Ned Hustus, 22, stout fellow, M, (Lieut. Eustace, [K.A. reg't.]). [Formerly slave] to John White, Camden, South Carolina; left him & joined the British troops early in 1781.

Will Hollyday, 33, [stout fellow], B, (Lieut. Smith, [K.A. reg't.]). [Formerly slave] to Joseph Hollyday, Nansemond, Virginia; left him in the year 1781 & joined the British troops.

Montague
bound for [St. John's]

Abraham Ness, 30, [stout fellow], (Adj't. Ness).

[Formerly slave] to James Brown, Camden, South Carolina, from whom Mr. Ness purchased him in the year 1782.

Lucy Ness, 29, stout wench, ([Adj't. Ness]). [Formerly slave] to Widow Payne, [Camden, South Carolina], from whom Mr. Ness purchased from the widow by Mr. Ness at Charlestown.

William Carden, 27, stout fellow, (Lieut. Col. DeVeber). [Formerly slave] to Joseph Taylor, Danbury, Connecticut; left him 7 years past & joined the troops there.

Diana Carden, 24, ordinary wench, ([Lieut. Col. DeVeber]). [Formerly slave] to Richard Burke, Rhode Island; left him 7 years ago.

William
bound for [St. John's]

Anthony, 32, [ordinary] fellow, (Lt. Barker, K.A. reg't.). [Formerly slave] to Ben Warren, Charlestown, South Carolina; left him year 1780 previous to the Siege of that Garrison.

Christopher, 28, [ordinary fellow], (Capt. Atwood, [K.A. reg't.]). [Formerly slave] to Alexander McAlister, East Florida; left him & joined the British troops at Savannah in 1780.

Apollo
bound for [St. John's]

Bob, 15, likely boy, (Adj. Cunningham). His property.

Jeff, 12, [likely boy], (Lieut. B. Ward). His own property.

Vinia, 25, stout wench, M, (Capt. Willmot). Capt. Willmot's property.

Harry, her [*Vinia's*] infant, ([Capt. Willmot]). Capt. Willmot's property.

Robert, her [*Vinia's*] infant, ([Capt. Willmot]). [Capt. Willmot's property.]

Two Sisters
bound for [St. John's]

Silvia, 20, likely wench, B. Capt. Brown of *2 Sisters*, claimant. (Capt. Brown). [Formerly slave] to Col. Lowe near Brunswick, New Jersey; left him in 1776 & joined the British troops.

Besse, 21, [likely wench], (D. Humphries, N.Y. Vols.). Lived with Capt. Atkins, Clown, South Carolina; left him about 4 years ago. Sold by the widow of said Atkins sometime after as the wench says.

Kitty, infant, M, ([Dr.
Humphries, N.Y. Vols.]). Her
infant.

Gull, 16, stout boy, B, ([Dr.
Humphries, N.Y. Vols.]).
[Formerly slave to Capt.
Atkins, Clown, South Carolina;
left him about 4 years ago.
Sold by the widow of said
Atkins.]

Ambrose Lewis, 19, stout
fellow, (Lieut. DeBeck). His
own property.

Esther
bound for [St. John's]

Maria, 21, stout wench. Capt.
Campbell of St. John's,
claimant. (Capt. Campbell).
[Formerly slave] to Mr.
McRae, Hatter, New Jersey,
who sold her to Mr. Burton,
New York, & has since been
purchased as she says by Capt.
Campbell.

Mingo, 3, infant. [Capt.
Campbell of St. John's,
claimant.] ([Capt. Campbell]).
[Formerly slave to Mr. McRae,
Hatter, New Jersey, who sold
her to Mr. Burton, New York,
& has since been purchased by
Capt. Campbell.]

Abraham, 21, stout fellow.
Capt. McLeod of [St. John's],
claimant. (Capt. McLeod). The
Captain's Property.

Mars
bound for [St. John's]

Mingo [], 27, ordinary fellow,
(Ensign Stanley). Cornelius
Munford, Long Island near
Flushing, returned to the
owner.

Diana [], 26, stout wench,
([Ensign Stanley]). [Cornelius
Munford, Long Island near
Flushing, returned to the
owner.]

Phebe [], 1 1/2, infant,
([Ensign Stanley]). [Cornelius
Munford, Long Island near
Flushing, returned to the
owner.]

Paul Moore, 36, ordinary
fellow, (Capt. McPherson).
Col. John Taylor, Richmond
County, Virginia; left him in
1777 & joined the British
troops.

Sarah Moore, 24, likely
wench, M, ([Capt.
McPherson]). Mary Meaks
near Warwick Town,
Maryland; left her 6 years ago.
GBC.

Prince Blake, 16, likely lad,
B, (Lieut. Robins). Capt.
Blake, Charlestown; left him
after the Siege of that place &
joined the British troops. GMC.

James Robinson, 30, stout
fellow, (Lieut. Sargen). Mr.
Robertson, Charlestown, South
Carolina; left him before the

Siege of that Garrison & joined [the British troops]. GBC.

John Fortune, 20, likely lad, (Capt. Gelder). Capt. Connor, Norfolk, Virginia; [left him before the Siege of that Garrison] & joined the British troops in 1779. [GBC]

Ned Ugee, 30, likely fellow. General Hugee, Charlestown, South Carolina; left him & joined [the British troops] before the Siege of that Garrison. [GBC]

Ned Thomas, 21, [likely] fellow, (Cornet Hovendon). Certified to be free by General Musgrave's Certificate.

---

13 September

Britain
bound for [St. John's]
John Allen

Nelly, 18, likely wench. Major Coffin of St. John's, claimant. (Major Coffin). Became his property by the marriage of Mrs. Coffin.

Fortune, 9, likely boy. [Major Coffin of St. John's, claimant.] ([Major Coffin]). [Became his property by the marriage of Mrs. Coffin.]

Sovereign
bound for [St. John's]
Stewart

Liberty, 25, stout fellow. Capt. Dunbar of St. John's, claimant. (Capt. Dunbar). Negro acknowledges to have been purchased by the Capt. at the West Indies 17 years ago.

Tim, 22, [stout fellow]. Capt. T. French of [St. John's], claimant. (Capt. T. French). Certified from the office of Police to be the Captain's property purchased from James Whitten, Charlestown.

Pompey Grant, 30, ordinary fellow (Delanceys). [Formerly slave] to Thomas Grant at New York; Gen. Musgrave's Certificate.

Tinah Leech, 25, stout wench, (Capt. French). [Formerly slave] to George Leach of Philadelphia; [Gen. Musgrave's Certificate].

Susannah, 35, ordinary wench. Capt. McPherson of St. John's, claimant. (Capt. McPherson). Property proved per Bill of Sale.

Michael Beacon, 25, stout fellow, (Ensign Boyle). [Formerly slave] to Andrew Thomson, New Kent, Virginia; left him about 3 years & joined Lord Cornwallis's Army.

Phillis Drove, 20, likely wench, B, (Capt. McCoy). Formerly the property of William Gardner near Charlestown, South Carolina; left him three years ago. GMC.

John Brown, 25, stout fellow, M, (Capt. McGill). Appears to be free.

Rosanna Mott, 25, stout wench, M, ([Capt. McGill]). [Formerly the property] of Jacob Mott, Charlestown, South Carolina; left him after the Siege of that Garrison. GMC.

Simon Adams, 38, ordinary fellow, B, (Capt. McCoy). [Formerly the property] of Thomas Fuller, Ashley river, [South Carolina; left him] 4 years ago. [GMC]

Emmy Adams, 26, likely wench, ([Capt. McCoy]). [Formerly the property] of Isaac Homes, John's Island, [South Carolina; left him 4 years ago]. GBC.

Hannah Jones, 20, stout wench, ([Capt. McCoy]). [Formerly the property] of James Nichol, Charlestown, [South Carolina]; left him in 1779; declared free by GMC.

James Fraser, 9, stout boy, (Ensign Height). [Formerly the property] of Mr. Frazer, Virginia; [left him] in 1780. GBC.

Lottie, 30, likely wench, (Capt. Carr). [Formerly the property] of John Walloby, Virginia; [left him] 8 years ago. [GBC]

Sandy Alexander, 21, stout fellow, (Lt. Howe). [Formerly the property] of William Matthews, Charlestown, South Carolina; [left him] 3 [years ago]. [GBC]

Ned, 25, [stout fellow], (Lt. Potts). Proved to be free.

Anthony Ferguson, 21, [stout fellow], (Lt. Holland). [Formerly the property] of John Ferguson, Wilmington, North Carolina; [left him] 5 [years ago]. GMC.

Gabriel Johnson, 27, [stout fellow], (Capt. Stephenson). [Formerly the property] of Jacob Petsworth, Quibble town, New Jersey, and joined the British troops. [GMC]

Nancy Bryan, 16, likely wench, (Ensign Matthewson). [Formerly the property] of Louis Bryan, Virginia; left him 5 years ago. [GMC]

Fortune Logan, 20, likely fellow, (Major Armstrong). [Formerly the property] of William Logan, [left him] 3 [years ago]. [GMC]

Diana, 22, [likely] wench. L.C. Robertson of St. John's, claimant. (Capt. Robertson). Proved the Colonel's property.

Samuel Wright, 30, middling fellow, (Capt. Carr). [Formerly the property] of Richard Goff, Charlestown, South Carolina; left him before the Siege of that Garrison. GBC.

Paris, 19, stout lad, (Cornet Merrell). [Formerly the property] of Col. Oree, [Charlestown, South Carolina; left him] 4 [years ago] & joined the British troops. GMC.

Joe, 25, stout fellow, (Dr. Gamble). [Formerly the property] of Robert Johnson, [Charlestown, South Carolina; left him] 5 [years ago]. [GMC]

Isaac York, 26, [stout fellow], (Ensign Murray). Appears to be free. [GMC]

John Jones, 37, [stout fellow], (Capt. McCoy). [Formerly the property] of Henry Crouch, South Carolina; [left him] in the year 1780. GBC.

Pallesier
bound for St. John's
James Smith

Jack, 14, likely boy. Capt. Mills of [St. John's], claimant. (Capt. Mills). Certified to be his property from the Office of Police.

Rose, 14, likely wench. [Capt. Mills of St. John's, claimant ([Capt. Mills]). [Certified to be his property from the Office of Police.]

Ham, 15, likely boy. Ensign Hubbard of [St. John's], claimant. (Ens. Hubbard). [Certified to be his property from the Office of Police.]

Warwick, 26, stout fellow, (Adj't. Carpenter). [Formerly the property] of Aaron Jellot, Charlestown, South Carolina; left him 5 years ago. GMC.

Jack, 9, likely boy. Ensign Carpenter of [St. John's], claimant. (Ens. [Carpenter]). Certified to be his property by the Office of Police.

Nancy Howthey, 14, ordinary wench, (Lieut. DeVeber). [Formerly the property] of Mr. Hawthey, Charlestown, South Carolina; left him 5 years ago. GBC.

Kate, 23, stout wench, (Ensign Carpenter). [Formerly the property] of John Williamson, [Charlestown, South Carolina; left him 5 years ago]. GMC.

Kate, 5, likely child. Lieut. DeVeber of [St. John's], claimant. (Lt. DeVeber). His property certified by the Mayor.

Mary, 41, ordinary wench. Ensign Cheace of [St. John's], claimant. (Ens. Cheace). [His property certified] by Mr. Walton.

Aurora
bound for Halifax

Hannah, 19, [ordinary wench]. Lt. Brackenback of Halifax, claimant. (Lt. Brackenback). Proved to be the Lieutenant's property by Bill of Sale.

Joseph, 1 1/2, her infant. [Lt. Brackenback of Halifax, claimant.] ([Lt. Brackenback]). Naturally the Lieutenant's property.

Nancy, 28, stout wench, (Henry Myer). [Formerly the property] of James Jerrads of South Carolina; left him before the Siege of Charlestown & joined the British troops.

Mercury, 20, likely lad. Dr. Wright of [Halifax], claimant. (Dr. Wright). Proved to be Dr. Wright's property by Bill of Sale.

Supply
bound for [Halifax]

Henry Arrington, 38, stout fellow, on his own bottom. Certified free by GMC.

Bridgewater
bound for St. John's

Hargar, 17, ordinary wench. Widow Brown of St. John's, claimant. (Widow Brown). [Formerly the property] of the late Dr. Middleton of New York; was after his death sold to the said Widow Brown.

Mars
bound for [St. John's]

Abraham, 16, stout lad, (Cornet Hovendon). [Formerly the property] of James Jenkins of Wappoo bridge, South Carolina; left him immediately after the Siege of Charlestown. GBC.

Charles, 18, stout fellow, ([Cornet] Coulter). [Formerly the property] of Job Morrell, St. John's parish, South Carolina; left him 3 years ago. GMC.

Murcer, 18, ordinary wench, ([Cornet] Hovendon). Lived with Widow Kitchum, Huntingdon, Long Island; certified by General Musgrave to be free.

In pursuance of two Orders from His Excellency, Sir Guy Carleton, K.B. General and Commander in Chief of His Majesty's Forces from Nova Scotia to West Florida inclusive both dated Head Quarters, New York, the one 15 April and the other 22d May 1783. We whose names are hereunto Subscribed Do Certify that we did carefully Inspect the aforegoing Vessels on the fifth, sixth, eighth and the thirteenth days of September 1783 and that on board the said Vessels we found the Negroes mentioned in the aforegoing Lists amounting to **sixty five men, thirty two women and thirty children** (besides the three mentioned in the list to have been returned to the owner) and to the best of our Judgement believe them to be all the negroes on board the said Vessels. And We enquired of the Master of each Vessel whether he had any Records, deeds or Archives or Papers or other property of the Citizens of the United States on board and to each enquiry we were answered in the negative. And we further Certify that we furnished the master of each Vessel with a Certified List of the negroes on board his Vessel and informed him that he would not be permitted to land any other Negroes than those mentioned in the List and that if any other negroes were found on board his Vessel he would be Severely punished and that we informed the Agent of Transports of this matter and desired him to use means for returning to this place all Negroes not mentioned in the List.

[*Signed*]: W. S. Smith, Col., on the Part of the United States; Samuel Jones, Secretary; ___ Armstrong, DJGP. Gen.; ___ Gilfillan, DVM Gen.

Inspection Roll

of

Negroes

Book No. 2

*[New York City
Book No. 2
September 22–November 19, 1783]*

22 September 1783

Spencer
bound for Port Roseway
Rob Valentine

William Scot, 24, stout fellow, M, (David Wright). Says he was born free at Charles City, Virginia; served till 21 years of age with Berry Harden. Pass from Mr. Matthews, Mayor.

James Vallentyne, 33, [stout fellow], pockmarked, B, ([David Wright]). [Says he was born free.] Lived with John Studvelt, Prince George County, Virginia; left it 3 years ago. GBC.

Jane, 28, stout wench, ([David Wright]). Formerly the property of David Cooper of Nansemond, Virginia; left him 3 [years ago]. [GBC]

Prosperous Amelia
bound for [Port Roseway]
Thomas Atkinson

Sue, 25, [stout wench], (James Alexander). Property of James Alexander.

Thom Bolton, 52, stout fellow, (Cornelius Rapelje). [Formerly the property] of Thomas Bolton, [Nansemond, Virginia]; left him 6 [years ago]. [GBC]

Charles, 23, [stout fellow], (James Alexander). Property of James Alexander.

Anny Bolton, 42, stout wench, ([James Alexander]). [Formerly the property] of Thomas Bolton, [Nansemond, Virginia]; left him 6 [years ago]. [GBC]

Scipio, 31, stout fellow, (Mr. Potts). [Formerly the property] of Philip Scuyler, Albany; left him 3 1/2 [years ago]. GMC.

Jenny Bolton, 11, stout girl, ([Mr. Potts]). Property of Mr. Potts.

Brig *Nancy*
bound for Annapolis Royal
Mich Cunningham

Prince, 22, stout fellow, (Chaplain Brown). [Property] of Chaplain.

Betty Rapelje, 21, stout wench, (Peter Brown). Says she was born free at Newtown, Long Island; lived 6 years with Abraham Rapelje.

Jim, 4, fine boy, ([Peter Brown]). [Says he was born free at Newtown, Long Island; lived 6 years with Abraham Rapelje.]

Lydia, 20, stout wench, (Maj. Millidge). [Formerly the property] of William Hopton, Charlestown, South Carolina; left him 4 [years ago]. [GMC]

Peter, 40, stout fellow, (Peter Brown). [Formerly the property] of John Bour, Suffolk

County, Virginia; left him 4 [years ago]. [GMC]

Pompey, 32, [stout fellow] with a wife & 2 children, (Jonathan Clawson). Property of Jonathan Clawson.

Eliza Ward, 7, fine girl, (Ebenezer Ward). [Property] of Ebenezer Ward.

Ship *Nancy*
bound for St. John's
Capt. Hammond

Lewis, 45, stout fellow, (Ben Lester). [Property] of Benjamin Lester.

Letitia, 16, stout wench, M, ([Ben Lester]). [Property of Benjamin Lester.]

Sam, 15, stout lad, B, ([Ben Lester]). [Property of Benjamin Lester.]

Hannibal, 11, [stout] boy, ([Ben Lester]). [Property of Benjamin Lester.]

Gill, 8, [stout boy], ([Ben Lester]). [Property of Benjamin Lester.]

Cuff Ben, 40, stout, thick set man (Jehiel Portelous). [Formerly the property] of George Ben of Norfolk, Virginia; left him 5 [years ago]. GBC.

John Walker, 34, stout fellow, M, (Matthew Portelous).

[Formerly the property] of John Ben of Nansemond, [Virginia]; left him 5 [years ago]. [GBC]

Grace Walker, 50, [stout] wench with a child 5 months old, ([Matthew Portelous]). [Formerly the property] of James Naylor, Hampton County, [Virginia]; left him 5 [years ago]. [GBC]

John & Jane
[*no destination*]
William Dawson

Francis, 40, very stout big fellow, B, (John Hajeman). [Formerly the property] of Samuel Moore, Newtown, Long Island, who has given him his freedom as per paper produced.

Ephraim, 60, stout man of his age, (Ludwick Syphle). Freeborn Indian.

Casar, 25, stout fellow, (Cornelius Van Dyne). Property of Cornelius Van Dyne.

William
bound for Port Roseway
Thomas Potts

Peggy, 20, stout wench, (Daniel Blair). [Formerly the property] of Major Robinson, Rappahannock, Virginia; left him 3 [years ago].

Grace, 7, fine girl, (John Turner). Born free. Indented to John Turner for 10 years from 18 February 1783.

Adam, 21, stout set fellow, (Adam Sutherland). [Formerly the property] of George Rivers of James's Island, South Carolina, who sold him to Adam Sutherland.

Vulean, 18, stout fellow, (Robert Andrews). Property of Robert Andrews.

Mercury
bound for St. John's
Thomas Dawson

Harry, 12, fine boy, (Samuel Peters). [Property] of Samuel Peters.

Phillis, 14, stout wench, (Charles Hale). [Property] of Charles Hale.

Peg, 22, [stout wench], (Sam Dickenson). [Property] of Samuel Dickenson.

Charming Nancy
bound for Port Roseway
John Clark

Toby Sams, 25, stout fellow, pock marked, (Lt. Serjeant). Formerly the property of William Sams of John's Island, South Carolina; left him 4 years ago. GBC.

Rebecca Izzard, 26, stout wench, ([Lt. Serjeant]). [Formerly the property] of Ralph Izzard, Esq. [of South Carolina]; left him 4 [years ago]. [GBC]

Nanny, 35, [stout wench], (Capt. Hickford). [Formerly the property] of Austin Graham, 9 Partners, New York Province; left him 7 [years ago]. [GBC]

Stephen Pottle, 26, stout fellow, M, (Thomas Dalton). [Formerly the property] of William Miles of Oyster Bay who died 4 years ago & left him free.

Lydia Johnson, 30, stout wench, (Lt. Serjeant). [Formerly the property] of John Brown, 9 Partners; left him 3 [years ago]. [GBC]

Clinton
bound for Port Roseway
Lt. Trounce

Hannah, 60, mulatto wench, (John Hoser). Free. Formerly slave to William Hilton, parish of Westmoreland, Island of Jamaica.

Samuel Croaker, 21, ordinary fellow, (Hugh Walker). Formerly slave to Richard Goff, South Carolina; left him in the year 1780. GBC.

Samuel Atkinson, 21, [ordinary fellow], ([Hugh Walker]).

[Formerly slave] to Joseph Atkinson, [South Carolina; left him in the year 1780]. [GBC]

Samuel White, 30, [ordinary fellow], ([Hugh Walker]). [Formerly slave] to William White, Port Royal, South Carolina; [left him in the year] 1779; joined the troops at Savannah. [GBC]

Minty Atkinson, 21, stout wench, ([Hugh Walker]). [Formerly slave] to William Sabbs, [South Carolina; left him in the year 1780] after the siege of Charlestown. [GBC]

Peggy Croaker, 24, ordinary wench, ([Hugh Walker]). Formerly slave to Jacob Garret, [South Carolina; left him in the year] 1779 & joined the troops at Savannah. [GBC]

Peggy White, 40, [ordinary wench], ([Hugh Walker]). [Formerly slave] to William White, Port Royal, [South Carolina; left him in the year] 1779 & joined the troops. [GBC]

Grand Dutchess of Russia **bound for [Port Roseway] Stephen Holman**

Plato, 20, stout fellow, (John Marshall). Property of John Marshall.

Richard Sloane, 40, [stout fellow], ([John Marshall]).

Born free at Rocky Hill in Jersey; left that three years ago.

Molly, 45, stout wench, ([John Marshall]). Free as certified from the Reverend Dr. Sayre.

Sally, 40, [stout wench], (Elliot). Property of Elliot.

John Warren, 45, stout fellow, (Isaac Read). [Formerly slave] to Mr. Warren of Antigua who gave him his freedom.

Dinah Archer, 42, stout wench, one eyed, (Mrs. Savage). [Formerly slave] to John Bayne, Norfolk County, Virginia; left him 5 years ago.

Basan Vaughan, 25, (Isaac Read). [Formerly slave] to William Vaughan of South Carolina.

Bill, 25, stout ugly fellow, (William Douglas). Property of William Douglas.

Leah, 4, fine child, (Isaac Reed). [Property] of William Wilbank, King's pilot.

Lilly, 30, stout wench, ([Isaac Reed]). [Property of William Wilbank, King's pilot.]

Caron **bound for Annapolis Royal David Balmanno**

Nancy, 23, [stout wench], (Alexander Haight). [Formerly

slave] to Stephen Tankard, Norfolk, Virginia; left him 5 years ago. GMC.

Anny Walters, 25, [stout wench], (Leonard Tarrant). [Formerly slave] to Lambert Reddick, Suffolk, [Virginia; left him 5 years ago]. [GMC]

Aberdeen, 40, stout fellow, (John Hicks). [Formerly slave] to Mary Bridger, Smithfield, Isle of Wight, Virginia; left her 8 [years ago]. GBC.

Nancy Aberdeen, 24, stout wench with 2 children, one 2 years the other 2 months, ([John Hicks]). [Formerly slave] to George Ben of Nansemond, [Virginia; left him] 8 [years ago]. [GBC]

Philip Morgan, 35, stout fellow, (Joseph Marvin). [Formerly slave] to William Molden, Cecil County, Maryland; [left him] 7 [years ago]. [GBC]

Robert Bias, 20, [stout fellow], (John Hicks). Born free; lived with Mr. Handford, Smithfield, Isle of Wight, Virginia; left him 4 months ago. GBC.

Friar, 30, [stout fellow], ([John Hicks]). [Formerly slave] to Hassen Pendtree, South Carolina; left him 4 years ago. GBC.

Jean, 15, stout wench, (Joseph Marvin). Property of Joseph Marvin.

Belinda, 43, [stout wench] with a boy 3 years old, (Gabriel Purdy). [Property] of Gabriel Purdy.

Sue, 21, stout wench, ([Gabriel Purdy]). [Property of Gabriel Purdy.]

Ned Moore, 45, stout fellow, ([Gabriel Purdy]). [Property of Gabriel Purdy.]

Peter, 19, [stout fellow], ([Gabriel Purdy]). [Property of Gabriel Purdy.]

Casar, 26, [stout fellow], (John Hicks). [Property] of John Hicks.

Joseph Gaul, 25, [stout fellow], on his own footing. Born free; served untill 21 years with Thomas Young, Oyster Bay.

Naoma Gaul, 18, stout wench, on her own footing. [Born free; served untill 21 years] with John Townsend, [Oyster Bay].

Amelia Hopewell, 21, [stout wench], (Lt. McDonald). Property of Lieutenant McDonald.

Anson, 21, stout fellow, ([Lt. McDonald]). [Property of Lieutenant McDonald.]

Joe, 14, fine boy, (Daniel Odell). [Property] of Daniel Odell.

Bob, 7, [fine boy], (Isaac Cooper). [Property] of Isaac Cooper.

Abigail, 7, fine girl, (Jacob Beeber). [Property] of Jacob Beeber.

Ship *Nancy*
[*no destination*]
Capt. Hammond

Joe, 25, stout fellow, (Northrop Marpole). [Formerly slave] to Abraham Ackerman, Paramus, New Jersey; left him 5 years ago. GBC.

Margaret, 19, stout wench with a girl 3 years old, (Timothy Clows). Property of Timothy Clows.

Peter Mattocks, 40, stout fellow, ([Timothy Clows]). [Formerly slave] to Andrew Lyons, Province of New York.

Ship *Friendship*
bound for Port Roseway
Charles Coldstream

Bob, 19, stout fellow, (James Frazer). Property of James Fraser.

Lilly, 12, fine girl, ([James Frazer]). [Property of James Fraser.]

Captain, 15, stout lad, M, (John Graff). [Property] of John Graff.

Bet, 10, stout girl, (John de Young). Property of John de Young.

Lord Townsend
bound for Annapolis Royal
James Hog

Samuel Penilack, 25, stout fellow, M, (Ens. Taylor). Formerly slave to Peter Schenck, Milstone, New Jersey; left him 7 years ago. GBC.

Sampson, 30, [stout fellow], B, (Capt. Raymond). [Formerly slave] to Robert McReady, Head of Elk; [left him] 7 [years ago]. [GBC]

Joe, 52, [stout fellow], (Major Tympany). [Formerly slave] to George Culbert of Savannah, Georgia; [left him] 7 [years ago]. GMC.

Jack, 28, [stout fellow], ([Major Tympany]). [Formerly slave] to William Moore, Dorchester, South Carolina; [left him] 8 [years ago]. GBC.

Rachel, 28, [stout] wench, (2nd Mast. Cloud). Born free nigh Flushing, Long Island; lived with Capt. Hicks.

Ned, 20, [stout] fellow, (Maj. John Vandyke). Property of Major John Vandyke.

Abraham, 23, [stout fellow], (Capt. Bowen). [Formerly

slave] to James Smith, Charlestown, South Carolina; left him in 1779. GMC.

Jack, 60, [stout fellow], (Major Tympany). [Formerly slave] to Samuel Covenhoven, Hackensack, New Jersey; [left him] 4 years ago.

Pompey Campbell, 50, ordinary fellow, (Capt. Thomas). [Formerly slave] to Arthur Campbell, Norfolk, Virginia; [left him] in 1776.

Sharper Cole, 20, likely lad, (Col. Cole). The Colonel's own property; certified by Office of Police.

Anthony Butler, 18, [likely lad], (Joseph Munford). [Formerly slave] to Captain Carter, 56th; certified to be free by General Birch.

Abraham Robertson, 15, [likely boy], (Capt. McDonald). [Formerly slave] to Col. Robertson, Virginia; left him 3 years ago. GMC.

Moses Caswell, 28, stout fellow, (Joseph Munford). [Formerly slave] to Col. Caswell, North Carolina; [left him] in the year 1780. GBC.

Sally, 10, ordinary wench, (Capt. Raymond). Capt. Raymond's property; certified by the Office of Police.

Susannah, 14, [ordinary wench], (Major Tympany).

[Formerly slave] to Dr. Middleton, Savannah; left him in the year 1780. GMC.

Sarah, 12, [ordinary wench], ([Major Tympany]). [Formerly slave to Dr. Middletown, Savannah; left him in the year 1780. GMC.]

Silvia, 30, [ordinary wench], (Col. Cole). Proved to be the Colonel's property by Certificate from Police.

Annie, 17, [ordinary wench], ([Col. Cole]). [Proved to be the Colonel's property by Certificate from Police.]

Abraham, 3, small boy, ([Col. Cole]). [Proved to be the Colonel's property by Certificate from Police.]

Flora Robins, 35, ordinary wench, (Major Tympany). [Formerly slave] to Dr. Middleton, Savannah; left him in the year 1780. GBC.

Tom Domaresh, 20, ordinary fellow, ([Major Tympany]). [Formerly slave] to John Demarsh, Hackensack, New Jersey; left him 5 years ago. GMC.

James Nicols, 27, stout fellow, (Col. Cole). [Formerly slave] to Philip Nichols, Fairfield, Connecticut; [left him] near 5 [years ago]. GBC.

Jenny Perry, 40, ordinary wench, (Capt. Hutten).

[Formerly slave] to Daniel Perry, Hackensack, New Jersey; [left him] 5 [years ago]. GMC.

Betts, 30, [ordinary wench]. Capt. John Longstreet, claimant. Capt. Longstreet's property proved.

Phillis, 15, likely wench. [Capt. John Longstreet, claimant. Capt. Longstreet's property proved.]

James, 19, stout fellow. Robert Cook, claimant. Robert Cook's property proved.

Kate, 50, ordinary wench, (Capt. Thomas). [Formerly slave] to Mr. Parks, James River, Virginia; [left him] in the year 1779. GBC.

Bill, 15, likely boy, (Lt. McLeod). Lieut. McLeod's property per the Major's Certificate & Bill of Sale.

Rachel, 32, ordinary wench, ([Lt. McLeod]). [Lieut. McLeod's property per the Major's Certificate & Bill of Sale.]

Clinton
bound for Port Roseway
Lt. Trounce

Nan, 7, fine girl, (Samuel Davenport). Property of Samuel Davenport.

Bet, 5, [fine girl], ([Samuel Davenport]). [Property of Samuel Davenport.]

Silvia, 30, stout wench, (James Collins). [Property] of James Collins.

Mary, 14, [stout wench], (Dr. Henry Mallow). [Property] of Henry Mallow.

Elizabeth, 24, stout wench with a small child, (Francis Wood). [Property] of Francis Wood.

Jude, 9, fine girl, ([Francis Wood]). [Property of Francis Wood.]

Jack, 15, stout lad, M, ([Francis Wood]). [Property of Francis Wood.]

William & Mary
bound for Halifax
William Moore, Master

Achabee, 60, stout fellow, (Dr. Bullen). Property of Dr. Bullen.

Catharina, 60, old stout wench, ([Dr. Bullen]). [Property of Dr. Bullen.]

Jenny, 40, stout wench, ([Dr. Bullen]). [Property of Dr. Bullen.]

Prince, 30, stout fellow, ([Dr. Bullen]). [Property of Dr. Bullen.]

Katy, 6, fine girl, ([Dr. Bullen]). [Property of Dr. Bullen.]

L'Abondance
bound for Port Roseway
Lt. Philips

Silvia, 30, stout wench, (Valentine Nutter). [Property] of Valentine Nutter.

Eve, 64, [stout wench], (Henry Guest). [Property] of Henry Guest.

Daniel, 13, stout boy, (William Black). [Property] of William Black.

Patty Turner, 23, stout wench, (Rob Thomson). Formerly slave to Willis Wilkinson, Nansemond, Virginia; left him 6 years ago. GBC.

David Lokes, 30, stout fellow, ([Rob Thomson]). [Formerly slave] to William Booker, Westbranch, [Virginia; left him 3 years ago]. [GBC]

Hester Wilkinson, 50, stout wench, (Andrew Murray). [Formerly slave] to Willis Wilkinson, Pigs point, Virginia. [GBC]

John Woodie, 23, stout lad, (John Tier). [Formerly slave] to Garabrands Van Houter, Totowa, New Jersey; [left him] 3 [years ago]. [GBC]

Nat Turner, 30, stout fellow, (Robert Thomson). [Formerly slave] to Pas Turner, Nansemond, Virginia; [left him] 5 [years ago]. [GBC]

Jacob Richards, 57, [stout fellow], (Benjamin Hart). [Formerly slave] to John Richards, Barbadoes Neck, New Jersey; [left him] in 1776. GMC.

Betty Richards, 55, stout wench, ([Benjamin Hart]). [Formerly slave to John Richards, Barbadoes Neck, New Jersey; left him in 1776. GMC.]

Sarah, 17, [stout wench], (Mrs. Johnson). [Property] of Mrs. Johnson.

Casar, 27, stout fellow, ([Mrs. Johnson]). [Property of Mrs. Johnson.]

Sam, 22, [stout fellow], tall, (Valentine Nutter). [Property] of Valentine Nutter.

Robert & Elizabeth
bound for Annapolis
John Milbank

Tempe, 9, likely wench, (Capt. Williams). [Property] of Capt. Williams; police certificate.

Sibbe, 11, [likely wench], (Moses Ward). [Property] of Moses Ward.

Jason
bound for St. John's
Thomas Appleby

Tamar, 13, ordinary wench, (Gilbert Pugsley). [Property] of Gilbert Pugsley.

Tom, 22, stout fellow, (Joseph Allen). [Property] of Joseph Allen.

Joe Miller, 12, likely boy, (Moses Miller). [Property] of Moses Miller.

Mary
bound for Port Roseway
George Bell

Sarah, 20, [likely] wench, (James Bogart). [Property] of James Bogart.

Susannah, 1/2, infant, ([James Bogart]). [Property] of James Bogart.

Bill, 12, likely boy, (Aury Vanvoorst). [Property] of Aury Vanvoorst.

Harry, 30, ordinary fellow, (Capt. Akerman). [Property] of Capt. Akerman.

Sam, 40, [ordinary fellow], ([Capt. Akerman]). [Property] of Capt. Akerman.

Sam, 35, [ordinary fellow], ([Capt. Akerman]). [Property of Capt. Akerman.]

William & Mary
bound for Halifax
Anthony Moore

Clarinda, 19, stout wench, (Dr. Bullen). [Property] of Dr. Bullen. Formerly slave to Harry Boyd, South Carolina; left him 4 years ago.

Jupiter, 33, [stout] fellow, ([Dr. Bullen]). [Property of Dr. Bullen.]

Nancy, 25, stout wench, ([Dr. Bullen]). [Property of Dr. Bullen.]

Sarah, 1/2, infant, ([Dr. Bullen]). [Property of Dr. Bullen.]

Diana, 22, ordinary wench, ([Dr. Bullen]). [Property of Dr. Bullen.]

Neptune
bound for St. John's
Sam Bilson

Sam, 15, [ordinary] lad, (Lt. Pleace). Formerly slave to Samuel Clark, South Carolina; left him in the year 1780.

Pleasant, 35, [ordinary] wench, (John McKee). [Formerly slave] to Elliphalet Lockwood, Norwalk, Connecticut; left him 4 years ago. GBC.

James, 1 1/2, infant, ([John McKee]). Born within the British lines.

York, 35, ordinary fellow,
(William Lewis). [Formerly
slave] to Tobias Green, Blue
Point, Long Island; [left him]
about 5 years ago.

Nancy
bound for Port Roseway
Rob Bruce

Prince, 20, stout fellow,
(Samuel Kirk). [Formerly
slave] to Joseph Mayo, James
River, Virginia; left him with
Gen. Arnold in 1781. GMC.

Ibby, 24, ordinary wench,
([Samuel Kirk]). Certified to
be free by General Birch.

Harry, 2, infant, ([Samuel
Kirk]). [Certified to be free by
General Birch.]

John Fortune, 62, ordinary
fellow, (Richard Boll).
[Formerly slave] to John
Bruckle, Virginia; left him 5
years ago. GBC.

Kate, 50, [ordinary] wench,
(Richard Boll). [Formerly
slave to John Bruckle,
Virginia; left him] with her
husband. [GBC]

L'Abondance
bound for Port Roseway
Lt. Philips

Eve, 56, stout wench, (Francis
Howse). Property of Francis
Howse.

Mary Johnson, 18, stout
wench, M, (John Tier). Born
free at New Rochelle.

Michael
bound for Annapolis
James Bishop

Ming, 26, stout fellow, (John
Morrison). Formerly slave to
Mr. Reynolds, Rhode Island
Government; left him with the
troops evacuating that
Garrison.

Mary Ann, 22, ordinary wench,
([John Morrison]). Born free;
from New Port Glasgow in
Scotland.

Tom, 26, stout fellow, (John
Ryerson). John Ryerson's
property proved.

Priscilla, 32, stout wench,
([John Ryerson]). [John
Ryerson's property proved.]

Sam, 2, an infant, ([John
Ryerson]). [John Ryerson's
property proved.]

Sarah, 22, stout wench, M,
(Francis Ryerson). Francis
Ryerson's [property proved].

Judith, 40, ordinary wench,
(Mrs. VanHorn). Mrs.
VanHorn's [property].

Dinah, 28, stout wench, (Capt.
Hornbrook). Capt. Hornbrook's
[property].

Cato, 2, an infant, (Capt. Hornbrook). Capt. Hornbrook's [property].

Cows, 22, ordinary fellow, M, (Mr. VanHorn). Mr. VanHorn's [property].

Sam, 22, [ordinary fellow], M, ([Mr. VanHorn]). [Mr. VanHorn's property.]

**Ship *Hope*
bound for [Annapolis]
Mat O'Brien**

Molly, 16, likely wench, M, (Daniel Hammond). Formerly slave to Dr. Taylor, Virginia; left him 4 years ago.

Mary, 20, [likely wench], B, (Capt. Polhemus). Property of Capt. Polhemus.

Dinah, 1/2, infant, ([Capt. Polhemus]). [Property of Capt. Polhemus.]

Elizabeth, 26, stout wench, (Capt. Hicks). [Property] of Capt. Hicks.

Tim, 1/2, infant, ([Capt. Hicks]). [Property of Capt. Hicks.]

Jack, 10, ordinary boy, ([Capt. Hicks]). [Property of Capt. Hicks.]

Phillis, 6, likely child, ([Capt. Hicks]). [Property of Capt. Hicks.]

William, 20, stout fellow, ([Capt. Hicks]). [Property of Capt. Hicks.]

Quaco, 22, [stout fellow], (Thomas Bannister). [Property] of Thomas Bannister.

Casar, 50, ordinary fellow, (Lt. Knipsgheld). Formerly slave to Casparus Maybee, Orangetown; left him 7 years ago. GMC.

Dick, 11, likely boy, (John Moore). Property of John Moore.

Lizzy Martin, 50, worn out, (Thomas Baldwin). Formerly slave to Benjamin Fowler, Horseshoe, South Carolina; left him early in 1780. GBC.

Sarah Allman, 20, likely wench, (Phil Adams). [Formerly slave] to Phil Allman, Savannah; left him at the siege of that place. [GBC]

Sam Van Wart, 44, ordinary fellow, (Thomas Rapelje). [Formerly slave] to Jacob Van Wart, Phillipsburgh, West Chester County, New York Province.

Rachel, 40, [ordinary] wench, ([Thomas Rapelje]). Free born.

Susannah, 11, likely child, ([Thomas Rapelje]). [Free born.]

Cudjoe Thomas, 40, ordinary fellow, (Daniel Hammond). Formerly slave to William

Thomas, South Carolina; left him in 1779 at the Siege of Savannah. GBC.

William Martin, 13, likely boy, (Thomas Baldwin). [Formerly slave] to Benjamin Fowler, South Carolina; left him early in 1780. [GBC]

John, 26, ordinary fellow, (Joseph Montgomery). Property of Joseph Montgomery.

Trepassey
bound for Fort Cumberland

Tom, 26, [ordinary fellow], (Capt. Palmer). [Formerly slave] to Tunis Denyse, Monmouth County, New Jersey; left him early in 1778.

Nero, 15, likely lad, ([Capt. Palmer]). Property of Capt. Palmer.

Jarvis, 22, [likely] fellow, ([Capt. Palmer]). [Formerly slave] to Isaac Frost, Cortlandts Manor; left him 4 years ago.

John, 23, [likely fellow], (Martin Clany). [Formerly slave] to Thomas Jacks, Virginia; left him 4 years ago by virtue of proclamation.

Jane, 33, ordinary wench, (Capt. Palmer). [Formerly slave] to Joseph Foster, Long Sing, Westchester County, New York Province; left him 4 years ago.

Mary, 17, likely wench, M, (Capt. Forshemy). Free born in the Captain's family.

---

3 October 1783

Joseph
bound for Annapolis
James Mitchel

Joe, 10, stout boy. Gilbert Tippet of Annapolis, claimant. (Gilbert Tippet). Property of Gilbert Tippet.

Nancy, 11, incurably lame, [Gilbert Tippet of Annapolis, claimant]. ([Gilbert Tippet]). [Property of Gilbert Tippet.]

---

7 October 1783

Kingston
bound for Port Roseway
John Atkinson

Lucy, 26, stout wench, (James Strahan). Formerly slave of Henry Scudder, East End of Long Island; left him in the year 1775. GBC. GMC.

Priscilla, 7, fine child, ([James Strahan]). Daughter to the above wench.

Eleanor Cross, 11, fine girl, (Joseph White). Born free; indented for 10 years by David Matthews to James White.

Hannah, 23, stout wench, (John Patton). Property of John Patton.

Jane Samson, 52, [stout wench], on her own footing. Born free at Morrisanaie.

Catharine, 25, sick, [on her own footing]. Daughter to the above.

Hannah, 21, stout pockmarked wench, (Patrick Wall). Property of Patrick Wall.

John Thomas, 15, stout lad, ([Patrick Wall]). [Property of Patrick Wall.]

Cuff Cummins, 24, stout fellow, (John Patton). [Formerly slave] of Mr. F__n of Philadelphia; left him 5 1/2 years ago. GBC.

Lettia, 5, fine child, (Patrick Wall). Property of Patrick Wall.

Selina
bound for [Port Roseway]
John McGee

Casar, 40, thin fellow, (Mr. Jenkins). [Property] of Mr. Jenkins.

Robert, 30, stout fellow, (Lawrence Van Buskirk). [Property] of Lawrence Buskirk.

Sally, 19, stout wench, (D. Landy). [Formerly slave] to

Mrs. Parker who left her free at New York about three years ago.

Dinah, 38, [stout wench], (L.V. Buskirk). Property of L.V. Buskirk.

Dinah, 20, [stout wench], (Richard Jenkins). [Property] of Richard Jenkins.

George, 14, stout boy, ([Richard Jenkins]). [Property of Richard Jenkins.]

Poll, 16, stout girl, (William Summers). [Property] of William Summers.

Brig *Hopewell*
bound for [Port Roseway]
George Garbut

Katy Profit, 32, stout wench, (James Dole). [Formerly slave] to Richard Van Dam of Stotterdam.

Joe, 8, child of the above wench, ([James Dole]).

Daniel, 9 months, child of the above wench [*Katy Profit*], ([James Dole]).

Edward Wan, 30, stout fellow, (Cook of the *Hopewell*). [Formerly slave] to Peter Delancey who gave him his freedom 12 years ago.

George Travelle, 23, [stout fellow], (Caleb Morgan). Born

free; formerly lived at Huntington, Long Island.

Mary
bound for St. John's
Thomas Rowbottom

Peg, 16, stout girl, lame of one leg, (George McCall). Property of George McCall.

Sally
bound for [St. John's]
William Bell

Moses Thompson, 20, stout fellow, (Justice Sherwood). Born free at Philadelphia; his father & mother free.

Mary, 36, stout wench, (John Van Winkle). Property of John Van Winkle.

Sally, 6 months old, children of the above wench, ([John Van Winkle]). [Property of John Van Winkle.]

Jackey, 3, children of the above wench [*Mary*], ([John Van Winkle]). [Property of John Van Winkle.]

Abraham, 30, ([John Van Winkle]). [Formerly slave] to Lewis Sniffon, Philips Manor; left him 7 years ago.

William Etherington, 13, stout boy, ([John Van Winkle]). [Formerly slave] to Col. Etherington; sold by Capt.

Munro, British Legion, to John Van Winkle which had no right to do.

Ned, 40, stout fellow, (Richard Carman). Property of Richard Carman.

Jenny, 40, stout wench, ([Richard Carman]). [Property of Richard Carman.]

Alexander
bound for [St. John's]
Roger Alderson

Cairo, 20, [stout wench], (James Peters). [Property] of James Peters.

Bella, 14, [stout wench], ([James Peters]). [Property of James Peters.]

Esther, 18, [stout wench], M, (Bartholomew Cranell). [Property] of Bartholomew Crannell.

Sam, 35, ([Bartholomew Cranell]). [Property of Bartholomew Crannell.]

Robert, 36, stout fellow, ([Bartholomew Cranell]). [Formerly slave] to Isaack Conklin, 9 Partners; left him 2 years ago.

Pompey, 25, [stout fellow], on his own bottom. Born free.

Prince of Orange
bound for Port Roseway
Thomas McCaull

William, 51, [stout fellow], (James Bergen). [Formerly slave] to William Robertson, Westmoreland, Virginia; taken by some whaleboats about 10 months ago.

Brig *Kingston*
bound for [Port Roseway]
J. Atkinson

William Ernist, 31, ordinary fellow, (Lt. Sullivan). Certified to be free by Charles Philips, Cooper in Broad Street in New York, with whom he served his time and by the office of Police.

Jane Cook, 41, [ordinary], M, ([Lt. Sullivan]). [Certified to be free] by her former Master, Thomas Ludlow, Jr., C. of New York & by GMC.

Sloop *Elk*
bound for Port Mattoon
Peter Slack

Grace, 26, stout wench, (W.M. General Dept.). [Formerly slave] to Richard Drew, Pennsylvania; left him with the British troops leaving Philadelphia.

Betsey, 22, ordinary [wench], ([W.M. General Dept.]). Born free, Southampton, Virginia; served her time to Richard Barrow.

Isabella, 22, [ordinary wench], ([W.M. General Dept.]). [Formerly slave] to Thomas White, Charlestown, South Carolina; left him before the siege of that town in 1780.

Molly, 21, likely wench, ([W.M. General Dept.]). [Formerly slave] to William Elliot, [Charlestown, South Carolina; left him before the siege of that town in 1780].

Jane, 24, ordinary wench, M, ([W.M. General Dept.]). Born free at Middletown, New Jersey.

Sukey, 21, stout wench, (W.M. General Dept.). Formerly slave to Thomas Smith, Charlestown, South Carolina; left him after the Siege in 1780.

Sukey, 21, ordinary wench, M, ([W.M. General Dept.]). Born free in the City of New York.

Fanny, 25, [ordinary wench], ([W.M. General Dept.]). [Formerly slave] to John Hope, Southampton, Virginia; left him in the year of 1779 & joined the British.

Katy, 22, stout wench, ([W.M. General Dept.]). [Formerly slave] to Mr. Lawrence of Charlestown, South Carolina; left him before the siege of said town & joined the British troops.

Mary, 17, ordinary [wench], ([W.M. General Dept.]). [Formerly slave] to Isaac Johnson of Philadelphia; left him & joined the British Troops in 1778.

Betty, 1, infant, ([W.M. General Dept.]). Born within the British lines.

Elijah, 1/2, [infant], ([W.M. General Dept.]). [Born within the British lines.]

Sukey, 1/2, [infant], ([W.M. General Dept.]). [Born within the British lines.]

---

11 October 1783

Inspected by Captains Gilfillan & Armstrong, Lieutenant Colonel Smith & Samuel Jones, Esquire, Secretary.

Mid Summer Blossom
bound for Halifax
Will Rayon

Kate, 16, stout wench, (Dr. Russell, 33 Reg't.). Formerly slave to Isaac Waite, John's Island, South Carolina; left him in 1779.

Will Hicks, 12, stout boy, M, ([Dr. Russell, 33 Reg't.]). Says he was born free at Port Royal, South Carolina; stolen from

thence by a Capt. McDonald, Master of a ship.

Solomon, 25, stout fellow, (Capt. Stewart, 33 [Reg't.]). [Formerly slave] to Chief Justice Howard of North Carolina; now understood to be property of Miss Howard, his daughter.

Dick, 21, [stout] fellow, (Lieut. Harvey, [33 Reg't.]). Formerly servant to John White, Charlestown; says he was born free.

Nancy, 37, stout wench, (Dr. Russell, [33 Reg't.]). [Formerly slave] to Isaac Waite, John's Island, South Carolina; left him in 1779. GBC.

Bristol, 25, stout fellow, ([Dr. Russell, 33 Reg't.]). [Formerly slave] to Isaac Waite, John's Island, South Carolina; left him in 1779.

Dutchess of Gordon
bound for [Halifax]
James Holmes, Master

William Simpson, 45, [stout fellow], (42nd Reg't.). [Formerly slave] to Benjamin Singleton, Charlestown, South Carolina; left him before the siege in 1780.

John Brown, 30, [stout fellow], (42nd Reg't.). [Formerly slave] to Peter Buckie, [Charlestown,

South Carolina; left him before the siege in 1780].

Punch, 25, [stout fellow], ([42nd Reg't.]). [Formerly slave] to Peter Porcher, [Charlestown, South Carolina; left him before the siege in 1780].

Saucy Ben
bound for [Halifax]
James Miller

Mingo Shiels, 24, [stout fellow], ([42nd Reg't.]). [Formerly slave] to Samuel Shiels, Portsmouth, [Virginia; left him] in the year 1780.

Sam McLeod, 29, [stout fellow], ([42nd Reg't.]). [Formerly slave] to Dr. Walter McLeod, Hampton, [Virginia; left him in the year 1780].

Rhinoceros
bound for [Halifax]

Whitehaven, 30, [stout fellow], ([42nd Reg't.]). [Formerly slave] to [blank] near Norfolk, [Virginia; left him in the year 1780].

---

14 October 1783

Sloop *Cato*
bound for Annapolis Royal

Joe Freeman, 35, [stout fellow], (Stephen Freeman). [Formerly slave] to Joseph Freeman, Little York; [left him] 4 years ago. GMC.

Ben Freebody, 35, ordinary fellow, ([Stephen Freeman]). [Formerly slave] to Samuel Freebody, New Port, Rhode Island; [left him] 7 [years ago]. [GMC]

John Doore, 50, stout fellow, ([Stephen Freeman]). [Formerly slave] to Dr. Ross, Prince George's County, Maryland; left him 4 years ago. [GMC]

William Freeman, 30, ordinary fellow, ([Stephen Freeman]). [Formerly slave] to Capt. Gayton, Royal Navy; says the Captain gave him his freedom. GBC.

Vigo, 30, stout fellow, ([Stephen Freeman]). Free by his former master as Certified by Justice Hamlin, Middletown, Connecticut.

James Brown, 21, [stout fellow], (Isaac Sweezie). [Formerly slave] to William Williamson, Black Swamp, South Carolina; left him 5 years ago. GBC.

Titus, 28, [stout fellow], (Stephen Sneadon). Property of Stephen Sneadon as per Bill of Sale.

Abigail, 20, stout wench, ([Stephen Sneadon]). [Property of Stephen Sneadon as per Bill of Sale.]

Massey Astin, 30, [stout wench], (Jacob Ross). [Formerly slave] to Joseph Tankins, Dutchess County, New York Province; [left him] 6 years ago. [GBC]

Nancy King, 19, ordinary [wench], (Widow Boyd). [Formerly slave] to Widow Campbell, Hampton, Virginia; [left her] 6 years ago. [GBC]

Joseph, 30, [ordinary] fellow, (John Moore). John Moore's property.

Timothy, 33, [ordinary fellow], (Jacob Frost). Property of Charles Thorne, Musquito Cove, Long Island.

**Sloop *Skuldham*
bound for [Annapolis Royal]
James Nicholson**

Cato, 35, stout fellow, (Godfrey Wainwood). Free.

Rose Wansworth, 30, [stout] wench, 2 children 12 & 5 years of age, ([Godfrey Wainwood]). [Formerly slave] to Daniel

Russel of New port, Rhode Island; left him 7 years ago.

Casar, 51, ordinary fellow, (Mrs. Grant). Property of Mrs. Grant by Bill of Sale.

Bill, 14, fine boy, ([Mrs. Grant]). Free.

Daniel, 5, fine boy, ([Mrs. Grant]). Free.

Hannah, 30, stout wench with child 2 years old, ([Mrs. Grant]). Free.

Yast Benson, 24, stout fellow, (Ephraim Stanford). [Formerly slave] to Sampson Benson of Haerlem; left him 7 years ago. [GBC]

Jenny, 20, fine wench with 2 children, 2 years old & one 1 month, (William Mot). Free.

Jane, 17, fine wench, (Bartholomew Haynes). [Formerly slave] to Bartholomew Gidney of White Plains; Haynes property by Bill of Sale.

Margaret, 15, [fine wench], (James Irwin). Property of James Irwin by Bill of Sale.

James Jackson, 36, ordinary fellow, (John Smith). [Formerly slave] to Silas Holly of Stamford, Connecticut; left him 7 years ago. [GBC]

Betsey Jackson, 16, fine girl, ([John Smith]). Free born.

---

15 October 1783

**Ship *Betsey*
bound for Annapolis Royal
William Gallillee**

Amy Ash, 26, stout wench, M, (John Hinzman). Free born.

Jim, 8, fine boy, ([John Hinzman]). Free born.

Jack, 22, stout fellow, ([John Hinzman]). Formerly slave to Mr. Furman, Prince George County, Virginia; left him 6 years. GBC.

Letitia, 25, squat stout wench, (Elias Bolner). Property of Elias Bolner per Bill of Sale produced.

Flanders Goff, 20, stout fellow, (William Young). [Formerly slave] to Richard Goff, Charlestown, South Carolina; [left] him 4 [years]. [GBC]

Sabinah, 35, stout wench, (Basil Jackson). [Formerly slave] to Ben Stratton of the Eastern Shore, Virginia; [left him] 5 [years]. [GBC]

Sam, 5, child of the above wench, ([Basil Jackson]).

Beck, 1, [child of the above wench], ([Basil Jackson]).

Black Bill, 35, stout fellow, ([Basil Jackson]). [Formerly slave to Ben Stratton of the Eastern Shore, Virginia; left him 5 years.]

Aaron, 15, stout boy, (Oliver Hicks). Property of Oliver Hicks.

George, 19, stout lad, (Edward O'Brien). [Formerly slave] to Thomas Mills nigh Charlestown, South Carolina; [left him] 4 [years]. [GBC]

John, free.

Mima, [free].

Glasgow, 45, stout fellow, (James Rankin). [Formerly slave] to Ben Stratton, Eastern Shore, Virginia; [left him] 5 [years]. [GBC]

Silvia Ben, 30, ordinary, (John Lewis). [Formerly slave] to Capt. Miller of New York who gave her her freedom.

Cander, 8, children of the above wench, ([John Lewis]).

John, 2, [children of the above wench], ([John Lewis]).

John Been, 48, ([John Lewis]). [Formerly slave] to [*blank*] of [*blank*] at Esopus, Province of New York.

John Jackson, 22, stout fellow, (Isaac Bonnel, Esq.). [Formerly slave] to Mr. Bunion, Charlestown, South Carolina; left him in 1780 after the siege.

Tertullus, 41, [stout fellow], (Jonathan Kirk). Free born South Hole.

15 October 1783

Ship *Betsey*
bound for Annapolis Royal
William Gallillee

Amy Ash, 26, stout wench, M, (John Hinzman). Free born.

Jim, 8, fine boy, ([John Hinzman]). Free born.

Jack, 22, stout fellow, ([John Hinzman]). Formerly slave to Mr. Furman, Prince George County, Virginia; left him 6 years. GBC.

Letitia, 25, squat stout wench, (Elias Bolner). Property of Elias Bolner per Bill of Sale produced.

Flanders Goff, 20, stout fellow, (William Young). [Formerly slave] to Richard Goff, Charlestown, South Carolina; [left] him 4 [years]. [GBC]

Sabinah, 35, stout wench, (Basil Jackson). [Formerly slave] to Ben Stratton of the Eastern Shore, Virginia; [left him] 5 [years]. [GBC]

Sam, 5, child of the above wench, ([Basil Jackson]).

Beck, 1, [child of the above wench], ([Basil Jackson]).

Black Bill, 35, stout fellow, ([Basil Jackson]). [Formerly slave to Ben Stratton of the Eastern Shore, Virginia; left him 5 years.]

Aaron, 15, stout boy, (Oliver Hicks). Property of Oliver Hicks.

George, 19, stout lad, (Edward O'Brien). [Formerly slave] to Thomas Mills nigh Charlestown, South Carolina; [left him] 4 [years]. [GBC]

John, free.

Mima, [free].

Glasgow, 45, stout fellow, (James Rankin). [Formerly slave] to Ben Stratton, Eastern Shore, Virginia; [left him] 5 [years]. [GBC]

Silvia Ben, 30, ordinary, (John Lewis). [Formerly slave] to Capt. Miller of New York who gave her her freedom.

Cander, 8, children of the above wench, ([John Lewis]).

John, 2, [children of the above wench], ([John Lewis]).

John Been, 48, ([John Lewis]). [Formerly slave] to [*blank*] of [*blank*] at Esopus, Province of New York.

John Jackson, 22, stout fellow, (Isaac Bonnel, Esq.). [Formerly slave] to Mr. Bunion, Charlestown, South Carolina; left him in 1780 after the siege.

Tertullus, 41, [stout fellow], (Jonathan Kirk). Free born South Hole.

John Pomp, 24, stout fellow, ([B. Pioneers]). [Formerly servant] to John Morris, Portsmouth, Virginia; [left him] in 1779.

Jacob, 34, [stout fellow], ([B. Pioneers]). [Formerly servant] to Willis Wilkinson, Nansemond, [Virginia; left him] in 1779.

Bob Harrison, 21, likely fellow, ([B. Pioneers]). [Formerly servant] to Benjamin Harrison, James River, [Virginia; left him] in 1779.

Tom, 60, ordinary [fellow], ([B. Pioneers]). [Formerly servant] to Colonel Conner, Valley Forge, Pennsylvania; [left him] in 1777.

Abraham Lesslie, 31, stout fellow, ([B. Pioneers]). [Formerly servant] to Richard Quints, Upper Town Creek, North Carolina; [left him] in 1776.

Quash, 39, ordinary rascal, ([B. Pioneers]). [Formerly servant] to Parker Quints, [Upper Town Creek, North Carolina; left him] in 1776.

Prince, 30, [ordinary] fellow with a wooden leg, ([B. Pioneers]). [Formerly servant] to Mr. Spooner, Philadelphia; [left him] in 1777.

Will, 50, [ordinary fellow], ([B. Pioneers]). [Formerly servant]

to Mr. Scarborough, Norfolk, Virginia; [left him] in 1778.

Pleasant, 17, likely wench, ([B. Pioneers]). [Formerly servant] to Willis Wilkinson, Nansemond, Virginia; [left him] in 1778.

George, 1, ([B. Pioneers]). Born within the British Lines.

Harry, 3, ([B. Pioneers]). [Born within the British Lines.]

Molly, 40, ordinary wench, incurably lame of left arm, ([B. Pioneers]). Formerly slave to Mr. Hogwood, Great Bridge near Portsmouth, Virginia; [left him] in 1779.

Jenny, 9, ([B. Pioneers]). [Formerly slave to Mr. Hogwood, Great Bridge near Portsmouth, Virginia; left him in] 1779.

Joseph, 7, (Black Pioneers). Formerly slave to Mr. Hogwood, Great Bridge near Portsmouth, Virginia; left him in 1779.

Charlotte, 18, stout wench, ([Black Pioneers]). [Formerly slave] to Alexander Foreman, [Great Bridge near Portsmouth, Virginia; left him] in 1779.

Grace, 20, ordinary [wench], ([Black Pioneers]). [Formerly slave] to Col. Carter, James River, [Virginia; left him] in 1779.

Sally, 27, [ordinary wench], ([Black Pioneers]). [Formerly slave] to Samuel Ash, Edisto, South Carolina; left him in 1779.

Tom, 12 1/2, likely boy, ([Black Pioneers]). [Formerly slave to Samuel Ash, Edisto, South Carolina; left him in 1779.]

Lidia, 7, [likely] wench, ([Black Pioneers]). [Formerly slave to Samuel Ash, Edisto, South Carolina; left him in 1779.]

Phillister, 20, born dumb, ([Black Pioneers]). [Formerly slave] to Benjamin Harrison, James River, Virginia; [left him] in 1779.

Phillis, 20, likely wench, ([Black Pioneers]). [Formerly slave] to Willis Wilson, Portsmouth, [Virginia; left him] in 1778.

Sam, 10, [likely] boy, ([Black Pioneers]). [Formerly slave to Willis Wilson, Portsmouth, Virginia; left him in 1778.]

Johnny, 1/2, infant, ([Black Pioneers]). Born within the British Lines.

Sarah, 42, ordinary wench, stone blind, ([Black Pioneers]). [Formerly slave] to Lord Dunmore. [Left him in] 1776.

Betsey, 36, [ordinary wench], ([Black Pioneers]). [Formerly slave] to William Conner, Crane Island near Norfolk, Virginia; [left him] in 1778.

Prudence, 11, likely girl, ([Black Pioneers]). [Formerly slave to William Conner, Crane Island near Norfolk, Virginia; left him in 1778.]

Mary, 20, [likely] wench, ([Black Pioneers]). [Formerly slave to William Conner, Crane Island near Norfolk, Virginia; left him in 1778.]

Silvia, 55, ordinary [wench], worn out, ([Black Pioneers]). [Formerly slave] to Joseph Hunt, Charlestown, South Carolina; left his service 20 years ago. Says she is free.

Sally, 32, [ordinary wench], ([Black Pioneers]). [Formerly slave] to Isaac Waite, [Charlestown, South Carolina]; left him in 1779.

August, 7, likely boy, ([Black Pioneers]). [Formerly slave to Isaac Waite, Charlestown, South Carolina; left him in 1779.]

Dinah, 25, stout wench, ([Black Pioneers]). [Formerly slave] to Phil Phelix, Philadelphia; [left him] in 1778.

Pleasant, 26, ordinary wench, ([Black Pioneers]). [Formerly slave] to Col. Godfrey, Norfolk, Virginia; [left him] in 1778.

Lettius, 11, likely child, ([Black Pioneers]). [Formerly slave to Col. Godfrey, Norfolk, Virginia; left him in 1778.]

Ned, 6, likely boy, ([Black Pioneers]). [Formerly slave to Col. Godfrey, Norfolk, Virginia; left him in 1778.]

Fanny Brown, 40, stout lump of a wench, ([Black Pioneers]). [Formerly slave] to Robert Gilmore, [Norfolk, Virginia]; left her with Lord Dunmore in 1776.

Patty, 6, likely girl, ([Black Pioneers]). Born within the British Lines.

Nancy, 36, ordinary wench, ([Black Pioneers]). [Formerly slave] to George Walden, Charlestown, South Carolina; [left him] in 1776.

John, 4 months, [ordinary] fellow, ([Black Pioneers]). Born within the British Lines.

John Cockburn, 56, [ordinary fellow], ([Black Pioneers]). Born free as appears by General Birch's Certificate.

---

31 October 1783

Inspected by Captains Gilfillan & Armstrong & Lieutenant Col. Smith.

**Brig *Joseph*
bound for Port Mattoon
Ben Coward**

Dolly Wilkinson, 62, stout wench, on her own bottom. Formerly slave to Willis Wilkinson, Nansemond, Virginia; left him in 1779. GBC.

Villotte Miller, 34, [stout wench], (W.M. General Department). [Formerly slave] to Rose Lloyd, Philadelphia; [left] her in 1778. GMC.

Abram [Miller], 40, ordinary fellow, ([W.M. General Department]). [Formerly slave] to William Hudson, [Philadelphia; left him in 1778]. GMC.

Sam Hawkins, 25, stout fellow, ([W.M. General Department]). [Formerly slave] to John Hawkins of Rye, New England; [left him] in 1779. [GMC]

Amie Orphan, 8, likely girl, ([W.M. General Department]). [Formerly slave] to Mr. Hughes near Charlestown, South Carolina; [left him] in 1780. [GMC]

Brig *Elijah*
bound for [Port Mattoon]
Alexander Buchanon

Lieut. Col. Bridges, 43, ordinary fellow, lame, ([W.M. General Department]). Free as appears by [GMC].

Reuben Simmons, 37, stout fellow, ([W.M. General Department]). [Formerly slave] to Abraham Wilson, Carlisle County, Virginia; [left him] in 1781. [GMC]

William Davis, 30, ordinary fellow, ([W.M. General Department]). [Formerly slave] to Lewis Burnel Martin, James River, [Virginia; left him] in 1779. [GMC]

March Jones, 40, [ordinary fellow], ([W.M. General Department]). [Formerly slave] to Mr. Jones, Santee, South Carolina; [left him] in 1779. [GMC]

Paul Johnson, 21, stout fellow, ([W.M. General Department]). Says he was born free; lived with Able Noble, Sterling, New Jersey; left him in 1776. [GMC]

Cato, 23, likely fellow, ([W.M. General Department]). [Formerly slave] to Thomas Harris, City of New York, who says he got his freedom when his Master died.

John Mosely, 25, [likely fellow], ([W.M. General Department]). Lived with John Cunningham, Portsmouth, Virginia, as a freeman; left him in 1776. GMC.

Solomon Lawson, 30, stout fellow, ([W.M. General Department]). [Formerly slave] to Col. Anthony Lawson, Princess Ann County, Virginia; left him in 1776. [GMC]

William Dean, 62, ordinary fellow, ([W.M. General Department]). [Formerly slave] to William Dean, Crane Island, Virginia; [left him] in 1779. [GMC]

Levi Johnson, 26, [ordinary fellow], ([W.M. General Department]). [Formerly slave] to William Smith, Accomack County, Virginia; [left him in 1779]. [GMC]

John Ballamay, 38, stout fellow, ([W.M. General Department]). Certified to be free. GBC.

Jacob Rowan, 26, [stout fellow], ([W.M. General Department]). [Formerly slave] to Arthur Upshaw, Accomack County, [Virginia]; left him in 1778. [GBC]

Tom Hunter, 22, [stout fellow], ([W.M. General Department]). [Formerly slave] to Bessel Mosely, Norfolk, [Virginia; left him] in [1778]. GMC.

Jacob Watson, 27, ordinary fellow. Formerly slave to Philip Watson, Richmond County, Virginia; left him in 1776. GBC.

George Price, 40, [ordinary fellow]. [Formerly slave] to Richard Barrisworth, Charlestown, South Carolina; [left him] in 1780. GMC.

Thomas Freeman, 31, stout fellow. [Formerly slave] to John Roots, Gloster County, Virginia; [left him] in 1781. GBC.

Peter Robertson, 24, ordinary [fellow]. [Formerly slave] to Frederick Jay, New York; left him in 1779. [GBC]

Roger Scot, 57, [ordinary fellow]. [Formerly slave] to Lord Dunmore; says he got his freedom from Lord Dunmore.

Henry Calls, 22, stout fellow. [Formerly slave] to George Hellis, Nansemond, Virginia; left him in 1779. GMC.

James Rea, 24, ordinary [fellow] without legs. [Formerly slave] to George Wilk, Williamsburg, [Virginia; left him] in 1779. [GMC]

Robert Cain, 19, likely lad. [Formerly slave] to William Harriot, Georgetown, [Virginia; left him] in 1777.

Silas Bright, 26, stout fellow. [Formerly slave] to William

Fife, Norfolk, [Virginia; left him] in 1776. GBC.

George Johnson, 29, ordinary fellow. Says he was free; served his time at Sterling Ironworks. [GBC]

Joseph Warrington, 25, stout [fellow]. [Formerly slave] to George Bundeck, Eastern Shore, Virginia; [left him] in 1780. GMC.

George Wise, 30, [stout fellow]. [Formerly slave] to Francis Thorowgood, Norfolk, Virginia; [left him] in 1778. GBC.

Robert Holt, 24, [stout fellow]. [Formerly slave] to William Holt, Williamsburgh, [Virginia; left him] in 1779. GBC.

Ben Frankham, 21, ordinary [fellow]. Says he was born free in Charlestown, South Carolina; certified by GMC.

Alexander Duke, 24, stout [fellow]. Says he was born free in Barbadoes; [certified by GMC].

Joseph Hartly, 20, [stout fellow]. [Says he was born free in] Virginia; [certified by GMC].

Richard Bush, 60, ordinary [fellow]. [Formerly slave] to Nancy Goddin, Nansemond, [Virginia]; left her in 1778. [GMC]

Samuel Saunders, 20, likely lad. [Formerly slave] to John Beans, Crane Island, [Virginia; left] him in 1778. GBC.

Betsey Elliot, 25, ordinary wench. Proved free by Bill of Sale produced.

Lucy Johnson, 25, [ordinary wench]. Says she was born free Rhode Island; certified by [GBC].

Peggy Minton, 22, likely wench, Quadroon. [Formerly slave] to William Black, Williamsburgh, Virginia; left him in 1779. [GBC]

Fanny Harris, 20, [likely wench] & daughter 7 months old. [Formerly slave] to Mrs. Bird, James river, [Virginia]; left her in 1779. GMC.

Nelly Bush, 54, ordinary wench. [Formerly slave] to Andrew Stewart, Princess Ann, [Virginia]; left him in 1777. GBC.

Jenny Fracklan, 24, [ordinary wench]. Says she was born free in the house of Mr. John Pen, Norfolk County, Virginia. GMC.

Nancy Basset, 28, likely wench, M. Proved to be free as Certified by GBC.

Patience Jackson, 23, very likely [wench], M. Says she was born free Rhode Island; certified by [GBC].

Rebecca Duke, 16, ordinary wench, M. Says she was born free; lived with Mr. Baird, Virginia; certified by GMC.

Jane Bush, 17, likely [wench], M. [Formerly slave] to Andrew Stewart, Crane Island, [Virginia]; left him in 1779. GBC.

Peggy Wise, 26, stout wench. [Formerly slave] to Humphrey Guin of Guin's Island; [left him] in 1776. [GBC]

Katy Bridges, 54, ordinary [wench], M. Born free as certified by [GBC].

Jane Bridges, 13, likely girl, quadroon. [Born free as certified by GBC.]

Hannah Linning, 34, ordinary wench, blind of an eye. [Formerly slave] to John Lynning, Charlestown, South Carolina; [left him] in 1780. GMC.

Mellia Johnson, 19, fine girl. Says she was born free, South Hampton, Long Island. GBC.

Since Dean, 62, ordinary wench. [Formerly slave] to Samuel Colbert, Norfolk, Virginia; [left him] in 1778. [GBC]

Dinah Johnson, 54, [ordinary wench]. [Formerly slave] to Mr. Henry Holland of New York who left her free at his death. [GBC]

Patty Vantyle, 21, fine wench. Proved to be free; certified by Mr. David Matthews, Mayor.

Massey Vantile, 4. [Proved to be free; certified by Mr. David Matthews, Mayor.]

Rebecca Scot, 20, ordinary wench. [Formerly slave] to Thomas Rutledge, Beaufort, South Carolina; left him in 1778. GMC.

Joseph Scot, 11, likely boy. [Formerly slave to Thomas Rutledge, Beaufort, South Carolina; left him in 1778.]

Mary [Scot], 1/2, an infant. Born free.

Mary Bright, 26, ordinary wench. [Born free] at Jamaica, Long Island; certified by Mr. Hugh Willis.

Matthew, 9. [Born free.]

Silas, 1 1/2, infant. [Born free.]

Esther Roberts, 28, ordinary wench. Free as proved per Bill of Sale produced.

Diana Roberts, 10, fine girl. [Free as proved per Bill of Sale produced.]

Peggy Rea, 25, likely wench. Formerly slave to David Shields, Norfolk, Virginia; left him in 1778. GMC.

Mimbo Scot, 21, ordinary fellow. [Formerly slave] to Joseph Scot, Charlestown,

South Carolina; [left him] in 1778. GBC.

Phebe Scot, 3 months. Born within the Lines.

Susannah, 23, stout wench. Formerly slave to Andrew Reynolds, Norfolk, Virginia; left him in 1779. GBC.

Eaddie, 5. [Formerly slave to Andrew Reynolds, Norfolk, Virginia.]

Chloe, 23, likely wench. [Formerly slave] to Thomas Bean, Nansemond, [Virginia; left him] in 1776. [GBC]

Priscilla, 21, stout [wench]. [Formerly slave] to Joshua Jolly, Norfolk County, Virginia; [left him] in 1777. GMC.

Dianah, 62, ordinary [wench]. [Formerly slave] to John Lynning, Charlestown, South Carolina; [left him] in 1780. [GMC]

Nancy Johnson, 36, stout [wench]. [Formerly slave] to William Smith, Accomack, Virginia; [left him] in 1777. [GMC]

Abigail, 35, ordinary wench & son Joseph, 5 years old. [Formerly slave] to Peter Barbery, New York; [left him] in 1776. GBC.

Sally Oxford, 22, [ordinary wench]. [Formerly slave] to William Sheppard,

Nansemond, Virginia; [left him] in 1777. [GBC]

Elizabeth, 27, stout wench, M. Says she was born free at St. Augustine.

Judith, 9 months, M. Born free.

Ellice, 17, stout wench. [Formerly slave] to Capt. McDonald, Santee river, South Carolina; [left him] in 1778. GMC.

James Campbell, 9 months. Born within the lines.

Patty Christopher, 30, stout wench, M. Free as proved by proper certificate.

Silvia, 14, likely [wench], M. [Free as proved by proper certificate.]

Cathern Scot, 40, stout wench. Formerly slave to Lord Dunmore. GBC.

Elizabeth Edwards, 26, ordinary [wench]. [Formerly slave] to General McDougall who left her in 1776. [GBC]

Elizabeth [Edwards], 4. Born within the Lines.

Jean Quack, 28, stout wench, M. Born free.

Elizabeth [Quack], 50, ordinary wench, M. [Born free.]

Sally Quack, 17, likely wench, M. [Born free.]

Mary Ann Thomson, 22, [likely wench]. Taken prisoner on her passage from Bermuda to Virginia; formerly slave to William Potts of Barbadoes. GBC.

Osmond Thomson, 8, likely boy. [Taken prisoner on his passage from Bermuda to Virginia; formerly slave to William Potts of Barbadoes.]

Cathern Hurbert, 30, [likely] wench, M. [Formerly slave] to Henry Lamot, Norfolk, Virginia; left him in 1776. GBC.

Fanny [Hurbert], 9. [Formerly slave to Henry Lamot, Norfolk, Virginia.]

---

3 November 1783

**Brig *Elizabeth*
bound for Cat Island
Robert Harrington**

Samuel Holmes, 32, ordinary fellow, (Ellias & Eve). [Formerly slave] to Joseph Holmes, Charlestown, South Carolina; [left him] in 1780.

John Thomson, 31, [ordinary fellow], ([Ellias & Eve]). [Formerly slave] to Anker Gardiner, [Charlestown, South Carolina]; left him in 1779. GMC.

John Lambert, 57, much worn out, ([Ellias & Eve]). [Formerly slave] to William Trusler, [Charlestown, South

Carolina]; taken prisoner by the British troops in 1778. [GMC]

Richard Smith, 21, likely lad ([Ellias & Eve]). [Formerly slave] to Capt. Robert Gail, Virginia; [left him] in 1776. [GMC]

Nuse Bagshaw, 31, stout fellow, ([Ellias & Eve]). [Formerly slave] to R. Komer, Matuxent, Virginia; [left him] in 1781. GBC.

James, 50, worn out, ([Ellias & Eve]). [Formerly slave] to George Grenal, Charlestown, South Carolina; [left him] in 1778. GMC.

Rachell, 40, ordinary wench, ([Ellias & Eve]). [Formerly slave] to John Collins, Santee, South Carolina; [left him] in 1778. GBC.

Nancy Lambert, 31, [ordinary wench], ([Ellias & Eve]). [Formerly slave] to William Maginnis, Hobbs Court House; [left him] in 1778. [GBC]

Charlotte David, 25, [ordinary wench], (Oswald & Eve). [Formerly slave] to George Godfrey, Georgia; [left him] in 1779. GMC.

Cyrus David, 47, ordinary fellow, ([Oswald & Eve]). [Formerly slave to George Godfrey, Georgia; left him in 1779. GMC.]

Clarinda, 5, ([Oswald & Eve]). Born free within the British lines. [GMC]

Sarah, 4, ([Oswald & Eve]). [Born free within the British lines. GMC.]

Chloe, 1 month, ([Oswald & Eve]). [Born free within the British lines. GMC.]

Joe, 41, ordinary fellow, ([Oswald & Eve]). [Formerly slave] to Paul Pritchard, Charlestown, South Carolina; [left him] in 1780. GBC.

Charles Rogers, 33, [ordinary fellow], ([Oswald & Eve]). Proved to be free by Certificate of Daniel Randall, Philadelphia.

Cubit, 38, ordinary fellow, (Oswald Eve). Property of said Oswald Eve.

Sarah, 30, stout wench, (Michael Clark). Free as per Certificate from her last owner, Thomas Brown of London.

Nero Denton, 40, stout fellow, (Cornet Gray, B. Legion). Formerly the property of William Denton of Goshen; left him in 1776. GMC.

Dalkeith, 25, [stout fellow], ([Cornet Gray, B. Legion]). [Formerly the property] of James Ronaldson, Smithfield, Virginia; [left him] in 1778. [GMC]

Henry Francis, 47, [stout fellow], (Ellis & Eve). [Formerly the property] of Simon Halward, Back river, [Virginia; left him] in 1779. [GMC]

Peter Quamina, 30, [stout fellow], ([Ellis & Eve]). [Formerly the property] of John Stanley, Newburgh, North Carolina; [left him] in 1778. [GMC]

Toney, 20, stout wench, (Cornet Gray, B. Legion). Property of Cornet Gray per Bill of Sale.

Jem, 1, ([Cornet Gray, B. Legion]). [Property of Cornet Gray per Bill of Sale.]

Nicholas, 20, stout fellow, ([Cornet Gray, B. Legion]). [Formerly the property] of Benjamin Fisher, Pennsylvania.

James Kilby, 21, [stout fellow], (Joseph Shoemaker). Says he was born free at [___], Island of Jamaica; lived with Lawyer Davis.

John Stephenson, 35, [stout fellow], ([Joseph Shoemaker]). Proved to be free; from the Island of Jamaica.

---

9 November 1783

Commerce
bound for Spithead
R. Strong

Bob Wheaton, 19, stout fellow. Formerly slave to Thomas Wheton, Norfolk, Virginia; left him in 1779. GMC.

Casar Nichols, 12, fine boy. [Formerly slave] to Ben Nichols, Rhode Island; [left him] in 1778. GBC.

Rose Nichols, 36, ordinary wench. [Formerly slave to Ben Nichols, Rhode Island; left him in 1778. GBC.]

Cathern Townsend, 17, likely wench, M. Served her time with [Ben Nichols] but says she was free. [GBC]

Pallacier
bound for [Spithead]
James Smith

Peter Britain, 17, stout lad. Formerly slave to William Sands, Charlestown, South Carolina; [left him] in 1779. [GBC]

Duke Richmond
bound for [Spithead]
Richard Davis

George Mintoes, 25, stout fellow. [Formerly slave] to

Thomas Gale, Morristown, New Jersey; [left him] in 1777. [GBC]

Hector Cockwell, 16, likely lad. [Formerly slave] to Mr. McReady, Charlestown, South Carolina; left him in the summer of 80.

Henry Rhodes, 24, ordinary fellow. Says he was free; served his time with John Grig, Gravesend, Long Island.

William, 14, likely boy. [Formerly slave] to Mr. Jackson, Charlestown, South Carolina; left him in 1780. GBC.

Peter George, 18, [likely boy]. [Formerly slave] to John Radcliffe, [Charlestown, South Carolina; left him] in 1780. [GBC]

Anthony Teunis, 19, ordinary lad. [Formerly slave] to Thomas Rybold, [Charlestown, South Carolina; left him] in 1780. [GBC]

Taby Gustus, 24, [ordinary wench]. [Formerly slave] to John Curtis, Eastern Shore, Virginia; [left him] in 1780. [GBC]

John Higgins, 20, likely fellow. [Formerly slave] to Dennis Higgins, Santee River, South Carolina; [left him] in 1779. [GBC]

Susannah, 21, likely wench. [Formerly slave] to John Stanyard, John's Island, [South Carolina; left him] in 1780. [GBC]

Sally, 11 weeks old, infant. Born within the British Lines.

Molly
bound for [Spithead]
G. Legyet

John, 13, ordinary fellow. [Formerly slave] to William Simmonds, Charlestown, South Carolina; [left him] in 1780. GMC.

Mary
bound for Ostend
Matthew Peacock

Sam, 20, likely fellow. [Formerly slave] to Thomas Winks, Norfolk, Virginia; [left him] in 1779. [GMC]

Aurora
bound for [Ostend]
Thomas Jackson

Molly, 20, [likely] wench. [Formerly slave] to Barney Beakman, Charlestown, South Carolina; [left him] in 1779. [GMC]

William Winter, 15, likely lad. [Formerly slave] to William Sams, John's Island, South

Carolina; [left him] in 1779.
[GMC]

Betsy, 24, [likely] wench,
(wife to the above). [Formerly
slave] to John Godfrey,
Charlestown, South Carolina;
[left him] in 1779. [GMC]

John Jack, 22, [likely] fellow.
[Formerly slave] to Ben Cattle,
Ashley River, South Carolina;
[left him] in 1779. [GMC]

Gilbert, 16, [likely fellow].
[Formerly slave] to John Ragg,
Charlestown, [South Carolina;
left him] in 1780.

Joseph
bound for Annapolis Royal
James Mitchell

Thomas Potters [*Peters*], 45,
ordinary fellow. (Black
Pioneers). [Formerly slave] to
William Campbell,
Wilmington, North Carolina;
[left him] in 1776. [GMC]

Murphy Steele, 34, [ordinary
fellow]. ([Black Pioneers]).
[Formerly slave] to Stephen
Daniel, [Wilmington, North
Carolina; left him] in 1776.
[GMC]

George Kendle, 35, [ordinary
fellow], ([Black Pioneers]).
[Formerly slave] to John
Kendle, Eastern Shore,
Virginia; [left him] in 1777.

Toby, 18, [ordinary] lad, (Capt.
Angus McDonald). [Formerly
slave] to Henry Tismore, Cape
Fear, North Carolina; [left him]
in 1780.

Sally Petters, 30, [ordinary]
wench, (Black Pioneers).
[Formerly slave] to Mr.
Bellinge, Ashepoo, [South
Carolina; left him] in 1779.
GBC.

Clara, 12, likely child, ([Black
Pioneers]). [Formerly slave to
Mr. Bellinge, Ashepoo, South
Carolina; left him in 1779.]

John, 1 1/2, infant. Born within
the lines.

John Salter, 35, stout fellow,
(Black Pioneers). [Formerly
slave] to D. Salter,
Philadelphia; [left him] in
1779. GMC.

Nancy Jenkins, 19, likely
wench, ([Black Pioneers]).
[Formerly slave] to Benjamin
Webb, Charlestown, South
Carolina; [left him] in 1780.

Lucy, 25, stout [wench], (Capt.
McDonald). Certified to be
free by Mr. Walton, Magistrate
of Police.

Abraham, 2, infant, ([Capt.
McDonald]). Born within the
Lines.

Judy Stewart, 49, ordinary
wench, (Black Pioneers).
Formerly slave to Alexander

Stewart; left him in New York in 1776. [GMC]

Frances Herbert, 65, worn out wench, (Black Pioneers). Certified to be free. Says she came from the West Indies. GBC.

Betsey Herbert, 44, ([Black Pioneers]). Says she was born free at Peter Van Dewater's, Bedford, Long Island. GBC.

James With, 24, stout fellow, (Col. Stewart). Formerly slave to George With, Hampton, Virginia; left him in 1779. GMC.

Peggy Fenwick, 19, fine wench, ([Col. Stewart]). [Formerly slave] to Edward Fenwick, Charlestown, South Carolina; [left him] in 1780. GBC.

Isaac, 28, ordinary fellow, (Capt. Alex McKay). [Formerly slave] to Mr. Devon, Savannah; [left him in] 1775. Walton, [GBC].

Sarah, 20, stout wench, ([Capt. Alex McKay]). [Formerly slave] to Samuel White near Charlestown; [left him] in 1780. [Walton, GBC.]

Lucy Howard, 23, ordinary [wench], (Maj. McLean). [Formerly slave] to Col. Thomas Howard, Indian Lands, South Carolina; [left him] in 1776.

Violet Moore, 30, stout [wench], (Col. Stewart). [Formerly slave] to William Hedden of New York; says he left her free.

Dorothy, 13, sickly [wench], ([Col. Stewart]). [Formerly slave to William Hedden of New York; says he left her free.]

Rose Wright, 25, ordinary [wench], (Black Pioneers). [Formerly slave] to Francis Wright, Norfolk, Virginia; left him in 1779. GBC.

Patience, 7, stout girl, ([Black Pioneers]). [Formerly slave] to [*blank*].

Judith, 9 months, ([Black Pioneers]). [Formerly slave] to [*blank*].

Phebe Budel, 30, lathy wench, ([Black Pioneers]). [Formerly slave] to John Budell, Santee, South Carolina; [left him] in 1779. GBC.

Timothy Withers, 26, stout fellow, ([Black Pioneers]). [Formerly slave] to William Withers, Goose Creek, [South Carolina; left him in 1779].

Betsey Bodel, 14, fine girl, ([Black Pioneers]). [Formerly slave] to John Budell, Santee, [South Carolina; left him in 1779]. [GBC]

Mary Steel, 24, fine wench, ([Black Pioneers]). [Formerly

slave] to Charles Cannon, Portsmouth, Virginia; [left him] in 1778. GMC.

Cutto, 55, ordinary [wench], ([Black Pioneers]). Free by proper Certificate.

James Bowles, 28, [ordinary] fellow, ([Black Pioneers]). Says he was born free; lived with Isaac Bowls. [Left him in] 1778.

Phillis, 23, fine wench, ([Black Pioneers]). [Formerly slave] to Moses Hays of Narraganset; [left him in] 1779.

Cato Motte, 21, fine lad, ([Black Pioneers]). [Formerly slave] to Christopher Motte, Peedee, South Carolina; [left him in] 1778.

Hannah Hannell, 35, stout wench, (Col. Stewart). Says she was born free.

Jenny Burton, 20, ordinary [wench], ([Col. Stewart]). [Formerly slave] to Andrew Burken, Savannah, Georgia; [left him in] 1779. GBC.

Benjamin Pandorus, 18, fine lad, (Major McLean). [Formerly slave] to Richard Pandorus, Ashley River, South Carolina; [left him in 1779]. [GBC]

Judah Johnson, 24, ordinary wench, ([Major McLean]). [Formerly slave] to William Walker, Savannah, Georgia; [left him in] 1781. GMC.

Stephen, 5, fine boy, ([Major McLean]).

Sam, 3, [fine boy], ([Major McLean]).

Richard Johnson, 33, ordinary lad, ([Major McLean]). [Formerly slave to William Walker, Savannah, Georgia.]

Nero, 25, stout lad, ([Major McLean]). [Formerly slave] to Paul Phipps of Santilena, South Carolina; [left him in] 1779. GBC.

Frank Cilley, 37, [stout lad], (Jacob Smith). [Formerly slave] to Richard Ireland, Hackensack, New Jersey; [left him] in 1778. GMC.

Ann, 27, stout wench, ([Jacob Smith]). [Formerly slave] to Jacob De Motte, English Neighbourhood; [left him in] 1781.

Sarah, 5, ([Jacob Smith]). [Formerly slave to Jacob De Motte, English Neighbourhood.]

Tom, 1 1/2, ([Jacob Smith]). [Formerly slave to Jacob De Motte, English Neighbourhood.]

Daphne, 11, fine girl, (Mrs. Kelly). Born free.

Susanna Motte, 44, stout wench, ([Mrs. Kelly]). Free as Certified by GBC.

Isabella, 5, ([Mrs. Kelly]). [Free as Certified by GBC.]

Sam, 3, ([Mrs. Kelly]). [Free as Certified by GBC.]

Jenny, 25, fine wench, (Black Pioneers). [Formerly slave] to Mrs. Dawson, Savannah; left her in 1779.

John Marian, 37, ordinary fellow, (Daniel Ray). [Formerly slave] to Peter Marian, Santee, South Carolina; [left him in 1779]. GMC.

Susannah, 25, stout wench, ([Daniel Ray]). [Formerly slave] to John Marian, [Santee, South Carolina; left him in 1779]. [GMC]

Diana, 7, [stout] girl, ([Daniel Ray]). [Formerly slave to John Marian, Santee, South Carolina.]

Sukey, 7 months, ([Daniel Ray]). Born within the Lines.

Sambo Crowell, 44, ordinary fellow, ([Daniel Ray]). [Formerly slave] to Nathaniel Crumwell, Goose Creek, South Carolina; [left him in 1779]. [GMC]

Phillis, 30, [ordinary] wench, ([Daniel Ray]). [Formerly slave to Nathaniel Crumwell,

Goose Creek, South Carolina; left him in 1779. GMC.]

Anthony, 8, stout lad, ([Daniel Ray]). [Formerly slave to Nathaniel Crumwell, Goose Creek, South Carolina; left him in 1779. GMC.]

Nancy, 6, [stout] girl, ([Daniel Ray]). [Formerly slave to Nathaniel Crumwell, Goose Creek, South Carolina; left him in 1779. GMC.]

Mariah, 1, [stout] girl, ([Daniel Ray]). Born within the Lines.

William Catchpole, 24, ordinary fellow, ([Daniel Ray]). Certified to be free by Mr. Matthews.

Joseph
bound for Annapolis
James Mitchell

Nancy Erwine, 32, fine wench, (Capt. McRea). Formerly slave to Charles Renk, South Carolina; left him 4 years ago.

Sally, 12, fine girl, ([Capt. McCrea]). [Formerly slave to Charles Renk, South Carolina; left him 4 years ago.]

Tom, 2, [fine] boy, ([Capt. McCrea]). [Formerly slave to Charles Renk, South Carolina.]

Sambo Frier, 24, ordinary fellow, (Daniel Ray). [Formerly slave] to George Frier, John's Island, South

Carolina; [left him] in 1779. GMC.

Tom Rivers, 43, stout fellow, ([Daniel Ray]). [Formerly slave] to Col. Rivers, James Island, [South Carolina; left him] beginning 1780. [GMC]

**Brig *Jenney*
bound for Port Mattoon
Ammerson**

Phil Birtley, 50, ordinary & worn out, (John Nash). [Formerly slave] to John Birtley, Mill town, South Carolina; left him early in 1780. GMC.

Charles Middleton, 57, [ordinary & worn out], ([John Nash]). [Formerly slave] to Arthur Middleton, Ashley River, South Carolina; [left him] in 1778. [GMC]

Abraham, 10, fine boy, ([John Nash]). Proved to be the property of John Nash by Bill of Sale.

Bina, 17, likely wench, ([John Nash]). [Proved to be the property of John Nash by Bill of Sale.]

Pompey, 4 months, ([John Nash]). [Proved to be the property of John Nash by Bill of Sale.]

November 19, 1783

**Ship *Nisbet*
bound for [Port Mattoon]
Wilson**

Henry Derling, 32, stout fellow, M, (Mr. Thomas Cutler). Free. Formerly the property of Garret Derling, Jamaica South, who gave him his freedom 6 years ago.

Philip Thompson, 24, [stout fellow], M, (Wagon Master General Department). Formerly the property of James Thompson, Clown, South Carolina; left him 4 years ago. GMC.

Andrew Izzard, 28, [stout fellow], B, ([Wagon Master General Department]). [Formerly the property] of Ralph Izzard, [Clown, South Carolina]; left him 5 [years ago]. [GMC]

Peter French, 93, remarkably stout of his age, ([Wagon Master General Department]). Free.

Jeff, 5, fine boy, M, (Mr. Thomas Cutler). Bound untill 21 years of age to Mr. Cutler.

Robert Conway, 51, stout fellow, ([Wagon Master General Department]). [Formerly the property] of David Alstin of Woodbridge, New Jersey; [left him] in the year 1776. [GMC]

Thomas James, 18, [stout fellow], ([Wagon Master General Department]). [Formerly the property] of John Stephens of St. Christophers; brought off by the Capt. of the *Alcide*. [GMC]

Samuel DeGraw, 24, [stout fellow], ([Wagon Master General Department]). [Formerly the property] of Land Degraw of Tappan, New Jersey; left him 5 years [ago]. [GMC]

George Wilkins, 53, [stout fellow], ([Wagon Master General Department]). [Formerly the property] of S. Wilkin, Princess Ann, Virginia; [*left him*] 5 [years *ago*]. [GMC]

Chris King, 28, [stout fellow], ([Wagon Master General Department]). [Formerly the property] of Thomas Reese near Valley Forge, Pennsylvania; [*left him*] 5 [years *ago*]. [GMC]

John Bass, 19, [stout fellow], ([Wagon Master General Department]). Free, born free; served some time with Ned Street, Nansemond, Virginia. [GMC]

John Townsend, 25, [stout fellow], ([Wagon Master General Department]). [Formerly the property] of Stephen Townsend, Delaware; [*left him*] 6 years [*ago*]. [GMC]

John Wright, 25, [stout fellow], ([Wagon Master General Department]). [Formerly the property] of Stephen Wright, Norfolk, Virginia; [*left him*] 6 [years *ago*]. [GMC]

Stephen Van Borun, 20, [stout fellow], ([Wagon Master General Department]). [Formerly the property] of Albert Ackerman, Paramus, New Jersey; [*left him*] 4 [years *ago*]. [GMC]

Andrew Whitehead, 29, [stout fellow], ([Wagon Master General Department]). [Formerly the property] of Hemed Whitehead, South Carolina; [*left him*] 6 [years *ago*]. [GMC]

Cato Brown, 31, [stout fellow], ([Wagon Master General Department]). [Formerly the property] of Samuel Hudson, Philadelphia; [*left him*] 7 [years *ago*]. [GMC]

Richard Jardine, 31, [stout fellow], ([Wagon Master General Department]). [Formerly the property] of Edward Jardin, Nansemond, Virginia; [*left him*] 4 [years *ago*]. [GMC]

Daniel Brown, 45, [stout fellow], ([Wagon Master General Department]). [Formerly the property] of Thomas Russel, Maryland; [*left him*] 4 [years *ago*]. [GMC]

Ben Astens, 56, [stout fellow], ([Wagon Master General Department]). [Formerly the property] of Alexander Atkins, Newcastle County; [*left him*] 5 [years *ago*]. [GMC]

John Longstreet, 45, [stout fellow], ([Wagon Master General Department]). [Formerly the property] of Derick Longstreet, Princetown, New Jersey; [*left him*] 7 [years *ago*]. [GMC]

Quash Shepherd, 29, [stout fellow], ([Wagon Master General Department]). [Formerly the property] of William Shepard, Nansemond, Virginia; [*left him*] 5 [years *ago*]. [GMC]

Prince Crosbie, 22, [stout fellow], ([Wagon Master General Department]). [Formerly the property] of Timothy Crosbie of Charlestown, South Carolina; [*left him*] 5 [years *ago*]. [GMC]

Thomas Boyle, 26, [stout fellow], ([Wagon Master General Department]). [Formerly the property] of Adam Boyle of Cecil County, Maryland; [*left him*] 6 [years *ago*]. [GMC]

Bristol Borden, 20, [stout fellow], ([Wagon Master General Department]). [Formerly the property] of John Borden, Northampton County,

Virginia; [*left him*] 3 [years *ago*]. [GMC]

Gab Morris, 23, [stout fellow], ([Wagon Master General Department]). [Formerly the property] of John Allen, Surry side, Virginia; [*left him*] 3 [years *ago*]. [GMC]

Rachel Wilson, 34, [stout] wench, ([Wagon Master General Department]). [Formerly the property] of William Curl of Hampton, Virginia; [*left him*] 5 [years *ago*].

Lucy Hart, 35, stout wench, ([Wagon Master General Department]). [Formerly the property] of Samson Levi of Philadelphia who gave her her freedom.

Amelia Connor, 19, [stout wench], ([Wagon Master General Department]). [Formerly the property] of James Vandross of Charlestown, South Carolina; [*left him*] 3 [years *ago*].

Sally, 16 months, ([Wagon Master General Department]). Born within the British Lines.

Pomp Wilson, 54, stout fellow, ([Wagon Master General Department]). [Formerly the property] of William Curl, Hampton, Virginia; [*left him*] 5 [years *ago*]. [GMC]

Sukey Dismal, 24, stout wench, ([Wagon Master

General Department]).
[Formerly the property] of B.
Guy, Norfolk, [Virginia]; [*left him*] 5 [years *ago*].

Nancy, 5, her children.

George, 11 months, her children.

Massey, 22, (Wagon Master General Department). Formerly slave to John Jay, Esq.; left him in 1778.

Elizabeth, 20, ([Wagon Master General Department]). Free born.

Hannah, 22, ([Wagon Master General Department]). [Formerly slave] to Stephen Wright, Norfolk, Virginia; [left him] in 1776.

Nancy, 15 months, ([Wagon Master General Department]). Her child.

Jenny Conway, 33, stout wench, ([Wagon Master General Department]). [Formerly slave] to Oxford Birt, Spanktown, New Jersey; [left him] in 1777.

Bristol, 12, ([Wagon Master General Department]). Her children.

Hannah, 10, ([Wagon Master General Department]). Her children.

Betty Westerfield, 28, stout wench, ([Wagon Master

General Department]). Born free at Rhode Island.

Phillis, 40, [stout wench], ([Wagon Master General Department]). [Born free at Rhode Island.]

Molly Sweney, 30, [stout wench], ([Wagon Master General Department]). [Formerly slave] to John Willoughby, Willoughby Point; [left him] in 1778.

Rose French, 16, [stout wench], ([Wagon Master General Department]). [Formerly slave] to Obadiah Bown, Shrewsbury, New Jersey; [left him in] 1778.

Phillis, 22, [stout wench], ([Wagon Master General Department]). [Formerly slave] to Thomas Erskine, Charlestown, South Carolina; [left him in] 1776.

Mary, 1, ([Wagon Master General Department]). Her child.

Nancy, 21, stout wench, ([Wagon Master General Department]). [Formerly slave] to John Miles, South Carolina; [left him] in 1781.

Sarah Stebbs, 22, stout wench, ([Wagon Master General Department]). Born free on Long Island.

John, 20 months, ([Wagon Master General Department]). Her child.

Dinah, 22, stout wench, ([Wagon Master General Department]). [Formerly slave] to John Rag, Charlestown, South Carolina; [left him] in 1778.

John, 2, ([Wagon Master General Department]). Her children.

Lakey, 7 months, ([Wagon Master General Department]). Her children.

Fanny, 30, stout wench, ([Wagon Master General Department]). [Formerly slave] to Dr. Bluefinch of Boston; [left him] in 1775.

Silvia Thompson, 23, [stout wench], ([Wagon Master General Department]). [Formerly slave] to Thomas Ladson, Charlestown, South Carolina; [left him] in 1778.

Hagar, 20, [stout wench], ([Wagon Master General Department]). [Formerly slave] to Thomas Broughton, Canonachee, South Carolina; [left him] in 1779.

Nanny, 26, [stout wench], ([Wagon Master General Department]). [Formerly slave] to Thacker Washington, Eastern Shore; [left him] in 1776.

Mary, 7 months, infant, ([Wagon Master General Department]). Her child.

Nancy, 20, stout wench, several scars in her face, ([Wagon Master General Department]). [Formerly slave] to Rutledge, Charlestown, South Carolina.

Jem, 9 months, infant, ([Wagon Master General Department]). Her child.

Hannah, 40, stout wench, ([Wagon Master General Department]). Free. Served 31 years with John Gale of Maryland.

Rose, 7, ([Wagon Master General Department]). Her child.

Lydia, 29, stout wench, ([Wagon Master General Department]). [Formerly slave] to Robert Murray, Senee, South Carolina; [left him] in 1776.

Bridget, 35, [stout wench], one eyed, ([Wagon Master General Department]). [Formerly slave] to James Murphy, Norfolk, Virginia; [left him] in 1775. GBC.

Nelly, 36, [stout wench], ([Wagon Master General Department]). Born free at Hackensack, New Jersey.

Ilinda, 19, [stout wench], M, ([Wagon Master General

Department]). Born free at Flushing, Long Island.

Rachel, 19, [stout wench], ([Wagon Master General Department]). Free. Formerly the property of Gov. Graham, Savannah.

Sally, 16 months, infant, ([Wagon Master General Department]). Her child.

Lydia, 23, stout wench, ([Wagon Master General Department]). Free. Formerly the property of John Alstin, Charlestown, South Carolina; [left him] in 1777.

Jenny, 3 months, infant, ([Wagon Master General Department]).

Peggy Waldron, 30, stout wench, ([Wagon Master General Department]). Free. [Formerly the property] of Isaac Waldron, Charlestown, South Carolina; [left him] in 1777. GBC.

Diana, 8, ([Wagon Master General Department]). Her children.

Benjamin, 1, infant, ([Wagon Master General Department]). Her children.

Peggy, 24, stout wench. Born free on Bahamas Island.

Betty, 3. Free.

Susannah, 65, stout wench.

John Ryerson, 36, [stout] fellow, one eyed. Formerly slave to John Ryerson, Hackensack, New Jersey; left him in 1776.

Kitty, 25, stout wench. [Formerly slave] to Peter Trumbly, [New Jersey; left him] in 1776.

Sam Cooper, 32, stout fellow. [Formerly slave] to John Cooper, New England. GMC.

Pompey Perkins, 30, [stout fellow]. [Formerly slave] to James Perkins, Boston. [GMC]

Simon Rutledge, 23, [stout fellow]. [Formerly slave] to Thomas Rutledge, Charlestown, South Carolina; left him in 1777. [GMC]

Charles Sweeney, 40, [stout fellow]. [Formerly slave] to Major Sweeney, Hampton, Virginia. [GMC]

Richard Price, 30, [stout fellow]. [Formerly slave] to James Price, [Hampton, Virginia; left him] in 1776. GMC.

York, 27, [stout fellow]. [Formerly slave] to John Borden, Eastern Shore, Virginia; [left him in 1776]. [GMC]

Hercules, 26, [stout fellow]. [Formerly slave] to Thomas Hanscomb, Charlestown, South

Carolina; [left him] in 1778. [GMC]

Charles Barren, 25, [stout fellow]. [Formerly slave] to James Barren, Hampton, Virginia; [left him in 1778]. [GMC]

Jacob Westerfield, 34, ordinary fellow. [Formerly slave] to Crisparus Westerfeldt, Bergen, New Jersey; [left him] in 1776. [GMC]

Benjamin, 23, stout fellow. [Formerly slave] to Isaac Waldron, Charlestown, South Carolina; [left him in 1776]. [GMC]

Nancy Savage, 17, [stout wench]. [Formerly slave] to Thomas Savage, [Charlestown, South Carolina; left him] in 1778. [GMC]

Ned Dickinson, 21, [stout fellow]. Says he was born free in West Indies; pressed on board a Man of War.

Charles Lamb, 30, [stout fellow]. [Formerly slave] to Frederick Hanson, Kent County, Maryland; left him in 1777. GMC.

Abraham Bayard, 30, [stout fellow]. [Formerly slave] to Samuel Bayard, Cecil County, Maryland; [left him in 1777]. [GMC]

Joseph Harris, 53, [stout fellow]. [Formerly slave] to

Joseph Harris, Rhaway neck, New Jersey; [left him] in 1775. [GMC]

Job Work, 22, [stout fellow]. [Formerly slave] to Anthony Work, Hemps Landing, Virginia; [left him] in 1778. [GMC]

Willis Page, 35, [stout fellow]. [Formerly slave] to John Driver, Nansemond, [Virginia; left him] in 1779. [GMC]

Polly, 14, fine girl. [Formerly slave] to Peter Trumbly, Springfield, New Jersey.

Peggy, 7, [fine girl].

Paul Jackson, 35, ordinary fellow. [Formerly slave] to Joe Jackson, Boston; [*left him in*] 1775.

Charles White, 25, stout [fellow]. [Formerly slave] to Dr. Dillehour, Charlestown, South Carolina; [left him] in 1777. [GMC]

Dick Roach, 55, [stout fellow]. [Formerly slave] to Lieutenant Col. DeLancey.

Benjamin Gerrow, 25, [stout fellow]. [Formerly slave] to Peter Gerrow, Charlestown, South Carolina.

Isaac Balton, 23, likely fellow. Formerly slave to Joseph Johnson, Norfolk, Virginia; left him in 1778. GMC.

Bacchus Erwin, 40, ordinary [fellow]. [Formerly slave] to David Irwin, Philadelphia; [left him] in 1778. [GMC]

William Goodwin, 45, ordinary [fellow]. [Formerly slave] to James Goodwin, Nansemond, Virginia; [left him] in 1780. [GMC]

Moses Mount, 20, [ordinary fellow]. [Formerly slave] to Michael Mount, Allentown, New Jersey; [left him] in 1776. [GMC]

Esther Clark, 35, [ordinary] wench. [Formerly slave] to Michael Clark, Philadelphia; [left him] in June 1778.

William Billinger, 23, likely fellow. [Formerly slave] to George Billinger, Ashley River, South Carolina; [left him] in May 1780. [GMC]

Joseph Harris, 53, ordinary [fellow]. [Formerly slave] to Mr. Harris, Rhaway, New Jersey; [left him] in 1776. [GMC]

Isaac Betty, 25, [ordinary fellow]. [Formerly slave] to John Betty, Charlestown, South Carolina; [left him] in 1780. [GMC]

Violet Parkin, 27, [ordinary] wench, (Mr. Parkin). Mr. Parkin's property.

Dick [Parkin], 1/2, ([Mr. Parkin]). [Mr. Parkin's property.]

Anthony Redhook, 25, likely lad. [Formerly slave] to Moses Redhook, Nansemond, Virginia; [left him] in 1779. [GMC]

Thomas Bruin, 30, ordinary fellow. Formerly slave to David Bruin, Hackensack, New Jersey; left him in 1779. GMC.

Joseph Bartlet, 31, stout man. [Formerly slave] to Gilbert Livingston, Poughkeepsie, New York; [left him] in 1779. [GMC]

Samuel Willis, 41, very ordinary fellow. [Formerly slave] to David Earle, Bergen, New Jersey; left him in 1779. GBC.

Rachel Willis, 30, [very ordinary wench]. [Formerly slave] to Increase Carpenter, Jamaica, Long Island; he left her in 1776. GMC.

Joseph Willis, 9 months. Her children.

Charles Willis, 5. Her children.

Jenny Willis, 3. Her children.

Ben Field, 38, ordinary fellow. [Formerly slave] to Jeremy Field, Piscataway, New Jersey; his master left him in 1776. GMC.

Eleanor Field, 27, stout wench. [Formerly slave to Jeremy Field, Piscataway, New Jersey; her master left her in 1776. GMC.]

Ben Field, 4. Her children.

Sarah Field, 2. Her children.

James Annie, 39, stout fellow. [Formerly slave] to John Annie, Rhode Island; left him in 1779. GMC.

Sam Smith, 36, [stout fellow]. [Formerly slave] to Col. Samuel Breese, Monmouth, New Jersey; [left him] in 1778. [GMC]

Sam Dismal, 31, [stout fellow]. [Formerly slave] to John Dismal, Somerset County, Maryland; [left him] in 1779. [GMC]

Garret Hart, 29, [stout fellow]. [Formerly slave] to Conrad Ralph near Reading, Pennsylvania; [left him] in April 1778. [GMC]

Isaac Warren, 25, ordinary fellow. [Formerly slave] to Thomas Warren, Charlestown, South Carolina; [left him] in May 1780. [GMC]

Thom Richardson, 32, stout fellow. [Formerly slave] to Edward Dawson, Aarons County, Maryland; [left him] in July 1777. [GMC]

Rachel Jordan, 30, stout wench. [Formerly slave] to

Solomon Slaughter, Nansemond, Virginia; [left him] in 1779. GBC.

Dempse [Jordan], 11, likely boy. Her children.

Judy Jordan, 9, [likely] wench. Her children.

Joseph Wingwood, 24, stout fellow. [Formerly slave] to Gilbert Wingwood, Wando, South Carolina; [left him] in 1780. GMC.

Flora Hill, 21, ordinary wench. [Formerly slave] to James Yard, Philadelphia; [left him] in 1778. [GMC]

John Green, 44, [ordinary] fellow. [Formerly slave] to Lucy Given, Norfolk County, Virginia; [left] in 1776. [GMC]

Nelly Lamb, 21, stout wench. [Formerly slave] to Col. Ruffin Jordan, [Norfolk County, Virginia; left him] in 1779. GBC.

Funky Hancock, 25, ordinary [wench]. [Formerly slave] to John Hancock, Princess Ann County, [Virginia; left him] in 1781. [GBC]

Arthur Boler, 34, stout fellow. [Formerly slave] to Medcalfe Bowler, Portsmouth, Rhode Island; [left him in 1781]. [GBC]

Phebe [Boler], 35, ordinary wench. Says she was born free,

[Portsmouth, Rhode Island].
[GBC]

Betsy [Boler], 12, likely girl.
[Says she was born free,
Portsmouth, Rhode Island.
GBC.]

Fan Barclay, 42, ordinary
wench. [Says she was born
free.] Certified by James
Henderson, Waggon Master.

Rachel [Barclay], 16, likely
girl. Her children.

Elizabeth [Barclay], 12, likely
quadroon. Her children.

George [Barclay], 8, likely
boy. Her children.

Israel [Barclay], 6. Her
children.

Tishy [Barclay], 3. Her
children.

Jane [Barclay], 1/2. Her
children.

Mary Stratton, 24, likely
wench. [Formerly slave] to Ben
Stratton, Eastern Shore,
Virginia; left him in 1779.
GBC.

Rose [Stratton], 8. Her
children.

Johnny [Stratton], 2. Her
children.

Peggy [Stratton], 4 months. Her
children.

Hannah Richardson, 22,
ordinary wench. [Formerly
slave] to Ben Bennet, Head of

Elk, Maryland; [left him] in
1779. GMC.

Nancy Sheppard, 40, stout
wench. [Formerly slave] to
Edward Buxton, Nansemond,
Virginia; [left him] in 1779.
GBC.

Priscilla, 8, ordinary. Her child.

Richard Redock, 39, ordinary
fellow. Formerly slave to Col.
Redock, Virginia; left him in
1778. GMC.

Charity [Redock], 14,
[ordinary] girl. [Formerly slave
to Col. Redock, Virginia.
GMC.]

Jenny [Redock], 12, [ordinary
girl]. [Formerly slave to Col.
Redock, Virginia. GMC.]

Betsy Palmerton, 20, stout
wench. [Formerly slave] to
Joseph Palmerton,
Charlestown, South Carolina;
[left him] in 1778. [GMC]

Billy [Palmerton], 4. Her child.

John Van Bruyck, 33, ordinary
fellow. [Formerly slave] to
Samuel Van Bruyck, Tappan,
New Jersey; [left him] in 1779.

Nancy [Van Bruyck], 28, stout
wench. [Formerly slave] to
David Edwards, [Tappan, New
Jersey; left him] in 1779.

Sarah [Van Bruyck], 5. Her
child.

Francis Wells, 24, stout lad.
[Formerly slave] to Thomas

Wills, Mulberry, Virginia; [left him] in 1780.

Thomas York, 31, stout fellow. [Formerly slave] to Col. Bird,

Reading, Pennsylvania; [left him] in 1777.

———————————

In pursuance of two Orders from His Excellency Sir Guy Carleton, K. B., General and Commander in Chief of His Majesty's Forces from Nova Scotia to West Florida inclusive, both dated Head Quarters, New York, the one the 15 April and the other the 22d May 1783. We whose names are hereunto Subscribed Do respectively Certify that on the 22d of September and the 7, 11, 14, 15, 21, and 31 of October and the 3d, 9th and 19th of November 1783 the aforegoing Vessels were carefully Inspected by us whose names are for that purpose respectively mention'd to have Inspected the said respective Vessels and that on board the said Vessels We found the Negroes mention'd in the aforegoing List amounting to **Two Hundred and ninety six men, two Hundred and fifty five women and one Hundred and ninety nine Children** and to the best of Judgement believe them to be all the negroes on board the said Vessels and We enquir'd of the Master of each Vessel whether he had any Records, Deeds or Archives or papers or other property of the Citizens of the United States on board and to each enquiry we were answer'd in the negative. And We further Certify that we furnish'd the master of each Vessel with a certified List of the Negroes on board his Vessel and inform'd him that he would not be permitted to Land any other Negroes than those mention'd in the List and that if any other negroes were found on board his Vessel, he would be severely punished and that we inform'd the Agent of Transports of this matter and desired him to use means for returning to this place all negroes not mention'd in the List.

[*Signed*]: Gilfillan; Armstrong; W. S. Smith, Col., on the part of the United States; Samuel Jones, Secretary.

By *his Excellency the Right Honourable* JOHN *Earl of* DUNMORE, *his Majesty's Lieutenant and Governour-General of the Colony and Dominion of Virginia, and Vice-Admiral of the same:*

A PROCLAMATION.

AS I have ever entertained Hopes that an Accommodation might have taken Place between *Great Britain* and this Colony, without being compelled, by my Duty, to this most disagreeable, but now absolutely necessary Step, rendered so by a Body of armed Men, unlawfully assembled, firing on his Majesty's Tenders, and the Formation of an Army, and that Army now on their March to attack his Majesty's Troops, and destroy the well-disposed Subjects of this Colony: To defeat such treasonable Purposes, and that all such Traitors, and their Abetters, may be brought to Justice, and that the Peace and good Order of this Colony may be again restored, which the ordinary Course of the civil Law is unable to effect, I have thought fit to issue this my Proclamation, hereby declaring, that until the aforesaid good Purposes can be obtained, I do, in Virtue of the Power and Authority to me given, by his Majesty, determine to execute martial Law, and cause the same to be executed throughout this Colony; and to the End that Peace and good Order may the sooner be restored, I do require every Person capable of bearing Arms to resort to his Majesty's S T A N-DARD, or be looked upon as Traitors to his Majesty's Crown and Government, and thereby become liable to the Penalty the Law inflicts upon such Offences, such as Forfeiture of Life, Confiscation of Lands, &c. &c. And I do hereby farther declare all indented Servants, Negroes, or others (appertaining to Rebels) free, that are able and willing to bear Arms, they joining his Majesty's Troops, as soon as may be, for the more speedily reducing this Colony to a proper Sense of their Duty, to his Majesty's Crown and Dignity. I do farther order, and require, all his Majesty's liege Subjects to retain their Quitrents, or any other Taxes due, or that may become due, in their own Custody, till such Time as Peace may be again restored to this at present most unhappy Country, or demanded of them for their former salutary Purposes, by Officers properly authorised to receive the same,

GIVEN under my Hand, on Board the Ship William, *off* Norfolk, *the 7th Day of* November, *in the 16th Year of his Majesty's Reign.*

D U N M O R E.

G O D SAVE THE K I N G.

Lord Dunmore's Proclamation, Virginia, 1775. Dunmore's famous proclamation was the only signal many slaves needed to flee from their masters and join the British army and military.

Theodor Kaufman, "On to Liberty." This later painting captures an essential quality of the Black Loyalist experience in the American Revolution —the flight of black women and children into war in search of freedom.

196   Oand MG I Vol. 948

NEW-YORK, 21 *April* 1783.

THIS is to certify to whomſoever it may concern, that the Bearer hereof *Cato Ramſay* a Negro, reſorted to the Britiſh Lines, in conſequence of the Proclamations of Sir William Howe, and Sir Henry Clinton, late Commanders in Chief in America ; and that the ſaid Negro has hereby his Excellency Sir Guy Carleton's Permiſſion to go to Nova-Scotia, or wherever elſe *He* may think proper. ⎯⎯

By Order of Brigadier General Birch,

Cato Ramsay's Pass from Brigadier General Samuel Birch, 1783. This is the only surviving example of the coveted passes British commanders awarded to Black Loyalists, which allowed them to begin their hegira of freedom.

These are sample pages from the original version of the Book of Negroes. Far down the left side may be seen entries for Stephen Blucke, his wife Margaret and daughter, Isabel Gibbons.

Daughter to Betsey Jackson, named in the British lines
Formerly the Property of John Willoughby of Norfolk Virginia, left him seven years agoe G B C
Formerly the Property of Lucas Powell of Williamsburgh Virginia, left him two years agoe Ditto
Son to Sally Dennis and born within the British lines
Formerly the Property of William Wilson of Somerset County Maryland, left him three years agoe Ditto
Formerly the Property of Joseph White of Charlestown South Carolina, left him five years agoe Ditto
Formerly the Property of Smith McKenzie of Savannah Georgia, left him four years agoe Ditto
Formerly the Property of Solomon Talbot of Norfolk Virginia, left him five years agoe Ditto
Formerly the Property of Bayley Gray of Norfolk Virginia, left him four years agoe Ditto
Formerly the Property of Thomas Dale of Norfolk Virginia, left him four years agoe Ditto
Formerly the Property of Samuel Holdhead of Norfolk County Virginia, left him seven years agoe Ditto
Formerly the Property of Edward Mealy of Princess Ann County Virginia, left him seven years agoe Ditto
Ditto Ditto Ditto
Formerly the Property of James Johnson of Savannah Georgia, left him two years agoe Ditto
Daughter to Jane Milligan and born within the British lines
Formerly the Property of John Willoughby of Norfolk County Virginia, left him seven years agoe Ditto
Ditto Ditto Ditto Ditto
Daughter of Molly Brown and born within the British lines
Formerly the Property of John Wigton of Norfolk County Virginia, left him four years agoe Ditto
Formerly the Property of Robert Brown of Norfolk County Virginia, left him three years agoe Ditto
Ditto Ditto Ditto Ditto
Ditto Ditto Ditto Ditto
Formerly the Property of John Walton of Norfolk Virginia, left him three years agoe Ditto
Formerly the Property of Thomas Brown of Portsmouth Virginia, left him four years agoe Ditto
She says she was born free and produces General Birch's Certificate. She came from Virginia three years agoe
Formerly the Property of Abraham Parks of Norfolk Virginia, left him Seven years agoe Ditto
Formerly the Property of Thomas Murch of Charlestown Virginia, left him three years agoe Ditto
Formerly the Property of George Gordon of Nancy Mumn Virginia, left him three years agoe Ditto
Formerly the Property of Miles Williamson of Charlestown South Carolina, left him five years agoe Ditto
She says she was born free in the Island of Barbadoes and produces General Birch's Certificate
Says she was born free in New Jersey Family of N York & bought her freedom fourteen years agoe Ditto
Margeret Blacks purchased her of Mrs Coventry's Daughter & says her freedom Ditto
Formerly the Property of John Mooter of Elizabeth Town New Jersey, left him seven years agoe Ditto
Formerly the Property of Mathew Phripp of Norfolk Virginia, left him six years agoe Ditto
Formerly the Property of Robert Morris of Philadelphia, left him six years agoe Ditto
She produces a certificate of freedom from Margret Eglees her former Mistress
Ditto Ditto Ditto Ditto
Ditto Ditto Ditto Ditto
Formerly the Property of Abraham Lissom of Albany State of N York, left him six years agoe G B C
Formerly the Property of Peter Messenborn of New York, left him six years agoe Ditto
Daughter to Sarah Sawward and born within the British lines
Son Ditto Ditto Ditto
Formerly the Property of John Fullerton of Philadelphia, left him five years agoe G B C

Rose Fortune, Black Loyalist. Courtesy of Public Archives of Nova Scotia.

Black Wood Cutter. Many Black Loyalists earned their keep in New York, Nova Scotia, and Sierra Leone by cutting wood.

YANKEE DOODLE.

OR

THE NEGROES FAREWELL TO AMERICA.

The Words and Muſic by T. L.

Now farewell my Maſſa my Miſ-ſey a - dieu   More blows or more ſtripes will

me e'er take from you   Or will me come hither or thither me go no help make you

CHO. Vivace.

rich by de ſweat of my brow   Yankee doodle Yankee doodle dandy I

vow   Yankee doodle Yankee doodle bow wow wow.

2

Farewell all de Yams & farewell de ſalt Fiſh
De Bran & Spruce Beer at you all me cry Piſh
Me feed upon Pudding Roaſt Beef & Strong Beer
In Englan' old Englan' when me do get dere.
　　　　　Yankee doodle, &c.

3

Farewell de Muſketo farewell de black fly
And Rattle Snake too who may ſting me to dye
Den Negroe go 'Ome to his friends in Guinee
Before dat old Englan' he 'ave a ſeen'e.
　　　　　Yankee doodle, &c.

4

Farewell de cold Winter de Froſt & de Snow
Which cover high Hills and de Valleys ſo low
And dangling & canting ſwearing & drinking
Taring and Feath'ring for ſer'ouſly thinking.
　　　　　Yankee doodle, &c.

5

Den Hey! for old Englan' where Liberty reigns
Where Negroe no beaten or loaded with chains
And if Negroe return O! may he be bang'd
Chain'd tortur'd & drowned — Or let him be hang'd.
　　　　　Yankee doodle, &c.

For the GUITTAR.

Andante.

Vivace.

T
C*S

"Yankee Doodle or the Negroes Farewell to America." A song popular in London in the
early 1780s.

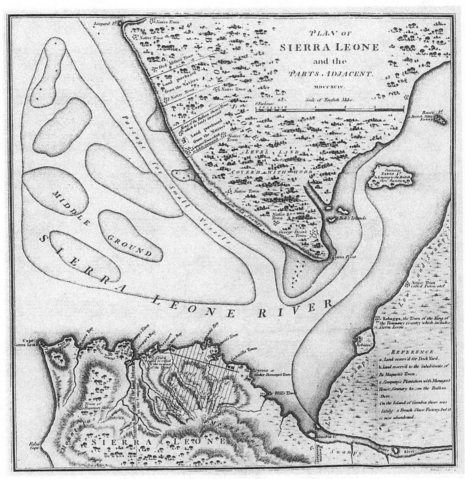

Plan of Sierra Leone and the Parts Adjacent, 1794. The port of Freetown with slave traders perched just above the city.

Inspection Roll

of

Negroes

Book No. 3

taken on board the under named vessels, on the 30th day of November 1783 at anchor near Statten Island, previous to their sailing for Port Mattoon in Nova Scotia

30 November 1783

Inspected by Captains Gilfillen and Armstrong

On Board the Ship *Peggy* James Beazley, Master

John Bucher, aged 23 years, stout fellow, goes with the Waggon Master General's department. Formerly slave to Mr. Webb, Charlestown, South Carolina; left him in 1776. General Musgrave's Certificate.

Fortune Rivers, 30 years, ordinary fellow, WMGD. Formerly slave to Molly Rivers, Charlestown, South Carolina; left her in 1776. GMC.

Sally Rivers, 30 years, ordinary wench, WMGD. Formerly slave to Molly Rivers, Charlestown, South Carolina; left her in 1776. GMC.

Jenny Rivers, 7 years, ordinary child, WMGD. Born free within the British lines.

Close Herring, 50 years, nearly worn out, WMGD. Formerly slave to Patton Herring, Tappan, New Jersey; left him and joined the British troops in 1778. GMC.

William Sampson, 28 years, likely fellow, WMGD. Formerly slave to James Jackson, New Windsor, New York Province; left him in 1777. GMC.

Peter Young, 21 years, ordinary fellow, WMGD. Formerly slave to Charles Conner, Crane Island, Virginia; left him in 1779. GMC.

Samuel Minton, 60 years, nearly worn out, WMGD. Formerly slave to Thomas Minton, Norfolk, Virginia; left him in 1779. GMC.

Prince Frederick, 32 years, stout fellow, WMGD. Formerly slave to Capt. Frederick, Boston, New England; left him in 1776. GMC.

Gilbert Lafferts, 21 years, likely lad, Mr. James Henderson's possession, proved to be the property of Mr. James Henderson, Waggon Master & Bill of Sale produced.

Jenny Frederick, 32 years, ordinary wench, WMGD. Certified to be free by Jonah Frederick of Boston, New England.

On Board The Ship *Danger* James Duncan, Master

Thomas Thomas, aged 36 years, stout fellow, Royal Artillery Department. Formerly slave to Charles Thomas, Nancy Mund, Virginia; left him in 1776. GBC.

Barry Sawyer, 25 years, stout fellow, Royal Artillery Department. Formerly slave to Charles Sawyer, Princes Ann County, Virginia; left him in 1776. GMC.

Shinea Sawyer, 33 years, stout wench, RAD. Formerly slave to John Ivie, Norfolk County, Virginia; left him in 1776. GMC.

Nelly Sawyer, 14 years, likely wench, RAD. Formerly slave to James Hickerson, Norfolk County, Virginia; left him in 1776. GMC.

Chloe Sawyer, 11 years, likely wench, RAD. Formerly slave to John Ivie, Norfolk County, Virginia; left him in 1776. GMC.

Tom Sawyer, 10 years, likely boy, RAD. Formerly slave to James Micherson, Norfolk County, Virginia; left him in 1776. GMC.

Tom Summer, 35 years, ordinary fellow, RAD. Formerly slave to Josiah Summer, Nancy Mund, Virginia; left him in 1779. GBC.

Pinna Summer, 21 years, likely wench, RAD. Formerly slave to Josiah Summer, Nancy Mund, Virginia; left him in 1779. GBC.

Cato Summer, 2 1/2 years, RAD, born free within the British Lines.

Michael Wallace, 38 years, likely fellow, RAD. Formerly slave to James Wallace, Norfolk, Virginia; left him and joined Lord Dunmore in 1777. GMC.

Hannah Wallace, 22 years, ordinary Wench, RAD. Formerly slave to William Arronstead, Gloucester, Virginia; left him in 1776. GMC.

Dick Wallace, 4 years, fine boy, RAD. Born free within the British lines.

Ralph Henry, 30 years, ordinary fellow, RAD. Formerly slave to Patrick Henry, Gloucester, Virginia; left him in 1776. GMC.

Miney Henry, 25 years, ordinary wench, RAD. Formerly slave to Joseph Convey, Philadelphia; left him in 1778. GMC.

Molly Henry, 4 years, fine child, RAD. Born free within the British lines.

James Reid, 33 years, stout fellow, RAD. Formerly slave to Doctor Reid, Norfolk, Virginia; left him & joined Lord Dunmore in 1776. GMC.

Patty Reid, 23 years, likely wench, RAD. Formerly slave

to Joseph Corrin, James River, Virginia; left him in 1777. GMC.

Bristow Garritt, aged 32 years, ordinary fellow, RAD. Formerly slave to James Garrett, Essex County, Virginia; left him and joined Lord Dunmore in 1776. GMC.

Rose Garritt, 20 years, likely wench, RAD. Formerly slave to Mrs. Wade, Charlestown, South Carolina; left her in 1780. GMC.

Anthony Cooper, 63 years, worn out, RAD. Formerly slave to Willis Cooper, Suffolk County, Virginia; left him in 1779. GMC.

Sarrah Cooper, 60 years, worn out, RAD. Formerly slave to Willis Cooper, Suffolk County, Virginia; left him in 1779. GMC.

Isaac Cooper, 14 years, likely boy, RAD. Formerly slave to Willis Cooper, Suffolk County, Virginia; left him in 1779. GMC.

Nancy Cooper, 4 years, fine child, RAD, born free within the British lines.

Hector Lewis, 40 years, ordinary fellow, RAD. Formerly slave to Frank Lewis, Charlestown, South Carolina; left him in 1779. GMC.

Judith Jackson, 53 years, ordinary wench, RAD. Formerly slave to John Clain, Norfolk, Virginia; left him early in 1779.

Silas Brown, 51 years, ordinary fellow, RAD. Formerly slave to Richard Brown, Portsmouth, Virginia; left him in 1779. GMC.

Murray Scott, 28 years, ordinary fellow, RAD. Formerly slave to Isaac Murray, Princes Ann County, Virginia; left him in 1779. GMC.

Molly Scott, 30 years, ordinary wench, RAD. Formerly slave to Christopher Godwine, West Branch, Virginia; left him in 1779. GMC.

Jack Tollberry, 26 years, ordinary fellow, RAD. Formerly slave to John Alexander, Roanock, North Carolina; left him in 1779. GMC.

Sillo Tollberry, 23 years, stout wench, RAD. Formerly slave to Isaac Barnett of Beaufort, South Carolina; left him in 1779. GMC.

Kate Godfrey, 30 years, ordinary wench, RAD. Formerly slave to Mathew Godfrey, Norfolk, Virginia; left him early in 1779. GMC.

Port Godfrey, 12 years, likely boy, RAD. Formerly slave to

Mathew Godfrey, Norfolk, Virginia; left him early in 1779. GMC.

Lucy Godfrey, 7 years old, ordinary child, RAD. Formerly slave to Mathew Godfrey, Norfolk, Virginia; left him early in 1779. GMC.

Salley Godfrey, 1 1/2 years, RAD, born free within the British lines.

Lewis Church, aged 27 years, stout fellow, RAD. Formerly slave to Robert Betty, Norfolk, Virginia; left him in 1779. GMC.

John Brown, 45 years, ordinary fellow, RAD. Formerly slave to Doctor Seaman, Norfolk, Virginia; left him in 1776, with Lord Dunmore. GMC.

Peggy Brown, 30 years, stout wench, RAD. Formerly slave to Colonel Godfrey, Norfolk, Virginia; left him in 1776, with Lord Dunmore. GMC.

Jenny Brown, 5 years, ordinary child, RAD. Born free within the British Lines.

James Brown, 2 years, RAD. Born free within the British Lines.

Nancy Brown, 1 1/2 years, RAD. Born free within the British Lines.

London Winters, 40 years, incurably lame, RAD. Formerly slave to Patrick

Singleton, North Landing, Virginia; left him in 1779. GBC.

James Tucker, 55 years, almost worn out, RAD. Formerly slave to Capt. McFipps, Norfolk, Virginia; left him in 1776 with Lord Dunmore. GMC.

Lewis Cornick, 30 years, ordinary fellow, RAD. Formerly slave to Lamber Cornick, Princes Ann County, Virginia; left him in 1776. GMC.

Rachel Cornick, 30 years, sickley wench, RAD. Formerly slave to William Tannable, Princes Ann County, Virginia; left him in 1776. GMC.

Tom Cornick, 1/2 year infant, RAD. Born free within the British lines.

Argill Killing, 22 years, stout fellow, RAD. Formerly slave to Adam Killings, Princes Ann County, Virginia; left him in 1779. GMC.

Peggy Thomas, 22 years, stout wench, RAD. Formerly slave to James Otter, Nancy Mund, Virginia; left him in 1779. GMC.

David Thomas, 5 years, likely boy, RAD. Formerly slave to James Otter, Nancy Mund, Virginia; left him in 1779. GMC.

Tony Carragan, 47 years, ordinary fellow, RAD. Formerly slave to Samuel Tryar, Charlestown, South Carolina; left him in 1779. GMC.

James Hector, aged 55 years, ordinary fellow, RAD. Formerly slave to William R. Currell, Hampton County, Virginia; left him in 1779. GBC.

Judy Hector, 30 years, stout wench, RAD. Formerly slave to Robert Bright, Hampton County, Virginia; left him in 1779. GBC.

Kate Hector, 8 years, likely child, RAD. Formerly slave to Robert Bright, Hampton County, Virginia; left him in 1779. GBC.

John Hector, 1 1/2 years, RAD. Born free within the British lines.

Sam Godfrey, 26 years, stout fellow, RAD. Formerly slave to Mathew Godfrey, Norfolk, Virginia; left him in 1779. GMC.

Sucky Godfrey, 22 years, stout wench, RAD. Formerly slave to Francis Rice, Hampton, Virginia; left him in 1776 & joined Lord Dunmore. GMC.

Salley Godfrey, 6 years, ordinary child, RAD. Born free within the British lines.

Robert Godfrey, 2 years, RAD. Born free within the British lines.

James Godfrey, 1 year, RAD. Born free within the British lines.

Sam Grayson, 32 years, stout fellow, RAD. Formerly slave to Colonel Grayson in Georgia; left him early in 1779. GBC.

Salley Grayson, 20 years, ordinary wench, RAD. Formerly slave to Colonel Grayson in Georgia; left him early in 1779. GBC.

James Anderson, 35 years, lame & ordinary fellow, RAD. Formerly slave to Mr. Anderson, Charlestown, South Carolina; left him early in 1780. GMC.

Dianach Anderson, 25 years, stout wench, RAD. Formerly slave to Mr. Anderson, Charlestown, South Carolina; left him early in 1780. GMC.

James Stewart, 29 years, stout fellow, RAD. Formerly slave to John Stewart, Sommerset County, Maryland; left him early in 1780. GMC.

Joseph Smith, 54 years, lame, RAD. Formerly slave to William Currier, Cecil County, Maryland; left him early in 1777. GBC.

Eliza Laston, 24 years, stout wench, RAD. Formerly slave

to Isaac Laston, Baltimore, Maryland; left him early in 1777. GBC.

Charles Laston, 4 years, RAD. Born free within the British Lines.

James Philip, aged 40 years, stout fellow, RAD, Capt. Symon's possession & proved to be the property of Capt. Symon.

Peter Stogdon, 19 years, stout lad, RAD, Widow Stogdon's and proved to be the property of Widow Stogdon.

Prince, 11 years, likely boy, RAD, Doctor McIntyre's and proved to be the property of Doctor McIntyre of General Hospital.

Amelia, 35 years, ordinary wench, Dr. McIntyre. Proved to be a free woman, and goes as a servant to the Gen'l Hospital.

Salley, 6 years, ordinary child, Dr. McIntyre. Proved to be a free woman and goes as a servant to the General Hospital.

Samuel Mixied, 45 years, stout fellow, RAD. Formerly slave to Thomas Brown of Portsmouth, Virginia; left him 4 1/2 years ago. GMC.

Moses Halstede, 30 years, stout fellow, RAD. Formerly slave to Henry Halstede,

Norfolk County, Virginia; left him 7 1/2 years ago. GMC.

York Nash, 50 years, stout fellow, RAD. Formerly slave to Thomas Nash, Norfolk County, Virginia; left him 5 years ago. GMC.

Mary English, 25 years, stout M wench, RAD. Formerly slave to George English, Charlestown, South Carolina; left him about 5 years ago. GMC.

King Tucker, 51 years, stout fellow, RAD. Formerly slave to Robert Tucker of Norfolk, Virginia; left him about 7 1/2 years ago. GMC.

Dianah Tucker, 22 years, stout wench, RAD. Formerly slave to Mathew Cuttonon, Charlestown, South Carolina; left him about 5 years ago. GMC.

Nezer Wright, 22 years, stout fellow, RAD. Formerly slave to Stephen Wright, Crane Island, Virginia; left him about 5 years ago. GMC.

Henry Givin, 33 years, stout fellow, RAD. Formerly slave to Henry Givin, Givins Island, Virginia; left him about 5 years ago. GMC.

Dublin Miller, 65 years, stout fellow, RAD. Formerly slave to Mason Miller of Norfolk, Virginia; left him about 7 1/2 years ago. GMC.

Samuel Hutchins, 39 years, stout fellow, RAD. Formerly slave to Joseph Hutchins of Norfolk, Virginia; left him about 5 years ago. GMC.

Lucy Hutchins, 30 years, stout wench, RAD. Formerly slave to Samuel Colbert of Norfolk, Virginia; left him about 5 years ago. GMC.

Garth Wright, 50 years, stout fellow, RAD. Formerly slave to Stephen Wright of Crane Island, Virginia; left him about 5 years ago. GMC.

Ben Poole, aged 43 years, stout fellow, RAD. Formerly slave to Edward Poole of Norfolk, Virginia; left him about 7 1/2 years ago. GMC.

Mary Poole, 40 years, stout wench, RAD. Formerly slave to Joseph Moore of Philadelphia; left him about 6 years ago. GMC.

Jack Ellis, 28 years, stout fellow, RAD. Formerly slave to Will Ellis of Ashely river, South Carolina; left him about 5 years ago. GMC.

Pompy Beacon, 30 years, stout fellow, RAD. Formerly slave to Samuel Beacon of Norfolk, Virginia; left him about 5 years ago. GMC.

Mary Halstead, 36 years, stout wench, RAD. Formerly slave to Francis Rice of Hampton, Virginia; left him about 7 1/2 years ago. GMC.

Phillis, 11 years, her daughter, RAD. Formerly slave to Francis Rice of Hampton, Virginia; left him about 7 1/2 years ago. GMC.

Charity Beacon, 36 years, stout wench, RAD. Formerly slave to Isaac Luke of Portsmouth, Virginia; left him about 6 years ago. GMC.

Charles Williams, 68 years, stout man, RAD. Formerly slave to Samuel Williams, New Port Comfort, Virginia; left him about 7 years ago. GMC.

Venus Williams, 50 years, stout woman, RAD. Formerly slave to George Gibson of Philadelphia; left him about 6 years ago. GMC.

Sally Stewart, 26 years, stout wench, RAD. Formerly slave to John Tassell of Williamsburgh, Virginia; left him about 7 1/2 years ago. GMC.

Moses Kelly, 37 years, stout fellow, RAD. Formerly slave to Mary Kelly, Portsmouth, Virginia; left her about 5 years ago. GMC.

Jenny Kelly, 32 years, stout wench, RAD. Formerly slave to Mathew Godfrey of Norfolk County, Virginia; left him about 5 years ago. GMC.

Petter, 6 years, fine boy, RAD. Formerly slave to Mathew Godfrey of Norfolk County, Virginia; left him about 5 years ago. GMC.

Bridget Godfrey, 55 years, stout wench, RAD. Formerly slave to Mathew Godfrey of Norfolk County, Virginia; left him about 5 years ago. GMC.

Salley Collins, 22 years, stout wench, RAD. Formerly slave to Maurice Seaman, George Town, North Carolina; left him about 5 years ago. GMC.

Jacob Collins, 40 years, stout fellow, RAD. Formerly slave to John Collins, Santee river, South Carolina; left him about 4 years ago. GMC.

Hannah Ellis, aged 20 years, stout wench, RAD. Formerly slave to William Ellis, Charlestown, South Carolina; left him about 5 years ago. GMC.

Abraham Herron, 4 years, RAD. Born free within the British lines.

Jack Robinson, 22 years, stout fellow, RAD. Formerly slave to Tully Robinson, Hamps landing, Virginia; left him about 5 years ago. GMC.

Quash English, 29 years, stout fellow, RAD. Formerly slave to John English, Charlestown, South Carolina; left him about 4 years ago. GMC.

Clarly English, 29 years, stout wench, RAD. Formerly slave to Col. Deavux of Beaufort, South Carolina; left him about 6 years ago. GMC.

Marian Maxico, 27 years, stout wench, RAD. Formerly slave to Thomas Brown of Portsmouth, Virginia; left him about 5 years ago. GMC.

Rachael Maxico, 8 years, RAD. Formerly slave to Thomas Brown of Portsmouth, Virginia; left him about 5 years ago. GMC.

Prince Robinson, 23 years, stout fellow, RAD. Formerly slave to Tully Robinson, Hempslanding, Virginia; left him about 5 years ago. GMC.

Hannah Robinson, 32 years, stout wench, RAD. Formerly slave to John Wheaton, South Branch, Virginia; left him about 5 years ago. GMC.

Peggy Robinson, 12 years, likely girl, RAD. Formerly slave to John Wheaton, South Branch, Virginia; left him about 5 years ago. GMC.

Tom Seaman, 50 years, stout fellow, RAD. Formerly slave to Morris Seaman, Charlestown, South Carolina; left him about 6 years ago. GMC.

Daniel Frip, 39 years, stout fellow, RAD. Formerly slave to Mathew Frip of Norfolk,

Virginia; left him about 5 years ago. GMC.

Rose Frip, 39 years, stout wench, RAD. Formerly slave to John Singletown of Norfolk, Virginia; left him about 5 years ago. GMC.

Lucy Frip, 9 years, likely girl, RAD. Formerly slave to John Singletown of Norfolk, Virginia; left him about 5 years ago. GMC.

Nicholas Forde, 60 years, stout fellow, RAD. Formerly slave to William Thorntown, King George County Virginia; left him about 6 years ago. GMC.

Dick Poole, 19 years, stout fellow, RAD. Formerly slave to Howard Poole of Norfolk County, Virginia; left him about 5 years ago. GMC.

Jacob Williams, 22 years, stout fellow, RAD. Formerly slave to Samuel Williams, Gloucester County, Virginia; left him about 2 years ago. GMC.

Quomo Robinson, aged 45 years, stout fellow. Formerly slave to David Robinson of Norfolk County, Virginia; left him about 5 years ago. GMC.

Betty Quomo, 50 years, stout wench. Formerly slave to Will Wilson of Norfolk County, Virginia; left him about 5 years ago. GMC.

Jack Neal, 23 years, little fellow, RAD. Formerly slave to James Robinson, Hempslanding, Virginia; left him about 7 1/2 years ago. GMC.

Frank Miller, 70 years, ordinary fellow, RAD. Formerly slave to Massey Miller, Norfolk County, Virginia; left him about 7 1/2 years ago. GMC.

Jenny Miller, 50 years, stout wench, RAD. Formerly slave to Joseph Coles, Portsmouth, Virginia; left him about 7 1/2 years ago. GMC.

Nancy Miller, 9 years, RAD. Formerly slave to Joseph Coles of Portsmouth, Virginia; left him about 7 1/2 years ago. GMC.

Pompy Clarke, 33 years, stout fellow, General Hospital's department. Formerly slave to Doctor William Clarke of Boston, New England; left him about 7 1/2 years ago. GMC.

Phillis Clarke, 30 years, stout wench, GHD. Formerly slave to Joseph Lagree, Santee river, South Carolina; left him about 7 1/2 years ago. GHD.

Joseph Dickson, 50 years, ordinary fellow, GHD. Formerly slave to William Dickson of Savannah, Georgia; left him about 4 1/2 years ago. GMC.

John Browne, 40 years, stout fellow, Artillery Department. Born free in Gloucester County, Virginia. GMC.

Cato Ramsey, 50 years, ordinary fellow, General Hospital Department. Formerly the property of Benjamin Ramsey, Cecil County, Maryland; left him about 5 years ago. GMC.

Suckey, 60 years, ordinary wench, GHD. Formerly slave to Benjamin Chine, Cecil County, Maryland; left him about 5 years ago. GMC.

Cato, 5 years, her son, GHD. Born free within the British lines.

Lucey Lambert, 28 years, stout wench, one eye, passenger in the ship. Born free in the City of New York.

Nancey Leonard, 26 years, stout wench, passenger in the ship. Formerly slave to Doctor Tucker, Long Island, New York Province; left him about 7 years ago. GMC.

Jacob Kemp, 40 years, stout fellow, passenger on the ship. Formerly slave to John Adams, Portsmouth, Virginia; left him about 4 years ago. GMC.

**Brig *Concord*
George Robinson, Master**

David Raymond, 40 years, stout fellow, Lt. S. Major. Formerly slave to John Raymond, of Norwalk, Connecticut; left him about 7 years ago. GBC.

Prince Baker, 39 years, stout fellow, Nathaniel Marks. Formerly slave to Nathaniel Baker of Boston, New England; left him about 7 years ago. GMC.

Dorothey, 30 years, stout wench, Nathaniel Marks. Formerly slave to Ralph Stoddart of Boston, New England; left him about 7 years ago. GMC.

John Goseman, 23 years, stout fellow, Mr. Weir. Formerly slave to Daniel Lathem of New London, New England; left him about 4 years ago. GBC.

Charles Harrison, 25 years, stout fellow, Nathaniel Marks. Formerly slave to Charles Kelly of New Georgia, South Carolina; left him about 4 years ago. GBC.

Daniel Proffitt, 23 years, stout fellow, Maurice Salt. Formerly slave to Thomas Hunter of Rapphannack, Virginia; left him about 5 years ago. GMC.

Sibe Proffitt, 32 years, stout wench, Maurice Salt. Formerly slave to Isaac Packley, White Plains, New York Province; left him about 5 years ago. GMC.

Rose Gozeman, 24 years, stout wench, Mr. Weir. Formerly slave to John Easton, Rhode Island; left him about 4 years ago. GMC.

Fanney Gozeman, 5 months old, Mr. Weir's. Born free within the British lines.

Peter Dorram, 25 years, lost his right arm, Mr. Robinson's. Born free at the head of Elk.

Harry Blauvett, 32 years, stout fellow, Lt. S. Majers, free as per voucher produced from Hermanus Blauvelt. GBC.

Dorras Scudder, 20 years, stout wench, Maurice Salt. Formerly slave to Isaac Scudder of Norwich, Connecticut; left him about 6 years ago. GBC.

Andrew Dickson, 11 years, fine boy, John Dickson's. Born free.

Peter Mercer, 54 years, ordinary fellow, Mr. Morrell's. Formerly slave to John Mercer, Stafford County, Virginia; left him about 6 years ago. GMC.

Thomas Ormond, aged 25 years, stout fellow, Capt. Hubble. Formerly slave to Aaron Ormond, Nancy Mund, Virginia; left him about 7 years ago with Lord Dunmore. GBC.

Toney Bartram, 25 years, stout fellow, Capt. Hubble. Formerly slave to Joal Bartram, Fairfield, Connecticut; left him about 4 years ago. GBC.

John Fredrick, 24 years, stout fellow, Mr. Ellis's. Born free in the Island of Jamaica, West Indies. GBC.

Peter Sampson, 19 years, stout fellow, Mr. Bready. Formerly slave to David Core, North Carolina; left him about 4 years ago. GMC.

Thomas Thomson, 20 years, stout fellow, Mr. Ellis. Formerly slave to Andrew Middleton, Ashley river, South Carolina; left him about 4 years ago. GMC.

Prince Perry, 45 years, ordinary fellow, Capt. Hubble. Formerly slave to Colonel Perry, Fairfield, Connecticut; left him about 7 years ago. GBC.

Daniel Payne, 22 years, ordinary fellow, Maurice Salt. Formerly slave to Gen. Washingtown, Virginia; left him about 4 years ago. GMC.

Polly Groves, 26 years, likely wench, Capt. Hubble. Born free in Barbadoes, West Indies as certified by B: General Birch.

Darcas, 28 years, stout wench, Capt. Hubble. Born free at Flushing on Long Island as certified by David Mathews, Esq., Mayor of New York.

On Board The *Diannah* Will Browne, Master [*Port Mattoon*]

Scipio Conner, 22 years, stout fellow, WMG Department. Formerly slave to John Conner, Santee river, South Carolina; left him about 3 1/2 years ago. GMC.

John Broughton, 21 years, stout fellow, Wagon Master General Department. Formerly slave to Thomas Broughton, New England; left him about 3 1/2 years ago. GMC.

Suckey Broughton, 20 years, stout wench, WMGD. Formerly slave to Thomas Broughton, New England; left him about 3 1/2 years ago. GMC.

Thomas Summers, aged 39 years, stout fellow, Thomas Clarke. Formerly slave to Thomas Summers, Charlestown, South Carolina; left him about 3 1/2 years ago. GBC.

Sarrah Miller, 39 years, stout wench, James Clarke. Formerly slave to Thomas Summers, Charlestown, South Carolina; left him about 3 1/2 years ago. GBC.

Suzanah Turnbull, 23 years, stout wench, James Clark.

Born free at Providence in the West Indies as appears by GBC.

Sam Turnbull, 10 years, likely boy, James Clark. Born free at Charlestown, South Carolina as appears by GBC.

Titus Eldridge, 21 years, stout fellow, Wagon Master General's Department. Formerly slave to Joseph Eldridge, New York, who left the Negroes in 1776. GMC.

Prince Aldrich, 34 years, ordinary fellow, WMGD. Formerly slave to Timothy Crosby, Charlestown, South Carolina; left him about 4 years ago. GBC.

Betsey Aldrich, 33 years, ordinary wench, WMGD. Her freedom given her by James Way, farmer at Newtown landing on Long Island. GMC.

Tabby Rogers, 20 years, stout wench, WMGD. Formerly slave to William Allen, Western Shore, Virginia; left him about 6 1/2 years ago. GBC.

Betsey Rogers, 2 years, WMGD. Born free within the British lines.

Easter Rogers, 10 years, likely girl, WMGD. Former slave to William Allen, Western Shore, Virginia; left him about 6 years ago. GBC.

Cato Cox, 26 years, stout fellow, WMGD. Born free at Frankford, Province of Pennsylvania.

John Cox, 10 years, likely boy, WMGD. Born free at Frankford, Province of Pennsylvania.

Jenny Cox, 24 years, ordinary wench, WMGD. Formerly slave to John Dykman, New York Island, who left her free at his death. GMC.

Betsey Forsyth, 22 years, stout wench, WMGD. Formerly slave to George Townsend of New York who left her in 1776. GMC.

John Forsyth, 22 years, stout fellow, WMGD. Formerly slave to George Rapalje of New York who left said slave in 1776. GMC.

Lydia Forsyth, 1 year, WMGD. Born free within the British lines.

Isaac Spencer, 43 years, stout fellow, WMGD. Formerly slave to Henry Tromble, Chester County, Pennsylvania; left him about 5 years ago. GBC.

Jack Scotty, aged 32 years, stout fellow, WMGD. Formerly slave to John Scolly of Boston, New England; left him about 7 1/2 years ago. GBC.

Phebe Scotty, 25 years, stout wench, WMGD. Formerly slave to Arnold Wills of Boston, New England; left him about 7 1/2 years ago. GBC.

Jupiter, 35 years, stout fellow, WMGD. Formerly slave to Jasper Harmer of Brunswick, New Jersey; left him about 6 years ago. GBC.

Robert Backhus, 26 years, stout fellow, WMGD. Formerly slave to Hugh Alson of James Island, South Carolina; left him about 4 years ago. GBC.

Molly Backhus, 21 years, stout wench, WMGD. Formerly slave to Thomas Litcon of John's Island, South Carolina; left him about 5 years ago. GBC.

Phillis Farmer, 30 years, stout wench, WMGD. Formerly slave to Richard Jackwish of Brunswick, New Jersey; left him about 7 years ago. GBC.

Cato Rogers, 44 years, stout fellow, WMGD. Formerly slave to William Rogers of New Port, Rhode Island; left him about 5 years ago. GBC.

Robert Dalton, 36 years, stout fellow, WMGD. Formerly slave to James Dalton of Boston, New England; left him about 7 1/2 years ago. GBC.

Nelly Dalton, 26 years, stout wench, WMGD. Formerly slave to Joseph Lagree of

Charleston, South Carolina; left him about 7 1/2 years ago. GBC.

Suzan Dalton, 2 years, WMGD. Born free within the British lines.

Peter Tarbett, 32 years, stout fellow, WMGD. Formerly slave to Joseph Tarbett of Boston, New England; left him about 7 1/2 years ago. GBC.

Peggy King, 28 years, stout wench, WMGD. Formerly slave to Fraser of Chester County, Pennsylvania; left him about 5 years ago. GBC.

Robert King, 4 years, WMGD. Born free within the British lines.

Richard Samson, 25 years, stout fellow, WMGD. Formerly slave to John Bushell of Portsmouth, Virginia; left him about 5 1/2 years ago. GBC.

Daniel Reading, 28 years, stout fellow, WMGD. Formerly slave to Hans Miller of Walkhellen, New York Province; left him about 6 years ago. GMC.

Mary Reading, 19 years, stout wench, WMGD. Born free at New York.

Will Hannabill, 25 years, stout fellow, WMGD. Born free at Paramus, New Jersey.

Sarah Hannabill, 21 years, stout wench, WMGD. Born free at Fl___, New Jersey.

On Board His Majesty's Ship *L'Abondance* Lt. Phillips

Robert Bowland, 35 years, stout fellow, Black Brigade. Formerly slave to Champion Travers of Jamestown, Virginia; left him about 3 1/2 years ago. GMC.

Thomas Russall, 24 years, stout fellow, BB. Formerly slave to Doctor Wast of Charlestown, South Carolina; left him about 5 years ago. GMC.

Sam Wedder, 30 years, stout fellow, BB. Formerly slave to Doctor Wedder of Goose Creek, South Carolina; left him about 5 1/2 years ago. GBC.

John, 21 years, stout fellow, BB. Formerly slave to Isaac Vorcheen, Hackensack, New Jersey; left him about 7 1/2 years ago. GBC.

John Nicholas, 21 years, stout fellow, BB. Born free in Gloucester County, Virginia.

John Jackson, 19 years, stout fellow, BB. Formerly slave to Rabo, Glocester County, Virginia; left him about 4 years ago. GBC.

Lewis Freeland, 29 years, stout fellow, BB. Formerly slave to John Scuyler, Second river, New Jersey; left him about 6 years ago. GBC.

Elizabeth Freeland, 22 years, stout wench, BB. Born free nigh Parramus, New Jersey.

Lewis, 32 years, stout fellow, BB. Formerly slave to Mr. VerPlank of Cortlands Manner, New York Province; left him about 3 years ago. GBC.

Richard Jarrett, 30 years, stout fellow, BB. Born free at East Chester, New York Province.

Sam Van Nostrant, 53 years, ordinary fellow, BB. Formerly slave to C. Van Nostrant of Acquickenack, New Jersey; left him about 6 years ago. GBC.

Sarrah Van Nostrand, 50 years, ordinary wench, BB. Formerly slave to C. Van Nostrant of Acquickenack, New Jersey; left him about 6 years ago. GBC.

Sarrah Van Nostrant, aged 20 years, ordinary wench, BB. Formerly slave to C. Van Nostrant of Acquackeneck, New York; left him about 6 years ago. GBC.

Isaac Howard, 27 years, stout fellow, BB. Formerly slave to George Howard nigh Lewistown, Pennsylvania; left him about 4 years ago. GBC.

Morris Seaman, 21 years, stout fellow, BB. Formerly slave to Saul Paul of Georgetown, South Carolina; left him about 4 years ago. GBC.

Sarrah, 70 years, ordinary wench, BB. Formerly slave to Captain Wilson of Grenadas.

Belinda, 50 years, ordinary wench, BB. Formerly slave to P. N. Brooke Livingston, who gave her freedom.

Moses Kelty, 20 years, stout fellow, BB. Formerly slave to George Kelty of Norfolk, Virginia; left him about 4 years ago. GMC.

Thomas Cooper, 20 years, stout fellow, BB. Formerly slave to Cornelius Vanyinkle of Acquackinack, New Jersey; left him about 3 1/2 years ago. GBC.

Jane, 30 years, ordinary wench, BB. Formerly slave to John Sears of New Ark, New Jersey; left him about 8 years ago. GBC.

Aaron Jones, 42 years, stout fellow, BB. Formerly slave to Hendrick Smith, Monmouth County, New Jersey; left him about 6 years ago. GBC.

Isaac Jones, 10 years, fine boy, BB. Formerly slave to Richard Stout of Monmouth County, New Jersey; left him about 6 years ago. GBC.

Sarrah Jones, 42 years, stout wench, BB. Formerly slave to Richard Stout of Monmouth County, New Jersey; left him about 6 years ago. GBC.

Thomas Drake, 17 years, likely lad, BB. Formerly slave to Thomas Thurman of Monmouth County, New Jersey; left him about 5 years ago. GBC.

Tom, 17 years, likely lad, BB. Formerly slave to Nicholas Cyphrus, a French Merchant.

John Hamilton, 24 years, stout fellow, BB. Formerly slave to Mr. James Hamilton of Barbadoes; left him about 5 years ago. GBC.

Kate Walters, 40 years, stout wench, BB. Formerly slave to Rebecca Ramsburgh, who gave her freedom. GBC.

Will Robinson, aged 19 years, stout lad, BB. Born free in the City of New York.

Adam Green, 23 years, stout lad, BB. Formerly slave to John Brown of Portsmouth, Virginia; left him about 5 years ago. GBC.

Latice Young, 20 years, stout wench, BB. Formerly slave to William Young of Welltown, South Carolina; left him about 5 years ago. GMC.

Jack Williams, 24 years, stout fellow, BB. Formerly slave to William Williamson Horse,

Savannah, South Carolina; left him about 5 years ago. GMC.

Judith Dewitt, 22 years, stout wench, BB. Formerly slave to John Dewitt of Charlestown, South Carolina; left him about 4 years ago. GMC.

Dublin Moore, 31 years, ordinary fellow, BB. Formerly slave to John Moore of James Island, South Carolina; left him about 5 years ago. GBC.

John Charles Clap, 35 years, stout fellow, BB. Born free in New Cursesaw.

Thomas Holmes, 22 years, stout fellow, BB. Formerly slave to ___ Cairnes of Charlestown, South Carolina; left him about 7 1/2 years ago.

Jacob Brady, 40 years, stout fellow, BB. Formerly slave to Archibald Brodie of Chesterfield, Warwick County, Virginia; left him about 4 years ago. GBC.

Daniel Elliott, 29 years, stout fellow, BB. Formerly slave to Gen. Sumpter of Santee river, South Carolina; left him about 6 years ago. GBC.

Stanle Platt, 29 years, stout fellow, BB. Formerly slave to Peter Thorn Platt, Charlestown, South Carolina; left him about 5 years ago. GMC.

Peggy, 30 years, stout wench, BB. Formerly slave to Martin Joice, Norfolk County, Virginia; left him about 7 1/2 years ago.

Peter, her son, 2 years, BB. Born free within the British lines.

Sally Wilson, 18 years, stout wench, BB. Formerly slave to William Fredericks, Island of Providence; left him about 3 years ago.

James Russell, 20 years, stout fellow, BB. Born free; lived with John Mansburgh, Norfolk County, Virginia.

Capt. George Fraction, 27 years, stout fellow, BB. Formerly slave to David Leach of James river, Virginia; left him about 5 years ago. GBC.

John Cooper, 27 years, stout fellow, BB. Formerly slave to Martmas Cooper of Livingston Manner, New York Province; left him about 6 years ago. GBC.

Betsey Robinson, aged 40 years, ordinary wench, BB. Formerly slave to John Robinson of Charlestown, South Carolina, who gave her freedom.

Mingo Leslie, 34 years, ordinary fellow, BB. Formerly slave to John Leslie, Charlestown, South Carolina;

left him about 3 1/2 years ago. GMC.

Dianah Johnson, 18 years, likely wench. Formerly slave to William Johnson of Goose Creek, South Carolina; left him about 3 1/2 years ago. GMC.

Martin Cox, 44 years, nearly worn out, BB. Formerly slave to Col. Cox, Surry County, Virginia; left him about 4 years ago. GBC.

Lymus Pandorrus, 52 years, nearly worn out, BB. Formerly slave to Richard Pandorrus, New river, South Carolina; left him about 4 years ago. GBC.

Maria Pandorrus, 32 years, ordinary wench, BB. Formerly slave to William Jones of Savannah in Georgia; left him about 4 years ago. GBC.

Oliver Vinson, 30 years, stout fellow, BB. Formerly slave to John Freeman, Monmouth County, New Jersey; left him about 6 1/2 years ago. GBC.

Dianah Vinson, 28 years, stout wench, BB. Formerly slave to Samuel Rutt, Thourough-fair neck, Pennsylvania; left him about 6 1/2 years ago. GBC.

Judith Mozely, 28 years, likely wench, BB. Formerly slave to Col. Mozely of Princes Ann County, Virginia; left him about 5 years ago. GBC.

Peggy Mozely, 18 years, likely wench, BB. Formerly slave to Colonel Mozely, Princes Ann County, Virginia; left him about 5 years ago. GBC.

Isaac Taylor, 39 years, ordinary fellow, BB. Formerly slave to John Van Horn, Communepaw, New Jersey; left him about 7 1/2 years ago. GBC.

John Hedler, 26 years, likely fellow, BB. Born free as appears by a certificate from Brigadeer General Birch.

Dianah Hedler, 27 years, ordinary wench, BB. Born free as appears by a certificate from Brigadeer General Birch.

James Hedler, 6 years, ordinary boy, BB. Born free as appears by a certificate from Brigadeer General Birch.

Charlotte Hedler, 1 year, BB. Born free as appears by a certificate from Brigadeer General Birch.

Cato Winslow, aged 49 years, ordinary fellow, BB. Formerly slave to Mr. Winslow at New York; left him about 7 1/2 years ago. GMC.

Rose Winslow, 40 years, ordinary wench, BB. Formerly slave to Captain Valantine, Boston, New England; left him about 7 1/2 years ago. GMC.

Toby Winslow, 11 years, likely boy, BB. Formerly slave to Capt. Valantine, Boston, New England; left him about 7 1/2 years ago. GMC.

Hannah Winslow, 4 years, ordinary child, BB. Born free within the British lines.

Mary Thomson, 54 years, nearly worn out, BB. Born free at Newark as certified by Brigadeer General Birch.

Margaret Thomson, 25 years, stout wench, BB. Born free at Newark as certified by Brigadeer General Birch.

Polly Thomson, 10 years, ordinary child, BB. Born free at Newark as certified by Brigadeer General Birch.

Rachell Thomson, 3 years, ordinary child, BB. Born free at Newark as certified by Brigadeer General Birch.

Sally Thomson, 1 year, ordinary child, BB. Born free at Newark as certified by Brigadeer General Birch.

Betsey, 50 years, ordinary wench, BB. Proved to be free & voucher produced at the time of inspection.

George Wilkinson, 19 years, stout fellow, BB. Formerly slave to Willis Wilkinson, Nancy Munn County, Virginia; left him about 4 years ago. GMC.

Toney, 34 years, ordinary fellow, BB. Formerly slave to Rymer Suydam at Brooklyn, who left said negro in 1776 to shift for himself. GMC.

Hager Kennedy, 29 years, ordinary wench, BB. Formerly slave to Mathew Hardey, Augusta County, Georgia; left him about 4 years ago. GBC.

Sam her son, 1 year, BB. Born free within the British lines.

Peter Harding, 28 years, stout fellow, BB. Formerly slave to James Paul, Northumberland County, Virginia; left him about 4 years ago. GBC.

Kate Harding, aged 40 years, ordinary wench, BB. Formerly slave to Mr. Armsted, Gloucester County, Virginia; left him about 7 years ago. GBC.

Ebenezer Harding, 2 1/2 years, BB. Born free within the British Lines.

John Jackson, 30 years, stout fellow, BB. Formerly slave to

Peter Curtinas, Morristown, New Jersey; left him about 7 years ago. GMC.

Hannah Jackson, 30 years, stout wench, BB. Formerly slave to Aaron Gilbert, Morristown, New Jersey; left him about 7 years ago. GBC.

Pompy Colt, 27 years, ordinary fellow, BB. Formerly slave to Mr. Colt, Santee river, South Carolina; left him about 3 1/2 years ago. GMC.

Toby Castington, 33 years, stout fellow, BB. Formerly slave to John Conner, Kent County, Virginia; left him about 7 years ago, with Lord Dunmore. GBC.

Cloe Mann, 34 years, ordinary wench, BB. Formerly slave to Samuel Griggory, Virginia; left him about 7 years ago. GBC.

Bettsey Mann, 5 years, BB. Born free within the British Lines.

In pursuance of two orders from His Excellency Sir Guy Carleton, K. B., General & Commander in Chief of His Majesty's Forces, from Nova Scotia to West Florida inclusive, both dated head Quarters, New York, the one the fifteenth day of April and the other the Twenty second day of May Seventeen hundred and Eighty three years, we whose names are hereunto subscribed do certify that we did carefully inspect the aforegoing vessels on the thirtyeth day of November one thousand Seven Hundred & eighty three years, And that on board the said vessels we found the Negroes mentioned in the aforegoing list, Amounting to **one Hundred and Forty two men, Ninety women and fifty four Children**, And to the best of our Judgement believe them to be all the Negroes on board the said Vessels, And we enquired of the Master of each Vessel, whether he had any records, Deeds, or Archives, or papers, or other property of the Citizens of the United States on board and to each enquiry we were answered in the negative. And we further certify that we furnished each Master of a vessel, with a Certified List of the Negroes on board the vessel, And informed him that he would not be permitted to Land in Nova Scotia any other Negroes, than those contained in the List, And that if any other Negroes were found on board the vessel, he would be severely punished. And that we informed the agent for Transports of this Matter And desired him to use means for returning back to the Port of New York all Negroes not mentioned in the Lists.

London, 19th Febry. 1784

William Armstrong & T. Gilfillan

No. 47, Inspection rolls of Negroes

Recapitulation of the number of Negroes who have availed themselves of the Late Commander in Chiefs Proclamations by comming in with the British Lines in North America, which numbers distinguishing Men, Women and Children have been Inspected by the Commissioner appointed by His Excellency Sir Guy Carleton K.B. Commander in Chief, for that Purpose, on Board the Several Vessels in which they were Embarked previous to their Time of Sailing from the Port of New York in North America, between the 23rd April and the 30th November 1783 Both Days Inclusive.

Appendix 1

Tables

Table 1

All Negroes Who Claimed To Be Born Free

Colony	Men	Women	Boys	Girls	Gender Unknown
Unknown	12	14	26	35	3
New York	18	32	32	34	5
Virginia	19	9	1	8	2
Penn.	4	0	1	1	1
S. Carolina	11	6	2	3	1
N. Carolina	0	0	0	0	0
Georgia	0	1	0	0	0
N. Jersey	0	13	4	3	6
N. England	1	2	0	0	0
Maryland	4	1	2	0	0
Conn.	4	2	1	0	0
Rhode Is.	0	7	2	2	0
West Indies	6	1	0	0	0
Jamaica	7	1	2	0	0
Barbados	4	1	0	0	0
Antigua	0	1	0	0	0
England	1	1	0	0	0
Madagasgar	1	0	0	0	0
Bahamas	0	2	1	0	0
Bermuda	1	0	0	0	0
St. Augustine	0	1	0	1	0
St. Croix	1	0	0	0	0
Grenades	2	0	0	0	0
Canada	0	1	0	0	0
Total	96	96	74	87	18

Table 2

All Negroes Who Claimed To Have Escaped

Colony	Men	Women	Boys	Girls	Gender Unknown
Unknown	7	3	0	0	1
New York	23	12	4	1	7
Virginia	149	105	33	35	29
Penn.	20	9	2	1	4
S. Carolina	77	70	23	16	6
N. Carolina	7	3	0	0	4
Georgia	21	8	0	1	3
N. Jersey	40	26	6	6	5
N. England	6	6	1	1	0
Maryland	6	1	0	2	0
Conn.	4	0	0	0	0
Rhode Is.	2	2	0	0	2
West Indies	0	1	0	0	0
Jamaica	5	0	0	0	0
Barbados	2	0	0	0	0
England	0	0	0	0	0
St. Augustine	1	0	0	0	0
Grenades	0	1	0	0	0
Canada	1	0	0	0	0
Florida	1	0	0	0	0
Total	372	247	69	63	61

Table 3

All Negroes Who Were Free By Proclamation

Colony	Men	Women	Boys	Girls	Gender Unknown
Unknown	18	8	7	2	0
New York	33	22	6	8	1
Virginia	234	143	41	52	15
Penn.	13	9	1	1	0
S. Carolina	129	77	24	9	4
N. Carolina	13	6	2	1	2
Georgia	25	15	3	4	0
N. Jersey	61	21	9	6	0
N. England	13	4	2	0	0
Maryland	26	4	0	1	0
Conn.	19	4	1	0	3
Rhode Is.	11	4	3	1	0
West Indies	1	1	0	0	0
Jamaica	2	3	1	1	0
Barbados	1	1	1	0	0
St. Augustine	1	0	0	0	0
Grenades	1	0	0	0	0
Total	601	322	101	86	25

Table 4

Negroes Boarding Ships As Emancipated Slaves

Colony	Men	Women	Boys	Girls	Gender Unknown
Unknown	23	25	11	9	7
New York	14	20	8	9	7
Virginia	4	2	1	0	0
Pennsylvania	4	2	1	0	0
S. Carolina	8	3	1	0	0
N. Carolina	1	0	0	0	0
Georgia	2	5	2	2	1
New Jersey	5	1	0	0	0
N. England	2	1	0	0	0
Maryland	0	1	0	1	0
Connecticut	2	2	0	0	0
Rhode Island	3	2	0	1	0
West Indies	3	1	1	0	0
Jamaica	1	1	0	0	0
Barbados	1	0	0	0	0
Antigua	0	2	0	0	0
England	1	1	0	0	0
Total	74	69	25	22	15

Table 5

All Negroes Who Were Still Slaves

Colony	Men	Women	Boys	Girls	Gender Unknown
Unknown	53	56	43	41	7
New York	31	29	31	29	6
Virginia	2	0	2	5	0
Pennsylvania	1	0	0	0	0
S. Carolina	5	1	1	3	0
N. Carolina	1	0	1	0	0
Georgia	0	0	0	1	0
New Jersey	1	0	0	0	0
N. England	1	0	0	0	0
Maryland	3	0	2	2	0
West Indies	2	0	0	0	0
Canada	0	1	1	1	0
Amboy	1	1	0	1	0
Total	101	88	81	83	13

Table 6

All Negroes Who Were Indentured For Future Service

Colony	Men	Women	Boys	Girls	Gender Unknown
Unknown	0	0	0	3	0
New York	7	0	2	0	0
Virginia	1	0	0	0	0
Pennsylvania	0	0	0	0	0
S. Carolina	8	0	0	0	0
N. Carolina	0	0	0	0	0
Georgia	1	0	0	0	0
New Jersey	2	0	0	0	0
N. England	0	0	0	0	0
Connecticut	1	0	0	0	0
Jamaica	2	0	0	0	0
Antigua	2	0	0	0	0
Total	24	0	2	3	0

Table 7

All Negroes Who Were Released On Their Master's Death

Colony	Men	Women	Boys	Girls	Gender Unknown
Unknown	2	3	0	0	0
New York	7	6	1	0	0
Virginia	1	1	1	0	0
S. Carolina	8	3	1	0	0
Georgia	1	1	0	0	0
New Jersey	2	0	0	0	0
N. England	1	0	0	0	0
Rhode Island	1	1	0	1	0
Jamaica	2	0	0	0	0
Total	25	15	3	1	0

Table 8

All Negroes Who Were Free Or Unknown

Colony	Men	Women	Boys	Girls	Gender Unknown
Unknown	7	2	—	2	2
New York	—	3	—	2	1
Virginia	—	—	—	—	2
Pennsylvania	6	1	—	—	—
Total	13	6	—	4	5

Table 9

Those Slaves Who Were Abandoned

	Men	Women
New York	5	2

Appendix 2

The London Black Poor

An Alphabetical List of the Black People Who have Received the Bounty from Government. Source: PRO T1/638

1. John Adams
2. George Adams & Child
3. John Ashfield
4. James Anderson
5. Archibald Anderson
6. John Albert
7. William Anderson
8. Ebenezar Anderson
9. William Agnew
10. Thomas Ashworth
11. James Annison
12. Thomas Adams
13. John Anthony
14. Sylva Ablin
15. James Atkins
16. Samuel Allen
17. Thomas Ansley
18. Turese Ambo
19. Timothy Allenby
20. Joseph Allambazi
21. Harry Armstrong
22. Joshua Allamazi
23. Henry Alexander
24. Daniel Allington
25. Gaub Annand
26. Charles Adams
27. Jack Anthony
28. Joseph Anderson
29. Syllavo Augustavas
30. John Adams
31. Abram Allison
32. Samuel Adamson
33. John Aberdeen
34. Ann Allamaze
35. Robert Ashfield
36. Jack Andrew
37. John Ashfield
38. Jack Anthony
39. Joseph Anthony
40. John Anthony
41. John Brown
42. Joseph Brown
43. Thomas Bruce
44. John Beckett
45. William Barnes
46. George Broomfield
47. William Bird
48. Benjamin Brown
49. Joseph Barley
50. William Blue
51. George Brown
52. Joshua Brown
53. Aaron Brooks
54. John Bell
55. Peter Bristow
56. John Brandy
57. Jacob Boss
58. David Brown
59. Anthony Burgess
60. Richard Bristow
61. Henry Butler
62. John Britain
63. Hamil Bendiver
64. Isaac Benn
65. Johanna Bryan
66. George William Bryan
67. Edward Brown
68. William Bond
69. Thomas Britain
70. Henry Beale
71. John Bridges
72. Robert Black
73. John Blake
74. James Batty
75. John English Brown
76. John Black
77. John Bristow
78. James Bailey

79. Joseph Benthew
80. George Berwick
81. John Brown
82. James Barnes
83. William Boarham
84. Billy a Boy from Africa
85. Benjamin Burgess
86. Francis Broughton
87. John Brown
88. William Barnes
89. John Bristow
90. George Bernard
91. Thomas Brown
92. Pete Bastian
93. Richard Bradley
94. Sylva Besantee
95. James Brown
96. Patient Baldwin
97. Francis Bastion
98. David Bricker
99. Thomas Brown
100. John Brown
101. John Baptist
102. John Bamptiser
103. John Brown
104. John Brown
105. Isaac Brunhard
106. James Boston
107. John Cambridge
108. Richard Cooper
109. Thomas Clements
110. Joseph Curry
111. Paul Clark & his wife
112. John Comyns
113. Charles Chilcoth
114. James Collins
115. John Currigut
116. James Crisby
117. Francis Chase
118. John Carrol
119. James Chilton
120. William Carey
121. Thomas Clark
122. Henry Carter
123. Henry Cane
124. George Clark
125. Daniel Cooper
126. Thomas Cummins
127. Daniel Christopher
128. Charles Carvat
129. Benjamin Clark & Wife
130. Robert Clayton
131. Thomas Criswill
132. John Cane
133. John Coleman
134. William Cole
135. Benjamin Clark
136. Charles Castor
137. John Coleman
138. Richard Crooks
139. William Collinson
140. William Cloase
141. Andrew Carey
142. David Cunningham
143. George Clark
144. Robert Carey
145. Shadrack Clark
146. James Charles
147. George Clark
148. William Clark
149. George Comfortable
150. William Campbell
151. Thomas Ceasor
152. Thomas Cox
153. James Cox
154. Thomas Damaine
155. Peter Dickson
156. John Davis
157. William Dennison
158. William Dean
159. James Dran
160. John Dobbs
161. James Douglas
162. William Davis
163. ___ Davis, Wife
164. John Dublin

165. William Dover
166. Henry Demaine
167. David Draper
168. George Douglass
169. Anthony Drewsaw
170. D A Silea
171. Thomas Davis
172. John Dandridge
173. Patrick Duke
174. Francis Durham
175. Richard Denham
176. James Davis
177. David Davidson
178. Stephen Dorset
179. Desantee Syllabos
180. John Dyer
181. David Dickson
182. John Dobson
183. William Duett
184. Joseph Doming
185. Anthony Domingo
186. Benjamin Elliott
187. Thomas Earle
188. George Elliott
189. Abraham Ellis
190. John Ellis
191. George Etty
192. Joseph Francis
193. George Truman
194. Thomas Franks
195. Peter Francis
196. John Truman
197. George Foster
198. Thomas Freeman
199. John Fortune
200. William Field
201. Samuel Francis
202. Benjamin Freeman
203. George Ferguson
204. Samuel Ford
205. John Ferrell
206. Thomas Foreman
207. Thomas Foreman

208. Henry Field
209. Henry Fitzgerald
210. Thomas Fruman
211. Simon Ford
212. Samuel Francis, Jr.
213. John Francis
214. Jonathan Fenwick
215. John Frederick
216. James Francis
217. George Ford
218. William Fenn
219. William Green
220. ___ Green, Wife
221. Matthew Gale
222. William Gordon
223. Thomas Grant
224. John Grovis
225. Abraham Elliott Griffith
226. John George
227. Peter Githam
228. William Gorman
229. John Green
230. James Green
231. John Goss
232. John Green
233. Richard Green
234. William George
235. John Gostel
236. William Green
237. John Green
238. Charles Gilbert
239. John Gay
240. David Gasgoine
241. John Green
242. Arthur Gilbert
243. Thomas Green
244. Anthony Grayson
245. Arthur Grayham
246. Archibald Grayham
247. Emanuel Gumbee
248. Thomas Gray
249. Joseph Glover
250. Peter Grant

251. Robert George
252. John George
253. Anthony Gray
254. Joseph Grovis
255. William Green
256. Francis Gordon
257. William Green
258. John Horn
259. ___ Horn, Wife
260. Edward Hamilton
261. Thomas Hooper
262. William Hamilton
263. James Hartford
264. ___ Hartford, Wife
265. John Walter Harvis
266. Thomas Hudson
267. Moses Henley
268. ___ Henley, Wife
269. Thomas Holder
270. William Hudson
271. ___ Hudson, Wife
272. George How
273. James Hadwick
274. ___ Hadwick, Wife
275. George Hill
276. John Hall
277. Thomas Holder
278. John Hughes
279. Edward Hamilton
207. Thomas Holder *
208. John Hughes
209. Edward Hamilton
210. John Harris
211. John Houghlin
212. James Harris
213. William Harrison
214. William Hoskins
215. John Hill
216. Joseph Harrison
217. James Harris
218. William Hughes
219. John Hamilton

220. James Hazzard
221. Francis Holland
222. John Hamilton (Child)
223. Tom Harris
224. John Harvey
225. Thomas Hall
226. James Harris
227. Peter Harris
228. Thomas Hall
229. William Higgins
230. Peter Harris
231. Peter Hill
232. John Hamilton
233. Richard Hall
234. Edward Hunnicutt
235. Josiah Horace
236. Edward Jackson
237. Daniel Johnson
238. William Jones
239. Joseph Jordon
240. Charles Jones
241. ___ Jones, Wife
242. Jacob Jackson
243. ___ Jackson, Wife
244. Henry Jones
245. Anthony Jochn
246. James Johnson
247. George Isaac
248. John Johnson
249. Joseph James
250. John Jackson
251. Thomas Jackson
252. John James
253. John Jacob
254. John Johnson
255. William Johnson
256. George Jamison
257. John Johnson
258. Joseph Johnson
259. William Johnson
260. George Jones
261. John Jacob

262. Jacob Johnson
263. John Jones
264. William Jackson
265. John Jacob (Child)
266. John Jupetor
267. Thomas Jordon
268. John Johnson
269. William Johnson
270. Jacob Jennings
271. Thomas Johnson
272. John Ceasor Johnson
273. Joseph Innis
274. Thomas Jackson
275. James Jackson
276. William Jack
277. Thomas Jack
278. Jack Jones
279. Joseph Jenkins
280. William Jackson
281. William Joseph
282. John Jenkins
283. Daniel Jones
284. William Jobson
285. Jonathan Jackson
286. James Johnson
287. Robert Jones
288. Robert James
289. John Jones
290. John James
291. William James
292. William James
293. Andrew James
294. David King
295. Robert Knight
296. William Kelly
297. Lewis Kivinor
298. John Limbrick
299. William Lee
300. Francis Lee
301. ___ Lee, Wife
302. George Lawrence
303. James Lowther
304. John Lampley
305. William Lawrence
306. William Limbrick
307. John Lemmon
308. William Lampley
309. Samuel Lewis
310. John Lewis
311. John London
312. Thomas London
313. John London
314. Thomas Lowther
315. Lewis Latoueh
316. Lewis Latoueh, Jr.
317. Alex Learmouth
318. George Lewis
319. James Lowther
320. James Lucas
321. William Lampley
322. Patrick Lawson
323. Abram Lumby
324. Daniel Lawrence
325. John Lewis
326. John Lynch
327. Andrew Littney
328. John Lucas
329. John Lawrence
330. John Lewis
331. Robert Moore
332. Lewis Morris
333. George Minor
334. William Manshaw
335. Charles Murren
336. John Manewell
337. John McHannon
338. Abraham McKay
339. William Martin
340. Laban Morris
341. Richard Markfield
342. William Moody
343. ___ Moody, Child
344. James Murray
345. Lewis Murphy
346. Daniel Mathews
347. Christian Minor

348. Jacob Miles
349. William Murphey
350. Charles Molineux
351. James March
352. John Murray
353. Joseph Maniwell
354. George Mead
355. Daniel Lawrence
356. William Munday
357. Thomas Marlin
358. John Morris
359. John Maniwell
360. James Maxfield
361. Thomas Martin
362. James Mellington
363. James Mitchell
364. Cornelius Manley
365. Simon Maron
366. David Murray
367. John Millick
368. John Monson
369. Richard McKay
370. James Marlin
371. Abram Mathews
372. James Millingly
373. Anthony Madare
374. John Munday
375. John Marshall
376. William Mullindee
377. Jon Murren
378. Hezekiah Neekens
379. Thomas Neale
380. George Newton
381. Thomas Nottingham
382. John Needam
383. James Nipper
384. John Nicholas
385. George Newland
386. Thomas Nelson
387. James Nesbit
388. John Nicholas
389. John Nicholas
390. James Neptune

391. James Newman
392. Joseph Newman
393. William Newman
394. Daniel Norman
395. George Ogram
396. ___ Ogram, Wife
397. John Osman
398. John Oliver
399. James Owann
400. Francis Oatsby
401. John Oxford
402. Ralph Oram
403. Peter Oramfield
404. William Ormfield
405. James Oliver
406. John Promise
407. John Promise
408. James Promise
409. William Powell
410. George Pimbrook
411. Abram Parado
412. Joseph Poole
413. Manuel Parado
414. George Peters
415. James Parker
416. Thomas Parker
417. John Peggs
418. George Prince
419. John Parford
420. Anthony Perry
421. Hanibal Polydore
422. George Phillips
423. Kinnett Pearcey
424. Jervis Prince
425. Thomas Plumb
426. Robert Prince
427. Benjamin Paby
428. Thomas Peter
429. John Peters
430. Thomas Pallas
431. Samuel Page
432. Peter Parker
433. William Prince

434. Joseph Phillip
435. Thomas Pearce
436. James Passmore
437. William Prince
438. Thomas Peasor
439. John Peasey
440. John Pompey
441. Mary Promise
442. John Provey
443. John Pompey, Jr.
444. John Peters
445. Emanuel Philips
446. Charles Prince
447. William Raper
448. Edward Robinson
449. James Richard
450. John William Ramsay
451. John Ramsey
452. John Riddle
453. John Robertson
454. Joseph Roberts
455. Jacob Richardson
456. Lewis Rose
457. James Robertson
458. Charles Richardson
459. Henry Rhodes
460. Stephen Roberts
461. James Roberts
462. William Richardson
463. William Roberts
464. James Rowland
465. James Reid
466. Robert Robertson
467. Nathaniel Richardson
468. Thomas Richardson
469. John Richards
470. Charles Richmond
471. Edward Russer
472. Thomas Robinson
473. Benjamin Richardson
474. Walter Rose
475. John Robinson
476. William Robinson
477. James Robinson
478. John Robinson
479. William John Redin
480. James Robert
481. Charles Stoddart
482. John Speak
483. ___ Speak, Wife
484. John Spears
485. ___ Spears, Wife
486. Francis Steward
487. ___ Steward, Wife
488. James Seymour
489. Anthony Smith
490. John Swithin
491. John Steward
492. James Strong
493. John Smith
494. William Sedgwick
495. Alexander Swinton
496. Lewis Sterling
497. Robert Stevens
498. Anthony Smith
499. John Simmons
500. John Solloman
501. Francis Swinton
502. Anthony Setine
503. George Samuel
504. John Smith
505. John Steven
506. Thomas Seppey
507. Henry Shaw
508. Benjamin Stevens
509. York Steward
510. Charles Searli
511. Samuel Skinner
512. John Stacey
513. George Steward
514. George Sharp
515. James Stepney
516. William Smith
517. John Solomon
518. David Smith

519. Joseph Simms
520. Francis Solomon
521. Charles Stonestreet
522. John Smith
523. John Stephens
524. George Selly
525. William Stephenson
526. George Samuel
527. Thomas Stanley
528. Abram Steward
529. John Simpson
530. Anthony Smith
531. Francis Sylva
532. Thomas Samo
533. John Smith
534. John Skinner
535. John Simpson
536. Robert Shirley
537. Abraham Silvarus
538. Martin Servantus
539. John Shrimpton
540. George Stephenson
541. George Shepherd
542. Dick Simmons
543. John Sereen
544. William Sampson
545. Isaac Sears
546. William Smith
547. Charles Stephenson
548. John Spring
549. Abraham Smith
550. Lilli Simon
551. Barbara Solomon
552. Mary Simms
553. John Smith
554. Thomas Smith
555. William Santhin
556. John Smith
557. Emanuel Saunders
558. John Smith
559. John Smith
560. Jack Simpson
561. Thomas Starling

562. Anthony Sylva
563. Adam Southerland
564. John Strong
565. Thomas Sampson
566. Abram Spears
567. William Smith
568. Thomas Sylva
569. Thomas Thompson
570. John Thomas
571. John Thomas
572. John Thomas
573. Anthony Thomas
574. John Thomas
575. John Thomas
576. John Thomas
577. John Thomas
578. William Thomas
579. John Thomas
580. Robert Thomas
581. Moses Thomas
582. James Thomas
583. John Thomas
584. Daniel Tallow
585. Thomas Thompson
586. George Turner
587. John Twine
588. Thomas Thompson
589. James Thompson
590. William Thompson
591. Joseph Thompson
592. Joseph Taylor
593. John Thompson
594. John Tatham
595. William Taylor
596. John Thomas
597. James Titus
598. Barret Thompson
599. William Theodore
600. Jack Thomas
601. Thomas Tucks
602. John Thomas
603. John Ceasor Thomas
604. Edward Thompson

605. John Thompson
606. Charles Thomas
607. Charles Thompson
608. Thomas Thompson
609. Alexander Thompson
610. John Thomas
611. Samuel Thompson
612. Edward Thompson
613. John Thompson
614. John Thomas
615. Jonathan Vincent
616. Edward Vaughn
617. Francis Vastian
618. William Williams
619. Robert Williams
620. John Williams
621. Peter Wilson
622. John Waters
623. Robert Wood
624. George Williams
625. Michael Wright
626. ___ Wright, Wife
627. Joseph Wilkinson
628. [*blank*]
629. Thomas Woodman
630. Alexander Williams
631. John Williamson
632. James Williams
633. William Williamson
634. Robert Wilson
635. John Wilks
636. John Wilson
637. [*blank*]
638. John Williams
639. Benjamin Wyllie
640. Francis Williams
641. William Williams
642. Philip Warren
643. Thomas Williams
644. William Williams
645. Samuel Ward
646. William Williamson
647. Thomas Williams

648. Philip White
649. Thomas Winkham
650. Jeremiah Williams
651. Samuel Wells
652. John Warwick
653. John Williams
654. James Watson
655. Lewis White
656. Joseph Williams
657. Richard Weaver
658. John Williams
659. John Williams
660. John Walton
661. Philip White
662. James White
663. John White
664. John Willis
665. Michael Waters
666. William Warkimon
667. Henry Williams
668. John Windsor
669. Edward Warren
670. Henry Williams
671. Samuel Williamson
672. Thomas Williamson
673. John White
674. John Williams
675. John Williamson
676. Samuel Wood
677. George Wright
678. John William
679. John Wood
680. Joseph Wilson
681. Abraham Wallace
682. Thomas Woodley
683. Peter Williams
684. Robert Walker
685. John Williams
686. Robert Wood
687. John Williams
688. John Wilkes
689. John Wilkes
690. James White

691. John Williams
692. John Williams
693. John Weekes
694. Joseph Williams
695. William Williams
696. John Wilson
697. George Young
698. John York & Wife
700. Samuel Young
701. Benajmin York
702. Robert Young
703. James Yarrow
704. John Zumbartus

Women and Men Weekly

1. March Kingston
2. Peggy Thompson
3. Lucy Bannister
4. Thomas Johnson & Wife
5. Betsy Johnson
6. Joseph Grovis
7. John Aaron Robinson
8. Elizabeth Douglas

Women

9. Phebe Andover
10. Mary Amos
11. Ann Allamaze
12. Mary Ann
13. Pam Ashfield
14. Mary Butler
15. Rosehanna Bryan
16. Mary Barwill
17. Jane Baptist
18. Jane Brown
19. Elizabeth Brown
20. Mary Brown
21. Jane Bord
22. Susanha Brown
23. Margaret Brown

24. Lililia Briggs
25. Helene Briggs
26. Charles Briggs
27. Catherine Brown
28. Hana Blear
29. Lydia Barrell
30. Johanna Bryan
31. Amelia Bowden
32. Elizabeth Burtonan
33. Ann Bennel
34. Elizabeth Baptist
35. Catherine Bateman
36. Ann Bennoh
37. Ann Berwick
38. Elizabeth Baldwin
39. Judith Bank
40. Ann Cogan
41. Ellis Cook
42. Mary Char
43. Ann Campbell
44. Maria Chapman
45. Sophia Cato
46. Amelia Clark
47. Hebanally Clara
48. Mary Clement
49. Judith Cambridge
50. Elizabeth Carr
51. Peggy Coleman
52. Rachel Coventry
53. Catherine Cardell
54. Ann Dean
55. Ann Dunlop
56. Mary Denwal
57. Elizabeth Dunbridge
58. Sarah Dunning
59. Susan Deserter
60. Bella Davis
61. John Davis, her Son
62. Judith Derry
63. Elizabeth Davis
64. Charlotte Edward
65. Ann Forbes
66. Philis Frankland

67. Susan Frankland
68. Mary Ford
69. Mary Fernandes
70. Elizabeth Francis
71. Susan Forbes
72. Sarah Frederick
73. Ann Gospors
74. Phebe Graham
75. Hanna Goodell
76. Diana Grans
77. Charlotte Glover
78. Martha Grans
79. Mary Grosvenor
80. Mary Green
81. Catherine Green
82. Elizabeth Green
83. Rebecca Gregory
84. Eleanor Hamilton
85. Elizabeth Hudson
86. Mary Hunt
87. Fanny Hunt
88. Clarissa Harlow
89. Mary Hadwick
90. Mary Harvey
91. Mary Harvey
92. Elizabeth Jones
93. Sarah Jones
94. Mary Jones
95. Catherine James
96. Margaret Johnson
97. Mary Johnson
98. Ann Johnson
99. Mary James
100. Mary Jones
101. Sarah Jones
102. Charlotte Kemp
103. Abigail King
104. Mary King
105. Mary Lawrence
106. Sarah Lee
107. Nancy Lynn
108. Ann Catherine Lewis
109. Sarah Lampton
110. Sarah Lasket
111. Mary Louch
112. Ann La Cruze
113. Ann London
114. Lucy Monron
115. Mary Markfield
116. Ann McKay
117. Ann Mary
118. Ann Moore
119. Elizabeth Molineux
120. Charlotte McKay
121. Ann Manswill
122. Sophia Manewill
123. Elizabeth Manwill
124. Ann Moore
125. Rachel Noble
126. Mary Nipper
127. Catherine Ogram
128. Ann Owens
129. Susan Owens
130. Elizabeth Ormfield
131. Elizabeth Peaser
132. Mary Prince
133. Peggy London
134. Kinnet Percy
135. Elizabeth Payton
136. Ann Page
137. Fanny Porter
138. Mary Promise
139. Ann Perry
140. Mary Pool
141. Mary Parker
142. Charlotte Pearse
143. Maria Pearce
144. Ann Provey
145. Louisa Provey
146. Ann Queen
147. Elizabeth Robinson
148. Betsy Robinson
149. Sarah Reese
150. Catherine Robertson
151. Ann Richardson
152. Elizabeth Rose

153. Sylvia Raper
154. Ann Beekman
155. Judith Samo
156. Isabella Sterling
157. Mary Simms
158. John Simms, Child
159. Susan Smith
160. Hanna Steward
161. Hester Simpson
162. Diana Strong
163. Barbara Solomon
164. Mary Simms
165. Sarah Simpson
166. Isabella Simpson
167. Mary Simmons
168. John Simmons, Child
169. Mary Smith
170. Ann Skillman
171. Ann Scott
172. Elizabeth Samuel
173. Margaret Smith
174. Mary Thomas
175. Margaret Taylor
176. Hanna Twim
177. Rachel Thompson
178. Ann Thomas
179. Ann Thomas
180. Matthew Thomas
181. Mary Thomas
182. Ann Thompson
183. Maria Thomas
184. Margaret Williamson
185. Charlotte Williamson
186. Hester Williams
187. Elizabeth Warren
188. Margaret Williams
189. Ann William
190. Mary Williamson
191. Elizabeth White
192. Elizabeth Welsh
193. Margaret Williams
194. Mary Williams
195. Lucy Weaver

196. Mary Williamson
197. Maria Williams
198. Eleanor Waters
199. Rebecca Windsor
200. Susannah Wood
201. Celea Young
202. Elizabeth Young
203. Mary Young
204. Mary York

Memorandum of Agreement made the Sixth day of October In the year of our Lord One Thousand Seven Hundred and Eighty Six And in the Twenty-seventh year of Reign of His most excellent Majesty King George the Third over Great Britain & in manner and form following (that is to say) We the undersigned do herby undertake contract and agree to and with Joseph Irwin Conductor of a certain intended Settlement or Colony to be situated on the Grain Coast of Africa and to be called The Land of Freedom under the Protection of and by the Encouragement and support of the British Government as follows vitz We the Men Women and Children whose Names are undersigned being Seamen Labourers and of various other descriptions receiving the Charity from the Humanity of the British Government for and in Consideration of the several Sums of money already had and received and of the Emoluments Liberties and Privileges found and provided for such of us as we may choose and wish to be happily settled on the said Grain Coast of Africa and for divers other good causes and Considerations and hereunto severall especially moving HAVE and each and every one of us, HATH undertaken agreed and contracted and by these presents DO and each and every one of us DOTH undertake agree and contract with the said Joseph Irwin TO assist in Navigating and doing such work as we are severally capable of doing Or as the said Joseph Irwin shall reasonably direct on board of the Ship or vessel called the Bellesarius of London Captain Seal Or on board of the Ship or vessell called the Atlantic of London late the Dennis Captain Muirhead which said Ships or Vessels are now lying in the River Thames bound shortly by Gods permission from the Port of London to Sierra Leona on the Grain Coast of Africa or on board of either of them. And we do also severally undertake agree and contract to go be and continue on board of the said Ships or Vessells or either of them on or before the Twentieth Day of October Instant. And He the said Joseph Irwin in Consideration thereof (and by the approbation of the Committee appointed for this Charitable purpose) DOTH hereby undertake agree and contract with all and every undersigned Men Women and Children to find and provide for all and each of them The Necessary Cloathing Good Provisions and all other reasonable Necessaries for and during the said intended passage and voyage and Also for Four Months after the arrival of the said Ship or vessell or Ships or vessells on the Grain Coast of Africa aforesaid agreeable to a plan published by the late Mr. Henry Smeathman deceased by the direction of the said Committee reference being thereunto has will more full and at large appear. And also Shall and will provide for all and every of the undersigned Men Women Children proper certificates of their being Loyal Subjects to this said Majesty King George the Third his Heirs and Successors to be printed on Parchment and delivered in a Tin Box in order to preserve the same AS Witnessed over Hands the Day and Year first above written.

Source: PRO T1/638

Joseph Irwin

1. John Walter Harris	37. Elizabeth Ramsay
2. John Wilson	38. James Harris
3. Lewis Lalouch	39. James Brown
4. Charles Stoddart	40. John Wells
5. William Gorman	41. John Skinner
6. John Smith	42. Peter Grant
7. John William Ramsay	43. John Steward
8. Abraham Elliot Griffith	44. Daniel Moore
9. John Mandeville	45. Richard Gutterow
10. James Strong	46. John Murray
11. Thomas Holder	47. Thomas Woodle
12. James Read	48. James Johnson
13. William Johnson	49. Timothy Allenby
14. William Green	50. William Collinson
15. Joshua Brown	51. David Allington
16. Joseph Poole	52. Catherine Lawson
17. James Johnson	53. David Davidson
18. George Newton	54. Abraham Lumley
19. Lewis Rose	55. James Nesbit
20. Jacob Jackson	56. Anthony Smith
21. Paul Clarke	57. Thomas McHingham
22. William Raper	58. John Adams
23. Aaron Brooks	59. Robert Young
24. William Green	60. William Kelly
25. Elizabeth Green	61. James Owen
26. Elizabeth Peazer	62. John Hall
27. Benjamin Brown	63. Robert Martin
28. Joseph Innes	64. John Williams
29. Thomas Peter	65. Thomas Johnson
30. John Morris	66. Thomas Nelson
31. Mary Smith	67. William Munday
32. John Jacob	68. Henry Williamson
33. George Isaac	69. George Lewis
34. Robert Moore	70. Anthony Gilbert
35. Robert Clayton	71. James Jackson
36. Peter Harris	72. Abraham Ellis

73. Daniel Lawrence
74. Thomas Green
75. John Wood
76. Peter Wilson
77. Joseph Newman
78. James Stephney
79. John Francis
80. Anthony Drewsaw
81. Joseph Taylor
82. Peter Bastian
83. Andrew Litteny
84. David Draper
85. John Thomas
86. Thom Martin
87. Dick Simmons
88. George Brown
89. John Jupiter
90. William Theodore
91. James Titus
92. John Brandy
93. George Stevenson
94. Thomas Williamson
95. John Brown
96. James Parker
97. James Anderson
98. William Powell
99. John Solomon
100. John Groves
101. Henry Jones
102. John Promise
103. Grace Promise
104. Mary Promise, Child
105. John Promise, Child
106. James Promise, Child
107. William Jones
108. Charles James
109. Anthony Jack
110. John Thomas
111. Frank Durham
112. John Peter
113. John Riddle
114. James Richardson
115. Ann Baptist
116. Tureo Ambo
117. John Hill
118. John Peasey
119. George Comfortable
120. Maria Groves
121. Joseph Groves
122. William Smith
123. George Bromfield
124. John Walton
125. Matthew Gale
126. Anthony Perry
127. Robert Thomas
128. James Diran
129. Mary Parford
130. Charles Castor
131. Fanny Castor
132. Matthew Castor
133. John George
134. Frank Swinton
135. Joseph Francis
136. John Thomas
137. Catherine Thomas
138. Anthony Thomas
139. Anthony Tackey
140. Thomas Hosper
141. John Speak
142. Diana Speak
143. George Young
144. Peter Githam
145. James Thompson
146. John Ashfield
147. John Swithin
148. Stephen Dorset
149. Thomas Neal
150. John Williamson
151. William Gordon
152. Frank Sylva
153. Anthony Santh
154. Elizabeth Hartford
155. Patient Baldwin
156. Joseph Benthew
157. George Prince
158. Phillip White

159. William Campbell
160. Thomas Franks
161. James White
162. George Freeman
163. Francis Pardo
164. John Needham
165. Eleanor Hamilton
166. Mary Butler
167. John Smith
168. George Ely
169. Joseph Allamaz
170. Harriet Allamaz
171. Joshua Allamaz, Child
172. Ann Allamaz, Child
173. Jane McKay
174. Charlotte McKay
175. Samuel Francis
176. Samuel Francis, Child
177. Thomas Woodman
178. William Lee
179. Edward Hamilton
180. Joseph Knight
181. John Limerick
182. Lewis Sterling
183. Ann Sterling
184. Martha Green
185. James Green
186. William Bird
187. Jane Bird
188. John Thomas
189. William Limirick
190. John Thomas
191. Mary Thomas
192. Ann Williams
193. Thomas Freeman
194. Abigail King
195. Diana Strong
196. John Johnson
197. John J. Ceasor
198. James Thomas
199. John Goff
200. Mary Young
201. Hannah Steward

202. John Parford
203. Thomas Harris
204. Charlotte Harris
205. Thomas Johnson
206. George Minor
207. Elizabeth Minor
208. James Richards
209. John Thomas
210. Ann Thomas
211. John Hughes
212. Thomas Holder
213. Ann Holder
214. Elizabeth Carr
215. John Lynch
216. George Hough
217. Samuel Lewis
218. Emanuel Pardo
219. William Williamson
220. William Williams
221. Mary Brown
222. John Thomas
223. Shadrack Clark
224. Sylva Ablin
225. Thomas Bruce
226. John Stacey
227. Charles Sorrill
228. Thomas Ashworth
229. Richard Dunham
230. Mary Denham
231. Thomas Thompson
232. John Oliver
233. Martin Servantus
234. William Roberts
235. Besantee Sylva
236. James Brown
237. John Robinson
238. John Simpson
239. William Williams
240. James Barnes
241. Anthony Sylva
242. William Jack
243. John Robinson
244. John Manuel

245. Amelia Bolton
246. Thomas Brown
247. Thomas Paris
248. Robert Jones
249. Margaret Broughton
250. Francis Broughton
251. Elizabeth Rose
252. Edward Robinson
253. Thomas London
254. Jacob Johnson
255. John Aberdee
256. John William Reading
257. Mary Thompson
258. Charles Thompson
259. Thomas Thompson
260. John Thompson
261. Frank Bastian
262. John Millick
263. John Williams
264. Prince William
265. Mary William
266. Letitia Clark
267. James Hartford
268. Margaret Johnson
269. John Johnson
270. Rebecca Winsor
271. Thomas Foreman
272. John Thomas
273. John Brown
274. Mary Ann Poole
275. Isabella Davis
276. Mary James
277. William Workinson
278. George Selley
279. Peter Bromfield
280. William Bromfield
281. Elizabeth Ormsfield
282. William Richardson
283. Elizabeth Davis
284. John Cane
285. John Johnson
286. William Johnson
287. Thomas Johnson

288. Ann Moore
289. Robert Walker
290. Robert Wilson
291. John Harvey
292. Margaret Harvey
293. William Hughes
294. Joseph Wilson
295. Mary Johnson
296. Mary Johnson
297. Margaret Swansken
298. Mary Stevenson
299. Charles Chilcot
300. John Bristow
301. George Bernard
302. Emanuel Gumby
303. James Brisco
304. John Pompey
305. Robert George
306. John Winsor
307. Ann Thompson
308. Barret Thompson
309. John Blake
310. John Provey
311. Ann Provey
312. Louisa Ann Provey
313. George Peters
314. John Warrick
315. Alexander Thompson
316. John Hamilton
317. Edward Rusca
318. John Leman
319. Jane Reid
320. Peter Bristow
321. John White
322. Dick Williams
323. Thomas Jordan
324. Prince William
325. John Thomas
326. George Alexander
    Berwick
327. Mary Ann Berwick
328. James Bailey
329. James Millengen

330. Lewis Lalouch
331. George Clark
332. Mary Lalouch
333. John Thompson
334. George Williams
335. Francis Vastion
336. Ann Labruise
337. Thomas Smith
338. George Samuel
339. John Thomas
340. Archibald Steward
341. Elizabeth Dandridge
342. John Goslet
343. Elizabeth Samuel
344. George Samuel
345. Sarah Simpson
346. Thomas Williams
347. Samuel Skinner
348. Peggy Thompson
349. John Aaron Robinson
350. Ann Marnival
351. D.A. Silea Anthony
352. William Lampley
353. John Fortune
354. Henry Beal
355. Jane Ashfield
356. Catherine Brown
357. William Lampley
358. James Neptune
359. John William
360. York Steward
361. Elizabeth Baptist
362. John Wilks, Child
363. Edward Hamilton, Child
364. Jeremiah Williams, Child
365. Elizabeth Williams, Child
366. William Thomas, Child
367. James Davis, Child
368. Mary Hunt
369. Fanny Hunt, Child
370. Maria Thomas, Child

371. Ann Thomas
372. Jane Brown
373. Edward Brown
374. Rosanne Bryan
375. George William Bryan, Child
376. Johanna Bryan, Child
377. Mary York
378. Sarah Dunning
379. Elizabeth Oman, Child
380. James Hadwick
381. Mary Hadwick
382. Mary Hadwick, Child
383. Thomas Stanley
384. John Ramsay
385. Francis Oatley
386. Abraham Mamacus
387. Richard Bradley
388. Joseph Roberts
389. Thomas Robinson
390. John Corrigut
391. Joseph Pankin
392. George Sharp
393. Benjamin Elliot
394. John Bristow
395. Henry Alexander
396. William Moody
397. George Moody, Child
398. Peggy Coleman
399. James Oliver
400. George Adams
401. William Adams, Child
402. Daniel Johnson
403. Joseph Wilkinson
404. John York
405. Mary Ann York, Child
406. Samuel Williamson
407. Thomas Sippey
408. Richard Crooks
409. Prince William
410. Joseph Williams
411. Peggy London
412. James Martin

413. Robert Robertson
414. Elizabeth Robertson
415. Letitia Briggs
416. Charles Briggs, Child
417. Helena Briggs, Child
418. James Seymour
419. John Stephens
420. Ann Johnson
421. Mary Simmons
422. John Simmons, Child
423. Joseph Mitchell
424. John Green
425. John Lucas
426. Thomas Parker
427. Mary Parker, Child
428. Sarah Parker
429. John Carrol
430. Thomas Clarke
431. Jacob Bossea
432. Francis Lee
433. Sarah Lee
434. Robert Williams
435. Mary Williams
436. Joseph Harrison
437. Robert Woods
438. Robert James
439. Elizabeth Welch
440. Sarah Jones
441. Ann Moore
442. Jane Forbes
443. Joseph Williams
444. Charles Minor
445. George Pembroke
446. Joseph Phillips
447. John Williams
448. Mary Jones
449. John Wicks, Jr.
450. John Wicks, Sr.
451. Jane Gosport
452. John York
453. Jack Jones
454. William Anderson
455. Maria Pearce
456. Charlotte Pearce
457. Joseph Lowther
458. John Britain
459. John Williams
460. James Collins
461. Wilson Sampson
462. Mary Doneval
463. George Hill
464. Mary Adams
465. William Stephenson
466. Thomas William Hall
467. William Warkinson
468. David Bricker
469. William Manshaw
470. William Barnes
471. Thomas Creswell
472. John Sampley
473. Hester Williams
474. Maria Williams
475. Charlotte Glovell
476. Joseph Glovell, Child
477. Lydia Raper
478. William Cobe
479. James Atkins
480. Thomas Hudson
481. Charles Murrin
482. John Green
483. Jacob Richardson
484. John Cummins
485. William Santhin
486. William Hoskins
487. William Taylor
488. John Williams
489. Robert Price
490. John London
491. John Solomon
492. William Higgins
493. Joseph Jordan
494. Thomas Richardson
495. Joseph Manwell
496. John Lawrence
497. Charles Jones
498. Elizabeth Jones

499. John Smith
500. David Brown
501. John Smith
502. Ann Dean
503. Samuel Wood
504. John English Brown
505. Robert Stevens
506. John Twine
507. Hannah Twine
508. Margaret Taylor
509. Elizabeth Warren
510. Messick Wright
511. Hester Wright
512. Kermet Pearcey
513. John Ferrell
514. Mary Simms
515. John Simms, Child
516. Charlotte Kemp
517. James White
518. John Dyer
519. Isabella Simpson
520. Samuel Ward
521. Sarah Lampton
522. Susan Brown
523. Isaac Behm
524. Elizabeth Behm
525. John Bell
526. William Smith
527. Anthony Smith
528. John Jackson
529. Rachel Noble
530. George Mead
531. Lewis Morris
532. Hezekiah Nickins
533. Thomas Commins
534. Benjamin Burgess, Child
535. Anthony Burgess
536. John Jacob
537. John Jacob, Child
538. Edward Jackson
539. William Dover
540. Abraham Learmouth
541. Elizabeth Learmouth
542. George Shepherd
543. Charles Stevenson
544. John Pompey
545. Mary Spears
546. George Phillips
547. Margaret Smith, Child
548. Augustus Sylva
549. John Williams
550. Emanuel Saunders
551. John Jones
552. George Ford
553. Joseph Cox
554. Celia Young
555. William Thompson
556. John Green
557. Samuel Thompson
558. Thomas Brown
559. George Clarke
560. Isaac Sears
561. James Milligan
562. Daniel Coventry
563. Rachel Coventry
564. Richard Mackfield
565. William Duett
566. Elizabeth Douglass
567. Jane Baptist
568. John Spears
569. John Baptist
570. George Wrightson
571. Benjamin Clark
572. Robert Ashfield
573. John London
574. Margaret London
575. John Brown
576. Peter Francis
577. James Harris
578. Robert Bristow
579. Hannah Blear
580. William Hudson
581. Elizabeth Hudson
582. Amelia Clark
583. Elizabeth Brown
584. John Smith

585. John Munday
586. William Green
587. Jack Simpson
588. John James
589. Ann Cardell
590. Catherine Cardell
591. Francis Gordon
592. Thomas Thompson
593. Margaret Chase
594. John Williams
595. Rachel Thompson
596. Thomas Sterling
597. George Ogram
598. Elizabeth Ogram
599. Catherine Ogram, Child
600. Ebenezer Anderson
601. Joseph Anderson, Child
602. Andrew Jack
603. John Dandridge
604. George Jones
605. Judith Cambridge
606. Thomas Demain
607. Sarah Jones
608. James March
609. John Brown
610. John Horne
611. Christian Horne
612. Benjamin Clark
613. Lewis Revinos
614. Hannah Woods
615. Judith Banks
616. James Monsell
617. Lucy Monsell
618. William Clause
619. William Green
620. Joseph Brown
621. James Harris
622. Mary Harris
623. James Batty
624. Joseph Crisby
625. William Jones
626. William James
627. John Peters
628. John Hamilton
629. William Ferro
630. John Marshall
631. John Baptiste
632. Adam Sutherland
633. John Strong
634. William Mullenden
635. Joseph Yarrow
636. John Ashfield
637. Israel Yarrow, Child
638. John Yarrow, Child
639. Mary Yarrow, Child
640. Francis Weeks
641. Ann Lynch
642. Thomas Davis
643. Emanuel Phillips
644. Richard Hall
645. Joseph Williams
646. Thomas Simpson
647. Isaac Brunchard
648. John Murrain
649. Abraham Spears
650. Charles Prince
651. Joseph Boston
652. Francis Holland
653. Benjamin Wycuff
654. Ann Thomas
655. Jane Thomas
656. Edward Honeycut
657. Joseph Domingo
658. Jack Anthony
659. Andrew James
660. John Adams
661. Joseph Anthony
662. John Anthony
663. Domingo Anthony
664. Thomas Sylva
665. John Oman
666. Josiah Hosier
667. John Lewis
668. John Becket
669. Elizabeth Williams
670. Ann Wilks

671. John Thomas Squire
672. Francis Steward
673. Hannah Steward
674. John Wilson
675. Thomas Freeman

A List of the Black Persons embarked on board the *Bellsaurus*, Captain Sill, 22 November 1786. Source: PRO T1/638

1. William Hoskins
2. George Isaacs
3. Samuel Thompson
4. Alexander Thompson
5. Joseph White
6. Emanuel Saunders
7. John Steward
8. James Taylor
9. John Lawrence
10. Thomas Sims
11. William Theodore
12. Thomas Williams
13. Thomas Freeman
14. John Limerick
15. John Stepney
16. Peter Grand
17. Edward Honeycut
18. Joseph Newman
19. Francis Holland
20. John Murray
21. Samuel Skinner
22. Richard Bradley
23. Mary Bradley
24. James Neptune
25. William Richardson
26. Hannah Richardson
27. Edward Jones
28. Francis Durham
29. William Mullenden
30. George Ford
31. John Aberdeen
32. York Steward
33. Thomas Woodman
34. Jack Thomas
35. Henry Beal
36. Turee Ambo
37. John Solomon
38. John Pompey
39. Samuel Wood
40. Mary Wood
41. Paul Clark
42. John James
43. Jack Thomas
44. John Smith
45. Benjamin Elliot
46. John Hughes
47. John Hall
48. William Howell
49. Lewis Sterling
50. Robert Clayton
51. Thomas London
52. Charles Jones
53. Elizabeth Jones
54. George Brown
55. Elizabeth Brown
56. Richard Gullero
57. Archibald Steward
58. Hannah Steward
59. John Wilson
60. George Comfortable
61. Joseph George
62. Hannah George
63. John William Ramsay
64. Elizabeth Ramsay
65. John Provey
66. Ann Provey
67. Lewis Ann Provey
68. John William Harris
69. Andrew James
70. Mary Jones
71. Sarah Sampson
72. Thomas Damerain
73. Elizabeth Damerain
74. James Read
75. Jane Read
76. Anthony Still
77. George Newton
78. John Horne

79. Christiana Horne
80. Jacob Jackson
81. Rebecca Jackson
82. Thomas Freeman
83. Daniel Christopher
84. Edward Smith
85. John Thomas
86. John Riddle
87. George Hill
88. James Richardson
89. John Goslet
90. Frank Sherburne
91. John Wilson
92. Ann Watson
93. Shadruck Clark
94. William Green
95. Martha Green
96. James Green
97. George Adams
98. William Adams
99. Nancy Adams
100. George Broomfield
101. John Peters
102. Mary Adams
103. James Martin
104. Barbara Thomas
105. Christopher Friday

The Names of Men, Women & Children who are now on board the *Bellsaurus* Captain Till lying at the Motherbank 16 February 1787. Source: PRO T1/643

1. James Stephenson
2. Joseph Taylor
3. William Threads
4. James White
5. Peter Grant
6. Edward Honeycut
7. James Murry
8. Joseph Newman
9. James Neptune
10. George Jones
11. James Seaman
12. John Thomas
13. Truro Ambo
14. John Solomon
15. Joseph Bromley
16. Misheck Wright
17. Abram Mathews
18. Lewis Sterling
19. Charles Jones
20. George Brown
21. William Hoskins
22. William Williams
23. John Thomas
24. John Thomas
25. Richard Guthrow
26. Archibald Stewart
27. John Lawrence
28. John William Ramsay
29. James Reid
30. Anthony Hill
31. William Anderson
32. William Smith
33. John Home
34. Edward Smith
35. George Hill
36. John Thomas
37. John Lewis
38. John Hull
39. John Wilson
40. William Green
41. Joseph Green, Jr.
42. Thomas Simms
43. Thomas Woodman
44. James Martin
45. William Richardson
46. Frank Durham
47. John Jones
48. Benjamin Elliot
49. John Marnine
50. James Marnine, Jr.
51. George Jones
52. Thomas Montague
53. John Peters
54. John Twine
55. Christian Friday
56. Thomas Holder
57. Thomas Holder, Jr.
58. John Stewart
59. John Lewis
60. Frank Barlian
61. John Ramsay
62. John Thomas
63. William Hudson
64. John Homan
65. Joseph Hartford
66. Thomas Truman
67. John Swinthin
68. Lewis Lalouch
69. Lewis Lalouch, Jr.
70. Abraham Elliot Griffith
71. Andrew James
72. Joseph George
73. William Close
74. George Comfortable
75. William Lee
76. John Jacob

77. John Jacob, Jr.
78. John James
79. William Bromfield
80. John Martin
81. Richard Bradley
    81 Black Men

Black Women Married to White Men

1. Nancy Hughes
2. Hester Wright
3. Elizabeth Jones
4. Jane Gosport
5. Hannah Stewart
6. Sarah Simpson
7. Christian Horn
8. Ann Watson
9. Martha Green
10. Hannah Richardson
11. Hannah Twine
12. Sarah Lee
13. Peggy Smith
14. Martha Smith
15. Elizabeth Richardson
16. Elizabeth Hartford
17. Jane Baptist
18. Mary James
    18 Black Women

White Women Married to Black Men

1. Mary Bradley
2. Margaret Allen
3. Barbary Thomas
4. Elizabeth Brown
5. Elizabeth Ramsey
6. Margaret Jackson
7. Mary Adams
8. Elizabeth Demain
9. Ann Holder

10. Amelia Homan
11. Margaret Lalouch
12. Ann Provey
13. Rebecca Griffith
14. Martina James
15. Mary Ann Lee
16. Mary Jacob
    16 White Women

White Women Wanting to be Married

1. Mary Allen
2. Jane Gosport
3. Mary Adams
4. Elizabeth Robinson
5. Milly Simmons

White Men

1. Doctor Alexander Hackney
2. Doctor Thomas William Young
3. M. Graham, Purser
4. Robert Sterling, Pursers Mate
5. Richard Henry Duncobe, Surveyor
6. Thomas Newburn, Passenger
7. Rubin Talon, Black Smith
8. William Ricketts, Nurseryman and Seedsman
9. John Drage, Taylor
10. Joseph Leccock, Gardiner
11. White People

A List of all the Names of those People who are now on board the
Vernon laying at Motherbank Sunday 18 February 1787.
Source: T1/643

1. Richard Weaver
2. William Shrying
3. Abraham Ashmore
4. John Scott
5. John Cain
6. George Francis
7. George Harris
8. Mummy Sueby
9. John Bucks
10. Thomas Clements
11. John Williamson
12. Valentine Russell
13. Thomas Wooders
14. William Bond
15. William Child
16. John James
17. Jacob Johnson
18. Daniel Andrews
19. John Smith
20. John Cambridge
21. Adam Tabb
22. John Millick
23. John Ballester
24. Thomas Brown
25. William Stephenson
26. Charles Stoddart
27. George Isaac
28. James Drain
29. Thomas London
30. John Hughes
31. Samuel Wood
32. Samuel Skinner
33. John Smith
34. Thomas Warren
35. James York
36. Alexander Thompson
37. John Pompey
38. William Limbrick

39. James Francis
40. George Ford
41. Thomas Johnson
42. Emanuel Sanders
43. James Stepney
44. John Lalouch
45. Thomas Williams
46. John Andrews
47. William Mullender
48. John Wilson
49. John Brown
50. James Atkins
51. John Walton
52. Archibald Madera
53. James Tomlinson
54. William Cooper
55. John Lynch
56. James Valentine
57. William Smith
58. John Brandy
59. Martin Lemanthus
60. Anthony Drewsaw
61. John Anthony
62. John Lemmon
63. Lewis White
64. John Jupiter
65. George Selly
66. James Harris
67. Joseph Benthew
68. Thomas Richardson

68 Men

Black Women

1. Lucy Weaver
2. Lucy Ashmore
3. Margaret Francis

4. Sarah Williamson
5. Elizabeth Selly
6. Mary Smith
7. Judeah Banks
8. Sarah Stoddart
9. Isabella Smith
10. Elizabeth Lynts

White Women Married to
Black Men

1. Sarah Whycuff Husband
   dead
2. Sarah Cambridge
3. Mary Tabb
4. Mary Tomlinson
5. Elizabeth Lemmon
6. Ann Thompson
7. Elizabeth Andrews

Black Children

1. Judeah Weaver
2. George Lawrence

White Women Married to
White Men

1. Ann Drew
2. Ann Schenckel
3. M A Smith
4. Sarah Horn Sister to Ann
   Drew

White Children

1. Ann Schenckel
2. Richard [Schenckel]
3. Rosina [Schenckel]
4. Ann Hackett

Two White Women More to be
Married

White Men and their
Occupations

1. William Craig, Parish
   Sexton
2. William Drew, Smith and
   Armorer
3. John Schenckel, Bread
   Baker
4. Fardon Willsford,
   Carpenter
5. Hugh Smith, Flax Dresser
6. George Kern, Husband
   Man
7. Fred Kerkner, [Husband
   Man]
8. William Willesford,
   Waterman
9. Robert Bower, Tanner
10. James Baker, Purser
11. Thomas Bettsworth,
    Weaver
12. William Kennedy,
    Brushmaker
13. John Hodgkins,
    Brickmaker

The Whole Number of Black Men is 68
Black Women is 10
White Women 7
Black Children 2

White Women 4
White Children 4
White Men 13

In all 108
2 White Women 2
                                                                 110

List of Black Poor Embarked for Sierra Leone (Delivered by Captain Thompson, 30th December, 1788. Source: T1/643

1. Reverend Mr. Fraser
2. Mr. Daniel Curry, Dead
3. William Cahill
4. John Gesau, Dead
5. Mary Gesau, Dead
6. John Irwin, Discharged
7. John Smeathman, Discharged
8. Benjamin Phillips, Dead, Discharged
9. William Watts, Dead, Discharged
10. John Wrigglesworth, Dead, Discharged
11. John Bethell, Dead
12. Anthony Smith
13. Henry Graves
14. Peter Hill
15. David Draper
16. George Smith
17. John Stephenson
18. James Cox
19. John Green, Dead, Discharged
20. John Pomposend, Dead, Discharged
21. James Oliver, Dead, Discharged
22. John Groves, Run
23. Joseph Grant
24. John Anderson
25. John Thomas
26. James Owen
27. Robert Walker
28. Henry Domain
29. John Wilkes
30. George Minor, Dead, Discharged
31. Jacob Richardson
32. Dick Simmons
33. John Adams
34. Daniel More
35. John Bristow
36. Thomas Creswell
37. Henry Alexander
38. Isaac Benn
39. John Lucas
40. John Daley, Dead, Discharged
41. George Pembroke
42. William London
43. William James
44. Daniel Johnson
45. William Warner, Dead, Discharged
46. Aaron Brookes
47. James Johnson
48. William Dover
49. John Ashfield
50. James Harris
51. Joseph Fortune
52. Josiah Hosier, Dead, Discharged
53. William Working
54. Edward Thompson, Dead, Discharged
55. George Prince, Dead, Discharged
56. George How
57. John Stacey, Run
58. Charles Thompson
59. Robert Robinson
60. Lewis Rose, Dead
61. Benjamin York
62. John Spears
63. James Parker, Dead, Discharged
64. Nathaniel Goughing

65. John London
66. Prince William, Dead, Discharged
67. John Williams, Dead, Discharged
68. John Dyer, Dead, Discharged
69. John Windsor
70. William Gorman
71. William Raper, Dead
72. Domingo Antona, Dead, Discharged
73. John Lewis
74. Anthony Madiera
75. John Morris
76. Jacob Potter, Dead, Discharged
77. William Higgins
78. James Johnson (2), Dead, Discharged
79. William Thompson
80. Charles Marien
81. Thomas Green
82. James Atkins
83. William Green
84. Wilson Sampson
85. George Agram
86. William Stephenson
87. John Blake, Dead, Discharged
88. Robert Moore
89. Emanuel Parado
90. Francis Parado, Dead, Discharged
91. John Carigut, Dead, Discharged
92. Paul Clark, Dead, Discharged
93. John Banks
94. Edward Dominico
95. Joseph Poole, Dead, Discharged
96. John Williams, Run

97. William Green, Dead
98. Peter Victory
99. William Stafford
100. Henry Jones, Dead, Discharged
101. Peter Armsfield
102. Joseph Jordan
103. Thomas Peters
104. James Titus
105. John Simpson
106. James Harris (2)
107. Charles Chilcoth
108. James Crane
109. Samuel Green
110. Robert Price
111. Thomas Hooper
112. William Jones
113. William Green, Dead
114. William Williams, Dead, Discharged
115. John W. Harris
116. William Newton
117. James Dolphin, Dead, Discharged
118. John Dyer
119. Margaret Domain, Dead, Discharged
120. Mary Morris, Dead
121. Rebecca Innis
122. Mary Thompson
123. Ann Wilkes, Dead, Discharged
124. Elizabeth Dyer, Dead, Discharged
125. Elizabeth Williams, Dead
126. Elizabeth Robinson
127. Dorcas Brookes
128. Peggy Higgins
129. Jane Working
130. Lydia Raper, Dead
131. Mary Spears
132. Elizabeth Williams (2), Dead, Discharged

133. Ann Windsor, Dead,
     Discharged
134. Mary Johnson, Dead
135. Elizabeth Agram
136. Elizabeth How, Dead,
     Discharged
137. Ann Parado
138. Elizabeth Minor, Dead,
     Discharged
139. Sara Parker, Dead,
     Discharged
140. Elizabeth Benn, Dead,
     Discharged
141. Sara Thomas, Dead,
     Discharged
142. Diane Speake
143. Elizabeth Dover
144. Mary Johnson (2)
145. Mary Prince, Dead,
     Discharged
146. Mary Price, Dead,
     Discharged
147. Amelia Moore
148. Sarah Hooper, Dead
149. Lydia Clarke
150. Sarah Parado
151. Susan Ross
152. Mary James
153. Elizabeth Armsfield
154. Ann Jordan, Dead,
     Discharged
155. Bridget Williams
156. Sarah Pells, Dead,
     Discharged
157. Sophia Williams, Dead
158. Polly Dominica
159. Elizabeth Thompson
160. Ann Carigatt, Dead,
     Discharged
161. Mary Ashfield, Dead,
     Discharged
162. Sarah Potter
163. Mary Harris

164. Catherine Victory
165. Mary Poole, Dead,
     Discharged
166. Jane Newton
167. Sarah Dolphin
168. Ann Hughes
169. Elizabeth Chilcoth
170. Elizabeth Madeira, Dead,
     Discharged
171. Joseph Greves, Dead
172. Francis Broughton, Dead,
     Discharged
173. John Thompson
174. Catherine Robinson
175. John Wilkes, Dead,
     Discharged
176. Betsey Green, Dead
177. Mary Ann Clark
178. William Orsmfield, Dead,
     Discharged
179. Mary Howe, Dead,
     Discharged
180. Elizabeth Innis, Dead,
     Discharged
181. Thomas Thompson, Dead
182. John Britain
183. John Riddle
184. Betsey Gesau, Dead,
     Discharged
185. William Harris
186. Mr. Joseph Irwin, Dead,
     Discharged
187. Miss Irwin, Dead
188. Miss Betsey Irwin, Dead
189. Mr. Hills
190. Robert Bowers, Dead,
     Discharged
191. William Craig, Dead
192. Joseph Clifton, Dead
193. Thomas Davis, Dead,
     Discharged
194. James Baker, Dead,
     Discharged

195. Richard Weaver
196. Frederick Kirkner, Dead,
     Discharged
197. Abraham Ashmore
198. Lucy Ashmore
199. John Scott
200. John Cain
201. George Francis, Dead,
     Discharged
202. George Harris
203. Mummy Subby
204. John Bucks
205. George Laurence
206. William Thryning, Dead,
     Discharged
207. John Williamson
208. Margaret Francis
209. Valentine Russell
210. William Drew, Dead,
     Discharged
211. Ann Drew
212. Sarah Howe, Dead,
     Discharged
213. Lucy Weaver
214. Hugh Smith, Dead,
     Discharged
215. Hugh Smith, Dead,
     Discharged
216. Mary A. Smith
217. Sarah Wycuff, Dead,
     Discharged
218. Thomas Wooders
219. William Child
220. John James
221. Jacob Johnson, Dead,
     Discharged
222. Daniel Andrews
223. Thomas Clements
224. John Shenkell, Dead,
     Discharged
225. Ann Shenkell, Dead,
     Discharged

226. Richard Shenkell, Dead,
     Discharged
227. Ann Shenkell
228. Rosina Shenkell
229. George Kein, Dead,
     Discharged
230. William Bond
231. Elizabeth Silly
232. John Cambridge
233. Sarah Cambridge, Dead,
     Discharged
234. Mary Smith, Dead,
     Discharged
235. Adam Sabb
236. Mary Sabb, Dead,
     Discharged
237. Ann Hackett, Dead,
     Discharged
238. Mary Harris, Dead,
     Discharged
239. John Minnick
239. Judith Weaver **
240. John Battester
241. William Stephenson
242. Joseph Hodd, Dead,
     Discharged
243. John Valentine
244. Charles Stoddard
245. Thomas Warren
246. Samuel Wood
247. James York
248. George Isaacs
249. John Hughes
250. Emanuel Saunders
251. John Wilson
252. John Pompey
253. George Ford
254. Thomas London
255. William Mullender
256. John Smith
257. James Stepney, Run
258. John Matue, Dead,
     Discharged

259. Thomas Williams
260. William Limrick
261. James Francis
262. Ann Adams
263. Alexander Thompson
264. Elizabeth Turner, Dead
265. Elizabeth Savory
266. John Andrews
267. Samuel Skinner
268. James Drain
269. William Kennedy, Run
270. Thomas Betworth, Run
271. James Price
272. John Hodgkins
273. William Cooper
274. Anthony Dreusaw, Run
275. Thomas Brown, Dead,
    Discharged
276. Martin Vanshaw
277. John Jupiter, Dead,
    Discharged
278. John Brandy
279. Valentine Xanthus
280. John Anthony
281. John Brown
282. Anthony Madeira, Run
283. John English, Dead,
    Discharged
284. John Lynch
285. James Thomlinson
286. Thomas Richardson
287. Lewis White
288. John Walton
289. James Atkins, Run
290. John Francis
291. Augustine Barrows, Dead,
    Discharged
292. John Vaughn, Dead
293. William Smith
294. Isabella Smith
295. Sarah Wilkinson, Dead,
    Discharged
296. Alice Cook, Run
297. John George, Dead,
    Discharged
298. Joseph Smith, Run
299. Anthony Joice, Dead,
    Discharged
300. George Clarke
301. Elizabeth Clarke
302. M. A. Clarke
303. John Needham
304. John Smyth
305. Elizabeth Lynch
306. Mary Tomlinson, Run
307. Sarah Needham
308. John Sheerman, Run
309. John Lemon
310. Elizabeth Lemon
311. Thomas Bowline, Dead,
    Discharged
312. Sarah Bowline, Dead,
    Discharged
313. Isaac Blure
314. Peter Smith
315. John Darby
316. James Charles
317. James Harris
318. John Peesey
319. John Williams
320. Thomas Smith, Dead,
    Discharged
321. Fardon Wilsford, Dead,
    Discharged
322. Jacob Philips
323. Jeffery Amherst
324. Emanuel Crapp, Dead,
    Discharged
325. Margaret Jackson, Dead
326. Ann Harris
327. Mary English, Dead
328. Elizabeth Smith, Dead,
    Discharged
330. Peter Palmer
331. William Wilsford
332. John Bethel

333. John Bethel
334. Joseph Groves, Dead, Discharged
335. Ann Cook
336. Elizabeth Parsons
337. Mr. Alexander Hackney
338. Thomas W. Young, Run
339. Richard H. Dunscombe
340. Monkhouse Graham, Dead
341. Thomas Mewbourne, Dead
342. William Green, Dead, Discharged
343. Martha Green
344. James Green, Dead, Discharged
345. Ann Watson, Dead, Discharged
346. Thomas Simmons, Dead, Discharged
347. John Drage, Dead, Discharged
348. Abraham E. Griffith
349. Rebecca Griffith, Dead, Discharged
350. Andrew James
351. Martha James, Dead, Discharged
352. John W. Ramsay
353. Elizabeth Ramsay, Dead, Discharged
354. George Brown
355. Elizabeth Brown
356. Sarah Simpson
357. Lewis Latouch
358. Mary Latouch, Dead, Discharged
359. Lewis Latouch, Dead, Discharged
360. John Marien
361. Elizabeth Marien, Dead, Discharged
362. John Marien, Dead, Discharged
363. Mesech Wright
364. Hester Wright
365. Benjamin Elliot
366. Abraham Mathews
367. Hannah Irvine
368. William Smith
369. John Murray
370. Rubin Taton, Dead, Discharged
371. Christopher Friday
372. Joseph Lucock, Dead, Discharged
373. Joseph George
374. George Comfortable, Dead, Discharged
375. William Close
376. Jane Baptist
377. William Lee
378. Mary A. Lee
379. Richard Bradley
380. Mary Bradley
381. William Williams
382. Thomas Holder
383. Ann Holder, Dead, Discharged
384. Elizabeth Hudson
385. John Homan
386. Christian Horn
387. Robert Stirling, Dead
388. Thomas Holder
389. William Ricketts, Dead, Discharged
390. Isaac Jones, Dead, Discharged
391. Amelia Homan, Dead, Discharged
392. Mary S. Jones, Dead
393. Joseph Taylor, Dead, Discharged
394. William Richardson
395. Hannah Richardson

396. James Harford
397. Elizabeth Harford
398. Thomas Freeman, Run
399. John Swithen
400. John Peters
401. James Neptune
402. Edward Smith
403. George Hill, Dead, Discharged
404. John Lewis
405. Edward Honeycutt, Dead, Discharged
406. William Anderson, Run
407. Joseph Newman
408. Richard Guttero, Dead, Discharged
409. George Bromfield
410. Jane Gosport
411. Anthony Smith
412. Peggy Smith, Dead, Discharged
413. Sarah Lee
414. Thomas Montague
415. James White, Dead, Discharged
416. James Walker
417. James Stephens
418. Jack James
419. John Bromley
420. Tony Ambo, Dead, Discharged
421. Joseph Seaman
422. Thomas Fisher
423. Peggy Fisher
424. John Steward
425. John Ramsay, Run
426. Francis Baxthian
427. Lewis Stirling
428. Charles Jones, Dead, Discharged
429. Elizabeth Jones
430. William Hoskins
431. Elizabeth Hoskins
432. James Read
433. Anthony Hill
434. John Jacobs
435. Mary Jacobs, Dead, Discharged
436. John Jacobs, Dead, Discharged
437. Peter Grant
438. John Wilson, Run
439. Mary James
440. Martha Smith, Dead, Discharged
441. Thomas Mallady

Died   122

Discharged   28

Ran   23

Remaining at the Time His Majesty's Sloop *Nautilus* Left Sierra Leona
                    268

Number Embarked   441

* Repetitive and incorrect enumeration in original

** Double count in original

Selected Bibliography

Primary Sources

British Library, London

"Petition of the Settlers of the New Colony of Sierra Leon," "John Clarkson Papers," 4 vols, Additional Manuscripts 41263

Clements Library, University of Michigan

Frederick Mackensie Papers

Green Manuscripts

Library of Congress

Force Papers

Ralph Wormeley to John Robinson, April 19, 1783, Misc. Manuscripts.

New Bedford, Massachusetts Public Library

Paul Cuffe Papers

New-York Historical Society

Richard Varick Papers

New York State Library, Albany

Eliott Papers

Pennsylvania State Archives, Harrisburg, Pennsylvania

A List of Negroes belonging to the Citizens of Pennsylvania Carried Away by the British

Public Archives of Canada

Muster Book of Free Blacks, Settlement of Birchtown, 1784

Public Archives of Nova Scotia

A List of Those Mustered at Shelburne, Nova Scotia in the Summer of 1784

Annapolis Royal, Annapolis St. Luke's Anglican Church, Baptismal Register, 1782–1786

Anglican Church Records, Shelburne, Nova Scotia, Vestry Records, 1769–1868

Digby Township Records

Extracts from the General Sessions of Shelburne

Fergusson Papers

Journal of Reverend William Jessop, 1788

Samuel Skinner Papers

Shelburne Baptism from Reverend Dr. Walters' Records

State of the Provisions Sent by Reverend Mr. Brundle, 1783–84

Trinity Church Records

Public Record Office, London

Carleton Papers CO 30/55

Minutes of the Committee in Relief of the Black Poor, 1786

Plan of a Settlement to be Made Near Sierra Leone on the Grain Coast of Africa by Henry Smeatham, Esq, 1786

The Honorable Memorial and Petition of Thomas Peters, CO/217/63/54

Rhodes Library, Oxford University

Dr. Bray's Associates/Canada File

Newspapers and Magazines

> *Halifax Gazette*
> *Philanthropist* (London)
> *Royal Gazette* (New York)
> *St. John Gazette*

Printed Works

An Account of the Colony of Sierra Leone from its First Establishment in 1793 being the Substance of a Report Delivered to the Proprietors. London: Printed and Sold by James Philips, 1795.

An Account of the Designs of the associates of the late Dr. Bray with an Abstract of their Proceedings. London: Printed in the Year 1785.

"An Account of the Life of Mr. David George, from Sierra Leone in Africa; given by himself in a Conversation with Brother Rippon and Brother Pearce of Birmingham," in *The Baptist Annual Register for 1790–93*. London: By John Rippon,1793.

Falconbridge, Anna Maria. *Narration of Two Voyages to the River Sierra Leone during the Years, 1791–1792.* 2nd ed. London: L.I. Higham, 1802.

Fergusson, Charles Bruce, ed. *Clarkson's Mission to America, 1791–1792.* Public Archives of Nova Scotia, Publication no. 11. Halifax: Public Archives of Nova Scotia, 1971.

Fitzpatrick, John C., ed. *The Writings of George Washington from the original manuscript sources, 1745–1799.* Prepared under the Direction of the United States George Washington Bicentennial Commission and published by authority of Congress. Washington: Government Printing Office, 1931–1944.

Fyfe, Christopher, ed. *Our Children Free and Happy: Lettters from Black Settlers in Africa in the 1790s.* Edinburgh: Edinburgh University Press, 1991.

Hoare, Prince. *Memoirs of Granville Sharp, Esq. Composed from his own Manuscripts and other Authentic Documents in the possession of his Family of the African Institution* . . . London: Printed for H. Colburn and Company, 1820.

"Memoirs of the Life of Boston King, a Black Preacher," *Methodist Magazine* for March, 1798.

Papers of George Washington. Confederation Series, ed. W.W. Abbot and Dorothy Twohig. 2 vols. Charlottesville: University Press of Virginia, 1992.

Revolution in America: Confidential Letters and Journals, 1776–1784 of Adjutant General Major Bauermeister of the Hessian Forces. trans. and ed. by Bernard A. Uhlendorf. New Brunswick, NJ: Rutgers University Press, 1957.

Sharp, Granville. *A Representation of the Injustice and Dangerous Tendency of Treating Slavery or of Admitting the Least Claim of Private Property in the Persons of Men in England, in Four Parts.* London: Printed for B. White and R. Horsfield, 1769.

David T. Valentine, ed. *Valentine's Manual for the City of New York, 1870.* New York: Printed for the City of New York, 1870.

Wadstrom, C[arl] B[ernhard]. *An Essay on Colonization Particularly Applied to the Western Coast of Africa with Some Thoughts on Cultivation and Commerce . . .* London: Printed for the Author by Darton and Harvey, 1794.

____. *Report to the Directors of the Sierra Leone Company.* London, 1791.

Secondary Sources

Allen, Robert S., ed. *The Loyal Americans; the Military Role of the Loyalist Provincial Corps and their Settlement in British North America.* Ottawa, Canada: National Museum of Man, 1983.

Berlin, Ira and Hoffman, Ronald. *Slavery and Freedom in the Age of the American Revolution.* Charlottesville: Published for the United States Capitol Historical Society by the University Press of Virginia, 1983.

Blackburn, Robin. *The Overthrow of Colonial Slavery.* New York: Verso Books, 1988.

Brooks, George E. *The Kru Mariner in the Nineteenth Century.* Newark, Del.: Liberian Association in America, 1972.

Buckley, Roger. *Slaves in Red Coates: The British West India Regiments.* New Haven: Yale University Press, 1979.

Byers, Mary and McBurney, Mary. *Atlantic Hearth: Early Homes and Families of Nova Scotia*. Toronto: University of Toronto Press, 1994.

Campbell, Mavis C. *Back To Africa: George Ross & the Maroons*. Trenton, N.J.: Africa World Press, 1993.

____. *The Maroons of Jamaica, 1655–1796*. Trenton, N.J.: Africa World Press, 1990.

Cohen, Abner. *The Politics of a Power Elite: Explorations in the Dramaturgy of Power in a Modern African Society*. Berkeley, Ca.: University of California Press, 1981.

Cox-George, N.A. *Finance and Development in West Africa: The Sierra Leone Experience*. London: Dobson, 1961.

Creel, Margaret Washington. *"A Peculiar People": Slave Religion and Community Culture Among the Gullahs*. New York: New York University Press, 1988.

Crow, Jeffrey J. *The Black Experience in Revolutionary North Carolina*. Raleigh: Division of Archives and History, North Carolina Department of Cultural Resources, 1977.

Curtin, Philip, ed. *Africa Remembered: Narratives by West Africans from the Era of the Slave Trade*. Madison: University of Wisconsin Press, 1976.

____. *The African Slave Trade: A Census*. Madison: University of Wisconsin Press, 1969.

____. *The Image of Africa: British Ideas and Action, 1780–1850*. Madison: University of Wisconsin Press, 1964.

Davidson, Stephen Eric. "Leaders of the Black Baptists of Nova Scotia, 1782–1832," B.A. Honors Thesis, Arcadia University, 1975.

Du Bois, W.E.B. *The Suppression of the African Slave Trade*. Cambridge, Mass.: Harvard University Press, 1896.

Fingard, Judith. *The Anglican Design in Loyalist Nova Scotia, 1783–1816*. London: Published for the Church Historical Society [by] S.P.C.K.,1972.

Foote, Thelma Wills. "Black Life in Colonial Manhattan, 1664–1786." Ph.D. diss., Harvard University, 1992.

Frey, Sylvia. *Water from the Rock: Black Resistance in a Revolutionary Age*. Princeton: Princeton University Press, 1991.

Fryer, Peter. *Staying Power: The History of Black People in Britain.* Atlantic Highlands: Academic Press, 1984.

Fyfe, Christopher. *A History of Sierra Leone.* London: Oxford University Press, 1962.

____. "The Countess of Huntingdon's Connection in 19th Century Sierra Leone," *Sierra Leone Bulletin of Religion,* 4 (1962), 53–61.

George, Carol V. *Segregated Sabbaths: Richard Allen and the Rise of Independent Black Churches, 1760–1840.* New York: Oxford University Press, 1973.

Gilroy, Paul. *The Black Atlantic: Modernity and Double Consciousness.* Cambridge, Mass., Harvard University Press, 1993.

Hair, P.E.H. "Africanisms: The Freetown Contribution," *Journal of Modern African Studies,* 4 (1967), 521–39.

____. "Sierra Leone and the Bulama, 1792–1794," *Sierra Leone Bulletin of Religion,* 6 (1964), 56–67.

Harvey, Evangeline. "The Negro Loyalists," *Nova Scotia Historical Quarterly* 1 (1971).

Hodges, Graham Russell, ed. *Black Itinerants of the Gospel: The Narratives of John Jea and George White.* Madison: Madison House Publishers, 1993.

____. *Black Resistance in Colonial and Revolutionary Bergen County, New Jersey.* River Edge, N.J.: Bergen County Historical Society, 1989.

____. "Black Revolt in New York City and the Neutral Zone," in *New York in the Age of the Constitution,* eds. Paul A. Gilje and William Pencak. Cranbury, N.J.: Associated University Presses, 1992, pp. 20–48.

____. *New York City Cartmen, 1667–1850.* New York: New York University Press, 1986.

____. *Slavery and Freedom in the Rural North: African Americans in Monmouth County, New Jersey, 1660–1870.* Madison: Madison House Publishers, 1995.

Hodges, Graham Russell and Brown, Alan Edward, eds. *"Pretends to be Free": Runaway Slave Advertisements from Colonial and Revolutionary New York and New Jersey.* New York: Garland Publishing, Inc. 1994.

Kruger, Vivien. "Born to Run: The Black Family in New York in Slavery and Freedom, 1625–1827." Ph.d. diss., Columbia University, 1985.

Kuczynski, R.R. *Demographic Survey of the British Empire.* 3 vols. London: Oxford University Press, 1948–1953.

Lascelles, E.C.P. *Granville Sharpe and the Freedom of Slaves in England.* London, 1928.

Lindsay, Arnett G. "Diplomatic Relations between the United States and Great Britain Bearing on the Return of Negro Slaves, 1783–1828," *Journal of Negro History* 5 (1920), 391–419.

Little, K.L. "The Significance of the West African Creole for Africanist and Afro-American Studies," *African Affairs,* 49 (1950), 308–19.

Nash, Gary B. *Forging Freedom: the Formation of Philadelphia's Black Community, 1720–1840.* Cambridge, Mass.: Harvard University Press, 1988.

Norton, Mary Beth. "The Fate of Some Black Loyalists of the American Revolution," *Journal of Negro History,* 58 (1973).

Oliver, Pearleen. *A Brief History of the Coloured Baptists of Nova Scotia, 1782–1953.* Halifax: 1953.

Porter, Arthur T. "Religious Affiliation in Freetown, Sierra Leone," *Africa* 23 (1953).

Quarles, Benjamin. *The Negro in the American Revolution.* Chapel Hill, N.C.: University of North Carolina Press, 1960.

Rawley, James A. *The Transatlantic Slave Trade.* New York: W.W. Norton, 1981.

Rawlyk, George A. *Ravished by the Spirit: Religious Revivals, Baptists, and Henry Alline.* Kingston, Ontario: McGill-Queens University Press,1984.

Raymond. W.O. "The Founding of Shelburne: Benjamin Marston at Halifax and Miramiche," *New Brunswick Historical Society Collections,* 3 (1907).

Robertson, Marion. *King's Bounty: A History of Early Shelburne, Nova Scotia.* Halifax: Nova Scotia Museum,1975.

Smith, T. Watson. "The Slave in Canada," *Collections of the Nova Scotia Historical Society,* 10 (1896–98), 1–161.

Sweet, David G. and Nash, Gary B., eds. *Struggle and Survival in Colonial America.* Berkeley, Ca.: University of California Press, 1981.

Syrett, David. *Shipping and the American War, 1775–1783: A Study of British Transport Organization.* London: The Athlone Press, 1970.

Thomas, C.E. "The Work in Nova Scotia of the Society for the Propagation of the Gospel in Foreign Parts," *Nova Scotia Historical Society*, 38 (1973).

Thomas, Lamont. *Rise to be a People: A Biography of Paul Cuffe.* Urbana: University of Illinois Press, 1986.

Troxler, Carol. "The Migration of Carolina and Georgia Loyalists to Nova Scotia and New Brunswick." Ph.D. diss., University of North Carolina, 1974.

Wilentz, R. Sean. *Chants Democratic: New York City & the Making of the American Working Class, 1788–1850.* New York: Oxford University Press, 1984.

Walker, James W. St. G. *The Black Loyalists: The Search for a Promised Land in Nova Scotia.* New York: Africana Publishing Company, a division of Holmes & Meier, Inc., 1976.

____. "Blacks and American Loyalists: The Slave's War for Independence." *Historical Reflections/Reflections Historique.* 2 (1975), 51–57.

Walvin, James. "The Public Campaign in England Against Slavery," in David Eltis and James Walvin, *The Abolition of the Atlantic Slave Trade.* Madison: University of Wisconsin Press, 1981, 63–83.

White, E. Francis. *Sierra Leone's Women Traders: Women on the Afro-European Frontier.* Ann Arbor: University of Michigan Press, 1987.

Wilson, Ellen Gibson. *The Loyal Blacks.* New York: G.P. Putnam's Sons, 1976.

Winks, Robin. *The Blacks in Canada: A History.* New Haven, Ct.: Yale University Press, 1971.

Wyse, Akintola. *The Krio of Sierra Leone: An Interpretation.* London, 1990.

Index

(First names only given in Inspection Roll)

Aaron, 164
Aberdeen, 149
Abigail, 21, 149, 163, 172
Abraham, 7, 8, 136, 140, 150, 151, 159, 177, 181
Achabee, 152
Adam, 60, 68, 126, 147
Almin, 8
Amelia, 200
Amoretta, 47
Andrew, 134
Ann, 60, 179
Anna, 67, 69
Annie, 151
Anson, 149
Anthony, 135, 180
August, 167
Beck, 164
Belinda, 149, 209
Bella, 159
Ben, 39, 71, 123
Benjamin, 48, 186, 187
Bess, 122
Besse, 135
Bet, 150, 152

Betsey, 93, 116, 129, 131, 160, 167, 212
Betsy, 122, 177
Betts, 152
Betty, 58, 59, 68, 161, 186
Bill, 40, 148, 152, 154, 163
Billy, 228
Bina, 181
Black Bill, 164
Bob, 121, 135, 149, 150
Boston, 49
Bridget, 185
Bristol, 24, 63, 161, 184
Cairo, 159
Cander, 164
Captain, 150
Carolina, 127
Casar, 58, 123, 146, 149, 153, 156, 158, 163
Catharina, 152
Catharine, 9, 19, 113, 158
Cato, 63, 155, 163, 169, 204
Ceasor, 7
Charity, 165
Charles, 31, 37, 62, 140, 145

Charlotte, 166
Chloe, 134, 172, 174
Christopher, 135
Clara, 6, 177
Clarinda, 154, 174
Cornwallis, 121
Cows, 156
Cubit, 174
Cudja, 24
Cuffie, 60
Cutto, 179
Cyrus, 118
Dalkeith, 174
Dan, 75
Daniel, 153, 158, 163
Daphne, 179
Darcas, 205
Darkas, 9
David, 38, 71, 119
Dian, 36
Diana, 127, 134, 136, 138, 154, 180, 186
Dianah, 172
Dick, 35, 76, 156, 161
Dinah, 42, 48, 59, 68, 69, 71, 155, 156, 158, 167, 185

Dolly, 60
Dorothey, 204
Dorothy, 130, 178
Eaddie, 172
Effy, 49
Elijah, 161
Elizabeth, 66, 152, 156, 165, 173, 184
Ellice, 173
Emanuel, 25
Ephraim, 146
Esther, 95, 159
Eve, 153, 155
Fanny, 15, 28, 160, 185
Fortune, 7, 48, 78, 129, 137
Francis, 39, 50, 146
Friar, 149
George, 8, 120, 121, 124, 126, 134, 158, 164, 166
Gilbert, 177
Gill, 146
Glasgow, 164
Grace, 110, 146, 160, 166
Guinea, 15
Gull, 136
Hagar, 185

Ham, 139
Hannah, 8, 42,
  62, 120, 123,
  124, 140, 147,
  157, 158, 163,
  184, 185
Hannibal, 146
Hargar, 140
Harry, 7, 22,
  135, 147, 154,
  155, 166
Henry, 8
Hercules, 68,
  126, 186
Hope, 164
Ibby, 155
Ilinda, 185
Isaac, 8, 18, 178
Isabella, 25, 55,
  125, 160, 180
Jack, 50, 59, 68,
  118, 125, 132,
  139, 150, 151,
  152, 156, 164
Jackey, 159
Jacob, 33, 59,
  68, 165, 166
James, 54, 58,
  77, 93, 134,
  152, 154, 174
Jane, 123, 145,
  157, 160, 163,
  209
Jarvis, 157
Jean, 149
Jeanis, 122
Jeff, 77, 135, 181
Jeffery, 75
Jem, 175, 185
Jemima, 60
Jenny, 57, 79,
  152, 159, 163,
  166, 180, 186
Jeremy, 19
Jim, 29, 78, 145,
  164
Joe, 8, 9, 41, 59,
  78, 139, 149,
  150, 157, 158,
  174
John, 80, 120,
  122, 157, 164,

168, 176, 177,
  185, 208
Johnny, 167
Joseph, 6, 18,
  140, 163, 166,
  172
Joshua, 58
Joyce, 5
Juba, 127
Jude, 59, 152
Judith, 76, 155,
  173, 178
July, 120
Juno, 123
Jupiter, 154, 207
Kate, 8, 15, 125,
  139, 152, 155,
  161
Katy, 152, 160
Kezzia, 68
Kitty, 120, 135,
  186
Lakey, 185
Larry, 165
Leah, 148
Letitia, 146, 164
Letitie, 7
Lettia, 158
Lettius, 167
Levitia, 165
Lewis, 146, 209
Liberty, 137
Lidia, 167
Lilley, 80
Lilly, 148, 150
London, 42, 59,
  123, 134
Lottie, 138
Lucas, 126
Luce, 128
Lucia, 74
Lucinda, 77
Lucretia, 47
Lucy, 120, 130,
  157, 177
Lydia, 145, 185,
  186
Margaret, 105,
  150, 163
Maria, 104, 136
Mariah, 180
Marianna, 47

Mary, 8, 47, 52,
  58, 75, 139,
  152, 156, 157,
  159, 161, 167,
  184, 185
Mary Ann, 28,
  66, 80, 155
Mary Anna, 80
Massey, 184
Matthew, 172
Melinda, 134
Mercury, 140
Michael, 122
Mima, 57, 164
Ming, 155
Mingo, 120, 136
Minnus, 38
Molly, 60, 148,
  156, 160, 166,
  176
Moriah, 19
Moses, 9
Murcer, 140
Nan, 19, 152
Nancy, 19, 37,
  66, 71, 93, 121,
  126, 128, 140,
  148, 154, 157,
  161, 168, 180,
  184, 185
Nanny, 147, 185
Nathaniel, 134
Ned, 138, 150,
  159, 168
Nell, 118
Nelly, 137, 185
Nero, 157, 179
Nicholas, 175
Paris, 128, 139
Patience, 178
Patty, 128, 168
Paul, 6
Peg, 147, 159
Peggy, 31, 46,
  120, 128, 146,
  186, 187, 211
Peter, 7, 20, 119,
  121, 124, 145,
  149, 211
Petter, 202
Phebe, 7, 136
Philip, 60

Phillis, 19, 118,
  147, 152, 156,
  167, 179, 180,
  184, 201
Phillister, 167
Plato, 132, 148
Pleasant, 154,
  166, 167
Poll, 158
Polly, 93, 187
Polydore, 122
Pompey, 146,
  159, 181
Primus, 42, 134
Prince, 44, 145,
  152, 155, 166,
  200
Princessa, 99
Priscilla, 155,
  157, 172, 190
Prudence, 167
Punch, 162
Pusie, 132
Quaco, 156
Quash, 166
Rachel, 38, 118,
  150, 152, 156,
  186
Rachell, 174
Rebecca, 80,
  128
Reuben, 5
Robert, 135, 158,
  159
Rosanna, 118
Rose, 109, 121,
  126, 139, 185
Rosetta, 74
Sabinah, 46, 164
Salley, 200
Sally, 42, 62, 68,
  78, 120, 148,
  151, 158, 159,
  166, 167, 176,
  180, 183, 186
Sam, 35, 48, 50,
  60, 146, 153–
  156, 159, 164,
  165, 167, 176,
  179, 180
Sampson, 150

Sarah, 58–60,
68, 120, 151,
153–155, 165,
167, 174, 178,
179
Sarrah, 209
Scipio, 49, 145
Seelah, 95
Sentry, 28
Sharp, 126
Sibbe, 153
Silas, 49, 172
Silvia, 58, 135,
151–153, 167,
173
Simon, 49, 77

Solomon, 48,
161
Stach, 78
Stephen, 179
Suckey, 204
Sue, 145, 149
Sukey, 5, 23, 31,
50, 59, 67, 70,
160, 161, 180
Sunbury, 132
Susannah, 134,
137, 151, 154,
156, 172, 176,
180, 186
Sylvia, 39
Tamar, 154

Tampier, 74
Tempe, 153
Tertullus, 164
Thomas, 165
Tim, 137, 156
Timothy, 163
Titus, 163
Toby, 76, 121,
177
Tom, 37, 58, 76,
77, 126, 154,
155, 157, 166,
167, 179, 180,
210
Toney, 72, 175,
213

Venus, 8, 36,
128
Vigo, 162
Vinia, 135
Violett, 45
Vulean, 147
Wallace, 34
Warwick, 139
Whitehaven, 162
Will, 118, 121,
166
William, 7, 22,
44, 156, 160,
176
York, 59, 121,
132, 154, 186

(First and last names given in Inspection Roll)

Abbot
George, 93
Aberdee
John, 243
Aberdeen
John, 227, 249
Nancy, 149
Ablin
Sylva, 227, 242
Acker
Isaac, 70
Ackerman
Abraham, 150
Albert, 182
Ackland
Phil, 41
Adam
Owen, 122
Adams
Ann, 260
Charles, 227
Emmy, 138
George, 227,
244, 250
Jacob, 97
John, 45, 204,
227, 240, 247,
256

Lewis, 10
Mary, 245,
250, 252
Nancy, 250
Phil, 156
Simon, 138
Thomas, 227
William, 250
William
(Child), 244
Adamson
John, 25, 65,
69
Samuel, 227
Addie
Frank, 132
Addinot
Daniel, 130
Adnitt
Daniel, 59
Agnew
William, 227
Agram
Elizabeth, 258
George, 257
Aitken
Kassey, 61
Akerman

Capt., 154
Garret, 113
Albert
John, 227
Samuel, 34
Alderson
Roger, 159
Aldrich
Betsey, 206
Prince, 206
Alexander
Henry, 227,
244, 256
James, 145
John, 93, 197
Sandy, 138
Allamaz
Ann (Child),
242
Harriet, 242
Joseph, 242
Joshua (Child),
242
Allamaze
Ann, 227, 236
Allamazi
Joshua, 227
Allambazi

Joseph, 227
Allen
Barbary, 5
Charles, 10
Col., 25
Isaac, Lt. Col.,
5
Job, 25
John, 137, 183
Joseph, 61, 62,
154
Margaret, 252
Mary, 252
Polly, 25
Samuel, 227
William, 77,
206
Allenby
Timothy, 227,
240
Allington
Daniel, 227
David, 240
Allison
Abram, 227
John, 56
Allman
Phil, 156

Sarah, 156
Alson
   Hugh, 207
Alstin
   David, 181
   John, 186
Ambo
   Tony, 262
   Truro, 251
   Turee, 249
   Tureo, 241
   Turese, 227
Ambruse
   Lieut., 134
Amherst
   Jeffery, 260
   Ammerson, 181
Amos
   Mary, 236
Ancram
   George, 33
Anderson
   Archibald, 70,
   227
   Dianach, 199
   Ebenezar, 227
   Ebenezer, 247
   Isaac, 43
   James, 199,
   227, 241
   John, 20, 22,
   256
   Joseph, 227
   Joseph (Child),
   247
   Mr., 199
   Sarah, 43
   William, 227,
   245, 251, 262
Andover
   Phebe, 236
Andrew
   Jack, 227
Andrews
   Daniel, 253,
   259
   Elizabeth, 254
   George, 122
   John, 253, 260
   Robert, 147
Ann
   Mary, 236

Annand
   Gaub, 227
Annie
   James, 189
   John, 189
Annis
   John, 165
Annison
   James, 227
Ansley
   Thomas, 227
Anthony
   D. A. Silea,
   244
   Domingo, 247
   Jack, 227, 247
   James, 12
   John, 227, 247,
   253, 260
   Joseph, 227,
   247
   Mathew, 101
Antill
   George, 128
Antona
   Domingo, 257
Appleby
   Thomas, 154
Archer
   Daniel, 117
   Dinah, 148
   Thomas, 117
Archie
   Captain, 19
Armsfield
   Elizabeth, 258
   Peter, 257
Armsted
   Mr., 213
Armstrong, 191
   ___, 141
   Capt., 161,
   165, 168
   Harry, 227
   Major, 138
   P., 63
   William, 51,
   61, 130, 214
Arnold
   Gen., 21, 31,
   155

General, 6, 30,
   67, 134
   Jacob, 37
   Matthew, 126
Arrington
   Henry, 140
Arronstead
   William, 196
Ash
   Amy, 164
   John, 127
   Samuel, 165,
   167
Ashe
   Cato, 42
   Esther, 42
   Mary, 42
   William, 42
Ashfield
   Jane, 244
   John, 227, 241,
   247, 256
   Mary, 258
   Pam, 236
   Robert, 227,
   246
Ashmore
   Abraham, 253,
   259
   Lucy, 253, 259
Ashworth
   Thomas, 227,
   242
Astens
   Ben, 183
Astin
   Massey, 163
Aston
   John, 113
Atken
   Eli, 62
Atkins
   Alexander, 183
   Capt., 135, 136
   James, 227,
   245, 253, 257,
   260
   Widow, 135,
   136
Atkinson, 65
   J., 160

John, 26, 46,
   78, 157
   Joseph, 148
   Minty, 148
   Samuel, 147
   Thomas, 145
Atwood
   Capt., 135
August
   Betsey, 85
Augustavas
   Syllavo, 227
Augustus
   Prince, 69
Ayoner
   Sarah, 126
Ayres
   Leddleton, 117
   Sovereign, 108
Babus
   John, 92
   Nancy, 94
Bacchus
   Flora, 29
   Jenny, 29
   Mary, 29
   Thomas, 29
   William, 29
Backhus
   Molly, 207
   Robert, 207
Badger
   Rev. Mr., 59
Bagout
   ___, 94
Bagshaw
   Nuse, 174
Bailey
   Barney, 103
   Charles, 103
   James, 227,
   243
Bailie
   Hampstead, 21
Bailley
   Joe, 12
   Nancy, 12
   Silvia, 12
Baird
   Mr., 171
Baker

James, 254, 258
Nathaniel, 204
Prince, 204
Baldwin
Elizabeth, 236
Patient, 228, 241
Stephen, 17, 20
Thomas, 156, 157
Balford
General, 10
Ball
Anthony, 83
Benjamin, 92
Richard, 31
Thomas, 26, 87
Willis, 91
Ballad
William, 20
Ballamay
John, 169
Ballantine, 6
Ballard
Francis, 83
Ballester
John, 253
Ballingall
Robert, 77
Balmanno
David, 148
Baltimore
Lord, 11
Balton
Isaac, 187
Bamptiser
John, 228
Banbury
John, 110
Lucy, 111
Bank
Judith, 236
Banks
Ens., 132
Ensign, 132
John, 257
Judeah, 254
Judith, 247
Banmord
Samuel, 119
Bannister

Col., 134
Lucy, 236
Thomas, 156
Banter
Albert, 14
John, 14
Thomas, 14
Baptist
Ann, 241
Elizabeth, 236, 244
Jane, 236, 246, 252, 261
John, 228, 246
Baptiste
John, 247
Bar
George, 84
Barbaree
Capt., 132
Barber
Daniel, 5
Sam, 5
Barbery
Peter, 172
Barclay
Andrew, 30, 31
Elizabeth, 190
Fan, 190
George, 190
Israel, 190
James, 53
Jane, 190
John Wallis, 128
John Willis, 128
Mrs., 129
Rachel, 190
Tishy, 190
Barclett
James, 52
Kate, 52
Barker
Lt., 135
Mr., 13
Barley
Joseph, 227
Barlian
Frank, 251
Barlow
Jesse, 128

Barnes, 68
George, 121
James, 228, 242
Rachel, 121
William, 227, 228, 245
Barnett
Isaac, 197
Barns
D., 31
Robert, 91
Barrell
Lydia, 236
Barren
Charles, 187
James, 187
Barret
Joseph, 58
Barrett
Robert, 104, 105
Barrisworth
Richard, 170
Barron
Robert, 87, 88
Barrow
James, 113
Richard, 160
Barrows
Augustine, 260
Barry
Daniel, 43
Bartlet
Joseph, 188
Bartram
Joal, 205
Toney, 205
Barwill
Mary, 236
Bass
John, 182
Basset
Nancy, 171
Thomas, 106
Bastian
Frank, 243
Pete, 228
Peter, 241
Bastion
Francis, 228
Bateman

Catherine, 236
Batt
Jean, 46
Nathaniel, 106
Battester
John, 259
Batty
James, 227, 247
Baxter
James, 67
Baxthian
Francis, 262
Baxton
Matthew, 104
Bayard
Abraham, 187
Major, 118
Peter, 16
Sam, 16
Samuel, 187
William, 118
Bayley
George, 106
William, 106
Bayne
John, 148
Baynes
John, 95, 114
Bazely
Scipio, 65
Beach
Daniel, 30
Henry, 30
Beacon
Charity, 201
Michael, 137
Pompy, 201
Samuel, 201
Beadle
Mrs., 134
Beakman
Barney, 176
Beal
Henry, 244, 249
Beale
Henry, 227
Bean
Peter, 35
Thomas, 68, 120, 172

Beans
  John, 171
Beardsley
  John, Rev., 65
  Peter, 65
  Rev. Mr., 68
Beariman
  Sally, 127
Beattie
  Edward, 68
Beauman
  Thomas, 127
Beazley
  James, 195
Becket
  John, 247
Beckett
  John, 227
Beckle
  Nicholas, 5
Beeber
  Jacob, 150
Beekman
  Ann, 237
Been
  John, 164
Behm
  Elizabeth, 246
  Issac, 246
Bell
  Capt., 45
  Edmond, 104
  George, 154
  Jane, 104
  John, 20, 104,
  105, 107, 227,
  246
  Rachel, 104
  Sarah, 107
  Thomas,
  Captain, 51
  William, 77,
  159
Bella
  Mary, 32
Bellinge
  Mr., 177
Beman
  Ebenezer, 60
Ben
  Cander, 164
  Cuff, 146

George, 111,
  146, 149
  John, 146, 164
  Silvia, 164
  Thomas, 83
Bendiver
  Hamil, 227
Benn
  Elizabeth, 258
  Isaac, 227, 256
Bennel
  Ann, 236
Bennet
  Ben, 190
  John, 165
  William, 42
Bennoh
  Ann, 236
Benson
  B., 36
  Christopher, Jr.,
  59
  Egbert, 61
  Sampson, 163
  Yast, 163
Benssis
  Ben, 45
Benthew
  Joseph, 228,
  241, 253
Bentley
  George, 32
Bergen
  James, 160
Bernard
  George, 228,
  243
Berry
  Isaac, 65
  James, 14
  Josiah, 53
  Lieut., 14
  Tabitha, 53
Berwick
  Ann, 236
  George, 228
George
  Alexander, 243
  Mary Ann, 243
Besantee
  Sylva, 228
Best

Henry, 116
Bethel
  John, 260, 261
Bethell
  John, 256
Bettle
  John, 6
Betts
  Richard, 70
  Thomas, 70
Bettsworth
  Thomas, 254
Betty
  George, 30
  Isaac, 188
  John, 188
  Robert, 198
Betworth
  Thomas, 260
Beuff
  Francis, 30, 31
Bias
  Robert, 149
Bibbin
  George, 114
Biddle
  John, 114
  Stephen, 132
Billinger
  George, 188
  William, 188
Billings
  Capt., 11
Bilson
  Sam, 154
Bing
  Hannah, 96
  Robert, 95
  Thomas, 95
Birch
  Brig. Gen., 212
  Daniel, 101
  General, 205
Bird
  Col., 191
  Colonel, 99
  Jane, 242
  Mrs., 171
  William, 227,
  242
Birdny
  Peter, 108

Birmingham
  Richard, 27
Birt
  Oxford, 184
Birtley
  John, 181
  Phil, 181
Biscoe
  George, 125,
  126
Bishick
  George, 75
Bishop
  James, 155
Biverout
  Mary, 99
Biverowdt
  Henry, 98
Black
  Ann, 5
  Betsey, 35
  Effy, 26
  Elizabeth, 5
  George, 5, 35
  John, 227
  Nathaniel, 26
  Robert, 227
  William, 35,
  40, 153, 171
Blackston
  Isaac, 53
Blackwell
  Thomas, 117
Blaes
  Alexander, 18
Blair
  Daniel, 146
  Hannah, 110
  John, 108, 165
Blake
  Capt., 136
  John, 227, 243,
  257
  Litrop, 87
  Prince, 136
Blanchard
  Cornelius, 127,
  128, 129
Bland
  Theodric, 89
Blane
  John, 130

Blauvelt
  Hermanus, 205
  Jack, 18
  Mr., 18
Blauvett
  Harry, 205
Blavalt
  John, 17
Blavelt
  Dinah, 18
Blear
  Hana, 236
  Hannah, 246
Blew
  Phillis, 19
  Robert, 16
Bloom
  Lucy, 71
  Michael, 71
Blowfield
  Mr., 6
Bloy
  London, 38
Blucke
  Margaret, 88
  Stephen, 88
Blue
  William, 227
Bluefinch
  Dr., 185
Blure
  Isaac, 260
Boarham
  William, 228
Bocebeck
  Col., 34
Bodel
  Betsey, 178
Boden
  Cato, 25
  John, 86
  Peg, 26
  Peter, 109
Boder
  Peter, 109
Bogart
  James, 154
  John, 17
Bogert
  William, 17
Boggard
  Cornelius, 35

Boggs
  John, 71
Bogle
  William, 59
Boler
  Arthur, 189
  Betsy, 190
  Phebe, 189
Boll
  Richard, 155
Bolner
  Elias, 164
Bolton
  Amelia, 243
  Anny, 145
  Jenny, 145
  Thom, 145
  Thomas, 145
Bond
  Dick, 81
  John, 81
  Rose, 81
  William, 227,
    253, 259
Bonnel
  Isaac, Esq., 164
Bonta
  Albert, 118
Booker
  William, 153
Boon
  Celia, 74
  Dick, 74
  Elsee, 74
  Samuel, 74
Bord
  Jane, 236
Borden
  Bristol, 183
  John, 183, 186
Boss
  Jacob, 227
Bossea
  Jacob, 245
Bostick
  Solomon, 62
Boston
  James, 228
  Joseph, 247
Bosworth
  Thomas, 59
Bour

John, 145
Bourdet
  Harry, 58
Bourdett
  Oliver, 58
Bowden
  Amelia, 236
  Dempsey, 65
  Sally, 65
  Sealia, 65
Bowen
  Capt., 150
Bower
  Robert, 254
Bowers
  Robert, 258
Bowland
  Robert, 208
Bowler
  Medcalfe, 189
Bowles
  James, 179
Bowline
  Sarah, 260
  Thomas, 260
Bowls
  Isaac, 179
Bowman
  Thomas, 85
Bown
  Obadiah, 184
Boyd
  Harry, 154
  Widow, 163
Boykin
  Mrs., 134
Boyle
  Adam, 183
  Ensign, 137
  Thomas, 183
Bracey
  Jonas, 73
  Thomas, 73
Brackenback
  Lt., 140
Bracy
  Henry, 35
Bradford
  Joseph, 128
Bradley
  Mary, 249,
    252, 261

Richard, 228,
  244, 249, 252,
  261
Brady
  Jacob, 210
Brandy
  John, 227, 241,
    253, 260
Braveboy
  Mary, 57
Bready
  Mr., 205
Breese
  Samuel, Col.,
    189
Brew
  Captain, 16
Brewer
  Jeremiah, 119
  Moses, 56
Brian
  Luke, 15
Bricker
  David, 55, 228,
    245
Bridger
  Mary, 149
Bridges
  Jane, 171
  John, 227
  Katy, 171
  Lieut. Col., 169
  Thomas, 24
Bridgewater
  John, 62, 63
Briggs
  Charles, 236
  Charles
    (Child), 245
  Helena
    (Child), 245
  Helene, 236
  Letitia, 245
  Lililia, 236
  William, 49
Bright
  Mary, 172
  Robert, 199
  Silas, 30, 70,
    170
Brinkerhoff
  Jack, 130

Brinkerhoof
  Thomas, 35
Brinoly
  Silvester, 36
Brisbane
  Mr., 45
Brisco
  James, 243
Bristow
  John, 227, 228,
  243, 244, 256
  Peter, 227, 243
  Richard, 227
  Robert, 246
Britain
  Hagar, 65
  John, 227, 245,
  258
  Lt., 132
  Peter, 175
  Thomas, 227
Britton
  Lt., 133
  Thomas, 69
Broadstreet
  General, 98
Broden
  John, 97
Brodie
  Archibald, 210
Bromfield
  George, 241,
  262
  Peter, 243
  William, 243,
  252
Bromley
  John, 262
  Joseph, 251
Brookes
  Aaron, 256
  Dorcas, 257
  Richard, 60
Brooks
  Aaron, 227,
  240
  Basil, 10
Broome
  John, 120
Broomfield
  George, 227,
  250

Brothers
  Betsy, 6
  Sam, 6
Broughton
  Ben, 17
  Francis, 228,
  243, 258
  John, 206
  Margaret, 243
  Nancy, 20
  Suckey, 206
  Thomas, 185,
  206
Brow
  Mary, 116
Brown
  Abby, 87
  Benjamin, 227,
  240
  Capt., 135
  Catherine, 236,
  244
  Cato, 182
  Chaplain, 145
  Daniel, 182
  David, 227,
  246
  Dinah, 87
  Edward, 227,
  244
  Elizabeth, 236,
  246, 249, 252,
  261
  Fanny, 168
  George, 227,
  241, 249, 251,
  261
  Harry, 108
  Isaac, 63
  Isaac, Dr., 63
  James, 129,
  135, 162, 198,
  228, 240, 242
  Jane, 236, 244
  Jenny, 198
  John, 6, 54,
  138, 147, 161,
  198, 210, 227,
  228, 241, 243,
  246, 247, 253,
  260

John English,
  227, 246
  Joseph, 114,
  227, 247
  Joshua, 227,
  240
  Major, 61, 62
  Margaret, 236
  Marmory, 115
  Mary, 18, 236,
  242
  Nancy, 88, 198
  Patty, 115
  Peggy, 198
  Peter, 129, 145
  Pompey, 11
  Richard, 89,
  197
  Robert, 26
  Samuel, 108
  Silas, 197
  Susan, 246
  Susanha, 236
  Thomas, 36,
  70, 88, 174,
  200, 202, 228,
  243, 246, 253,
  260
  Widow, 140
  William, 124
Browne
  Bill, 37
  Capt., 54
  Dinah, 23, 37
  J. J., 6
  Jack, 23
  John, 14, 26,
  204
  Moses, 54
  Nicholas, 37
  Richard, 5, 6
  Sarah, 31
  Thomas, 17
  Will, 206
Brownell
  Josiah, 54
Bruce
  Betsey, 33
  Edmund, 60
  Edward, 21
  James, 129
  Jenny, 33

Rob, 155
Robert, 77, 109
Thomas, 227,
  242
Bruckle
  John, 155
Bruen
  Eliza, 61
  Hagar, 62
Bruens
  Henry, 61
Bruff
  Charles O., 18,
  19
  Charles Oliver,
  17, 18
  Robert, 96
Bruin
  David, 188
  Thomas, 188
Brunchard
  Isaac, 247
Brunhard
  Isaac, 228
Bryan
  George
  William, 227
  George
  William
  (Child), 244
  Johanna, 227,
  236
  Johanna
  (Child), 244
  Louis, 138
  Nancy, 138
  Rosanne, 244
  Rosehanna,
  236
Bryant
  William, 10
Buchanon
  Alexander, 169
Bucher
  John, 195
Buckel
  Jasper, 58
Buckie
  Peter, 161
Buckley
  Darcas, 54
  Jack, 54

Jonathan, 54
Prince, 55
Bucks
John, 253, 259
Budel
Phebe, 178
Budell
John, 178
Bull
Cazar, 52
Gov., 126
Jemima, 52
Lieut., 134
Millia, 52
Mr., 52
Philip, 52
Bullen
Dr., 152–154
Bullet
John, 25
Sall, 25
Bummele
Jacob, 97
Bundeck
George, 170
Bunion
Mr., 164
Buntin
Joshua, 125
Bunyan
Sarah, 18
Burges
Nathaniel, 106
Timothy, 128
Burgess
Anthony, 227,
246
Benjamin, 228
Benjamin
(Child), 246
Henry, 90
Burgis
Jeffery, 106
John, 64
Matthew, 128
Molly, 106
Burgoyne, 123
Benedict, 126
John Lewis,
120, 121
Burke
Mr., 117

Richard, 135
Burken
Andrew, 179
Burnett
George, 32
Burrell
Lucas, 86
Burtis
Paul, 98
Burton
Jenny, 179
Judith, 94
Mr., 136
Burtonan
Elizabeth, 236
Bush
Adam, 27
Andrew, 117
Benjamin, 89
Charity, 27
Cuffie, 57
Dorothy, 90
Flora, 124
Isaac, 104, 124
Jane, 171
Jenny, 82
Judith, 82
Lucy, 104
Mr., 27
Nelly, 171
Richard, 170
Sampson, 27
Samuel, 82,
89, 90
William, 57,
73, 117
Bushell
John, 208
Buskirk
John, 6, 9
L. V., 158
Lawrence, 158
Mr., 5
Susannah, 57
Buskirk, Jr
Mr., 5
Butler
Anthony, 151
Beggert, 42
George, 41
Henry, 227
Mary, 236, 242

Sukey, 41
William, 47
Buxton
Dempsey, 97
Edward, 190
James, 97
Mr., 41
Nathaniel, 98
Scipio, 41
Bybank
John, 124
Caesor
Sarah, 14
Cahill
William, 256
Cain
John, 253, 259
Robert, 170
Sillah, 112
Tom, 111
Cairnes
___, 210
Cakrean
Lewis, 101
Cald
John, 101
Calder
Andrew, 41
Caldwell
Unis, 107
Callighan
Widow, 48
Calls
Henry, 170
Cambridge
Charles, 58
John, 228, 253,
259
Judith, 236,
247
Sarah, 254, 259
Cameron
Duncan, 78, 79
John, 129
Campbell, 46
Ann, 236
Archibald, 46
Arthur, 151
Capt., 136
Clara, 105
James, 40, 112,
173

Moses, 112
Peggy, 111
Pompey, 151
Robert, 26
Widow, 163
William, 46,
75, 177, 228,
242
William, Lord,
33
Cane
Henry, 228
John, 228, 243
Cannon
Cato, 35
Charles, 179
John, 35
Carberry
Philip, 83
Cardell
Ann, 247
Catherine, 236,
247
Carden
Diana, 135
William, 135
Carey
Andrew, 228
Col. Mrs., 108
Jenny, 83
Lydia, 106
Polly, 83
Robert, 228
Thomas, 106
William, 228
Carigatt
Ann, 258
Carigut
John, 257
Carle
Dr., 132
Carleton
Col. Mrs., 103
Guy, Sir, 50,
61, 63, 72, 76,
118, 129, 140,
191, 213
Carlyne
Richard Wyatt,
59
Carman
Richard, 159

William, 19
Carnel
  Colonel, 112
Carney
  Barnaby, 82
Carpenter
  Adj't., 139
  Benjamin, 120
  Ensign, 139
  Increase, 188
Carr
  Capt., 138, 139
  Elizabeth, 236,
  242
Carragan
  Tony, 199
Carraway
  James, 82
Carrey
  Amos, 108
Carrol
  John, 228, 245
Carson
  William, 18,
  131
  Carter, 25
  Capt., 151
  Charles, Col.,
  165
  Col., 134, 166
  Henry, 69, 228
  John, 41
  Lewis, 13
  Lt., 123
Cartwright
  Lawrence, 124
  Thomas, 125,
  126
Carvat
  Charles, 228
Cary
  Charlotte, 83
  Daniel, 59
Casey
  Andrew, 93
  Dr., 68
Casoner
  Charles, 40
Casor
  John, 65
Cassells
  William, 19

Cassels
  William, 16,
  18
Cassidy
  Thomas, 41
Castington
  Toby, 213
Castor
  Charles, 228,
  241
  Fanny, 241
  Matthew, 241
Caswell
  Col., 151
  Moses, 151
Catchpole
  William, 180
Cato
  Sophia, 236
Cattle
  Ben, 177
Causins
  William, 92
Ceasor
  John J., 242
  Thomas, 228
Cevils
  Hannah, 85
  Zilpah, 85
Chace
  George, 45
Chandler
  Nat, 118
  William, 45
Channel
  Thomas, 67
Channell
  Abraham, 67
  John, Dr., 79
  Penny, 67
  Thomas, 78
Channill
  Clarissa, 79
Chapman
  John, 62, 113
  Maria, 236
Char
  Mary, 236
Charles
  James, 228,
  260
Charleson

Mr., 75
Charlotte
  Edward, 236
Chase
  Francis, 228
  Margaret, 247
  Pompey, 36
  Reuben, 36
Cheace
  Ensign, 139
Cheese
  Anna, 85
  William, 85
Cheeseman
  Thomas, 117
Chetwine
  William, 33
Chew
  Benjamin, 97
Chilcot
  Charles, 243
Chilcoth
  Charles, 228,
  257
  Elizabeth, 258
Child
  William, 253,
  259
Childs
  Mr., 113
Chillar
  Robert, 64
Chilton
  James, 228
Chine
  Benjamin, 204
Chipcot
  Agent, 73
Christeen
  Job, 90
  Judith, 91
Christian
  Capt., 117
  Michael, 108
  Toney, 108
Christie
  Edward, 132
  John, 52
Christopher
  Daniel, 228,
  250
  Patty, 173

Church
  Lewis, 198
Churchill
  Mr., 15
  William, 78
Churchwell
  Benjamin, 15
Cilley
  Frank, 179
Clain
  John, 197
Clany
  Martin, 157
Clap
  John Charles,
  210
Clara
  Hebanally, 236
Clark, 133
  Amelia, 236,
  246
  Benjamin, 228,
  246, 247
  Benjamin
  (Mrs.), 228
  Esther, 188
  General, 17
  George, 228,
  244
  James, 206
  John, 64, 147
  Joseph, 20, 22,
  67
  Letita, 243
  Mary Ann, 258
  Michael, 174,
  188
  Paul, 228, 249,
  257
  Paul (Mrs.),
  228
  Samuel, 77,
  154
  Shadrack, 242
  Shadruck, 228,
  250
  Thomas, 228
  William, 228
Clarke
  Archibald, 36
  Dr., 60
  Elizabeth, 260

George, 246,
260
James, 206
Lydia, 258
M. A., 260
Paul, 240
Phillis, 203
Pompy, 203
Sam, 78
Samuel, 77, 78
Thomas, 206,
245
William, Dr.,
203
Clarkely
Steven, 18
Clarkson
Mr., 131
Clause
William, 247
Clawson
Jonathan, 146
Clayton
John, 45, 90
Robert, 228,
240, 249
Clement
Mary, 236
Clements
Thomas, 228,
253, 259
Clifton
Joseph, 258
Clinton
Gen., 32
H., Sir, 20
Henry, Sir, 12,
22
Lt., 9
Clirby
John, 28
Cloase
William, 228
Close
William, 251,
261
Closs
Casar, 60
Cloud
2nd Mast., 150
Clouse
Lena, 74

Nicholas, 74
Clows
Lt., 133
Timothy, 150
Cob
John, 53
Cobbwine
Bristol, 6
Cobe
William, 245
Cochran
John, 60
Cockburn
John, 101, 168
Cockrill
Robert, 74
Cockwell
Hector, 176
Codbert
Thomas, 102
Coddamus
Jenny, 102
Coduise
Christopher, 97
Coffin
Major, 7, 137
Mrs., 137
Paul, 7
Cogan
Ann, 236
Coggle
Capt., 132
Colb
Mr., 10, 11
Colbert
Captain, 40
Cornelius, 125
Samuel, 171,
201
Coldstream
Charles, 150
Cole
Andrew, 97
Ben, 97
Col., 151
Colonel, 126
Edward, 79
Elizabeth, 79
Henry, 67
Jenny, 67
Jeremiah, 79
Richard, 57

Sharper, 151
William, 57,
228
Coleman
John, 228
Peggy, 236,
244
Sukey, 28
Coles
Joseph, 203
Mary, 98
Coley
David, 59
Jack, 59
Colhoun
Jack, 96
Samuel, 96
Collet
Violet, 114
Colley
Ebenezer, 14
Ishmael, 14
Collin
James, 21
Collins
Betsey, 9
Charles, 18
Hanna, 27
Jacob, 202
James, 152,
228, 245
John, 174, 202
Joseph, 9
Mary, 27
Nancy, 46
Robert, 46
Salley, 202
Collinson
William, 228,
240
Colt
Mr., 213
Pompy, 213
Colvill
John, 132
Comfortable
George, 228,
241, 249, 251,
261
Commins
Thomas, 246
Comyns

John, 228
Conel
Col., 21
Conklin
Isaack, 159
Samuel, 54
Conley
Widow, 131
Connaway
Walker, 90
Conner
Charles, 93,
107, 195
Colonel, 166
Dinah, 107
John, 206, 213
Scipio, 206
William, 167
Connor
Amelia, 183
Betsey, 82
Capt., 137
Charles, 19,
82, 114
Isaac, 18
James, 82
Jane, 82
Teresa, 82
William, 92
Connors
Charles, 18
Connoway
Peter, 89
Convey
Joseph, 196
Conway
Ben, 78
Bristol, 184
Hannah, 184
Jenny, 184
Robert, 181
Cook
Alice, 260
Ann, 261
Ellis, 236
Henry, 115
Jane, 160
John, 57, 126
Robert, 152
Wilbar, 61, 63,
72
Cooke

John, 67, 126
Cooper
  Anthony, 197
  Daniel, 228
  David, 145
  Edward, 114
  Ged, 45
  Grizzy, 84
  Harry, 116
  Isaac, 149, 197
  Jack, 45
  John, 134, 186, 211
  Lt., 130
  Martmas, 211
  Mr., 58, 130
  Nancy, 197
  Ned, 42
  Nelly, 58
  Richard, 228
  Sam, 186
  Sarrah, 197
  Thomas, 28, 209
  William, 253, 260
  Willis, 197
Copper
  Thomas, 83
Core
  David, 205
Corie
  Hagar, 7
  Isaac, 7
Corneck
  Henry, 15
Cornel
  Col., 21
Cornet
  James, 70
Cornick
  Lamber, 198
  Lewis, 198
  Rachel, 198
  Tom, 198
Cornwall
  Andrew, 55
  Frances, 41
  Ichabod, 40
Cornwell
  Jack, 54
  Prudence, 54

Corrigut
  John, 244
Corrin
  Joseph, 197
Coslin
  John, 44
Cottarge
  John, 111
Cotton
  James, 21
Coulson
  Mr., 48
  William, 48
Coulter
  Cornet, 140
Courtland
  Mrs., 5
Courtney
  Amanda, 47
Covenhoven
  Harry, 5
  John, 103
  Mr., 5
  Peter, 132
  Samuel, 151
  Vaughan, 132
Coventry
  Daniel, 246
  Mrs., 88
  Rachel, 236, 246
Coward
  Ben, 168
Cowley
  Ebenezer, 10
Cowling
  John, 52, 53
Cox
  Cato, 207
  Col., 211
  James, 228, 256
  Jenny, 207
  John, 97, 207
  Joseph, 124, 246
  Lieut., 134
  Lt., 134
  Martin, 211
  Michael, 117
  Ned, 103
  Nelly, 98

Peter, 73
  Thomas, 228
Coxeter
  Bartholomew, 80
Craig
  William, 254, 258
Crane
  James, 257
  Stephen, 19
Cranell
  Bartholomew, 159
Crannell
  Bartholomew, 159
Cranney
  Samuel, 106
Crapp
  Emanuel, 260
Craven
  Thomas, 75
Crawford
  Israel, 12
  Mr., 11
Creamer
  Andrew, 55
  Ben, 55
  Bethaser, 55
  Mary, 55
  Sarah, 55
Creswell
  Thomas, 245, 256
Crisby
  James, 228
  Joseph, 247
Criswell
  Hector, 129
Criswill
  Thomas, 228
Croaker
  Peggy, 148
  Samuel, 147
Crocker
  Samuel, 165
Cromwell
  Abner, 40
Crook
  Harriet, 22, 23
Crooks

Richard, 228, 244
Cropper
  Thomas, 53, 64, 93, 96
Crosbie
  Prince, 183
  Timothy, 183
Crosby
  Timothy, 206
Croser
  Jane, 74
Cross
  Eleanor, 157
  Mrs., 127
  Sarah, 36
  William, 9
Crouch
  Henry, 139
Crowell
  Sambo, 180
Cruden
  Col., 11
  Henry, 11
Cruger
  Col., 12
Crumline
  Chloe, 26
  Frank, 26
  Harry, 26
  Mingo, 26
Crumwell
  Dorcas, 116
  Nathaniel, 180
  Peggy, 116
Crutchley
  Phillis, 99
  William, 99
Cry
  Abraham, 112
Culbert
  George, 150
Cummins
  Cuff, 158
  James, 66
  John, 245
  Thomas, 228
Cunningham
  Adj., 135
  Capt., 18
  David, 228
  John, 169

Mich, 145
Mr., 15
Curl
  William, 122,
  183
Curle
  Mr., 41
  William, 113
  Zaccheus, 41
Currell
  William R.,
  199
Currier
  William, 83,
  199
Currigut
  John, 228
Curry
  Daniel, 256
  Joseph, 228
Curt
  Wilson, 108
Curtinas
  Peter, 213
Curtis
  John, 176
Cuthbert
  Dr., 28, 29
  John, 42
  Joseph, 42
  Lucinda, 42
  Sam, 42
Cutler
  John, 8
  Mr., 181
  Thomas, 181
Cuttonon
  Mathew, 200
Cuyler
  Mrs., 134
Cyphrus
  Nicholas, 210
Dale
  John, 19
Daley
  John, 256
Dalton
  Abraham, 67
  David, 67
  James, 207
  Nelly, 207
  Robert, 207

Suzan, 208
Thomas, 147
Damaine
  Thomas, 228
Damerain
  Elizabeth, 249
  Thomas, 249
Dandridge
  Elizabeth, 244
  John, 229, 247
  William, 60
Daniel
  John, 49
  Robert, 49
  Stephen, 177
Danvers
  Thomas, 36
Darby
  John, 260
Darling
  Thomas, 75
Davenport
  Samuel, 152
David
  Charlotte, 174
  Cyrus, 174
Davids
  Lt., 133
  Nancy, 49
Davidson
  David, 229,
  240
  Lt., 11
Davis
  (Mrs.), 228
  Anna, 114
  Anthony, 40
  Bella, 236
  Caleb, 112
  David, 35
  Edward, 16
  Elias, 127
  Elizabeth, 236,
  243
  Isabella, 243
  James, 123,
  229
  James (Child),
  244
  John, 26, 42,
  121, 129, 228,
  236

Lawyer, 175
Mark, 40
Mr., 116
Richard, 175
Thomas, 229,
247, 258
Tom, 27
William, 114,
169, 228
Dawson
  Charles, 110
  Edward, 189
  Mrs., 180
  Thomas, 147
  William, 146
Day
  John, 24, 59
De Motte
  Jacob, 179
De Young
  John, 150
Dean
  Alexander,
  127, 128
  Ann, 236, 246
  Benjamin, 122
  Harry, 122
  Since, 171
  Solomon, 65
  William, 169,
  228
Deane
  Mr., 7
Deaton
  Unus, 73
Deavux
  Col., 202
DeBeck
  Lieut., 136
DeBois
  Col., 6
DeBose
  S., Major, 119
DeDalmack
  Caspar, 68
Degraw
  Land, 182
  Samuel, 182
Degree
  Nathaniel, 86
Delahant
  Mrs., 79

DeLancey
  Lt. Col., 187
  Peter, 158
  Reed, Lt., 8
  Stephen, 131
Delanse
  Mr., 131
Demain
  Elizabeth, 252
  Thomas, 247
Demaine
  Henry, 229
Demarsh
  John, 151
Demce
  Charles, 44
Demill
  Dr., 58
  John, 58
Dempse
  John, 27
Dempsey
  Capt., 78
  William, 74
Denham
  Mary, 242
  Richard, 229
Dennis
  John, 86
  Sally, 86
Dennison
  William, 228
Denny
  David, 102
Denton
  Nero, 174
  William, 174
Denwal
  Mary, 236
Denyse
  Tunis, 157
Der Tuck
  Lt. Col., 123
Derling
  Garret, 181
  Henry, 181
Derry
  Judith, 236
  London, 54
Descan
  Daniel, 22
Deserter

Susan, 236
Deshee
  William, 19
Devaux
  James, 62, 63
DeVeber
  Lieut., 139
  Lieut. Col., 135
DeVois
  Col., 6
Devon
  Mr., 178
Devonshire
  David, 119
Dewit
  Mr., 15
Dewitt
  James, 19
  John, 210
  Judith, 210
Dibble
  Tyler, 50
Dick
  John, 40
Dickenson
  Gabriel, 11
  Mr., 52
  Nathaniel, 59
  Samuel, 147
Dickinson
  Ned, 187
  Philip, 110
  Phillip, 110
  Sam, 15
Dickson
  Absolom, 46
  Acky, 23
  Andrew, 205
  Capt., 128
  Clara, 23
  David, 229
  James, 129
  John, 205
  Joseph, 24, 203
  Peter, 228
  William, 203
  Dilforth, 122
Dillehour
  Dr., 187
Dimry
  Anthony, 102
Diran

James, 241
Dismal
  George, 184
  John, 189
  Nancy, 184
  Sam, 189
  Sukey, 183
Dixon
  Benjamin,
    Capt., 129
  Charles, 29
  Dick, 29
  Dolly, 29
  Fortune, 96
  John, 125
  Luke, 29
  Myles, 29
  Nancy, 125
  Richard, 43
  Sally, 30
  Sophia, 30
  William, 12
Dobbins
  John, 48
Dobbs
  John, 228
Dobson
  John, 229
Dole
  James, 158
Dollyer
  Peter, 75
Dolphin
  James, 257
  Sarah, 258
Domain
  Henry, 256
  Margaret, 257
Domaresh
  Tom, 151
Doming
  Joseph, 229
Domingo
  Anthony, 229
  Joseph, 247
Dominica
  Polly, 258
Dominico
  Edward, 257
Doneval
  Mary, 245
Donglish

William, 33
Donnel
  Peter, 32
Doore
  John, 162
Dorram
  Peter, 205
Dorset
  Stephen, 229,
    241
Doughty
  Ben, 13
  Elsia, 13
Douglas
  Effie, 13
  Elizabeth, 236
  James, 228
  William, 148
Douglass
  Elizabeth, 246
  George, 229
Dove
  Mr., 19
  Robert, Capt.,
    165
Dover
  Elizabeth, 258
  William, 229,
    246, 256
Dowell
  James, 16–19
Drage
  John, 261
Dragoon
  H. A., 13
Drain
  James, 253,
    260
Drake
  Benjamin, 93
  Thomas, 210
Dran
  James, 228
Draper
  David, 229,
    241, 256
Drayton
  Cath, 37
  Mrs., 37
  Samuel, 37
Dreusaw
  Anthony, 260

Drew
  Ann, 254, 259
  Richard, 160
  William, 254,
    259
Drewsaw
  Anthony, 229,
    241, 253
Driscoll
  James, 32
Driver
  John, 187
Drove
  Phillis, 138
Drummond
  Capt., 65
  Donald, 68
Dublin
  John, 228
Ducheel
  Joseph, 58
Duet
  James, 74
  Phillis, 74
Duett
  Judith, 74
  William, 229,
    246
Duffey
  Joseph, 49
Duke
  Alexander, 170
  Patrick, 229
  Rebecca, 171
Dunbar
  Capt., 137
Dunbridge
  Elizabeth, 236
Duncan
  James, 78, 195
Duncobe
  Richard Henry,
    252
Dungey
  Nat, 40, 41
Dunham
  James, 36
  John, 36
  Richard, 242
Dunk
  William, 17
Dunlap

Jack, 33
Dunlop
  Ann, 236
Dunmore
  Lord, 20, 24,
  32, 40, 65, 66,
  167, 168, 170,
  173, 196, 198,
  205, 213
Dunn
  Benjamin, 79
  Hugh, 22
  James, 71, 123
  John, 48
Dunning
  Sarah, 236, 244
Dunscombe
  Richard H., 261
Dupont
  J., 49
  Joseph, 49
Durffey
  Joseph, 49
Durham
  Francis, 229,
  249
  Frank, 241, 251
Dursey
  Josiah, 53
Duryea
  John, 98
Duryee
  Abraham, 113
  Jacob, 165
  John, 125
Dye
  Derrick, 103
  Rachel, 103
Dyer
  Elizabeth, 257
  Jeremy, 12
  John, 229, 246,
  257
  Keatie, 13
  Mr., 13
  Samuel, 12
Dykman
  John, 207
Eagle
  Hugh, 34
Earl
  Peter, 115

Earle
  David, 188
  Thomas, 229
Easton
  John, 205
Eden
  Medcalf, 22
  Edison, 22
Edmond
  Samuel, 12
Edmonds
  Dinah, 37
  Mr., 37
  Samuel, 119
  Thomas, 37
Edwards
  David, 103,
  190
  Elizabeth, 173
  Mr., 8
  Samuel, 52
  Sarah, 103
  Thomas, 55,
  123
Egerson
  William, 100
Eilbeck
  Jonathan, 9
  Mr., 9
Eldridge
  Joseph, 206
  Titus, 206
  Ellias, 173, 174
Elliot, 148
  Ben, 97
  Benjamin, 244,
  249, 251, 261
  Betsey, 171
  Charles, 37, 47
  George, 126
  Henry, 98
  Joe, 126
  John, 81
  Joseph, 81, 97,
  98
  Nancy, 81
  Samuel, 94
  William, 69,
  160
Elliott
  Benjamin, 229
  Daniel, 210

George, 229
Ellis, 175
  Abraham, 229,
  240
  Dinah, 39
  Hannah, 202
  Henry, 78
  Jack, 201
  John, 229
  Lucy, 39
  Mr., 205
  Samuel, 39
  Thomas, 39
  Will, 201
  William, 202
Ellison
  Abner, 45
  Arnet, 117
  Ed, Capt., 35
Elwin
  John, 124
Ely
  George, 242
  Emanuel, 25
English
  Clarly, 202
  George, 200
  John, 202, 260
  Mary, 200, 260
  Quash, 202
Enslow
  Isaac, 38, 48
Ernast
  John, 50
Ernist
  William, 160
Erskine
  Thomas, 184
Erwin
  Bacchus, 188
Erwine
  Nancy, 180
Etherington
  Col., 159
  William, 159
Etteridge
  James, 58
Ettridge
  James, 58
Etty
  George, 229
Euinge

Patience, 82
Eustace
  Lieut., 134
Evans
  Andrew, 110
  Judith, 111
  Sarah, 111
  Thomas, 110
  Eve, 173–175
  Oswald, 174
Everley
  Thomas, 13
Everly
  Judith, 13
  Mr., 13
  Sam, 13
F___n
  Mr., 158
Fairchild
  Cuff, 53
  George, 53
Fairweather
  Frank, 35
  Thomas, 35
Fall
  Adam, 105
  Dorothy, 105
Farmer
  Peter, 112
  Phillis, 207
  Sally, 99
  Samuel, 98
  Sarah, 5
Farmier
  Hernet, 60
Farque
  Dr., 54, 55
Faucet
  William, 79
Faucitt
  David, 79
Faulkner
  Ralph, 80
Fenn
  William, 229
Fenwick
  Edward, 105,
  178
  Jonathan, 229
  Peggy, 178
Ferguson
  Anthony, 138

George, 229
John, 138
Fergusson
   James, 45
   Thomas, 50
Fernandes
   Mary, 236
Ferrel
   Charles, 57
Ferrell
   John, 229, 246
Ferrill
   Thomas, 57
Ferro
   William, 247
Few
   Judah, 21
   Prince, 21
Fickins
   John, 47
Ficklin
   Stephen, 47
Field
   Ben, 188, 189
   Eleanor, 189
   Henry, 229
   James, 16
   Jeremy, 188,
   189
   P., 34
   Sarah, 189
   Widow, 24
   William, 229
Fife
   William, 170
Fillifitas
   Sarah, 42
Finch
   John, 15
Fisher
   Benjamin, 175
   Peggy, 262
   Thomas, 97,
   262
Fitt
   Thomas, 114
Fitzgerald
   Henry, 229
   Lt., 119
FitzSimmons
   Peter, 64
Flanders

George, 73
Fleck
   Lieut., 122
   Lt., 122
Flee
   Sarah, 103
Fleet
   Pompey, 28
   Sam, 28
   Thomas, 28
Fleming
   Eleanor, 100
   Hannah, 92
   Robert, 90
   Thomas, 18
Flemming
   Samuel, 100
Flowers
   Woodward, 41
Floyd
   Fanny, 98
   Henry, 97
   William, 97
Forbes
   Ann, 236
   Jane, 245
   Susan, 237
Ford
   Charles, 81
   Dennis, 104
   George, 229,
   246, 249, 253,
   259
   Hannah, 81
   Keziah, 81
   Mary, 236
   Patience, 104
   Samuel, 229
   Simon, 229
   Thomas, 40
   William, 44
Forde
   Nicholas, 203
Foreman
   Alexander, 166
   Thomas, 229,
   243
Forman
   David, 40
Forrester
   Captain, 59
   Joseph O., 59

Forshemy
   Capt., 157
Forsyth
   Betsey, 207
   John, 207
   Lydia, 207
Fortune
   John, 137, 155,
   229, 244
   Joseph, 256
   Primus, 127
   Ursula, 77
   William, 16,
   54
Foster
   Eleanor, 15
   George, 229
   Joseph, 157
   Thomas, 15
Fountain
   Betsey, 52
   Thomas, 79
Fowler
   Ben, 36, 121
   Benjamin, 156,
   157
   Daniel, 64
   Dublin, 45
   Gabriel, 78
   Joseph, 25
   Mary, 25
   Mr., 25, 57
   Richard, 78
   Thomas, 23
Fox
   Charles, 20
   John, 20, 77,
   121
   Rachel, 20
   Robert, 38
   Sarah, 6
Fracklan
   Jenny, 171
Fraction
   George, Capt.,
   211
   Prince, 37
Francis
   Billy, 33
   Charles, 19, 33
   Elizabeth, 237

George, 253,
259
   Henry, 175
   James, 229,
   253, 260
   Jenny, 101
   John, 101, 229,
   241, 260
   Joseph, 229,
   241
   Margaret, 253,
   259
   Peter, 229, 246
   Samuel, 229,
   242
   Samuel
   (Child), 242
   Samuel, Jr.,
   229
   Thomas, 33
   William, 32
Frankham
   Ben, 170
Frankland
   Philis, 236
   Susan, 236
Franks
   Thomas, 229,
   242
Franswa
   Mr., 24
Fraser, 208
   Hugh, 40
   James, 15, 138,
   150
   Reverend Mr.,
   256
   Simon, 48
Frazer
   Alexander, 43
   James, 150
   John, 80
   Mr., 138
Frederick
   Capt., 195
   Jenny, 195
   John, 11, 229
   Jonah, 195
   Prince, 195
   Sarah, 237
Fredericks
   William, 211

Fredrick
John, 205
Freebody
Ben, 162
Samuel, 162
Freeland
Elizabeth, 209
Lewis, 209
Freeman
Benjamin, 229
Cornet, 11, 13
George, 242
Joe, 130, 162
John, 211
Joseph, 162
Patience, 85
Robert, 30
Stephen, 162
Thomas, 170,
229, 242, 248–
250, 262
William, 162
French
Capt., 137
Peter, 181
Robert, 15
Rose, 184
T., Capt., 137
Friday
Christian, 251
Christopher,
250, 261
Friend
Lydia, 96
Widow, 96
Frier
George, 180
Sambo, 180
Frink
Capt., 134
Mrs., 134
Frip
Daniel, 202
Lucy, 203
Mathew, 202
Rose, 203
Frost
Isaac, 157
Jacob, 163
Fruen
Harry, 113
Fruman

Thomas, 229
Fuller
Thomas, 138
Fullerton
John, 89
Fulton
Capt., 11, 12
Samuel, 127
Furbs
Isaac, 64
Furman
Mr., 164
Fyer
Lt., 47
Gable
Major, 122
Gail
Robert, Capt.,
174
Gairway
Simon, 14
Gale
John, 185
Matthew, 229,
241
Thomas, 176
Gallilee
Robert, 76
Gallillee
William, 164
Gamble
Dr., 139
Garbut
George, 158
Gardiner
Anker, 173
Doctor, 98
Joseph
Leccock, 252
Gardner
John, 49
William, 138
Garish
Enoch, 60
Garret
Ben, 68
Benjamin, 122
Jacob, 148
Richard, 108
Garrett
James, 197
Garrison

Pat, 102
Garritt
Bristow, 197
Rose, 197
Gasgoine
David, 229
Gaul
Joseph, 149
Naoma, 149
Gautter
Nicholas, 107
Gay
John, 229
Gayton
Capt., 162
Gelder
Capt., 137
George
Hannah, 249
John, 229, 230,
241, 260
Joseph, 249,
251, 261
Peter, 176
Robert, 230,
243
William, 229
Gerrido
James, 42
Gerrow
Benjamin, 187
Peter, 187
Gesau
Betsey, 258
John, 256
Mary, 256
Getcheus
Jacob, 61, 62
Gibb
Frank, 48
Robert, 48
Gibbons
Isabel, 88
John, 49
Joseph, 49
Gibbs
Robert, 48
William, 28
Gibson
Andrew, 37
George, 201
James, 112

Patty, 114
Robt. Capt., 10
Gidney
Bartholomew,
163
Gilbert
Aaron, 213
Anthony, 240
Archibald, 13
Arthur, 229
Charles, 229
Col., 7
David, 17
Gilchrist
George, 96
Giles
John, 119
Gilfillan, 191
—, 141
Capt., 161,
165, 168
T., 51, 61, 214
Gill
Joseph, 78
Robert, 23, 66,
70
Gilles
Neal, 49
Gillman
Major, 35
Gills
Captain, 16
Gilman
Anthony, 35
Gilmore
Robert, 168
Githam
Peter, 229, 241
Given
Lucy, 189
Givin
Henry, 200
Glair
Joseph, 108
Glasgow
Hannah, 57
Jonathan, 113
Judith, 57
Pamela, 113
Richard, 57
Glenn
Mr., 12

Glocestor
  George, 123
Glovell
  Charlotte, 245
  Joseph (Child),
  245
Glover
  Charlotte, 237
  Joseph, 229
  William, 85
Goddard
  John, 49
Goddin
  Celia, 84
  Eleazer, 97
  Eliza, 67
  George, 66
  James, 82
  Manney, 21
  Nancy, 170
  Sarah, 84
Godfrey
  Abigail, 24
  Betsey, 24
  Bridget, 202
  Bristol, 96
  China, 39
  Col., 23, 24,
  39, 167, 168
  Colonel, 198
  Edward, 95
  Elizabeth, 23
  George, 174
  Jacob, 82
  James, 199
  Jeffry, 23
  John, 82, 177
  Kate, 82, 197
  Kitty, 96
  Lucy, 198
  Mathew, 197–
  199, 201, 202
  Matthew, 95,
  96
  Murphey, 38
  Ned, 23
  Port, 197
  Robert, 199
  Salley, 198,
  199
  Sally, 82
  Sam, 199

Sucky, 199
Valentine, 95
Godray
  Matt, 23
Godwine
  Christopher,
  197
Goff
  Flanders, 164
  John, 242
  Richard, 139,
  147, 164
Gold
  Betsey, 22
  Joe, 22
  Sukey, 23
  Thomas, 128
Goldthwait
  William, 124
Goodell
  Hanna, 237
Goodman
  Charles, 48
  Isaac, 48
Goodrich
  Mr., 30
Goodwin
  James, 188
  William, 188
Gordon
  Benjamin, 15
  Christopher,
  115
  Dublin, 110
  Edie, 115
  Francis, 230,
  247
  George, 88
  Jack, 15
  Jasper, 33
  John, 41, 60,
  92
  Mary, 84
  Philip, 88
  Phillis, 93
  Priscilla, 84,
  88
  Robert, 55, 109
  Sarah, 33
  Silvia, 111
  William, 229,
  241

Wynce, 93
Gore
  Capt., 8
Gorman
  William, 229,
  240, 257
Gosbeck
  James, 67
Goseman
  John, 204
Goslet
  John, 244, 250
Gospors
  Ann, 237
Gosport
  Jane, 245, 252,
  262
Goss
  John, 229
Gostel
  John, 229
Goughing
  Nathaniel, 256
Gozeman
  Fanney, 205
  Rose, 205
Graff
  John, 150
Graham
  Austin, 147
  Betsey, 131
  Captain, 32
  Charles, 107
  Gov., 186
  James, 41
  John, 61, 131
  Joseph, 36
  M., 252
  Monkhouse,
  261
  Mr., 13, 19
  Phebe, 237
  Sara, 18
  T., 122
Grand
  Peter, 249
Grandon
  Daniel, 40
Grans
  Diana, 237
  Martha, 237
Grant

Alexander, 71
Joe, 124
Joseph, 256
Major, 6
Mrs., 163
Peter, 229,
240, 251, 262
Pompey, 137
Thomas, 137,
229
Grassman
  Caspar, 49
Graves
  Henry, 256
Gray
  Abby, 15
  Anthony, 230
  Cornet, 174,
  175
  Dick, 22
  Harry, 15
  John, 32, 83
  Thomas, 229
  William, 78
Grayham
  Archibald, 229
  Arthur, 229
Grayson, 8
  Anthony, 229
  Capt., 9
  Captain, 9
  Colonel, 199
  James, 9, 69,
  70, 73
  James, Capt., 9
  Salley, 199
  Sam, 199
Green
  (Mrs.), 229
  Adam, 210
  Betsey, 258
  Catherine, 237
  Daniel, 12
  Edward, 69
  Elizabeth, 237,
  240
  James, 229,
  242, 250, 261
  John, 80, 189,
  229, 245, 246,
  256
  Joseph, Jr., 251

Martha, 242,
250, 252, 261
Mary, 237
Richard, 229
Samuel, 257
Thomas, 229,
241, 257
Tobias, 155
William, 229,
230, 240, 247,
250, 251, 257,
261
Greenard
George, 11
Mr., 12
Greentree
Mr., 7
Gregory
Rebecca, 237
Grenal
George, 174
Greves
Joseph, 258
Grey
Ben, 70
Griffin
Cyrus, 77
Dinah, 94
Francis, 98
John, 12
Sal, 94
Griffith
Abraham E.,
261
Abraham
Elliot, 240, 251
Abraham
Elliott, 229
Jack, 54
Rebecca, 252,
261
Robert, 53, 54
Griffiths
Joseph, 64
Grig
John, 176
Grigg
Glasgow, 57
John, 57
Thomas, 56, 57
Griggory
Samuel, 213

Griggs
August, 43
Samuel, 43
Grimes
John, 60
Philip, 103
Grimmill
Matt, 47
Griswell
Thomas, 129
Grosvenor
Benjamin, 49
Jupiter, 112
Mary, 237
Samuel, 112
Groves
John, 241, 256
Joseph, 241,
261
Maria, 241
Polly, 205
Grovis
John, 229
Joseph, 230,
236
Guest
Henry, 153
Guideste
Frazer, Capt.,
77
Guin
Humphrey, 171
Gullero
Richard, 249
Gullet
Samuel, 19
Gumbee
Emanuel, 229
Gumby
Emanuel, 243
Gunn
Enos, 62
Tom, 62
Gustus
John, 92
Taby, 176
Guthrow
Richard, 251
Guttero
Richard, 262
Gutterow
Richard, 240

Guy
B., 184
Bayley, 87
Benjamin, 91
John, 53
Gwin
Humphrey, 83
Hackett
Ann, 254, 259
Hackney
Alexander, 261
Alexander,
Doctor, 252
Haddin
Lt., 132
Hadwick
(Mrs.), 230
James, 230,
244
Mary, 237, 244
Mary (Child),
244
Hagan
Dennis, 8
Haight
Alexander, 148
Haines
Tony, 70
William, 70
Hairran
Stephen, 36
Hajeman
John, 146
Haldin
General, 16
Hale
Charles, 147
Hall
Elihu, 26
John, 42, 123,
230, 240, 249
Richard, 230,
247
Thomas, 230
Thomas
William, 245
Towerhill, 26
Halladay
Jane, 91, 92
Peter, 92
Halliday
Thomas, 104

Hallstead
Christopher, 92
James, 87
Sally, 87
Samuel, 87
Hallyar
Simon, 126
Haln
Anthony, 5
Halstead
Mary, 201
Peggy, 93
Phillis, 93
Philomel, 92
Halstede
Henry, 200
Moses, 200
Halward
Simon, 175
Ham
William, 115
Hamilton
Edward, 230,
242
Edward
(Child), 244
Eleanor, 237,
242
James, 210
John, 119, 210,
230, 243, 247
John (Child),
230
Robert, 122
William, 230
Hamlin
Justice, 162
Hammer
Walter, 96
Hammond
Abraham, 117
Capt., 146, 150
Charlotte, 111
Daniel, 156
John, 95, 111
Thomas, 66
Hancock
Barbara, 90
Funky, 189
Jacob, 110
John, 189

Robert Bray, 90
Stepney, 89
William, 89, 92
Handell
    Mr., 44
Handford
    Joseph, 60
    Mr., 149
Hanley
    Thomas, 66
Hannabill
    Sarah, 208
    Will, 208
Hannah
    Edward, 36, 37
    Nathaniel, 36
Hannell
    Hannah, 179
Hanscomb
    Thomas, 186
Hanson
    Frederick, 187
    Mr., 11
    William, 11
Harbeck
    John, 15
Harbert
    Charles, 66
    David, 66
    Hanna, 66
    Isaac, 66
    J. Martin, 66
    Jenny, 66
    London, 66
    Mr., 66
    Rose, 66
    T. Martin, 66
    Venus, 66
Harboard
    Thomas, 68
Harbords
    John, 99
Harden
    Berry, 145
    William, 97
Hardey
    Mathew, 213
Harding
    Ebenezer, 213
    George, 36

Kate, 213
Peter, 213
William, 98
Hare
    Alexander, 131
Harford
    Elizabeth, 262
    James, 262
Hargrove
    Willis, 83
Harkham
    Ellis, 102
Harleston
    Isaac, 126
Harlow
    Clarissa, 237
Harmer
    Jasper, 207
Harrand
    Howard, Capt., 32
Harrington
    Harry, 87
    Robert, 173
    Sally, 87
Harriot
    William, 170
Harris
    Ann, 260
    Benjamin, 126
    Charlotte, 242
    Fanny, 171
    George, 253, 259
    Hannah, 131
    James, 230, 240, 246, 247, 253, 256, 257, 260
    John, 230
    John W., 257
    John Walter, 240
    John William, 249
    Joseph, 187, 188
    Mary, 247, 258, 259
    Mr., 188
    Peter, 230, 240
    Polly, 131

Thomas, 169, 242
Tom, 230
William, 258
Harrison
    Benjamin, 85, 166, 167
    Bob, 166
    Charles, 133, 204
    Jack, 75
    Joseph, 230, 245
    Thomas, 6
    William, 230
Harry
    Harry, 44
Hart
    Benjamin, 153
    Charles, 27
    Garret, 189
    Lucy, 183
Hartford
    (Mrs.), 230
    Elizabeth, 241, 252
    James, 230, 243
    Joseph, 251
Hartley
    James, 120
    Thomas, 37
Hartly
    Joseph, 170
Hartshorne
    Lawrence, 5
Harvey
    John, 230, 243
    Lt., 161
    Margaret, 243
    Mary, 237
Harvis
    John Walter, 230
Hascomb
    William, 52
Hatheway
    Luther, 62
Hawkins
    John, 168
    Phil, 9
    Sam, 168

Thomas, 108
Hawthey
    Mr., 139
Hay
    A., 113
Haynes
    Bartholomew, 163
    Cloe, 66
    Dinah, 66
    Isaac, Col., 34
    Joseph, 109
    Nancy, 66
    Patrick, 110
    Sally, 109
Hays
    Hugh, 19
    Jacob, 51
    Moses, 179
    Sally, 41
Haywood
    Thomas, 16, 45, 129
Hazard
    Ben, 39
    Hana, 38
Hazell
    Charles, 124
Hazzard
    James, 230
Hearns
    John, 112
Heartley
    Thomas, 12
Hector
    James, 199
    John, 199
    Judy, 199
    Kate, 199
Hedden
    William, 178
Hedler
    Charlotte, 212
    Dianah, 212
    James, 212
    John, 212
Heid
    J., 126, 127
Height
    Ensign, 138
Heit
    Joseph, 54

Helenbeck
  Simon, 131
Hellenbeck
  Casper, 131
Hellis
  George, 170
Helsick
  Richard, 59
Hemmings
  Jacob, 112
Hempstead
  William, 40
  Wynie, 40
Henderson
  James, 190,
  195
  John, 18, 70
Hendrick
  Elish, 121
Hendricks
  Conrad, 58
Henley
  (Mrs.), 230
  Moses, 230
Henry
  Miney, 196
  Molly, 196
  Patrick, 196
  Ralph, 196
  Richard, 97
  Tom, 53
Herbert
  Betsey, 87, 178
  Frances, 178
  Jenny, 87
  Lancaster, 88
  Peter, 88
  Rachel, 110
  William, 53,
  73
  Willis, 73
Hereditaire
  Prince, 123
Herman
  Caleb, 126
Herring
  Close, 195
  Daniel, 17, 18,
  97
  Patton, 195
  Simsa, 17
  Susanna, 18

Herron
  Abraham, 202
Heughston
  James, 57
Hevelin
  Benjamin, 88
Hevlin
  John, 88
Hewelett
  Jonah, 100
Hewell
  Lamb, 9
Hewlett
  Joseph, 7
Hewlins
  Abraham, 129
Hickerson
  James, 196
Hickford
  Capt., 147
Hicks
  Capt., 150, 156
  David, 54
  Eleanor, 8
  John, 149
  Mr., 165
  Oliver, 164
  Robert, 79, 80
  Thomas, 21
  Will, 161
Hide
  Jack, 35
  Tom, 50
Higgins
  Dennis, 176
  John, 176
  Peggy, 257
  William, 230,
  245, 257
Higginson
  Will, 11
Hildrith
  Isaac, 69
Hill
  Anthony, 251,
  262
  Benjamin, 6
  Capt., 57
  Edmund, 10
  Flora, 189

George, 230,
  245, 250, 251,
  262
  Jane, 82
  John, 230, 241
  Joshua, 30
  Nancy, 34, 74
  Peter, 230, 256
  William, 22
Hilliard, 35
Hills
  (Mr.), 258
Hilton
  Andrew, 10
  William, 147
Hinzman
  John, 164
Hirst
  John, 94
Hobbs
  Mathew, 10
Hodd
  Joseph, 259
Hodges
  John, 104
  William, 81,
  106
Hodgkins
  John, 254, 260
Hodgson, 32
Hodson
  Michael, 122
Hog
  J., 73
  James, 150
Hogg
  James, 64, 65,
  67
Hoggart
  Thomas, 54
  Tom, 54
Hoggarth
  Andrew, 38, 39
Hoggat
  Thomas, 17
Hogwood
  James, 101
  Mr., 166
  Simon, 101
  Thermer, 20
Hogworth
  Mr., 113

Hoke
  John, 15
Holchapan
  William, 56
Holder
  Ann, 242, 252,
  261
  Thomas, 230,
  240, 242, 251,
  261
  Thomas, Jr.,
  251
Holland
  Francis, 230,
  247, 249
  Henry, 98, 171
  John, 98
  Lt., 138
  Richard, Lt., 62
Holloway
  John, 90
Holly
  Silas, 163
Hollyday
  Joseph, 134
  Will, 134
Holman, 117
  Stephen, 13,
  148
Holmes
  Betsey, 103
  James, 60, 161
  Joel, 58
  Joseph, 50, 173
  Samuel, 173
  Thomas, 210
Holt
  Robert, 170
  William, 109,
  170
Homan
  Amelia, 252,
  261
  John, 251, 261
Home
  John, 251
Homes
  Isaac, 138
  William, 102
Honeycut
  Edward, 247,
  249, 251

Honeycutt
    Edward, 262
Hooper
    Sarah, 258
    Thomas, 230,
    257
Hope
    John, 160
Hopewell
    Amelia, 149
    Hopkins, 51
    Sam, 10
Hopper
    Garret, 113
Hopton
    William, 145
Horace
    Josiah, 230
Horn
    (Mrs.), 230
    Christian, 252,
    261
    John, 230
    Sarah, 254
Hornbrook
    Capt., 155, 156
Horne
    Christian, 247
    Christiana, 250
    John, 247, 249
Horse
    William, 210
Horton
    Nathan, 72
Hoser
    John, 147
Hosier
    Josiah, 247,
    256
Hoskins
    Elizabeth, 262
    William, 230,
    245, 249, 251,
    262
Hosper
    Thomas, 241
Hotchinson
    Henry, 65
Hough
    George, 242
Houghlin
    John, 230

Housterman
    M., 77
    Manuel, 77
Houston
    John, 127
Hovendon
    Cornet, 137,
    140
How
    Elizabeth, 258
    George, 230,
    256
Howard
    Chief Justice,
    161
    George, 209
    Isaac, 209
    J., 29
    Jacob, 29
    John, 65
    Lucy, 178
    Miss, 161
    Nancy, 64
    Sarah, 29
    Thomas, Col.,
    178
Howe
    General, 128
    Lord, 33
    Lt., 138
    Mary, 258
    Sarah, 259
    W. W., Sir, 8
    William, Sir,
    8, 132, 133
Howell
    Nicholas, 58
    William, 249
Howse
    Francis, 155
Howthey
    Nancy, 139
Hoyt
    William, 79
Huams
    Peter, 62
Hubbard
    Ensign, 139
    Nat, 117, 118
    Nathaniel, 118
Hubbert
    Benjamin, 77

Hubble
    Capt., 205
Huddleston
    Captain, 16
Hudson
    (Mrs.), 230
    Elizabeth, 237,
    246, 261
    John, 31
    Samuel, 182
    Thomas, 230,
    245
    Tyna, 62
    William, 168,
    230, 246, 251
Huge
    George, 120
Hugee
    General, 137
Huggenel
    Cato, 131
Huggenell
    Daniel, 131
Hughes
    Ann, 258
    John, 230, 242,
    249, 253, 259
    Mr., 168
    Nancy, 252
    William, 230,
    243
Hull
    John, 43, 251
Hullet
    Captain, 96
Humble
    Capt., 12
Humphries
    D., 135
    Dr., 136
    John, 131
    Thomas, 124
Humphry
    Dr., 6
Hunnicutt
    Edward, 230
Hunt
    Elnathan, 64
    Elthen, 102
    Fanny, 237
    Fanny (Child),
    244

Joseph, 167
    Mary, 237, 244
    Thomas, 15
Hunter
    Francis, 15
    James, 90
    Jenny, 91
    Q.M., 120
    Samuel, 90
    Thomas, 204
    Tom, 169
    William, 95
Huntley
    Thomas, 55
Hurbert
    Cathern, 173
Hustus
    Ned, 134
Hutchins
    Col., 24
    Elizabeth, 82
    Jo., 32
    John, 107, 128
    Joseph, 201
    Kingston, 107
    Lucy, 201
    Samuel, 97,
    201
    Sarah, 98
Hutchinson
    Tom, 127
Hutten
    Capt., 151
Huyck
    John, 132
Hyde
    Col., 132
    John, 50
    Joseph, 35
Inglish
    Joseph, 18
Ingram
    Abraham, 57
    Charles, 113
Ingrim
    George, 86
Inman
    John, 49
Innes
    Joseph, 240
Innis
    Elizabeth, 258

Joseph, 231
Rebecca, 257
Ireland
Richard, 179
Iron
James, 122
Irvine
Hannah, 261
Irving
Captain, 47
Irwin
(Miss), 258
Betsey, 258
David, 188
James, 163
John, 256
Joseph, 258
Thomas, 73
Isaac
August, 24
George, 230,
240, 253
Isaacs
George, 249,
259
Isdale
George, 108
Ives
Samuel, 9
Ivey
Hilley, 33
Samuel, 70
Ivie
John, 196
Ivory
John, 108
Priscilla, 109
Izzard
Andrew, 181
George, 109
Ralph, 181
Ralph, Esq.,
147
Rebecca, 147
Jack
Andrew, 247
Anthony, 241
John, 177
Thomas, 231
William, 231,
242
Jacks

Thomas, 157
Jackson, 70
(Mrs.), 230
Basil, 164
Betsey, 163
Binah, 85
Bob, 117
Captain, 47
Dick, 10
Dinah, 39
Edward, 69,
230, 246
Fonlove, 39
Hannah, 66,
109, 117, 213
Harry, 20
Henry, 53, 128
Jacob, 230,
240, 250
James, 20, 69,
100, 163, 195,
231, 240
Joe, 187
John, 82, 96,
105, 127, 164,
208, 213, 230,
246
Jonathan, 231
Judith, 20, 197
London, 20
Margaret, 252,
260
Mr., 176
Nancy, 52
Ned, 39
Nelly, 21
Patience, 171
Paul, 187
Peggy, 100
Peter, 133
Rebecca, 250
Rose, 34
Sarah, 66
Sebro, 21
Thomas, 71,
73, 85, 176,
230, 231
Will, 53
William, 231
Zolpher, 21
Jackwish
Richard, 207

Jacob
John, 230, 240,
246, 251
John (Child),
231, 246
John, Jr., 252
Mary, 252
Thomas, 26
Jacobs
John, 262
Mary, 262
Jakeway
John, 49
Jakeways
John, 49
James
Aaron, 99
Andrew, 231,
247, 249, 251,
261
Benjamin, 69
Catherine, 237
Charles, 241
Henry, 102
Isaac, 34
Jack, 262
James, 33
Jane, 99
John, 100, 230,
231, 247, 249,
252, 253, 259
Joseph, 230
Martha, 261
Martina, 252
Mary, 237,
243, 252, 258,
262
Q.M., 132
Rachel, 33
Robert, 33, 98,
231, 245
Thomas, 182
William, 231,
247, 256
Jamison
George, 230
January
John, 132
Jardin
Edward, 182
Jardine
Richard, 182

Jarrett
Richard, 209
Jarridar
James, 31
Jarvis
Anthony, 65
Betsey, 65
Hannah, 132
James, 31, 32
John, 26
Samuel, 98
Susanna, 6
Jay
Frederick, 170
John, Esq., 184
Jellot
Aaron, 139
Jenkins
Bella, 13
Benjamin, 11
Charles, 46
Christian, 78
Daniel, 33
James, 11, 140
John, 67, 231
Joseph, 231
Mr., 158
Nancy, 177
Richard, 158
Robert, 30
Scipio, 11
Thomas, 46
Jennia
Thomas, 43
Jennings, 59
Jacob, 231
Jerrads
James, 140
Jerret
Ephraim, 115
Jessup
Moses, 90
Job
John, 125
Jobson
William, 231
Jochn
Anthony, 230
Johns
Marshal, 89
Johnson

Andrew, 23,
91, 127
Ann, 237, 245
Ben, 131
Betsey, 88
Betsy, 236
Bob, 95
Charles, 125
Chloe, 95
Colin, 51
Daniel, 111,
230, 244, 256
Dianah, 211
Dinah, 171
Eisha, 51
Fanny, 95
Gabriel, 138
George, 170
Guy, 131
Hannah, 95,
126
Hester, 105
Isaac, 161
Jack, 127
Jacob, 230,
243, 253, 259
James, 53, 62,
87, 230, 231,
240, 256, 257
Jenny, 23
Jingo, 99
John, 105, 230,
231, 242, 243
John Ceasor,
231
Joseph, 187,
230
Judah, 179
Judith, 36, 94
Kate, 127
Leven, 51
Levi, 169
Lucy, 171
Luke, 40, 95
Lydia, 147
Margaret, 51,
237, 243
Mary, 155,
237, 243, 258
Mellia, 171
Mrs., 153

Nancy, 91, 95,
172
Nanny, 95
Ned, 129
Patty, 27, 51,
83
Paul, 169
Peter, 36, 80,
88, 89, 125
Rachel, 100
Richard, 179
Robert, 93,
100, 126, 139
Samuel, 83
Sarah, 51
Simon, 134
Sukey, 89
Thomas, 51,
231, 236, 240,
242, 243, 253
Thomas (Mrs.),
236
William, 14,
15, 62, 80, 100,
211, 230, 231,
240, 243
Johnston
John, 131
Nancy, 83
Prima, 83
Joice
Anthony, 260
Martin, 211
Jolly
James, 46
Joseph, 81,
105, 106
Joshua, 172
Richard, 46
Jones
(Mrs.), 230
Aaron, 209
Adam, 31
Anthony, 28
Benjamin, 105
Betsey, 91
Binah, 80
Casar, 131
Cesar, 112
Charles, 230,
245, 249, 251,
262

Charlotte, 32
Daniel, 231
David, 39
Edward, 249
Elizabeth, 237,
245, 249, 252,
262
Francis, 88,
112
Gabriel, 36
George, 230,
247, 251
Hannah, 138
Henry, 105,
230, 241, 257
Isaac, 209, 261
Jack, 231, 245
James, 105,
124
John, 32, 35,
101, 129, 133,
139, 230, 231,
246, 251
Lt., 12
Lucretia, 32
March, 169
Marianna, 28
Mary, 237,
245, 249
Mary S., 261
Mr., 169
Peggy, 30
Q.M., 132
Richard, 32
Robert, 231,
243
Sally, 124
Samuel, 61,
63, 72, 77, 130,
141, 191
Samuel, Esq.,
161
Sarah, 104,
237, 245, 247
Sarrah, 210
Shadrick, 30
William, 211,
230, 241, 247,
257
Jordan
Ann, 258
Anny, 105

Dempse, 189
George, 116
Jack, 125
John, 94, 128,
129
Joseph, 245,
257
Joshua, 116
Judy, 189
Laker, 116
Miles, 95
Mingo, 92
Rachel, 189
Richard, 82,
92, 93, 95, 105
Robert, 125
Ruffin, Col.,
189
Thomas, 243
Venus, 125
William, 96,
105
Jordon
Joseph, 230
Thomas, 231
Joseph
James, 122
William, 231
Josephson
Jack, 54
Junius
Amey, 63
Brutus, 62
Grace, 63
Jupetor
John, 231
Jupiter
John, 241, 253,
260
Justice
Ralph, 53
Kain
James, 127
Kart
Charles, 47
Kassery
John, 45
Kearstead
Johnson, 8
Johnston, 8
Keayton
John, 121

Keeling
Anny, 104
Captain, 104
Grumbelly, 90
Pindar, 91
Robert, 104
William, 90
Kein
George, 259
Kelley
Joseph, 10
Kelly
Cary, 78
Charles, 204
Jenny, 201
Mary, 201
Moses, 201
Mrs., 179, 180
William, 231, 240
Kelty
George, 209
Moses, 209
Kemp
Charlotte, 237, 246
Jacob, 204
Kempe
John Tabor, 58
Kendle
George, 177
John, 177
Kennedy
Capt., 125
Hager, 213
Patrick, 124, 126
Patrick, Capt., 124, 125
William, 254, 260
Kent
George, 14
Keriche
John, 49
Kerkner
Fred, 254
Kern
George, 254
Ketcham
Jere, 35
Samuel, 35

Ketchin
John, 35
Phillis, 35
Ketrick, 20
Ketteltas
Abraham, 98
Kid
Capt., 59, 64
Kilby
James, 175
Killing
Argill, 198
Killings
Adam, 198
Kimberly
Ozel, 107
Kimme
Isaac, 66
Kindle
Col., 101
Kineschmidt, 119
King
Abigail, 237, 242
Boston, 86
Chris, 182
Col., 45
David, 231
Henry, 52
John, 27
Jupiter, 45
Mary, 237
Michael, 53
Nancy, 163
Peggy, 208
Robert, 208
Violet, 85
Kingsland
Casar, 102
Dinah, 103
Mr., 69
Roger, 101
William, 99
Kingston
John, 33, 34
March, 236
Kinty
William, 127
Kipp, 9
Abraham, 43
Capt., 56

Captain, 56
Daniel, Capt., 15
Henry, 43
John, 9
Kirby
Hannah, 96
John, 96
Lewis, 96
Kirk
Jonathan, 164, 165
Samuel, 155
Kirkham
William, 101
Kirkner
Frederick, 259
Kitchin
John, 35
Kitchum
Widow, 140
Kivinor
Lewis, 231
Kloproth, 75
Knapp
James, 109
Mr., 109
Knepp
Allice, 56
Captain, 56
Dinah, 56
Job, 56
Knight
Joseph, 242
Robert, 231
Tom, 18
Knipsgheld
Lt., 156
Knoblauch, 120–124
Knowland
Billy, 52
George, 52
Knyphanson, 119
Komer
R., 174
Kosporth
M. Gen., 119
La Cruze
Ann, 237
Labruise
Ann, 244

Lacy
Fanny, 15
George, 15
Kate, 15
Ladson
Elijah, 48
Thomas, 185
Lafferts
Gilbert, 195
Lafferty
Daniel, 41
Lagree
Joseph, 203, 207
Nathan, 25
Samuel, 165
Thomas, 110
Venus, 111
Laingeh
Frederick, 27
Lalouch
John, 253
Lewis, 240, 244, 251
Lewis, Jr., 251
Margaret, 252
Mary, 244
Lamb
Charles, 187
Nelly, 189
Lambert
John, 173
Lucey, 204
Nancy, 174
Lamorce
Jesse, 70
Lamot
Henry, 173
Lampley
John, 231
William, 231, 244
Lampton
Sarah, 237, 246
Land
Francis, 114
Landy
D., 158
Langford
Capt., 78
James, 78
Langley

Esther, 84
Johnson, 84
Langleyn
  James, 114
Langston
  Gerrit, 36
Lashley
  John, 103
Lasket
  Sarah, 237
Laston
  Charles, 200
  Eliza, 199
  Isaac, 200
  Moses, 26
Lathem
  Daniel, 204
Latouch
  Lewis, 261
  Mary, 261
Latoueh
  Lewis, 231
  Lewis, Jr., 231
Laurence
  Dinah, 109
  George, 259
  John, 109
Lautten
  Richard, 17
Lavender
  Robert, 79
Lawrance
  Gabriel, 89
Lawrence
  Betsey, 89
  Catharine, 89
  Daniel, 231,
  232, 241
  Dick, 109
  Dinah, 89
  George, 231,
  254
  Jac, 26
  John, 26, 57,
  231, 245, 249,
  251
  Mary, 237
  Mr., 160
  Peter, 44
  Rollins, 85
  William, 231
  York, 89

Lawson
  Anthony, Col.,
  169
  Captain, 13
  Catherine, 240
  Col., 15
  Jacob, 15
  Ned, 26
  Patrick, 231
  Robert, 60
  Ruth, 15
  Solomon, 169
Layon
  Paul, Captain,
  20
Leach
  David, 211
  George, 137
Lear
  Jesse, 38
Learmouth
  Abraham, 246
  Alex, 231
  Elizabeth, 246
Leccock
  Joseph, 252
Lechmore
  Cornet, 10
Lee
  (Mrs.), 231
  Capt., 132
  Charles, 91
  Francis, 231,
  245
  John, 22
  Mary A., 261
  Mary Ann, 252
  Robert, 55
  Sarah, 237,
  245, 252, 262
  William, 90,
  231, 242, 251,
  261
Leech
  Tinah, 137
Leffers
  Sukey, 110
Legree
  James, 110
Legyet
  G., 176
Leich

Dick, 21
Grace, 21
Ruth, 21
Leman
  John, 243
Lemanthus
  Martin, 253
Lemmon
  Elizabeth, 254
  John, 231, 253
Lemon
  Elizabeth, 260
  John, 260
Leonard
  George, Esq.,
  14
  Nancey, 204
Lerner
  William, 124
Leslie
  John, 211
  Mingo, 211
Lesslie
  Abraham, 166
Lester
  Ben, 146
  Benjamin, 146
Letchmore
  Lucy, 13
Letson
  Robert, 58
Leven, 51
Levi
  Samson, 183
Lewis
  Ambrose, 136
  Ann Catherine,
  237
  Frank, 197
  George, 231,
  240
  Hector, 197
  John, 25, 164,
  231, 247, 251,
  257, 262
  Samuel, 231,
  242
  William, 155
Libby
  John, 45
Lightfort
  Lambert, 109

Limbrick
  John, 231
  William, 231,
  253
Limerick
  John, 242, 249
Limirick
  William, 242
Limrick
  William, 260
Linden
  Pompey, 53
Lindsay
  Capt., 49
  Nathaniel, 10
  Robert, 43
Lindsey
  James, 48
Ling
  Valentine, 98,
  99
Linning
  Hannah, 171
Linus
  Cato, 47
Litcon
  Thomas, 207
Litteny
  Andrew, 241
Littney
  Andrew, 231
Liverpool
  James, 97
Livingston
  Brooke, P.N.,
  209
  Catharine, 99
  Gilbert, 188
  Robert, 99
Lloyd
  Affy, 46
  Col., 10
  Edward, 10
  John, 73, 81,
  117, 118
  Phillis, 46
  Rose, 168
  Thomas, 46
Lockart
  Mr., 14
Lockwood
  Elliphalet, 154

Locum
  William, 165
Logan
  Fortune, 130, 138
  William, 112, 121, 138
Lokes
  David, 153
London
  Ann, 237
  John, 57, 231, 245, 246, 257
  Lettice, 128
  Margaret, 246
  Peggy, 237, 244
  Thomas, 47, 231, 243, 249, 253, 259
  William, 256
Long
  Henry, 111
Longley
  John, 125
Longshore
  Jolly, 8, 9
Longstreet
  Derick, 183
  John, 183
  John, Capt., 152
Looseley
  Charles, 55
Loosely
  Jack, 55
  Mr., 55
Loosley
  Mr., 55
Lord
  Phil, 107
Lott
  Widow, 37
Louch
  Mary, 237
Lounse
  Lawrence, 39
Lounz
  Capt., 25, 26
Loveat
  John, 91
Low

George, 32
Isaiah, 124
Lowe
  Col., 135
  Cornelius, 48
  Jacobus, 98
Lowell
  Mr., 6
  Lowerhele, 33
Lownds
  Rowland, 123
Lownse
  Lawrence, 39
Lowther
  James, 231
  Joseph, 245
  Thomas, 231
Loyal
  Anthony, 40
  Hagar, 40
Lucas
  Cuffy, 125
  James, 231
  John, 231, 245, 256
Lucock
  Joseph, 261
Ludlow
  Gabriel W., 54
  Thomas, Jr., 160
Luke
  Isaac, 201
Lukes
  Ann, 125
Lumby
  Abram, 231
Lumley
  Abraham, 240
Lusam
  Peter, 70
Lydacre
  Fanny, 34
  Lucy, 33
  William, 33
Lydecker
  Garret, 73
  Thomas, 73
Lykes
  Lucey, 14
Lynch
  Ann, 247

Elizabeth, 260
Jacob, 7
John, 6, 231, 242, 253, 260
Mr., 6, 7, 9, 16
Peggy, 9
Peter, 44
Phebe, 7
Sally, 44
Tinnia, 44
Lyndon
  Josias, 53
Lynn
  Nancy, 237
Lynning
  John, 171, 172
Lynts
  Elizabeth, 254
Lyon
  Andrew, 9
  Henry, 9
  James, 9
  Phebe, 9
  Phillis, 9
  Walter, 79
Lyons
  Andrew, 150
Mackfield
  Richard, 246
Madare
  Anthony, 232
Madeira
  Anthony, 260
  Elizabeth, 258
Madera
  Archibald, 253
Madiera
  Anthony, 257
Maginnis
  William, 174
Mahan
  Timothy, 43
Maitland
  Mrs., 52
Majers
  S., Lt., 205
Major
  Edward, 69
  S., Lt., 204
Malby
  Thomas, 101
Malcombe

William, 82
Mallady
  Thomas, 262
Mallard
  Thomas, 79
Mallery
  William, 65
Mallory
  Caleb, 9
Mallow
  Henry, 152
  Henry, Dr., 152
Mamacus
  Abraham, 244
Mandeville
  John, 240
Manewell
  John, 231
Manewill
  Sophia, 237
Maniwell
  John, 232
  Joseph, 232
Manley
  Cornelius, 232
Mann
  Bettsey, 213
  Cloe, 213
  Samuel, 34
Mannan
  William, 16
Mansburgh
  John, 211
Manshaw
  William, 231, 245
Manswill
  Ann, 237
Manuel
  John, 242
Manwell
  Joseph, 245
Manwill
  Elizabeth, 237
March
  James, 232, 247
Marian
  John, 180
  Peter, 180
Marien
  Charles, 257

Elizabeth, 261
John, 261
Marion
  General, 11
Markfield
  Mary, 237
  Richard, 231
Marks
  Nathaniel, 204
Marlin
  James, 232
  Thomas, 232
Marnine
  James, Jr., 251
  John, 251
Marnival
  Ann, 244
Maron
  Simon, 232
Marpole
  Northrop, 150
Marrant
  Amelia, 57
  Ben, 57
  John, 56
  Mellia, 56, 57
Marren
  Thomas, 8
Marrian
  Abraham, 11
Marron
  Thomas, 8
Marshal
  Frank, 101
Marshall
  Jane, 102
  John, 148, 232, 247
Martin
  James, 244, 250, 251
  John, 27, 106, 252
  Lewis Burnel, 169
  Lizzy, 156
  Peter, 34
  Robert, 34, 240
  Samuel, 17
  Thom, 241
  Thomas, 232

William, 157, 231
Martine
  John, 131
Marvin
  Joseph, 149
Mary
  Ann, 237
Marygault
  Gabriel, 128
Mason
  Joe, 165
  Kate, 117
  Polly, 25
  Samuel, 25
Massenburgh
  Humphrey, 125
Mathews
  Abraham, 261
  Abram, 232, 251
  Daniel, 231
  David, 206
Matthews
  David, 80, 157, 172
  General, 52
  John, 22
  Margaret, 131
  Mr., 145, 180
  Peter, 131
  William, 138
Matthewson
  Ensign, 138
Mattocks
  Peter, 150
Matue
  John, 259
Maxfield
  Hannah, 37
  Henry, 37
  James, 232
Maxico
  Marian, 202
  Rachael, 202
Maxwell
  Francis, 53
  John, 101
May
  George, 16
Maybee
  Casparus, 156

Sparrows, 17
Mayo
  Joseph, 155
McAdam
  John, 28
  William, 113
McAlister
  Alexander, 135
McAlpine
  John, 29
McCall
  George, 15, 159
McCaull
  Thomas, 160
McClaurin
  David, 92
McCoy
  Capt., 138, 139
McCrea
  Capt., 180
McCrimmond
  Donald, 80
McCulloch
  Captain, 31
  Nero, 38
  Robert, 21
McDonald
  Alexander, 52, 53, 66, 70, 71
  Angus, Capt., 177
  Capt., 131, 151, 161, 173, 177
  Lieutenant, 149
  Lt., 149
  Sarah, 82
  William, 128, 129
McDougall
  General, 173
McFarlane
  Miss, 122
McFipps
  Capt., 198
McGee
  John, 158
McGill
  Capt., 138
McGrigger
  Dinah, 19

Henry, 16
McGuire
  Simson, 6
McHannon
  John, 231
McHingham
  Thomas, 240
McIntire
  Bill, 48
  Cornelius, 48
  Lissey, 48
McIntyre
  Doctor, 200
  Dr., 200
McInzie
  John, 28
McKay
  Abraham, 231
  Alex, Capt., 178
  Andrew, 93
  Ann, 237
  Charlotte, 237, 242
  James, 86
  Jane, 242
  John, 108
  Nancy, 83
  Richard, 232
McKee
  James, 70
  John, 154
McKensie
  John, 116
McKenzie
  Casar, 116
  Smith, 87
McKnight
  William, 94
McKown
  John, 45
  William, 45
McLean
  Maj., 178
  Major, 179
McLeod
  Capt., 136
  Dan, Lieut., 30
  Dan, Lt., 30
  Donald, 80
  John, 31
  Lt., 31, 152

Sam, 162
Thomas, 91
Walter, Dr.,
162
William, 29,
30
McManus
Thomas, 43
McMullan
Mr., 45
McNeal
John, 14
McNeill
Mr., 108
McPherson
Capt., 136, 137
Charles, 67
Dugal, 72
Job, 14
John, 60
McQuay
Robert, 51
McRae
Mr., 136
McRea
Capt., 180
McReady
Mr., 176
Robert, 150
McRimen
Donald, 52
McVeaugh
Benjamin, 52
Mead
Betty, 93
David, 27, 92,
93
George, 232,
246
Isaac, 92
Nanny, 93
Meaks
Mary, 136
Melden
Francis, 78
Mellington
James, 232
Menzies
John, 68
Mercer
John, 205
Peter, 205

Mercereau
John, 73
Merrell
Cornet, 139
Merrick
Elizabeth, 62
Richard, 62
Samuel, 62
Merrill
Caleb, 62
Merrit
Israel, 56
Robert, 32, 33
Merselis
Ahasmerus, 17
Mewbourne
Thomas, 261
Micherson
James, 196
Micuro
Hector, 12
Middleton, 121
Andrew, 205
Arthur, 110,
111, 181
Charles, 115,
181
Dr., 140, 151
Harry, 98, 100
Henry, 115,
122
Sarah, 100
Thomas, 120
Middletown
Dr., 151
Middleworth
John, 67
Mifflin
Abraham, 71
Charles, 71,
125
Milbank
John, 153
Miles
Bellah, 110
Hagar, 115
Jacob, 16, 231
John, 95, 99,
115, 184
Mary, 99
Robert, 127
Sally, 110

Sampson, 99
Savinah, 115
Venus, 115
William, 147
Millengen
James, 243
Miller
Abram, 168
Capt., 164
Dublin, 200
Frank, 203
Hannah, 112
Hans, 208
James, 73, 162
Jenny, 131, 203
Jerry, 133
Joe, 154
John, 15
Mason, 200
Massey, 203
Moses, 154
Nancy, 203
Richard, 113
Sarrah, 206
Thomas, 115,
125
Venus, 87
Villotte, 168
Millick
John, 232, 243,
253
Millidge
Maj., 145
Milligan
James, 246
Jane, 87
Maria, 87
Milliner
Robert, 122
Titus, 112
Millingly
James, 232
Mills
Capt., 139
Jonathan, 73
Joseph, 70
Thomas, 164
Tom, 70
Minnick
John, 259
Minor
Charles, 245

Christian, 231
Elizabeth, 242,
258
George, 231,
242, 256
Mintoes
George, 175
Minton
Henry, 115
Peggy, 171
Samuel, 195
Thomas, 195
Mitchel, 6
Bristol, 90
Dinah, 6
Frank, 6
James, 157
Phillis, 96
Mitchell
Elizabeth, 133
Henry, 96
James, 177,
180, 232
John, 41, 96
Joseph, 90, 245
Mixied
Samuel, 200
Mocock
Thomas, 88
Moffat
James, 42
Molden
Frank, 33
William, 149
Molineux
Charles, 232
Elizabeth, 237
Moncrief
Lt. Col., 25
Monday
Jonathan, 30
Monron
Lucy, 237
Monsell
James, 247
Lucy, 247
Monson
John, 232
Montague
Thomas, 251,
262
Montgomery

Archibald, 48
Joseph, 157
Monzies
  Major, 134
Moody
  ___ , Child,
  231
  George
  (Child), 244
  Henry, 111
  Nancy, 111
  William, 231,
  244
Moore
  Abby, 110
  Amelia, 258
  Andrew, 77
  Ann, 237, 243,
  245
  Anthony, 154
  Austin, 5
  Daniel, 35, 84,
  240
  Dublin, 210
  Elizabeth, 84
  Esther, 127
  Godolphin, 52
  Hampton, 52
  Hannah, 91
  Harry, 90
  James, 5, 90
  John, 43, 84,
  156, 163, 210
  Joseph, 127,
  201
  Lewis, 25
  Mr., 5, 25
  Ned, 149
  Paul, 136
  Robert, 231,
  240, 257
  Samuel, 110,
  146
  Sarah, 136
  Tinah, 84
  Violet, 178
  William, 150,
  152
Moorfield
  James, 20
More
  Daniel, 256

Francis, 101
Skinker, 110
Morgan
  Caleb, 158
  James, 100
  John, 16
  Philip, 149
  Rose, 26
  Theophilas, 12
  Thomas, 12
Morrel
  James, 60
Morrell
  Job, 140
  John, 129
  Mr., 205
Morris
  Betsey, 28
  Charity, 73
  Charles, 47, 48
  Edward, 73
  Gab, 183
  Isaac, 73
  James, 107
  John, 166, 232,
  240, 257
  Laban, 231
  Lewis, 231,
  246
  Lucy, 109
  Mary, 257
  Mary Ann, 73
  Ned, 73
  Robert, 88, 102
  Sam, 28
  William, 79
Morrison
  John, 155
  Malcom, 7
Moseley
  Ishmael, 82
  William, 67
Mosely
  Bessel, 169
  Col., 115
  Colonel, 102
  Edward, 87,
  103
  Fanny, 67
  John, 169
  Kate, 8!
  Patty, 103

Tilla, 102
Tommy, 67
Moses
  James, 117
  Joyce, 13
  Peter, 10
  Tilley, 13
  William, 108
Moss
  Amos, 54
  Cornelius, 35
Mot
  William, 163
Mott
  Jacob, 123, 138
  Mrs., 8, 58
  Rosanna, 138
  Rosannah, 123
  William, 7
Motte
  Cato, 179
  Christopher,
  179
  Susanna, 180
Mount
  Michael, 22,
  188
  Moses, 188
Mowat
  Capt., 20, 21
Mowatt
  Captain, 51
Moy
  John, 123
Moyston
  Esq., 76
Mozely
  Col., 211
  Colonel, 212
  Judith, 211
  Peggy, 212
Mozley
  Aaron, 41
  Allen, 52
  Edward, 81
Mullenden
  William, 247,
  249
Mullender
  William, 253,
  259
Mullindee

William, 232
Mumford
  Bristol, 31
  Mrs., 31
  Nancy, 31
Munday
  John, 232, 247
  William, 232,
  240
Munford
  Cornelius, 136
  Joseph, 151
Munn
  John, 20
Munnall
  John, 19
Munns
  Alexander, 79
Munro
  Capt., 159
Murder
  James, 107
Murick
  John, 132
Murphey
  William, 231
Murphy
  James, 185
  John, 11, 109
  Lewis, 231
Murrain
  John, 247
Murray
  Alexander, 46
  Andrew, 153
  David, 232
  Ensign, 139
  Isaac, 116,
  128, 197
  James, 231
  Joan, 117
  John, 232, 240,
  249, 261
  Kitty, 107
  Maj., 11
  Major, 12, 13
  Moses, 107
  Richard, 85
  Robert, 185
Murren
  Charles, 231
  Jon, 232

Murrin
  Charles, 245
Murry
  Britton, 116
  James, 251
Musgrave
  Gen., 137
  General, 137,
  140
Myer
  Henry, 140
Myers
  Abram, 117
  Benjamin, 48
  Fredrick, 39,
  40
  Harry, 67
  John, 33, 49
Nagle
  William, 98
Nansberg
  Elizabeth, 33
Napier
  Mr., 54
  Robert, 54
Nash
  James, 127
  John, 181
  Thomas, 200
  York, 200
Nason
  Thomas, 102
Naylor
  James, 146
Neal
  Jack, 203
  Thomas, 241
Neale
  Thomas, 232
Needam
  John, 232
Needham
  John, 242, 260
  Sarah, 260
Neekens
  Hezekiah, 232
Nelis
  Benjamin, 93
  Jane, 94
  Jonathan, 94
  Sally, 94
Nelson

Thomas, 232,
  240
Neptune
  James, 232,
  244, 249, 251,
  262
Nerna
  Flora, 69
Nesbit
  James, 232,
  240
  John, 26
  Orchbert, 43,
  44
Ness
  Abraham, 134
  Adj't., 134, 135
  Lucy, 135
  Mr., 135
Newbold
  Chris, 57
  Peter, 57
Newburn
  Thomas, 252
Newcombe
  James, 117
Newland
  George, 232
Newman
  James, 232
  Joseph, 232,
  241, 249, 251,
  262
  William, 232
Newton
  Abigail, 112
  George, 232,
  240, 249
  Jane, 258
  Lambert, 83
  Lydia, 112
  Thomas, 90,
  91, 108, 115,
  117
  William, 257
Newtown
  Lambert, 112
Nichol
  James, 138
Nicholas
  John, 208, 232
Nicholls

Casar, 22
Nichols
  Ben, 175
  Casar, 175
  Philip, 151
  Rose, 175
Nicholson
  Cornet, 10
  James, 163
  William, 113
Nickins
  Hezekiah, 246
  James, 90
Nickinson
  Joseph, Capt.,
  107
  Patty, 109
  Robert, 107
  Willis, 116
Nicklin
  Samuel, 60
Nicollson
  Cornet, 11
Nicols
  James, 151
Nicolson
  Cornet, 11
Nightingale
  Nathaniel, 48
Nipper
  James, 232
  Mary, 237
Nixon
  William, 107
Noble
  Able, 169
  Rachel, 237,
  246
Nockle
  William, 74
Norgall
  Barin, 99
Norman
  Daniel, 232
Norris
  John, 165
Norstrandt
  John, 21
Nottingham
  Richard, 108
  Thomas, 232
Nunn

Sarah, 38
Nutter
  Valentine, 153
  William, 78
O'Brien
  Edward, 164
  Lewis, 165
  Mat, 156
O'Neale
  Will, 50
Oakes
  John, 75
Oatley
  Francis, 244
Oatsby
  Francis, 232
Oaxley
  William, 64
Odell
  Abraham, 101
  Daniel, 149
Ogden
  Barbara, 20
  Thomas, 17
Ogilvie
  Margaret, 88,
  89
Ogram
  (Mrs.), 232
  Catherine, 237
  Catherine
  (Child), 247
  Elizabeth, 247
  George, 232,
  247
Oliphant
  Dr., 54
  York, 54
Oliver
  James, 232,
  244, 256
  John, 232, 242
Oman
  Elizabeth
  (Child), 244
  John, 247
Opey
  Lincey, 124
Oram
  Ralph, 232
Oramfield
  Peter, 232

Oree
  Col., 139
Ormfield
  Elizabeth, 237
  William, 232
Ormond
  Aaron, 205
  Thomas, 205
Ormsfield
  Elizabeth, 243
  William, 258
Orphan
  Amie, 168
Orser
  Abigail, 74
  Joseph, 74
  Oliver, 74
Osman
  John, 232
  Oswald, 174
Otter
  James, 198
Owann
  James, 232
Owen
  James, 240,
  256
Owens
  Ann, 237
  Susan, 237
Oxford
  John, 232
  Sally, 172
Oxley
  William, 34,
  131
Paby
  Benjamin, 232
Packley
  Isaac, 205
Page
  Ann, 237
  Samuel, 232
  Willis, 187
Pallas
  Thomas, 232
Palmer
  Alpheus, 16–20
  Ben, 18
  Benjamin, 20
  Capt., 157
  Edmund, 37

Hana, 18
John, 122
Lewis, 65
Moses, 18
Peter, 260
Palmerton
  Betsy, 190
  Billy, 190
  Joseph, 190
Pandarves
  Josiah, 100
Pandorrus
  Lymus, 211
  Maria, 211
  Richard, 211
Pandorus
  Benjamin, 179
  Richard, 179
Pankin
  Joseph, 244
Parado
  Abram, 232
  Ann, 258
  Emanuel, 257
  Francis, 257
  Manuel, 232
  Sarah, 258
Pardo
  Emanuel, 242
  Francis, 242
Parford
  John, 232, 242
  Mary, 241
Paris
  Thomas, 243
Parker
  Daniel, 51, 61
  F., 65
  George, 83, 84
  James, 104,
  232, 241, 256
  Jenny, 79
  Mary, 237
  Mary (Child),
  245
  Miss, 51
  Mr., 15
  Mrs., 158
  Peter, 41, 42,
  44, 79, 232
  Sara, 258
  Sarah, 245

Thomas, 79,
232, 245
  William, 96
Parkin
  Dick, 188
  Mr., 188
  Violet, 188
Parks
  Cornet, 12
  Jane, 88
  Jonathan, 88
  Mr., 152
Parsons
  Elizabeth, 261
Passmore
  James, 233
Patrick
  Frank, 89
  Phebe, 40
  Thomas, 40
  William, 87
Patten
  George, 26
Patterson
  Betty, 113
  General, 14
  John, 43, 55
  Thomas, 113
Patton, 122
  George, 46
  John, 158
Paul
  Abby, 109
  James, 213
  John, 108
  Joseph, 124
  Saul, 209
  Susannah, 124
Pavell
  Susanna, 128
Payne
  Daniel, 205
  Widow, 135
Payton
  Elizabeth, 237
Peacock
  Matthew, 73,
  74, 176
  R., 74
  Robert, 35
Peacocke
  Capt., 35

Pearce
  Charlotte, 245
  Jane, 117
  Maria, 237,
  245
  Thomas, 117,
  232
Pearcey
  Kermet, 246
  Kinnett, 232
Pearse
  Charlotte, 237
Pearson
  Capt., 59
Peaser
  Elizabeth, 237
Peasey
  John, 233, 241
Peasor
  Thomas, 233
Peazer
  Elizabeth, 240
Peers
  Abraham, 43
Peesey
  John, 260
Peggs
  John, 232
Pell
  John, 22, 75
  Judah, 22
Pells
  Sarah, 258
Pembroke
  George, 245,
  256
Pen
  John, 171
Pendtree
  Hassen, 149
Penilack
  Samuel, 150
Pennington
  Lt. Col., 8
Pepperel
  William, Sir,
  103
Percy
  Kinnet, 237
Perkins
  Cato, 53
  James, 186

John, 53
Pompey, 186
Pero
Jerry, 49
Perrill
Captain, 38
Jenny, 38
Perrin
John, 92
Perrow
James, 18
Perry
Ann, 237
Anthony, 232, 241
Colonel, 205
Daniel, 152
Henry, 68
Jenny, 151
John, 91
Nicholas, 68
Preniah, 19
Prince, 205
Sturges, 51, 53
Perth
Casar, 116
Mary, 85
Pertrie
Mr., 23
Peter
John, 241
Thomas, 232, 240
Peterkin
Tobia, 86
Peters
D., 29
Frank, 41
George, 78, 232, 243
Hector, 115
James, 45, 159
John, 52, 232, 233, 247, 250, 251, 262
Nancy, 41, 110
Samuel, 147
Stephen, 24
Thomas, 257
Petery
William, 127
Petsworth

Jacob, 138
Petters
James, 35
Sally, 177
Pettitt
William, 49
Pew
Peter, 90, 91
Pharo
Peter, 113
Phelix
Phil, 167
Philcox
Gabriel, 78
Philip
James, 200
Philips, 62
Anthony, 44
Capt., 8, 44
Captain, 78
Charles, 160
Emanuel, 233
Gabriel, 30
Jacob, 260
James, 44
Jenkin, 14
Lt., 80, 153, 155
Mr., 37
Nathaniel, 61, 130
Phillip
Joseph, 232
Phillips
Benjamin, 38, 256
David, 27
Emanuel, 247
George, 38, 232, 246
John, 106
Joseph, 9, 245
Lt., 103, 208
Nathaniel, 72
Phipps
Paul, 179
Thomas, 110
Phips
Matthew, 88
Phrip
Matthew, 104, 107, 114

Pickhall
John, 76
Pierte
Griffin, 30
Piggot
Anthony, 34
Bill, 36
Casar, 34
John, 34
Sarah, 34
Pilgrim
Joseph, 126
Pimbrook
George, 232
Pimken
Joseph, 40, 41
Pinchon
Joseph, 42
Pinto
Joseph, 129
Pioneer, 10
Pitcairn
Capt., 20
Pitcher
Capt., 122
Moses, 53
Pitt
John, 51
William, 51
Platt
Peter Thorn, 210
Stanle, 210
Pleace
Lt., 154
Pleasant
Foreman, 28
Robert, 71, 134
Thomas, 71
Plumb
Charlotte, 43
Thomas, 41, 43, 232
Plummitty
Christopher, 100
Polhemus
Capt., 156
Polydore
Hanibal, 232
Pomp
John, 166

Pompey
John, 233, 243, 246, 249, 253, 259
John, Jr., 233
Polly, 38
Pomposend
John, 256
Ponthien
Mr., 28
Pool
Mary, 237
Thomas, 105
Poole
Ben, 201
Dick, 203
Edward, 201
Howard, 203
Joseph, 232, 240, 257
Mary, 201, 258
Mary Ann, 243
Pope
Ezekiel, Capt., 76
Porcher
Peter, 162
Portell
Thomas, 42
Portelous
Jehiel, 146
Matthew, 146
Porter
Elizabeth, 84
Fanny, 237
Portress
Josiah, 35
Post
Gilfin, 70
John, 103
Tommy, 103
Postell
Andrew, 70, 71
John, 70
Robert, 70
Potter
Cuff, 54
Jacob, 257
John, 70
Lucy, 70
Ralph, 54
Robert, 70

Sarah, 258
Potters
  Thomas, 177
Pottle
  Stephen, 147
Potts
  Lt., 138
  Mr., 145
  Thomas, 146
  William, 173
Powell
  Bob, 129
  John, 129
  William, 232,
  241
Powers
  Thomas, 30
Predun
  John, 37
Prentice
  Peter, 25
Preson
  Cathrine, 24
Preston
  Nancy, 53
Price
  George, 170
  James, 186,
  260
  Mary, 258
  Ned, 125
  Richard, 186
  Robert, 245,
  257
Prideaux
  Capt., 131
Prim
  John, 49
Prime
  John, 98
Primus
  John, 77
Prince
  Charles, 233,
  247
  George, 232,
  241, 256
  Jervis, 232
  Mary, 237, 258
  Robert, 232
  William, 232,
  233

Princes
  Elizabeth, 43
  Margaret, 43
  Nicholas, 43
  Prince, 43
Prior
  John, 31
  Mr., 62
Prison
  John, 24
Pritchard
  Paul, 174
Proffitt
  Daniel, 105,
  204
  Sibe, 204
Profit
  Daniel, 158
  Joe, 158
  Katy, 158
  Venus, 109
Profitt
  Dick, 108
Promise
  Grace, 241
  James, 232
  James (Child),
  241
  John, 232, 241
  John (Child),
  241
  Mary, 233, 237
  Mary (Child),
  241
Proutt
  William, 58
Provey
  Ann, 237, 243,
  249, 252
  John, 233, 243,
  249
  Lewis Ann, 249
  Louisa, 237
  Louisa Ann,
  243
Provost
  General, 16
Pruett
  Timothy, 26,
  27
Pugsley
  Gilbert, 154

William, 100
Punderson
  Isaac, 125
Purdie
  Gabriel, 56
  Lydia, 56
Purdy
  Gabriel, 149
Pursell
  David, 107
Pyate
  Mr., 12
Quack
  Elizabeth, 173
  Jean, 173
  Sally, 173
Quamina
  Peter, 175
Queen
  Ann, 237
Quig
  Hugh, 60
Quinby
  Mr., 23
Quince
  Abram, 114
  Parker, 67
  Patt, 24
  Richard, 114
Quints
  Parker, 166
  Richard, 166
Quomo
  Betty, 203
  Rabo, 208
Radcliffe
  John, 176
Raddick
  Henry, 54
Radlow
  Mr., 16
Rag
  John, 185
Ragg
  John, 177
Ralph
  Conrad, 189
Ramsay
  Elizabeth, 240,
  249, 261
  John, 244, 251,
  262

John W., 261
John William,
  233, 240, 249,
  251
Ramsburgh
  Rebecca, 210
Ramsey
  Benjamin, 204
  Betsey, 39
  Cato, 39, 204
  Dr., 22
  Elizabeth, 252
  James, 38
  Joe, 31
  John, 233
  John, Dr., 39
  Nelly, 39
Randall
  Adam, 91
  Andrew, 90
  Anthony, 89
  Daniel, 174
  John, 83
  Nancy, 90
  Peter, 16
  Phebe, 91
Randsberry
  Mrs., 115
Ranger
  John, 80
Rankin
  James, 164
Rapalje
  George, 17, 18,
  207
Rapelje
  Abraham, 145
  Betty, 145
  Cornelius, 145
  Thomas, 156
Raper
  Lydia, 245, 257
  Sylvia, 237
  William, 233,
  240, 257
Ravo
  Gabriel, 80
  Pompey, 80
Ray
  Daniel, 180,
  181
  James, 77

Mr., 16
Rayden
  Henry, 58
Raymond
  Capt., 150, 151
  David, 204
  John, 204
Rayon
  Will, 161
Rea
  James, 170
  Peggy, 172
Read
  Isaac, 148
  James, 240,
  249, 262
  Jane, 249
Reading
  Daniel, 208
  John William,
  243
  Mary, 208
Reddick
  Agnes, 94
  Elsey, 94
  Henry, 92
  Joseph, 93
  Katy, 117
  Lambert, 92,
  149
  Pleasant, 94
  Willis, 82
Redhook
  Anthony, 188
  Moses, 188
Redin
  William John,
  233
Redock
  Charity, 190
  Col., 190
  Jenny, 190
  Richard, 190
Reed, 27
  Bowes, 60
  Isaac, 148
  James, 66, 67
  John, 47, 116
  William, 106
Rees
  James, 32
Reese

Sarah, 237
Thomas, 182
Reid
  Doctor, 196
  James, 196,
  233, 251
  Jane, 243
  John, 54
  Patty, 196
  Thomas, 56
Remain
  Ellis, 39
Renck
  Kenneth, 18
Renk
  Charles, 180
Revinos
  Lewis, 247
Reynolds
  Andrew, 172
  Cornet, 10, 13
  Jenny, 23
  Mr., 155
Rhodes
  Henry, 176,
  233
Rice
  Anthony, 57
  Francis, 199,
  201
Richard
  Dick, 89
  James, 233
  Rose, 5
  Thomas, 5
Richards
  Bella, 31
  Betty, 153
  Charles, 8
  Dick, 18
  Esther, 91
  Jack, 53
  Jacob, 153
  James, 8, 91,
  102, 242
  John, 31, 101,
  102, 153, 233
  Libby, 31
  Mary, 18
  Nel, 108
  Peggy, 91
  Peter, 31

Polly, 102
Richard, 91
Richardson, 6
  Abigail, 38
  Ann, 237
  Benjamin, 233
  Capt., 6
  Catharine, 38
  Charles, 233
  Elizabeth, 252
  Hannah, 190,
  249, 252, 261
  Jacob, 233,
  245, 256
  James, 241,
  250
  Mr., 38
  Nathaniel, 233
  Richard, 133
  Thom, 189
  Thomas, 233,
  245, 253, 260
  William, 233,
  243, 249, 251,
  261
Richee
  John, 38
Richie
  Capt., 40
Richmond
  Charles, 233
Ricketts
  William, 252,
  261
Rickman
  James, 36
Ricks
  Anthony, 122
Riddick
  Josiah, 96
Riddle
  Ben, 64
  David, 64
  John, 233, 241,
  250, 258
Rinn
  Billy, 27
  Carsy, 27
  Charles, 27
  Mary, 27, 28
  Phillis, 28
Rippen

Isaac, 24
Risbeck
  Col., 120, 121
Ritchie
  John, 40
Ritchse
  Andrew, 6, 7
  James, 7
Rivers
  Col., 181
  Daphne, 127
  Fortune, 195
  George, 147
  Jenny, 195
  Kal, 24
  Mallaby, 111,
  112
  Molly, 195
  Sally, 195
  Sikes, 114
  Susannah, 114
  Tom, 181
Roach
  Dick, 187
  Matthew, 121
Robert
  James, 233
  Jane, 84
  Simon, 84
Roberts, 75
  Capt., 71
  Clarisa, 12
  Diana, 172
  Erasmus, 43
  Esther, 172
  George, 12,
  124
  Hannah, 12
  James, 233
  Jane, 111
  Joseph, 233,
  244
  Mark, 44
  Mr., 43
  Owen, 33
  Robert, 100
  Stephen, 233
  William, 233,
  242
Robertson
  Abraham, 151

Alexander, 28, 29
Betsey, 20
Capt., 138
Catherine, 237
Charles, 29
Col., 151
Elizabeth, 245
George, 114
James, 20, 233
John, 233
L.C., 138
Mr., 136
Peter, 170
Robert, 233, 245
William, 44, 160
Robins
Flora, 151
John, Major, 110
Lieut., 136
Robinson
Betsey, 211
Betsy, 237
Capt., 14
Catherine, 258
David, 203
Edward, 233, 243
Elizabeth, 237, 252, 257
George, 95, 204
Hannah, 202
Jack, 202
James, 30, 31, 50, 52, 136, 203, 233
Joe, 46
John, 211, 233, 242
John Aaron, 236, 244
Major, 146
Mr., 205
Peggy, 202
Peter, 42
Prince, 202
Quomo, 203
Rob, 112

Robert, 256
Thomas, 233, 244
Tully, 202
Will, 210
William, 233
Rogers
Baggerty, 107
Betsey, 206
Captain, 37
Cato, 207
Charles, 174
Easter, 206
Jack, 45
James, 45, 111
Jenny, 107
John, 37
Lt., 62
Mr., 80
Tabby, 206
Thomas, 65, 73
William, 207
Ronaldson
James, 174
Roots
John, 170
Rose
Elizabeth, 237, 243
James, 38
Lewis, 233, 240, 256
Peter, 8
Walter, 233
Ross
Alexander, 44
Andrew, 41
Donald, 51, 52
Dr., 162
Jacob, 163
Susan, 258
Rosser
John, 39, 40
Roughbottom
Francis, 40
Rowan
Jacob, 169
Rowbottom
Francis, 78
Thomas, 159
Rowland
James, 233

Roxby
John, 29, 74
Royal
Prince, 72
Ruffean
Robert, 101
Ruffin
James, 55
Ruggles
General, 44
Hester, 44
Jeffery, 44
Richard, 44
Rusca
Edward, 243
Ruscow
Col., 41
Russall
Thomas, 208
Russel
Daniel, 163
Thomas, 182
Russell
Dr., 161
James, 211
Valentine, 253, 259
Russer
Edward, 233
Rutledge, 185
Flora, 111
Gov., 111
John, 66
Pompey, 111
Simon, 186
Thomas, 172, 186
Rutt
Samuel, 211
Ryall
Nicholas, 109
Rybold
Thomas, 176
Ryerson
Francis, 155
John, 155, 186
Peter, 7, 8
Sabb
Adam, 259
Mary, 259
Sabbs
William, 148

Sally
Livsa, 103
Salt
Maurice, 204, 205
Salter
D., 177
John, 177
Samo
Judith, 237
Thomas, 234
Sampley
John, 245
Sampson, 54
Peter, 205
Samuel, 97
Sarah, 249
Thomas, 234
William, 195, 234
Wilson, 245, 257
Sams
Toby, 147
William, 147, 176
Samson, 54
Bacchus, 54
Catharine, 158
Jane, 158
Richard, 208
Stephen, 10
Samuel
Elizabeth, 238, 244
George, 233, 234, 244
William, 80
Sanders
Emanuel, 253
Sands
William, 175
Santh
Anthony, 241
Santhin
William, 234, 245
Sargen
Lieut., 136
Saunders
Abraham, 92
C., 122

David, 49
Emanuel, 234, 246, 249, 259
Gad, 17
Judith, 17
Mrs., 48
Olive, 114
Patty, 114
Samuel, 171
Thomas, 114
Savage
Jeremiah, 48
John, 102
Mary, 102
Mrs., 148
Nancy, 187
Thomas, 187
Savory
Elizabeth, 260
Sawyer
Barry, 196
Charles, 196
Chloe, 196
Nelly, 196
Shinea, 196
Tom, 196
Sayre
James, 35
Rev. Dr., 148
Rev. Mr., 118
Reverend, 118
Reverend Mr., 118
Scarberry
Betsey, 94
Peter, 94
Sarah, 94
Scarbery
George, 93
Scarborough
Mr., 166
Schenck
John, 48
Peter, 150
Schenckel
Ann, 254
John, 254
Richard, 254
Rosina, 254
Schuler
Col., 123
Schumaker

Samuel, 101
Scolly
John, 207
Scot
Cathern, 173
George, 41
Hesther, 126
James, 64
Joseph, 127, 172
Mary, 172
Mimbo, 172
Peter, 100
Phebe, 172
Phillis, 99
Rebecca, 172
Roger, 170
William, 145
Scott
Ann, 238
John, 253, 259
Molly, 197
Murray, 197
Scotty
Jack, 207
Phebe, 207
Scribbins
Thomas, General, 38
Scribner
Ebenezer, 8
Joseph, 8
Scudder
Dorras, 205
Henry, 157
Isaac, 205
Scull
John, 36
Scutcheon
Rachel, 23
Thomas, 23
Scuyler
John, 209
Philip, 145
Seabrook
Becky, 109
John, 109
Seaburry
David, 118
Seaman
Doctor, 198
James, 251

Joseph, 262
Maurice, 202
Morris, 202, 209
Tom, 202
William, 96
Searli
Charles, 233
Sears
Isaac, 234, 246
John, 209
Nancy, 24
Searum
Bill, 123
James, Dr., 123
Sedgwick
William, 233
Seeble
Ens., 122
Seep
John, 102
Selley
George, 243
Selly
Elizabeth, 254
George, 234, 253
Sepkins
Daniel, 113
Seppey
Thomas, 233
Sera
Daniel, 125
Sereen
John, 234
Serjeant
Lt., 147
Servantus
Martin, 234, 242
Setine
Anthony, 233
Seymour
James, 233, 245
Shadwell
Abner, 41
Shakespeare
Stephen, 36–40
Shanerhorn
Peter, 89
Sharp

Dick, 25
George, 233, 244
John, 113
Mr., 5
Sharpe
Jacob, 36
James, 113
Shaw
Henry, 233
Sheerman
John, 260
Sheets
Luke, 21
Shemby
John, 114
Shenkell
Ann, 259
John, 259
Richard, 259
Rosina, 259
Shepard
William, 183
Shepherd
David, 81
George, 234, 246
Israel, 30
Jane, 98
John, 97
Quash, 183
Silva, 30
Solomon, 89
William, 81, 97
Sheppard
Benjamin, 46
Kessiah, 107
Nancy, 190
Priscilla, 190
Saul, 107
Solomon, 46
Thomas, 113
William, 14, 107, 172
Shepperd
Joseph, 104
Lucy, 104
Saul, 94
Thomas, 104
Sherburne
Frank, 250

Sherwood
  Justice, 159
Shewbrick
  Patty, 38
Shields
  Daphne, 96
  David, 96, 172
  George, 107
  Thomas, 105
  William, 105
Shiels
  Mingo, 162
  Samuel, 162
Ship
  3 Friends, 62
  3 Sisters, 69,
  131
  Adventure, 12
  Alcide, 182
  Alexander, 159
  Amity's
  Production, 56
  Ann, 20, 22,
  64, 67, 133
  Ann &
  Elizabeth, 36,
  121
  Antelope
  Gordon, 75
  Apollo, 25, 45,
  65, 69, 135
  Ariel, 6
  Aurora, 5, 47,
  70, 73, 122,
  139, 176
  Baker & Atlee,
  43, 74
  Beaver, 44
  Bellsaurus, 249
  Belsaurus, 251
  Berwick, 131
  Betsey, 164
  Blacket, 29
  Blackett, 74
  Bridgewater,
  59, 130, 140
  Britain, 137
  Brunswick, 131
  Camel, 8, 74
  Caron, 148
  Cato, 34, 162

Charming
  Nancy, 147
  Clinton, 89,
  147, 152
  Commerce, 65,
  68, 130, 175
  Concord, 204
  Cyclops, 117
  Danger, 195
  Delight, 45
  Diannah, 206
  Dispatch, 37
  Duke of
  Richmond, 132
  Duke
  Richmond,
  133, 175
  Dutchess of
  Gordon, 60,
  161
  Dutchess of
  Hamilton, 49
  Eagle, 49, 130
  Elijah, 169
  Elizabeth, 32,
  66, 71, 122,
  133, 173
  Elk, 160
  Enterprise, 122
  Esther, 23, 66,
  70, 136
  Fishburn, 78
  Friends, 47, 48
  Friendship, 150
  Generous
  Friends, 55
  Grace, 34, 64,
  131
  Grand Dutchess
  of Russia, 13,
  117, 148
  Greg, 50
  Hesperus, 77,
  78
  His Majesty's
  Solitaire, 76
  Hope, 35, 74,
  156
  Hopewell, 58,
  158
  Jane, 27
  Jason, 153

Jenney, 181
John & Jane,
  146
Joseph, 65, 68,
  157, 168, 177,
  180
Katy, 44
King George,
  134
Kingston, 26,
  46, 78, 157,
  160
L'Abondance,
  80, 103, 153,
  155, 208
La Sophia, 51
Lady's
  Adventure, 10
Lehigh, 165
Little Dale, 20,
  58
London, 16, 75
Lord
  Townsend, 150
Lord
  Townshend, 64,
  67
Lucifer, 122
Lydia, 61, 62
Mars, 8, 66,
  69, 73, 133,
  136, 140
Mary, 40, 73,
  78, 154, 159,
  176
Mercury, 147
Michael, 155
Mid Summer
  Blossom, 161
Milford, 123
Minerva, 123
Molly, 176
Montague, 38,
  48, 70, 134
Nancy, 49, 77,
  145, 146, 150,
  155
Nautilus, 124
Neptune, 154
Nero, 32
New Blessings,
  75

Nicholas &
  Jane, 56
Nisbet, 181
Ocean, 75
Otter, 65, 75
Pallacier, 175
Pallesier, 139
Pearl, 49
Peggy, 7, 79,
  195
Polly, 14, 120
Prince of
  Orange, 159
Prosperous
  Amelia, 145
Providence, 38
Ranger, 44
Rebecca, 121,
  122
Rhinoceros,
  162
Robert &
  Elizabeth, 153
Roy Britton,
  123
Sally, 49, 77,
  159
Saucy Ben,
  162
Selina, 158
Skuldham, 163
Sovereign, 35,
  68, 137
Spencer, 6, 77,
  145
Spring, 5
St. Alban, 21
Stafford, 27,
  47, 80, 165
Supply, 140
Sybil, 119
Symmetry, 53
Tartar, 58
Thames, 57
The Brothers,
  48
Thetis, 55
Three Sisters,
  28
Townshend, 73
Tree Briton, 51
Trepassey, 157

Trident, 75
Two Sisters,
54, 135
Union, 50, 75
Venus, 27
Vernon, 253
Volcano, 123
William, 69,
135, 146
William &
Mary, 56, 152,
154
Shirley
Robert, 234
Shoemaker
John, 124, 126
Joseph, 175
Shrewsbury
Stephen, 85
Shrewstin
Mrs., 115
Shrimpton
John, 234
Shrying
William, 253
Shubrick
Thomas, 38
Sickles
Daniel, 65
Ethan, 58
Silea
D. A., 229
Sill
Captain, 249
Silly
Elizabeth, 259
Silvarus
Abraham, 234
Simmon
Nero, 24
Simmonds
William, 176
Simmons
Dick, 234, 241,
256
Dinah, 64
Edward, 56
John, 233, 238
John (Child),
245
Joseph, 82
Mary, 238, 245

Milly, 252
Mr., 30
Reuben, 169
Sippio, 16
Thomas, 261
William, 30
Simms
John, 238
John (Child),
246
Joseph, 233
Mary, 234,
238, 246
Thomas, 251
Simon
John, 69
Lilli, 234
Simonons, Esq.,
45
Simonsbury
John, 18
Simpson
Hester, 238
Isabella, 238,
246
Jack, 234, 247
John, 234, 242,
257
Sarah, 238,
244, 252, 261
Thomas, 247
William, 161
Sims
Thomas, 249
Simson
Moses, 14
Singleton
Benjamin, 161
Henry, 104
Hester, 19
John, 19
Patrick, 198
Singletown
John, 203
Sipe
John, 102
Sippey
Thomas, 244
Skidmore
Mr., 38
Skillman
Ann, 238

Skinner
John, 234, 240
Joseph, 44
Samuel, 233,
244, 249, 253,
260
Thomas, 44
Slack
Peter, 160
Slade
Jonathan, 45
Slaide
Freelove, 45
John, 45
Lotche, 45
Roger, 45
Slaughter
Dempse, 9
Solomon, 189
Slinne
John, 42
Sloane
Richard, 148
Smallwood
Nelly, 102
Robert, 101
Smeathman
John, 256
Smith, 64, 191
Abraham, 101,
234
Anthony, 233,
234, 240, 246,
256, 262
Burgess, 51
Capt., 34
Daniel, 75
David, 19, 233
Doctor, 58
Dr., 133
Edward, 250,
251, 262
Elizabeth, 260
Esther, 32
Eunis, 106
George, 256
Gerrit, 18
Hendrick, 209
Henry, 37
Hugh, 254, 259
Isabella, 254,
260

Jack, 14, 36
Jacob, 64, 179
Jacomiah, 14
James, 106,
139, 151, 175
John, 12, 19,
32, 41, 50, 101,
119, 131, 163,
233, 234, 240,
242, 246, 249,
253, 259
Joseph, 17,
199, 260
Josiah, 7
Lieut., 134
Lt. Col., 161,
165, 168
Luke, 106
M. A., 254
Major, 103
Margaret, 238
Margaret
(Child), 246
Martha, 252,
262
Mary, 238,
240, 254, 259
Mary A., 259
Miss, 54
Mr., 77
Peggy, 252,
262
Peter, 260
Richard, 174
Robert, 126
Rose, 106
Sam, 189
Saunders, 106
Sukey, 103
Susan, 238
Susannah, 106
Sylvia, 64
Thomas, 17,
50, 160, 234,
244, 260
W. L., 130
W. S., 61, 72,
77, 141
Whiteford, 47
William, 7, 30,
34, 36, 112,
116, 125, 132,

169, 172, 233, 234, 241, 246, 251, 253, 260, 261
Smithe
Lieut., 55
Smithers
James, 32
Smithfield, 149
Smyth
John, 260
Snail
George, 87
Sneadon
Stephen, 163
Sniffon
Lewis, 159
Snow
James, 124
Snowball
Mary, 85
Nathaniel, 85, 115
Timothy, 125
Violet, 85
Sobrisky
John, 91
Solloman
John, 233
Solomon
Barbara, 234, 238
Francis, 233
John, 233, 241, 245, 249, 251
Somerset
Jacob, 49
William, 49
Sorrill
Charles, 242
Southerland
Adam, 234
Southern
John, 25
Sparrow
China, 85
John, 19, 90
Nancy, 91
Nannis, 19
Peter, 90
Phillis, 19
Richard, 85

Sukey, 19
William, 112
Speak
(Mrs.), 233
Diana, 241
John, 233, 241
Speake
Diane, 258
Spears
(Mrs.), 233
Abraham, 247
Abram, 234
John, 233, 246, 256
Mary, 246, 257
Speed
Paul, 21
Speffen
Casar, 57
Speir
Cyrus, 84
Frank, 84
John, 69
Judith, 84
Patty, 84
Spencell
Harry, 36
Spencer
Abigail, 36
Isaac, 207
Jack, 27
Luke, 35
Oliver, 36
Robert, 27
Spooner
Mr., 166
Spring
John, 234
Sproule
Andrew, 90, 109
Squash
Deborah, 16
Harry, 16
Squire
John Thomas, 248
St. Louis, 45
Stewart, Capt., 36
Stacey

John, 233, 242, 256
Stafford
Bob, 5
William, 257
Stanford
Ephraim, 163
Stanley
Ens., 133
Ensign, 136
John, 175
Richard, 7
Thomas, 234, 244
Stanly
Parthenia, 8
Stanton
Ben, 53
Stanyard
John, 176
Mrs., 29
Starling
Thomas, 234
State
George, 56
Job, 56
Mary, 56
Statia
Thomas, 21
Stebbs
John, 185
Sarah, 184
Steel
Mary, 178
Steele
Murphy, 177
Stephens
James, 262
John, 182, 234, 245
Moses, 91
Sarah, 91
Stephenson
Capt., 138
Charles, 234
George, 234
James, 251
John, 175, 256
Major, 131
William, 234, 245, 253, 257, 259

Stephney
James, 241
Stepney
James, 233, 253, 259
John, 249
William, 56
Sterling
Ann, 242
Isabella, 238
Lewis, 233, 242, 249, 251
Robert, 252
Thomas, 247
Steven
John, 233
Stevens
Anthony, 89
Benjamin, 233
Dr., 35, 36
Richard, 11, 104
Robert, 233, 246
Sarah, 91
Thomas, 90
Stevenson
Charles, 246
George, 241
Mary, 243
Steward
(Mrs.), 233
Abram, 234
Archibald, 244, 249
Francis, 233, 248
George, 233
Hanna, 238
Hannah, 242, 248, 249
John, 233, 240, 249, 262
York, 233, 244, 249
Stewart, 137
Alexander, 178
Andrew, 19, 101, 102, 105, 171
Archibald, 251
Bland, 65

Capt., 11, 161
Christiana, 120
Col., 178, 179
Daniel, 101
Francis, 120
Hannah, 120,
252
James, 102,
199
John, 10, 34,
62, 199, 251
Joseph, 11
Judy, 177
Lt., 10
Matthew, 6
Peggy, 120
Randel, 101
Rose, 88
Sally, 201
Tamar, 102
William, 35,
68
Stiephon
Charles, 80
Still
Anthony, 249
Stirling
Lewis, 262
Robert, 261
Stoddard
Charles, 259
Stoddart
Charles, 233,
240, 253
Mr., 7
Ralph, 204
Sarah, 254
Stogdon
Peter, 64, 200
Robert, 64
Widow, 200
Stokes
A., 47
James, 37, 43
Martin, 68
Patty, 47
Stone
Ben, 97
Joe, 97
Stonestreet
Charles, 233
Storm

Bristol, 95
Storms
Garrett, 95
Stout
Martin, 65
Richard, 209,
210
Stoutenburg
William, 121
Strahan
James, 157
Stratton
Ben, 164, 190
Johnny, 190
Mary, 190
Peggy, 190
Rose, 190
Street
Ned, 182
Stretch
Sam, 62
Samuel, 62
Strong
Diana, 238,
242
Dinah, 103
James, 233,
240
John, 101, 234,
247
R., 175
Richard, 65,
68, 130
Strooger
Daniel, 14
Stuart
Alexander, 60
Andrew, 81,
101
William, 68
Studvelt
John, 145
Sturgis
Daniel, 105
Subby
Mummy, 259
Subsion
Richard, 133
Sueby
Mummy, 253
Sullivan
Dempse, 116

Lt., 160
Summer
Cato, 196
Josiah, 196
Peggy, 29
Pinna, 196
Tom, 196
Summers
Thomas, 206
William, 158
Sumner
Luke, 29
Sumpter
Gen., 210
Sutherland
Adam, 147,
247
Sutter
James, 14
Suydam
Charles, 19
Rymer, 213
Swan
Richard, 86
Swansken
Margaret, 243
Sweeney
Charles, 186
Major, 186
Sweepston
Richard, 100
Sweezie
Isaac, 162
Sweley
Jack, 79
Sweney
Molly, 184
Swift
Capt., 130
Swinthin
John, 251
Swinton
Alexander, 233
Francis, 233
Frank, 241
Swithen
John, 262
Swithin
John, 233, 241
Sygh
John, 132
Syllabos

Desantee, 229
Sylva
Anthony, 234,
242
Augustus, 246
Besantee, 242
Francis, 234
Frank, 241
Thomas, 234,
247
Symon
Capt., 200
Symons
Frank, 56
Patrick, 124
Sype
John, 103
Syphle
Ludwick, 146
Syrrus
William, 17
Tabb
Adam, 253
Mary, 254
Tackey
Anthony, 241
Tait
Thomas, 61
Talbot
Capt., 9
George, 87
James, 87
John, 26
Joseph, 14
Nancy, 14
Solomon, 87
Susannah, 87
Tallow
Daniel, 234
Talon
Rubin, 252
Tankard
Alice, 104
David, 95
Matthew, 16
Scarborough,
104
Stephen, 95,
149
Tankins
Joseph, 163
Tannable

William, 198
Tanyard
  James, 129
  Tom, 129
Tarbell
  Lt., 11
Tarbett
  Joseph, 208
  Peter, 208
Tardeal
  Lt., 44
Tarrant
  Leonard, 149
Taskew
  Nat, 107
Tassell
  John, 201
Tasswell
  John, 92
Tatham
  John, 234
Taton
  Rubin, 261
Tatum
  John, 93, 94
Taylor
  Courtney, 47
  Dr., 156
  Ens., 150
  George, 128
  Hannah, 128
  Isaac, 212
  Jack, 108
  James, 249
  John Drage, 252
  John, Col., 136
  Joseph, 135, 234, 241, 251, 261
  Margaret, 238, 246
  Mrs., 40
  Sally, 41
  Sam, 123
  Widow, 108
  William, 234, 245
Teaboult
  Mr., 28
Teggen
  Becca, 27

Temple
  Benjamin, 100
Tennant
  Captain, 15
Terhune
  Dinah, 21
  Nicholas, 10
  Samuel, 21
  Thomas, 21
Terrell
  Sally, 13
Terrill
  Charles, 11
Teunis
  Anthony, 176
Thatcher
  Capt., 132, 133
Theodore
  William, 234, 241, 249
Thewston
  Edward, 84, 85
Thomas
  Abraham, 51
  Amos, 110
  Ann, 238, 242, 244, 247
  Anthony, 234, 241
  Barbara, 250
  Barbary, 252
  Capt., 151, 152
  Catherine, 241
  Charles, 108, 195, 234
  Cudjoe, 156
  David, 198
  Elizabeth, 113
  George, 42
  Jack, 234, 249
  James, 234, 242
  Jane, 247
  John, 47, 60, 69, 111, 113, 125, 158, 234, 235, 241–244, 250, 251, 256
  John Ceasor, 234
  Juno, 111
  Lewis, 40

Maria, 238
Maria (Child), 244
Mary, 238, 242
Matthew, 238
Michael, 108
Moses, 234
Ned, 137
Peggy, 198
Robert, 234, 241
Samuel, 101
Sara, 258
Thomas, 195
William, 156, 234
William (Child), 244
Thomlinson
  James, 260
Thompson
  Alexander, 235, 243, 249, 253, 260
  Ann, 238, 243, 254
  Barret, 234, 243
  Captain, 256
  Charles, 86, 234, 243, 256
  Col., 12
  Edward, 234, 235, 256
  Elizabeth, 258
  James, 114, 181, 234, 241
  Jane, 115, 117
  John, 234, 235, 243, 244, 258
  Joseph, 234
  Mary, 243, 257
  Moses, 159
  Mr., 47
  Peggy, 236, 244
  Philip, 181
  Rachel, 238, 247
  Samuel, 235, 246, 249
  Silvia, 185

Thomas, 234, 235, 242, 243, 247, 258
William, 234, 246, 257
Thomson
  Andrew, 137
  Betty, 86
  Col., 7, 11
  Elizabeth, 86
  Grace, 84, 86
  Hagar, 61
  Isabella, 84
  Jack, 47
  John, 173
  Joshua, 97
  Lydia, 85
  Margaret, 212
  Mary, 212
  Mary Ann, 173
  Osmond, 173
  Polly, 212
  Rachell, 212
  Rob, 153
  Robert, 153
  Sally, 212
  Thomas, 205
Thorne
  Charles, 163
Thorntown
  William, 203
Thorowgood
  Francis, 170
Threads
  William, 251
Thryning
  William, 259
Thurman
  Thomas, 210
Thurston
  Latham, 21
Tier
  John, 153, 155
Till
  Captain, 251
Tiller
  James, 123
Timkins
  William, 133
Tin
  Samuel, 34
Tinker, 8

William, 74
Tinnibald
  James, 109
Tippet
  Gilbert, 157
Tismore
  Henry, 177
Titus
  James, 234,
  241, 257
Tollberry
  Jack, 197
  Sillo, 197
Tollman
  Cornelius, 74
  John, 72
Tomkin
  Richard, 93
  Samuel, 93
Tomkins
  Capt., 99
  Lydia, 64
  Mary, 99
  Mr., 132
  Sam, 64
Tomlinson
  James, 253
  Lt., 12
  Mary, 254, 260
Toner
  Peter, 60
Toney
  Jenny, 107
Totten
  Harry, 56
  James, 56
  Joseph, 56
  Peter, 56
Townass
  Anthony, 124
  Henry, 124
Townsend
  Cathern, 175
  George, 207
  John, 105, 110,
  149, 182
  Stephen, 119,
  182
Trail
  Major, 26
Tramell
  Joseph, 105

Silvie, 105
Travelle
  George, 158
Travers
  Champion, 208
Travess
  James, 35
Trewell
  Anthony, 106
  John, 106
Trigler
  Edward, 37
Tromble
  Henry, 207
Trounce
  Lt., 89, 147,
  152
Troup
  Robert, 60
Truman
  George, 229
  John, 229
  Thomas, 251
Trumbly
  Peter, 186, 187
Trumpeter, 10–
12
Trusler
  William, 173
Tryar
  Samuel, 199
Tucker
  Col., 117
  Dianah, 200
  Doctor, 204
  Jack, 34
  James, 198
  King, 200
  Robert, 20, 200
  Thomas, 96
  Tom, 96
Tucks
  Thomas, 234
Tugle
  William, 123
Tungate
  Robert, 55
Turnbull
  Robert, 22, 23
  Sam, 206
  Suzanah, 206
Turner

Elizabeth, 260
  George, 234
  John, 147
  Nat, 153
  Parson, 16
  Pas, 153
  Patty, 153
Turpin
  Luby, 50
Twim
  Hanna, 238
Twine
  Hannah, 246,
252
  John, 234, 246,
251
Tybout
  Francis, 101
Tyers
  Lt., 47
Tygner
  Phil, 27
Tympany
  Major, 150,
151
Tynes
  Betty, 43
  Timothy, 43
Tyng
  Bill, 13
  Colonel, 13, 14
  Dinah, 13
  John, 13
  Juliet, 13
Ugee
  Ned, 137
Ulon
  Mr., 126
Umberston
  Charity, 75
  Samuel, 75
Underwood
  Daniel, 107
Upham
  Hagar, 71
  John, 71
Upkins
  Reuben, 64
Upshaw
  Arthur, 169
Ustus
  John, 86

Valantine
  Capt., 212
  Captain, 212
Valentine
  A., 77
  James, 253
  John, 259
  Rob, 145
Vallantine
  Jonathan, 14
Vallentyne
  James, 145
Van Alstine
  Cuff, 131
  Major, 131
Van Alstyne
  Peter, 132
Van Borun
  Stephen, 182
Van Bruyck
  John, 190
  Nancy, 190
  Samuel, 190
  Sarah, 190
Van Buskirk
  Lawrence, 158
Van Dam
  Richard, 158
Van Dewater
  Peter, 178
Van Dyne
  Cornelius, 146
Van Horn
  John, 212
Van Horne
  Cornelius, 23
  Nancy, 32
Van Houter
  Garabrands,
153
Van Klock
  Leonard, 59
Van Meter
  Richard, 100
Van Norstrant
  Sam, 43
Van Nostrand
  Sarrah, 209
Van Nostrant
  C., 209
  Sam, 209
  Sarrah, 209

Stoffle, 43
Van Ryper
  Cornelius, 116
  Derrick, 115
  Henry, 100
Van Sant
  John, 43
Van Sayl
  Cathern, 81
  Cornelius, 81
  Mary, 81
  Peter, 81
Van Solinger
  Dr., 113
Van Wart
  Dick, 33
  Jacob, 156
  John, 33
  Sam, 156
Van Winkle
  John, 159
Van Wyck
  Dr., 22
  John, 32
VanBuren
  Dr., 9
Vancepes
  Daniel, 18
Vanderborough
  Richard, 59
Vanderveer
  John, 81
Vandewater, 126
Vandexter
  Thomas, 31
Vandross
  James, 183
Vandyke
  John, Maj., 150
VanDyne
  Donn, 59
VanHorn
  Mr., 156
  Mrs., 155
VanRyker
  Peter, 133
VanRyper
  Abraham, 100
  Jacob, 103
  Mary, 103
  Susanna, 102
Vans

John, 5
VanSant
  Winey, 43
Vansayl
  Catharine, 81
Vanshant
  Albert, 130
Vanshaw
  Martin, 260
Vansuyl
  Peter, 103
Vantile
  Massey, 172
Vantyle
  Patty, 172
Vanvoorst
  Aury, 154
Vanyinkle
  Cornelius, 209
Varse
  Jacob, 30
Vastian
  Francis, 235
Vastion
  Francis, 244
Vaughan
  Basan, 148
  William, 148
Vaughn
  Edward, 235
  John, 260
Veasey
  Joseph, 40
Vermilla
  Isaac, 33
Vermille
  Isaac, 59
Vernon
  Capt., 133
VerPlank
  Mr., 209
Veters
  Adam, 108
Victory
  Catherine, 258
  Peter, 257
Vincent
  Charles, 133
  Dick, 133
  Ens., 133
  Jonathan, 235
Vinson

Dianah, 211
Oliver, 211
Vinters
  Thomas, 60
Virginia
  Norfolk, 83
Voice
  John, 36
Voise
  Cal, 24
Vorcheen
  Isaac, 208
Wade
  Mrs., 197
  William, 19,
  105
Waide
  Mr., 165
Wainwood
  Godfrey, 163
Wait
  Amy, 99
  Chressy, 99
  Harry, 98
  Isaac, 98
  Israel, 99
Waite
  Isaac, 161, 167
Wakeman
  Gideon, 73
Walden
  George, 168
Waldron
  Benjamin, 186
  Diana, 186
  Isaac, 186, 187
  Peggy, 186
  Resolved, 55
Walk
  Anthony, 96
Walker
  Anthony, 93,
  102
  Chloe, 86
  Grace, 146
  Henry, 113
  Hugh, 147, 148
  James, 115,
  262
  John, 11, 146
  Lydia, 86
  Nancy, 21

Richard, 79, 80
Robert, 235,
243, 256
Samuel, 86
Tobias, 113
William, 48,
179
Wall
  Patrick, 158
Wallace
  Abraham, 235
  Dick, 196
  Hannah, 196
  James, 196
  Michael, 196
  Mr., 45
  Tom, 45
Waller
  Hardy, 116
Wallis
  Judith, 81
Walloby
  John, 138
Wallow
  John, 121
Walls
  Dempsee, 9
Wallus
  Margaret, 81
Walsh
  Thomas, 64
Walter, Esq., 123
Walters
  Anny, 149
  Kate, 210
Walton
  Hester, 11
  John, 235, 241,
  253, 260
  Mr., 139, 177
  William, 132,
  133
Wan
  Edward, 158
Wandry
  Chloe, 102
  Nathaniel, 102
Wansworth
  Rose, 163
Wanton
  Bridget, 129
  Jacob, 21

Joseph,
Colonel, 129
Pompey, 64
Stephen, 64
Ward
B., Lt., 135
Ebenezer, 146
Eliza, 146
John, 112, 165
Moses, 153
Samuel, 235,
246
Widow, 67
Warde
E., 68
Edmund, 67
Wardell
John, 28, 69,
131
Waring
Joseph, 71
Richard, 86
Thomas, 85
Walley, 71
Warkimon
William, 235
Warkinson
William, 245
Warmington
John, 58
Warner
Effie, 22
Isaac, 7, 127
Peter, 22
Richard, 126
Samuel, 41
William, 41,
105, 256
Warren
Ben, 135
Edward, 235
Elizabeth, 238,
246
Henry, 92
Isaac, 189
Ishmael, 46
John, 148
Joseph, 46
Judith, 94
Mr., 148
Peter, 92, 94
Philip, 235

Thomas, 189,
253, 259
Warrick
John, 243
Warring
L., 53
Warrington
Col., 80
Joseph, 170
Mr., 15
Warwick
Cuff, 28
John, 235
Lydia, 28
Washington
General, 16,
112
Harry, 111
John, Col., 52
Thacker, 185
Washingtown
Gen., 205
Wast
Doctor, 208
Waterhouse
Reuben, 64
Waters
Eleanor, 238
John, 235
Michael, 235
Watson
Alexander, 37
Ann, 250, 252,
261
Brass, 24
Capt., 47
Jacob, 170
James, 10, 235
John, 66, 71,
123
Master, 133
Moses, 53
Nancy, 24
Philip, 170
Robert, 27, 80,
165
Watters
John, 95
Watts
Hugh, 16, 75
William, 256
Way

Adam, 98
James, 21, 206
Wearin
Peter, 68
Thomas, 68
Weaver
Judeah, 254
Judith, 259
Lucy, 238, 253,
259
Richard, 235,
253, 259
Webb
Benjamin, 177
George, 128
James, 133
John, 133
Mr., 195
Wedder
Doctor, 208
Sam, 208
Weedon
Judy, 107
Weekes
John, 235
Weeks
Dinah, 109
Francis, 247
George, 50
Peter, 110
Weidersheim
Major, 76
Weir
Mr., 204, 205
Welch
Edward, 97
Elizabeth, 245
Wells
Francis, 190
John, 240
Mary, 32
Samuel, 235
William, 32
Welsh
Elizabeth, 238
Wescot
Molly, 109
West
Andrew, 69
James, 69
Thomas, 117
Westcott

Joseph, 108
Sharp, 108
Wright, 108,
109
Westerfeldt
Crisparus, 187
Westerfield
Betty, 184
Jacob, 187
Wheaton
Bob, 175
John, 202
Richard, 45, 46
Wheeler
Caleb, 100
Richard, 100
Wheton
Thomas, 175
Whillax
John, 115
White, 22
Alexander, 74
Charles, 187
Dr., 62
Elizabeth, 92,
238
George, 97
Gideon, 8
Hemus, 34
Isaac, 89
Jack, 60
James, 157,
235, 242, 246,
251, 262
John, 59, 60,
83, 134, 161,
235, 243
Joseph, 157,
249
Lewis, 235,
253, 260
Mary, 88
Peggy, 148
Philip, 235
Phillip, 241
Richard, 16, 19
Robert, 55
Samuel, 148,
178
Silvia, 83
Simon, 9
Thomas, 160

William, 105, 148
Whitehead
Andrew, 182
Charles, 126
Hemed, 182
Whitehill
David, 74
Whiten
Robert, 25
Whiting
Thomas, 19
Whitman
John, 10
Whitmore
Tim, 70
Whitten
Hannah, 116
Harry, 116
James, 137
John, 87, 88, 91, 105, 113, 116, 125
Nancy, 116
Samuel, 116
Thomas, 113
Whittfield
Jemma, 105
Whittin
Richard, 26
Whitting
Lucy, 41
Samuel, 41
Whycuff
Sarah, 254
Wickfall
Isaac, 128
Joseph, 128
Wicks
John, Jr., 245
John, Sr., 245
Wigfall
Jacob, 46
John, 20
Joseph, 46
Mr., 13, 26
Silvia, 46
Wiggan
Sam, 48
Wigsal
Prince, 26
Wilbank

George, 129
William, 148
Wilder
William, 86
Wilk
George, 170
Wilkes
Ann, 257
John, 235, 256, 258
Wilkin
S., 182
Toney, 114
Wilkins
Cara, 65
George, 182
Ichabod, 125
Isaac, 53
John, 53, 60, 99, 114
Michael, 69
Miley, 99
Phillis, 125
Robert, 69
Sarah, 114
Wilkinson
Dick, 81
Dolly, 168
George, 212
Hester, 153
John, 65, 114
Joseph, 235, 244
Melsey, 110, 116
Miles, 95, 111, 112
Molsey, 116
Molton, 132
Moses, 112
Mr., 5, 48
Patience, 114
Sarah, 260
Willis, 6, 29, 30, 84, 88, 114–116, 153, 166, 168, 212
Wilkison
Patience, 111
Wilks
Ann, 247
John, 235

John (Child), 244
Willesford
William, 254
Willet
Lemuel, 51
Lilley, 80
Nancy, 79, 80
Pomp, 79
Robert, 27
Sarah, 79, 80
William
Ann, 238
Betsey, 94
Isaac, 165
John, 235, 244
Mary, 243
Prince, 243, 244, 257
Williams, 8
Alexander, 235
Ann, 242
Betsey, 94
Bill, 80, 92
Billy, 5, 34, 115
Bridget, 258
Capt., 153
Captain, 12, 29
Cesar, 71
Charles, 201
Dick, 243
Elizabeth, 18, 247, 257
Elizabeth (Child), 244
Fanny, 71
Francis, 235
Fred, Capt., 55
George, 67, 235, 244
Harry, 83
Henry, 40, 235
Hester, 238, 245
Jack, 210
Jacob, 203
James, 235
Jane, 128
Jeremiah, 235
Jeremiah (Child), 244

Joe, 50, 52
John, 21, 47, 52, 98, 99, 235, 240, 243, 245, 246, 247, 257, 260
Joseph, 11, 235, 236, 244, 245, 247
Kimme, 66
Lizzy, 99
Lydia, 133
Margaret, 238
Maria, 238, 245
Mary, 85, 238, 245
Maurice, 127
Nancy, 71
Nathaniel, 118
Peter, 235
Polly, 67, 94
Prince, 55
Rebecca, 33
Richard, 41
Robert, 44, 235, 245
Rose, 83
Sally, 98
Sam, 15
Samuel, 133, 201, 203
Sill, 55
Sophia, 258
Thomas, 17, 132, 235, 244, 249, 253, 260
Venus, 201
William, 14, 80, 235, 236, 242, 251, 257, 261
Williamson
Charlotte, 238
Henry, 240
John, 10, 120, 121, 139, 235, 241, 253, 259
Kildare, 124
Margaret, 238
Mary, 238

Samuel, 235, 244
Sarah, 254
Thomas, 235, 241
William, 53, 162, 210, 235, 242
Willis
 Charles, 188
 George, 75
 Hester, 129
 Hugh, 172
 Jenny, 188
 John, 235
 Joseph, 188
 Peter, 89
 Rachel, 188
 Samuel, 188
 William, 129
Willmot
 Capt., 135
Willoughby
 Betsy, 48
 John, 85–87, 184
Wills
 Arnold, 207
 John George, Capt., 32
 Thomas, 191
Willsford
 Fardon, 254
Willus
 Margaret, 81, 82
Wilsford
 Fardon, 260
 William, 260
Wilson, 181
 Abraham, 169
 Betsy, 115
 Captain, 209
 Con, 50
 Consill, 75
 David, 25
 Dolly, 104
 George, 34
 Isaac, 52
 Jacob, 7, 79
 John, 18, 19, 47, 235, 236,

240, 248, 249, 250, 251, 253, 259, 262
Joseph, 235, 243
Luke, 104
Peter, 235, 241
Pomp, 183
Rachel, 183
Robert, 38, 48, 70, 235, 243
Sally, 211
Sam, 62
Solomon, 23
Will, 203
William, 33
Willis, 167
Wilton
 Thomas, 68
Windsor
 Ann, 258
 John, 235, 257
 Rebecca, 238
Wingfield
 Capt., 125
Wingwood
 Gilbert, 189
 Joseph, 189
Winkham
 Thomas, 235
Winks
 Thomas, 176
Winslow
 Cato, 212
 Col., 7, 8
 Hannah, 212
 Mr., 212
 Rose, 212
 Toby, 212
Winsor
 John, 243
 Rebecca, 243
Winter
 Betsy, 177
 Robert, 43
 Thomas, 30
 William, 176
Winters
 Humphry, 5
 London, 198
Wise
 Edward, 106

George, 170
Jupiter, 65
Peggy, 171
With
 George, 50, 178
 James, 178
Withers
 Timothy, 178
 William, 178
Wollerd
 Thomas, 65
Wolverton
 Thomas, 67
Wood
 Ben, 50
 Francis, 152
 John, 235, 241
 Mary, 249
 Robert, 235
 Samuel, 235, 246, 249, 253, 259
 Susannah, 238
 Thomas, 70
Woodberry
 John, 42
Wooders
 Thomas, 253, 259
Woodhouse
 Will, 38
 William, 38
Woodie
 John, 153
Woodle
 Thomas, 240
Woodley
 Philip, 101
 Thomas, 235
Woodman
 Gabriel, 103
 Thomas, 235, 242, 249, 251
Woodruff
 Isaac, 133
Woods
 Hannah, 247
 Robert, 245
Woodward
 John, 14
 Lambert, 62

Woolverton
 Thomas, 64
Work
 Anthony, 187
 Job, 187
Working
 Jane, 257
 William, 256
Workinson
 William, 243
Wriden
 John, 18
Wrigglesworth
 John, 256
Wright
 (Mrs.), 235
 David, 145
 Dr., 140
 Francis, 178
 Garth, 201
 George, 235
 Hester, 246, 252, 261
 James, 46, 80
 John, 182
 Mesech, 261
 Messick, 246
 Michael, 235
 Misheck, 251
 Mr., 76
 Nezer, 200
 Rose, 178
 Samuel, 139
 Stephen, 46, 182, 184, 200, 201
 William, 69
Wrightson
 George, 246
Wyatt
 John, 106
 Richard, 59
Wycuff
 Benjamin, 247
 Sarah, 259
Wykoff
 William, 40
Wyllie
 Benjamin, 235
 Samuel, 16
Wynah
 Susannah, 92

Xanthus
  Valentine, 260
Yard
  James, 189
Yarrow
  Israel (Child),
  247
  James, 236
  John (Child),
  247
  Joseph, 247
  Mary (Child),
  247
Yates
  Andrew, 58
Yeates
  Rose, 32
Yellow
  Dominick, 83
Yestown
  Lemuel, 38
York
  Benjamin, 236,
  256
  Betsey, 86
  Duskey, 86
  Isaac, 130, 139
  James, 253,
  259
  John, 236, 244,
  245
  John (Mrs.),
  236
  Mary, 238, 244
  Mary Ann
  (Child), 244
  Sally, 86
  Thomas, 191
Young
  Celea, 238
  Celia, 246
  Col., 86
  Elizabeth, 238
  George, 236,
  241
  James, 106,
  116
  Latice, 210
  Mary, 238, 242
  Peter, 195
  Robert, 236,
  240

Samuel, 236
Thomas, 149
Thomas W.,
261
Thomas
William,
Doctor, 252
William, 164,
210
Zerbel
  Anhalt, Lt., 75
Zumbartus
  John, 236

CPSIA information can be obtained
at www.ICGtesting.com
Printed in the USA
BVHW04214125052 3
664926BV00017B/115